C. D Maclean

Standing Information Regarding the Official Administration

of the Madras presidency in each department, in illustration of the yearly

administration reports

C. D Maclean

Standing Information Regarding the Official Administration
of the Madras presidency in each department, in illustration of the yearly administration reports

ISBN/EAN: 9783337403041

Printed in Europe, USA, Canada, Australia, Japan

Cover: Foto ©Suzi / pixelio.de

More available books at **www.hansebooks.com**

STANDING INFORMATION

REGARDING THE

OFFICIAL ADMINISTRATION OF THE MADRAS PRESIDENCY

IN EACH DEPARTMENT,

IN ILLUSTRATION OF THE YEARLY ADMINISTRATION REPORTS

PREPARED UNDER THE ORDERS OF GOVERNMENT.

BY

C. D. MACLEAN,

ADDITIONAL SUB-SECRETARY TO THE BOARD OF REVENUE.

———◆———

MADRAS:
PRINTED BY E. KEYS, AT THE GOVERNMENT PRESS.
1877.

PREFACE.

Some of the notices in the following pages have been taken from that portion of the Madras Administration Reports for 1872-73 and 1875-76 which dealt with standing as opposed to current information regarding the different departments. The greater number of the notices, however, and those which seemed the most important, have been written specially for the present volume. The account of the method of official administration in the Native State of Travancore has been taken from a paper written by the late Dewan of Travancore; it is given here as throwing light on the British administration of the Western Coast, especially with regard to the land revenue question. This volume does not attempt in any sense to be a Gazetteer of the Presidency; the few remarks of that nature which will be found, have been introduced only because there is at present no Presidency Gazetteer, and because a certain amount of information as to the state of the country seemed necessary for a proper understanding of the official machinery. The information is not brought down later than the 31st March 1876; it was necessary to fix one date for the whole, and a later date than this could not have been taken with any prospect of securing accuracy. An interleaved edition is published for the use of certain offices; in this such corrections can be made as are necessitated either by changes in the administration or by the imperfections of the present work. With corrections of this nature, the volume may perhaps be serviceable for some little time to come.

CONTENTS.

SECTION I.—GENERAL AND POLITICAL.

SECTION II.—ADMINISTRATION OF THE LAND.

SECTION III.—PROTECTION.

SECTION IV.—PRODUCTION AND DISTRIBUTION.

SECTION V.—REVENUE, FINANCIAL, AND ADMINISTRATIVE.

SECTION VI.—VITAL STATISTICS AND MEDICAL SERVICES.

SECTION VII.—INSTRUCTION.

SECTION VIII.—MISCELLANEOUS.

APPENDIX TO SECTION II.—ADMINISTRATION OF THE LAND.

SECTION I.

GENERAL AND POLITICAL.

AREA, PHYSICAL FEATURES, CLIMATE, CHIEF STAPLES, AND LINGUISTIC DIVISIONS.

THE territory included within the Presidency of Fort Saint George, or what is better known as the Madras Presidency, occupies a considerable area of the peninsula of India. The coast line extends on the east of the peninsula from Orissa, in Bengal, to Cape Comorin. On the west the narrow strip of country, which includes the Native States of Travancore and Cochin, forms the coast line from Cape Comorin to the town of Cochin, where Madras territory again extends along the coast until its junction with the Bombay Presidency at the northern extremity of the South Canara District. In the centre of the peninsula are the Nagpore country and Berar, the territories of His Highness the Nizam, known generally as the Deccan, and the province of Mysore; but all the centre of the peninsula, south and east of Mysore, belongs to the Madras Presidency. *General description.*

The Presidency occupies an area of 139,698 square miles; but within this is included 1,380 square miles belonging to the Puducottah territory, which is situated in the middle of one of the Revenue districts. *Area.*

The Presidency has a coast line of about 1,700 miles, and consequently a large area of country but little elevated above the level of the sea. Mountain ranges run northward from Cape Comorin along the Western Coast, attaining an elevation in some parts of from 4,000 to nearly 9,000 feet. Ranges of hills follow also the general line of the East Coast; but these, as a rule, are of lower elevation than the Western Ghauts. The drainage of the peninsula is for the most part from west to east into the Bay of Bengal, the area of country drained by rivers running westward being only the narrow strip of territory between the Western Ghauts and the sea. As a rule the country slopes gradually *Physical geography.*

from the eastern base of the western mountain chain down to the Coromandel Coast, while the fall is sudden and precipitous on the western side of the mountains. The centre of the peninsula consists generally of undulating table-lands from 1,000 to 3,000 feet above the level of the sea.

Influence of physical geography on climate. The peculiar physical geography of the peninsula of India, with a huge mountain chain running from north to south along its western boundary, is of importance in regard to climate and the productions of the various districts. These hills have the effect of arresting the lower strata of rain clouds brought up from the Indian ocean by the periodical winds of the south-west monsoon, and of causing excessive rain precipitation on the narrow strip of coast line on the western side of the peninsula. Where the mountain range is of great height, as between Malabar and Coimbatore, the rain clouds are almost entirely diverted from the districts immediately below the mountains on the eastern side, and while the annual rainfall on the western side may be one hundred and fifty inches, not more than twenty inches will be registered on the eastern side, immediately within the influence of the mountain ranges. Where the mountain chain is of lower elevation, the rain clouds pass over the hills, and rain is precipitated in uncertain and varying amount over the peninsula to the east of the Western Ghauts ; but, except in the northern districts, where the rainy season approximates to that of Bengal, the heaviest rainfall of the southern portion of the eastern division of the peninsula occurs during the period of the north-east monsoon. During the continuance of this monsoon, the western ranges of mountains have a similar effect in arresting the rain clouds, so that at the season of the year when the Carnatic is deluged by heavy rain, the Western Coast Districts enjoy fine clear weather.

Ditto on production. To the physical barrier of the Western Ghauts must be attributed not only the vast differences of climate, but also those in the nature of the productions, in the eastern and western divisions of the peninsula. In the former the uncertainty and capricious character of the rainfall has taught the cultivators of the soil the necessity of making provision for the storage of water for irrigation purposes, and the existence of innumerable tanks or reservoirs, scattered all over the country, testify to the fact that, from periods of the remotest antiquity, the inhabitants of the tracts of country which receive an irregular rainfall, have exercised great ingenuity and readiness of resource in the construction of public works for the artificial irrigation of the soil. On the western side of the mountains, however, the necessity for such works has never arisen. There the periodical rains fall with great regularity as to time and quantity, and the earth yields her fruits so abundantly that, although in certain exceptional years there may be partial failures of crops, absolute famine, as a result of bad seasons, is unknown. Only three of the twenty-one districts of which the Madras Presidency is composed lie within the influence of the never-failing rains of the south-west monsoon. In the remaining eighteen districts nature demands the assistance of art in the collection, storage, and distribution of the condensed moisture of the heavens. In some of these eighteen districts, however, as in the northern coast area, the periodic rains fall more regularly than in others, while in several of them the rivers running eastward, swelled by the south-west monsoon rains, are utilized in the fertilization of districts in which the natural moisture is defective.

The following table giving the mean average rainfall in each **Rainfall** district for a recent period of four years will throw light on the **throughout the Presi-** normal climate of the Presidency. An account of the scientific **dency.** operations of the Meteorological Department will be found under Section VII :—

Average Rainfall in Districts of Madras Presidency—Mean of Four Years, 1870-73.

Districts.	Number of Gauge-stations.	January.		February.		March.		April.		May.		June.		July.	
		Rain.	Days.	Rain.	Days.	Rain.	Days.	Rain.	Days.	Rain.	Days.	Rain.	Days.	Rain.	Days.
Bellary ...	17	0·09	0·25	0·01	0·00	0·07	0·25	0·70	1·50	2·26	4·25	2·71	6·25	2·05	5·75
Chingleput ...	7	1·32	1·25	2·64	1·50	0·39	0·75	0·61	0·75	1·99	1·25	2·23	4·75	3·77	8·50
Coimbatore ...	10	0·41	0·50	0·76	1·25	0·58	1·00	2·00	3·50	2·76	4·50	2·24	4·75	1·65	4·50
Cuddapah ...	10	0·51	0·75	0·27	0·50	0·27	0·50	0·30	0·50	2·16	2·75	2·15	5·00	2·74	6·00
Ganjam ...	13	0·39	0·75	0·13	0·25	0·75	1·25	1·51	3·00	1·61	3·50	6·70	7·25	6·24	10·75
Godavery ...	19	0·40	0·75	0·25	0·25	0·48	0·25	0·52	1·00	1·46	2·75	4·53	6·25	6·10	10·75
Kistna ...	11	1·09	0·75	0·07	0·25	0·36	0·25	0·30	0·50	1·10	2·50	2·71	5·50	4·62	9·50
Kurnool ...	9	0·20	0·75	0·00	0·00	0·04	0·00	0·28	0·50	1·49	3·50	2·98	6·00	4·08	9·00
Madras ...	1	1·75	2·60	1·65	2·00	0·73	1·00	0·76	1·25	1·12	1·25	3·60	10·00	4·88	15·25
Madura ...	13	1·08	2·00	0·96	2·00	0·50	1·25	1·68	3·00	1·83	2·25	1·19	2·00	0·84	2·00
Malabar ...	15	0·91	1·25	0·48	1·50	0·75	1·00	3·61	6·00	7·19	8·50	31·75	25·00	33·87	28·00
Nellore ...	18	1·30	1·25	0·70	0·25	0·17	0·25	0·15	0·25	1·05	1·75	1·18	3·00	2·71	5·75
North Arcot ...	9	0·55	0·75	1·54	0·75	0·73	0·50	0·42	1·00	3·72	2·75	1·97	4·50	3·20	6·00
Salem ...	10	0·16	0·50	0·61	1·00	0·75	0·75	1·21	2·75	4·16	5·00	2·41	4·75	2·82	5·50
South Arcot ...	8	0·43	0·75	2·04	1·50	0·26	0·25	1·19	1·00	2·64	2·25	1·78	3·25	3·20	5·25
South Canara ...	5	1·23	0·75	0·26	0·75	0·21	0·50	1·10	2·50	6·32	7·75	39·98	25·75	47·04	29·25
Tanjore ...	10	1·52	2·50	1·64	2·00	0·24	0·25	2·35	2·25	3·13	2·50	1·80	3·25	2·64	4·75
Tinnevelly ...	11	3·08	3·50	1·76	2·75	1·39	2·50	1·66	3·75	1·41	2·50	0·63	2·00	0·35	0·75
Trichinopoly ...	5	0·83	1·25	1·33	1·75	0·08	0·25	1·49	2·75	3·06	4·25	2·01	2·75	2·11	3·00
Vizagapatam ...	13	0·62	0·75	0·40	0·50	0·37	0·25	1·10	1·50	2·34	4·00	5·13	6·75	5·32	9·00

Average Rainfall in Districts of Madras Presidency—Mean of Four Years, 1870–73—(Continued).

Districts.	Number of Gauge-stations.	August.		September.		October.		November.		December.		Total.	
		Rain.	Days.	Rain.	Days.	Rain.	Days.	Rain.	Days.	Rain.	Days.	Rain.	Days.
Bellary ...	17	3·63	7·25	4·78	7·75	6·31	8·75	0·97	2·75	0·30	0·75	23·70	45·50
Chingleput ...	7	5·21	9·00	5·24	7·00	9·08	10·00	14·82	12·50	2·62	4·00	49·95	61·25
Coimbatore ...	10	2·43	4·75	2·94	5·75	4·94	8·25	4·35	7·25	0·57	2·00	25·53	47·50
Cuddapah ...	19	4·71	7·50	4·59	6·50	8·24	9·00	3·37	5·25	0·72	1·50	30·05	45·75
Ganjam ...	13	7·30	12·25	7·76	12·25	9·42	9·00	1·45	2·25	0·78	1·00	49·03	63·5
Godavery ...	19	5·06	8·00	8·24	10·25	10·82	10·75	1·95	2·50	0·55	0·75	40·34	54·20
Kistna ...	11	4·58	9·00	6·68	10·25	8·17	10·00	1·90	2·75	0·39	0·75	31·97	52·00
Kurnool ...	9	4·68	8·25	6·07	8·50	4·65	6·75	1·06	2·50	0·48	0·75	26·00	46·50
Madras ...	1	4·83	16·25	6·67	11·75	14·58	15·25	19·09	18·00	4·36	6·50	64·03	99·50
Madura ...	13	2·67	5·00	1·81	4·00	4·24	8·00	4·63	6·75	1·43	3·25	22·92	41·25
Malabar ...	15	11·60	18·75	9·49	14·50	8·25	12·25	3·74	6·25	0·81	1·50	112·97	124·50
Nelloro ...	18	3·73	5·75	3·92	5·25	11·02	9·25	9·78	8·00	1·76	2·00	40·36	42·50
North Arcot ...	9	4·94	8·50	6·22	9·25	8·00	10·25	7·65	8·50	1·39	3·25	35·57	54·75
Salem ...	10	4·99	8·00	6·62	6·25	7·09	9·50	3·28	5·75	1·44	2·75	46·63	55·50
South Arcot ...	8	5·59	8·25	5·32	19·75	8·87	10·25	11·79	12·25	3·66	4·25	46·63	55·50
South Canara ...	5	21·40	22·75	12·44	6·50	9·15	13·75	1·22	3·75	0·26	0·75	140·63	128·00
Tanjore ...	10	4·91	7·50	3·86	2·50	9·11	11·75	10·87	13·00	5·00	8·00	47·14	64·25
Tinnevelly ...	11	0·75	2·00	1·28	2·50	2·77	5·00	7·30	11·00	1·84	4·00	24·79	42·25
Trichinopoly ...	5	4·69	6·25	4·89	6·00	0·04	11·75	6·72	10·25	2·32	4·50	38·01	53·75
Vizagapatam ...	13	7·01	6·00	7·03	10·00	9·76	9·50	1·93	2·50	1·33	1·00	42·33	56·25

Chief staples.   The chief staples of the Presidency are rice, cholum (a kind of
maize), cumboo (a kind of millet), ragi, and varagu amongst
food-grains; gingelly amongst oil seeds; and chillies, tobacco,
sugar-cane, plantains, and betel leaf amongst garden crops.
Cotton, as a special crop, has a cultivation almost equal-
ling that of ragi. The trees most grown for their fruits are
cocoanut, areca nut, jack, tamarind, and mango. Rice, as might
be expected, is produced in the largest quantities in the alluvial
and highly-irrigated districts of Tanjore, Godavery, and Kistna
on the East Coast, and in Malabar and Canara on the West
Coast, where the rainfall is so abundant as to render irrigation
by artificial means almost unnecessary. Cholum is most abundant in the table-land districts of Bellary and Kurnool, while
cumboo and ragi are most extensively grown in the other inland,
but less elevated, districts, such as Salem and Coimbatore.
Cocoanut palms flourish most luxuriantly on the banks of the
estuaries and backwaters or salt-water lagoons of the western
districts of Malabar and Canara, and areca nut palms in the
valleys intersecting the lower slopes of the Western Ghauts.

**Linguistic
divisions.**   Within the Madras Presidency there are six well-defined
linguistic boundaries. In the northernmost district of Ganjam
is included a portion of the Ooriya-speaking population. The
Telugu language is commonly spoken by the people of the
Northern Circars, and in a portion of the Nizam's country,
Kurnool, Cuddapah, part of North Arcot, Nellore and some
parts of Bellary. Tamil is the common language of the districts
from a few miles north of Madras to the extreme south of the
eastern division of the peninsula. Malayalum is the language
of the Native States of Travancore, Cochin, and the Malabar
District. Tulu is spoken in a limited portion of the South
Canara District; and Canarese in certain portions of the Bellary,
Coimbatore, Salem, and South Canara Districts. Besides these
six Dravidian languages, the hill tribes of certain districts have
dialects of their own, also of a Dravidian type. In the whole
Presidency there are about 11,610,000 persons who speak the
Telugu language; Tamil, 14,715,000; Canarese, 1,699,000; Malayalum, 2,324,000; Tulu, 29,400; Ooriya and Hill languages,
640,000. From time to time colonies of Telugu and Canarese-
speaking people have found their way down to the southern or
Tamil country. In some cases they have been invited to settle
as cultivators in localities where waste lands were available. In
others they followed probably in the train of invading armies.

In the same way people from the Mahratta country have settled
in the south, and in all the large towns there are colonies of
silk-weavers from Gujirat, who speak a language of their own.
Along the border lines of the prevailing languages two or more
languages are indifferently spoken by the people. There is no
instance of the Tamil people pushing their colonies up towards
the north. The migrations appear to have been always from
north to south. In the large military cantonments of Secunderabad and Bangalore there are Tamil-speaking populations,
but these people have settled as camp-followers.

HISTORICAL SUMMARY.

The first attempt at the formation of an English Settlement
in the Madras Presidency was in conjunction with the Dutch at
Pulicat early in the seventeenth century, or about one hundred
years after the establishment of the Mahomedan kingdoms of
Bijapore and Golconda. Compelled to desist from this attempt,
the English formed a trading settlement at Masulipatam in
1620, and shortly afterwards at Armogum, about forty miles
north of Pulicat; and in 1639, after permission had been
obtained from the Hindu Rajah of Chandragherry, the first
English fortress on the Eastern Coast of India was erected at
Madras. In 1691 Fort St. David was built at Tegnapatam,
near Cuddalore, on a site purchased from a petty native prince.

*Military His-
tory—1620.*

Until the end of the first half of the following century the
English carried on their trading operations tolerably unmolested
in the midst of the continual wars between the Mussulman and
Mahratta conquerors of the old Southern Hindu powers; the
only event really affecting the future career of the settlements
being the acquisition by the French of the village of Pondicherry, which they purchased in 1672 from the King of Bijapore
shortly before his dynasty was overthrown by Aurungzebe. In
1744, war broke out between the French and English, and Fort
St. George fell—only to be restored again, however, at the
peace of Aix-la-Chapelle in 1749. The European war being
thus ended, the forces of the two powers found both occupation
and profit in the various wars between the native princes, and
it usually happened that their sympathies or their interests were
enlisted on opposite sides. Nearly the whole of Southern India
was then subject to the Nizam of Hyderabad, the country in

—1672.

the neighborhood of Madras being under the immediate rule of a tributary prince, called the Nabob of the Carnatic, while the Mahrattas still held supreme power in Tanjore and the adjacent country. The English first assisted a claimant to the Mahratta throne of Tanjore, and were rewarded by the cession of the town of Devicottah. The French took up the cause of Chanda Sahib, who, in alliance with Mirzapha Jung, opposed Mahomed Ali, Nabob of the Carnatic, and Nizam Nazir Jung. Chanda Sahib being an old enemy of the Tanjore Prince, the assistance of the English was again invoked and obtained, but Mirzapha Jung succeeded in securing the throne of the Nizam, and the triumph of the French under Dupleix was complete until Clive appeared upon the scene and changed the whole course of the war by seizing Arcot, the capital of the Carnatic, on the 30th August 1751, while Chanda Sahib and the French were besieging Mahomed Ali in Trichinopoly. He himself was besieged in turn, but repulsed all attacks and followed up his success by the victory of Arnee, which virtually placed the Carnatic once more under the ally of the English, although the siege of Trichinopoly was not formally raised until the French detachment, which had retreated to Srirungum, surrendered to Clive and Major Lawrence in June 1752. Chanda Sahib was eventually assassinated by a Mahratta, probably at the instigation of Mahomed Ali.

—1754.　　A quarrel next broke out between Mahomed Ali and Nunjeraj, the Minister of the Rajah of Mysore. The assistance of the latter had been procured by the Nabob by the promise to cede Trichinopoly if he were victorious, but, when he had got all he wanted, he declined to fulfil his agreement. Nunjeraj then had recourse to force, and, though the English at first hesitated to assist the Nabob under such circumstances, the conduct of Nunjeraj in other matters left them no alternative but to treat him as an enemy. The French supported the Mysoreans, and a succession of engagements took place, chiefly in the immediate vicinity of Trichinopoly, in which the English were almost uniformly successful. The recall of Dupleix on the 14th October 1754 led to a cessation of hostilities, but the English continued to aid the Nabob of the Carnatic in the internal management of his dominions, the Nizam Salabut Jung receiving similar assistance from the French under M. Bussy.

—1757.　　The theatre of action was then for some time transferred to Bengal, where Clive took command of the English army, but hostilities recommenced in Southern India in 1757 as soon as it

was known that war had again broken out in Europe between
the French and English. The French took advantage of the
English forces being dispersed in various expeditions, and made
an unsuccessful attack on Trichinopoly, while another detachment succeeded in gaining possession of Vizagapatam. In 1758
a French fleet appeared off Fort St. David, and the fort fell on
the 2nd June. Devicottah was next reduced, and the French
commander, Count de Lally, made a triumphal entry into
Pondicherry ; but here his success ended for the time, and an
expedition against Tanjore resulted in complete failure. In
December, however, he besieged Madras itself, and the siege
was not raised until two months afterwards, when an English
fleet appeared in the roads. In the meantime the English arms
under Colonel Forde were progressing satisfactorily farther
north, where Clive had sent a detachment to operate in a tract
called the Northern Circars, which had been ceded by the Nizam
to the French, and their successes culminated in the fall of
Masulipatam on the 7th April, by which the French influence
with the Nizam was destroyed, and a tract of territory around
Masulipatam, extending eighty miles along the coast and twenty
miles inland, was ceded by him to the English. The operations in the south were of a minor nature until the 22nd January
1760, when the French under Lally were completely defeated at
Wandewash, near Arcot, by Colonel Coote, who had arrived
with reinforcements from England. This was followed by the
capture within a fortnight of Gingee and Arcot. Minor forts
fell in rapid succession, and by May the English were in a
position to lay siege to Pondicherry. Lally then had recourse
to the services of Hyder Ali, an adventurer who subsequently
usurped supreme power in Mysore, but at that time merely held
high military command under the Rajah. An English detachment sent to meet the Mysoreans was totally defeated, and the
situation of the English might have become critical had not
home troubles recalled the Mysore troops to their own country.
Deprived of their aid, the French cause soon became hopeless,
and, on the 16th January 1761, Pondicherry surrendered.
With this event the French power in the Carnatic may be said
to have ended ; and, so far as the English were concerned, there
were no more military operations in Southern India until 1766
beyond granting such little aid as was, from time to time,
necessary to enable the Nabob of the Carnatic to keep down his
turbulent vassals. Negotiations were carried on with the
Nizam of Hyderabad for the cession of the Northern Circars,

but with no very satisfactory result; and in 1765 sunnuds trans-
ferring these tracts to the Company were obtained direct from
the Emperor of Delhi, whose paramount authority was recognized by the Nizam. The Madras authorities, however, hesitated
to avail themselves of the powers thus assigned to them except
with the consent of the Nizam ; and in 1766, although sending a
body of troops to secure their possession, they entered into a
treaty with Nizam Ali, agreeing to pay tribute for the Circars
and to defend the Nizam against his enemies. In the meantime
the Mysore adventurer, Hyder Ali, had succeeded, not only
in obtaining supreme power in that province, but in extending
his dominion on all sides, and the English were very soon called
on, under the treaty, to assist the Nizam and the Mahrattas in
checking the advance of Hyder in the direction of their territories. No sooner, however, had operations commenced than
Hyder Ali, by judicious expenditure of treasure, not only bought
off the Mahrattas, but actually induced the Nizam to desert his
allies and join him in a descent upon the Carnatic. Colonel
Smith, who commanded the English troops, finding himself thus
opposed to a force infinitely larger than his own, commenced a
retreat, followed by the allies who overtook him at Changamma.
The English repulsed the attack thus made, but were compelled
to continue their retreat to Trinomallee. On being attacked at
that place the victory of the English was decisive, the troops of
Hyder and of the Nizam retreating in the utmost confusion,
while bands of marauding horse, who had been plundering the
country up to the very gate of Madras under the command of
Hyder's son Tippoo, a boy of seventeen, considered their situation to be no longer secure, and drew off to rejoin the rest of the
army. Colonel Smith, however, was too weak to follow up his
victory, and withdrew his troops into cantonment for the rains,
which were now at hand. Hyder at once took advantage of this
inaction to reduce a few unimportant fortresses, but his movements were checked at the hill fort of Amboor, where Captain
Calvert, with a garrison of five hundred sepoys and fifteen
Europeans defied the utmost efforts of Hyder's armies for nearly
a month, when he was relieved by Colonel Smith on the 7th
December 1767. Hyder then drew off, and after a few skirmishes he retired above the ghauts, having learned that an
expedition from Bombay had captured his fleet in the harbours
of Canara and commenced hostile operations in his territories
on the Western Coast. Risking an invasion from the east,
Hyder hurried over to meet what to him seemed the more

imminent danger, and appeared suddenly before Mangalore in such force as to compel the re-embarkation of the expedition. In the meantime, though very imperfectly informed of Hyder's actual movements, the Madras Government resolved to commence offensive operations, and one body of troops under Colonel Wood proceeded to reduce the fortresses under the south-eastern slopes of the ghauts, while another entered Mysore proper under Colonel Smith. The movements of both detachments were at first completely successful, but just as they had united in August 1768, with the view of attacking Bangalore, Hyder returned from the Western Coast and made an attack on the camp of a Mahratta Contingent, which, though unsuccessful, was sufficient to show that there was no chance of reducing Bangalore unless a decisive victory could be first obtained over Hyder in the field. Various marches and counter-marches were undertaken with this object, but in vain, and after reconquering a number of the fortified places on the table-land, Hyder descended into the lowlands by passes unknown to the English, and speedily retook the fortresses in Coimbatore, the Baramahal, and Salem, which in almost all cases had been left most inadequately supplied with troops. He did not, however, care to risk an engagement in the field with Colonel Smith, and a treaty was concluded on the 4th April 1769, on the basis of a mutual restitution of conquests with the exception of Caroor, which was ceded to Hyder on the ground of its being an ancient dependency of Mysore.

From the date of this treaty until the year 1780 the only —1780. military operations in the south of India, beyond the usual work of assisting the Nabob of the Carnatic in keeping peace in his own dominions and in his quarrels with the Tanjore Rajah, were the capture of Pondicherry from the French in 1779, and the reduction of the French Settlement of Mahé on the Western Coast in 1779. The war which broke out again with Hyder in 1780 was attributable to the Nabob of the Carnatic failing to furnish the necessary supplies to enable the English to fulfil the stipulations of the treaty of 1769. Enraged at this apparent treachery and bad faith, Hyder succeeded in forming an alliance with the Nizam and the Mahrattas, and descended on the plains of the Carnatic in July 1780, burning crops and devastating villages, so that a cordon of blackened desert was formed around Madras, commencing at the lake of Pulicat, extending some fifty miles inland, and terminating a little to the north of Pondicherry. The English Commander-in-Chief, Sir Hector Munro, proceeded to Conjeveram, an open town 40 miles from Madras, and directed

Colonel Baillie to join him there with troops from the north. Hyder endeavoured to prevent the junction, and Sir Hector, seeing that Colonel Baillie was in danger, sent a detachment under Colonel Fletcher to his aid, which successfully eluded the enemy, and joined Colonel Baillie on the 9th September, only to be included, however, in the general massacre which took place when Colonel Baillie's force was attacked by overwhelming numbers on the following day. Sir Hector Munro considered Conjeveram no longer tenable when he heard the news of this disaster, and commenced a retreat to Madras, which he reached on the 14th September, leaving the field open to Hyder. On receipt of the intelligence at Calcutta, the then Governor-General Warren Hastings suspended the Governor of Madras and despatched Sir Eyre Coote with reinforcements. The latter arrived on the 1st November 1780, but was unable to take the field until the 17th January 1781. On the 19th he relieved Chingleput, and on the 21st retook Carangooly, which had the effect of raising the siege of Wandewash, which had been gloriously defended by Lieutenant Flint. Hearing of the arrival of a French fleet off Pondicherry he proceeded to that place, but, finding that the fleet had brought no land forces, he turned his attention to the protection of Cuddalore. Hyder had followed him down the coast, but moved off when the English general offered him battle, probably considering it more politic to endeavour to weaken the force by cutting off supplies, from the want of which the English army had already experienced considerable difficulty. Thus hampered, the troops remained almost inactive until the 18th June, when an ineffectual attempt was made to capture Chellumbrum. The news of this failure apparently emboldened Hyder to make a decisive attempt to annihilate the English army, and he accordingly advanced and took up a position close to Sir Eyre Coote's camp at Porto Novo, a small town on the coast about 14 miles south of Cuddalore. The battle commenced early on the morning of the 1st July 1781, an English fleet lying close in shore with the view of enabling the embarkation of the remnant of the army in the, by no means impossible, contingency of its being defeated in an encounter with an enemy at the very least eight times its numerical superior. The battle was long and severe, but by 4 P.M. the enemy were in precipitate retreat. The want of proper equipment rendered Sir Eyre Coote unable to take full advantage of the complete victory which he had gained, but he succeeded in again relieving Wandewash on the 18th July, after which he proceeded northwards and joined a detachment from Bengal at Pulicat, having eluded the force sent to intercept him by adopting a line of march hitherto supposed impassable for troops. Thus reinforced he marched against the fortress of Tripassore and procured its surrender on the 22nd August, just before Hyder's relieving army appeared on the field. A general action took place on the 27th, but with no very decisive result, though the English kept possession of the field. A month later, on the 27th of September, the English commander surprised the enemy near Sholinghur and gained such a victory as put him in a position to throw provisions into Vellore, which had been defended from the commencement of the war against the finest troops and strongest batteries which Hyder's resources could furnish. In November the English army retired for the monsoon to Madras, where it remained until the following January, when it had once more to advance to the relief of Vellore. Hyder then turned his attention to Cuddalore, and succeeded in reducing it with the assistance of a French Contingent which had landed at Porto Novo. Permacoil followed, but Sir Eyre Coote once more arrived in time to save Wandewash. In the meantime war had broken out with the Dutch as well as with the French, and the Dutch Settlements of Sadras, Pulicat, and Negapatam had been captured. A portion of the force employed for the reduction of the latter place was subsequently detached under Colonel Brathwaite to operate in Tanjore. Deceived by false spies, the little force was suddenly surrounded by superior numbers under Hyder's son, Tippoo, and only a small remnant escaped with their lives. To counterbalance this, a rebellion had broken out in Malabar, and a small force of English sent to their aid gained a considerable victory at Tellicherry, which necessitated the immediate despatch of Tippoo to the Western Coast, and Hyder Ali, feeling himself overmatched by Sir Eyre Coote, determined to quit the Coromandel Coast. The English commander then returned with his army to Madras, where he bid them a final farewell, and General Stuart assumed the command in his place. The English force on the Western Coast seemed hardly strong enough successfuly to oppose that brought against it, but the news of the death of Hyder at Chittoor on the 7th December 1782 led to Tippoo's speedy return to the head-quarters of the principal army, thereby leaving the field open to the English, who were shortly afterwards reinforced by a considerable number of troops from Bombay under General Matthews. Several places on the coast fell in rapid succession, and eventually the English penetrated to Bednore above the ghauts. Here, however, their success ended, Tippoo returning and compelling the surrender of the place on the 3rd May, after which he marched to the siege of Mangalore, where a small fort was in the occupation of Colonel Campbell. The garrison was insignificant and the material defences of the place contemptible, but Tippoo was unable to take it by assault and his large army remained for many months practically inactive, while his French allies under M. Bussy were being besieged in Cuddalore. On the receipt of the news of the conclusion of peace between France and England, an armistice was agreed upon under which Tippoo was bound to provision the garrison of Mangalore With but little more than a pretence of observing the letter of the convention, he deliberately broke the spirit by supplying provisions which were utterly unfit for consumption, and the garrison, completely broken down by famine and sickness, were obliged to capitulate on the 30th January 1784, the health of the commander being so undermined that he expired on the 23rd March following. After much evasion and delay, peace was ultimately concluded on the 10th March on the basis of mutual restoration of conquests. During this war many of the English prisoners, including General Matthews, were put to death by Tippoo by poison or still more inhuman means.

—1790.   After the conclusion of peace with the English, Tippoo seized about thirty thousand of the Christians of Canara, forcibly converted them to Islam, and deported them to the country above the ghauts. Subsequently, the many rebellions of the Nairs of Malabar on account of a somewhat similar exercise of fanatical zeal in that portion of his territory led to expeditions for the suppression of the several risings ; and many of the Nairs having taken refuge in Travancore, Tippoo resolved to invade that country in their pursuit, notwithstanding an intimation that such a proceeding would involve him in another war with the English. His first attempt to enter Travancore ended in failure. A second was more successful, and the country was overrun in the usual cruel manner; but, on his return to Coimbatore, he found an English army in the field at Trichinopoly under the command of General Medows, the Governor of Madras, who had also entered into alliances with the Mahrattas and the Nizam. Tippoo at first withdrew to Seringapatam, which he had established as the capital of his dominions, and the English met with little opposition in the reduction of the various forts along the south-eastern slopes of the ghauts until the 7th September, when their army was attacked by a force commanded by Tippoo in person, which had descended by the Gazalhatti pass. The attack was repulsed, but all General Medows' efforts to bring on a general action were evaded by Tippoo, and nothing but indecisive skirmishes took place, until the Governor-General, Lord Cornwallis, took the field in person, and, assuming the command on the 29th January 1791, at once commenced preparations for a march upon Bangalore, concentrating his army at Vellore. Tippoo hastened to intercept his advance, which he expected would be made by the passes near Amboor, but the demonstration in that direction was a mere feint, and the table-land was reached by the more northerly pass of Mooglee without a shot fired. The pettah or town of Bangalore fell early in March, and on the night of the 20th the fort was taken by assault after a severe contest of little over an hour. While these operations were going on in Mysore, Colonel Hartley from the Madras side had defeated the Sultan's troops near Calicut; and General Abercrombie, Governor of Bombay, had landed at Tellicherry with a considerable force, and reduced Cannanore without encountering much opposition. The name of Tippoo was so hated throughout the province that but little difficulty was met with in the operations in that neighborhood, and within a very short time the whole of Malabar was in the occupation of the English. Operations on a smaller scale were conducted in the north in concert with the Mahrattas and the Nizam, the latter having also despatched a body of about ten thousand horse to join Lord Cornwallis' army.

On the 4th of May the English army left Bangalore to march —1792. against Seringapatam; but the route was so difficult, the means of transport so limited, and the devastation of the country by Tippoo so thoroughly carried out, that, notwithstanding a successful engagement at Arikera, only nine miles from Seringapatam, Lord Cornwallis was compelled to abandon his plan of operations for the time and retire to the vicinity of Bangalore, where he occupied himself for some time in reducing a number of hill forts. The Nizam's troops and the Mahrattas having worked their way up from the north and reinforced his army with both men and supplies, Lord Cornwallis again appeared before the walls of Seringapatam on the 5th February 1792. On the night of the 6th, the outlying encampment and redoubts were carried and the city closely invested on two sides. Preparations were made for the vigorous conduct of the siege, and on the 16th the army was joined by that of General Abercrombie from Malabar. A few days previously Tippoo had made overtures for peace, but the negotiations did not lead to a cessation of preparations for the siege, and it was evident that the fall of Seringapatam was close at hand when, on the 24th February, orders were issued for the discontinuance of all hostilities, peace having been agreed upon on the basis of a cession to the allies of one-half of the dominions of which Tippoo was in possession before the war, the payment of three crores and thirty lakhs of rupees, and the restitution of all prisoners including those retained from the time of Hyder. Under this treaty the English came into possession of the Baramahal, Dindigul, Malabar, and Coorg, the latter being restored to the Rajah, who had rendered essential aid to the English in the course of the war.

—1789.   Though thus severely disabled, Tippoo was not rendered completely powerless. He lost no time in commencing a series of intrigues with the view of winning over those who had been the allies of the English, and even despatched an embassy to Paris to try and obtain the assistance of the French. His overtures being rejected by Louis XVI., he renewed them after the revolution had broken out, and a paltry contingent of ninety-nine men from the Mauritius landed at Mangalore in 1798. The aid thus received was contemptible, but the object of applying for it was manifest, and the then Governor-General, Lord Mornington, resolved to act at once instead of waiting till Tippoo had matured his plans. Instructions were despatched for the immediate adoption of such measures as were necessary to place the Madras army on a satisfactory footing, and an alliance was entered into with the Nizam. The object of the Governor-General was to obtain possession of the maritime territory still under Tippoo, and thus preclude him from communication with the French ; and, before commencing the war, an opportunity was afforded him of averting it by timely concession, but all efforts at negotiation were futile, and offensive operations were determined on. The army of the Carnatic was placed under the command of General Harris, while another force from Malabar under General Stuart ascended into Coorg early in March 1799. Tippoo directed his first efforts against this latter army, but was beaten at Sedasseer near Periapatam, and in the meantime General Harris and the Nizam's troops crossed the Mysore frontier. Tippoo turned to

meet them, and was defeated with severe loss in a general action
at Malvelly on the 27th March. He then retired to Seringapatam, and the allies advanced to the siege, which lasted for a
month before a practicable breach was made. The assault commenced at one o'clock on the 4th May, and before evening Tippoo
was dead, and the whole town in the possession of the English.
The dynasty of Hyder and Tippoo having practically come to
an end with the fall of the latter, the settlement of the country
was effected by the restoration of Mysore proper to the representative of the ancient royal family whose rights had been usurped
by Hyder. The greater part of the remainder was then divided
between the English and the Nizam, the districts of Canara,
Coimbatore, and Wynaad falling to the share of the former. A
portion was also reserved for the Peishwa, with the view of its
forming a basis for a new treaty with the Mahratta Empire.
Arrangements were at the same time made by which Mysore
could never again become a great military power, and, to provide
against the most remote contingencies, it was stipulated that
the heads of all the passes on the table-land should remain for
ever in the hands of the British. The military history of the
Madras Presidency may be said to cease with the treaty of
1799, all subsequent addition of territory, with one exception,
having been peacefully acquired. Before noting these, a brief
recapitulation will be made of the territorial acquisitions already
alluded to.

As stated in the opening paragraph, a trading settlement **Acquisition**
was established at Masulipatam in 1620, and in 1639 and in **of Territory down to 1799.**
1691 Forts St. George and St. David were built at Madras
and Tegnapatam, respectively, by the permission of the ruling
Hindu princes. The fort of Tellicherry, in Malabar, was
similarly established in 1708. The first footing in Tanjore was
gained by the cession of Devicottah in 1749, as a reward for
assistance rendered to a successful claimant to the throne. The
Nizams Mirzapha Jung and Salabut Jung had ceded Masulipatam and portions of the Northern Circars to the French; but,
on the capture of Masulipatam by the English in 1757, the
influence of the French was broken, and the town of Musulipatam
and a considerable tract of the surrounding territory was made
over to the English. In 1765 sunnuds ceding the whole of the
Northern Circars were obtained direct from the Emperor of
Delhi, but the Madras Government thought it more politic to
obtain the consent of the Nizam also, and in 1766 the five
Circars of Ellore, Chicacole, Rajahmundry, Moostafarnugger.

and Moortizanugger or Guntoor were ceded by treaty on the English agreeing to pay an annual subsidy of nine lakhs, or to furnish military assistance when required. A life-interest in the Circar of Guntoor was retained on behalf of the Nizam's brother Bazalut Jung, and it did not come into the possession of the English until 1768, six years after the death of Bazalut Jung. The Dutch settlements of Pulicat, Sadras, and Negapatam were annexed in 1781. The earlier wars with Hyder and Tippoo were concluded with a peace on the basis of mutual restitution of territory, but by the treaty of 1792 the districts of Malabar and Salem and the Dindigul division of Madura were acquired by the English, and on the partition of Tippoo's territory in 1799 the districts of Canara and Coimbatore fell to the share of the British Government.

Subsequent history.

During the wars of the eighteenth century the English more than once interfered in the disputes between the Rajah of Tanjore and the Nabob of the Carnatic, and in 1776 a treaty was concluded by which Nagore and 277 villages were ceded to the Company. The internal affairs of the kingdom continued to go on from bad to worse, and, after a turbulent period of disputed succession, the rightful claimant to the throne, on being put into power in 1799, executed a treaty resigning the administration of the kingdom into the hands of the British, on the understanding that he would receive a provision of one lakh of pagodas and one-fifth of the net revenues. The titular dignity became extinct in 1855 through failure of heirs. In 1800 a new treaty was entered into with the Nizam, by which a considerable increase was made in the British Subsidiary Force, on account of which the Nizam ceded all the territories he had acquired by the Mysore treaties of 1792 and 1799, together with the taluq of Adoni and all other taluqs situated to the south of the rivers Toombuddra and Kistna. These are known by the name of the Ceded Districts, and comprise the provinces of Bellary and Cuddapah. The English having in all the earlier wars of the peninsula supported the cause of Mahomed Ali, Nabob of the Carnatic, and having in fact secured him both the original possession of his kingdom and the power of retaining it, the revenues of the Carnatic were looked to for the defrayal of the expenses of the wars, and with this view the present district of Chingleput, then known as "the Jaghire," was made over to the Company in 1763. This was rented to the Nabob for some time, but in 1780 the British Government took the management into their own hands. As new wars arose fresh agreements were made, and a series of treaties were executed culminating in that of 1792, three years before the death of Mahomed Ali, and the accession of Omdut-ool-Oomrah, by which the Nabob agreed to pay a large subsidy, and, in order to secure punctual payment, the English were authorized to collect tribute direct from a large number of the poligars or local chiefs. In the event of the balance not being paid, the English were further authorized to assume the management of certain specified districts. In accordance with this treaty, tribute was collected throughout a great part of the Tinnevelly and Madura Districts, and in 1795 the Company assumed the entire management of the Ramnad division of the present district of Madura. On the fall of Seringapatam in 1799 it was discovered that both Mahomed Ali and Omdut-ool-Oomrah had been carrying on a treasonable correspondence with Mysore, and the treaty of 1792 having thus been infringed, the British Government resolved to assume the entire management of the Carnatic, and proposed a treaty for the purpose. Omdut-ool-Oomrah having died before arrangements were concluded, and his reputed son Ali Hoossain having rejected the terms offered him, another grandson of Mahomed Ali, named Azeem-ood-Dowlah, was declared his successor, and an arrangement was entered into on the 31st July 1801, by which he resigned the government of the country into the hands of the British, retaining the titular dignity and receiving a liberal stipend. The effect of this treaty was to bring under British rule the whole of the country from the Northern Circars to Cape Comorin, with the exception of the French settlements of Pondicherry and Karikal and the Danish settlement of Tranquebar. The titular dignity of Nabob of the Carnatic was continued until 1855, when there was a failure of direct heirs. The present representative of the family bears the title of Prince of Arcot, and has the position of the first native nobleman of Madras. In 1838 internal mismanagement and suspicion of treasonable intrigue on the part of the Nabob of Kurnool led to the occupation of his territory by an armed force and to its subsequent annexation. Tranquebar was ceded by the Danes in 1845, since which time there has been no accession of territory to the Madras Presidency. The district of North Canara was transferred to the Bombay Presidency in 1862.

CIVIL DIVISIONS OF THE BRITISH TERRITORY.

Districts grouped.

The Madras Presidency, according to existing boundary divisions, is made up of twenty-one districts, grouped as below :—

*Technical names of groups of Districts.	Districts.	Area in Square Miles.	Position.
Northern ...	1. Ganjam	8,313	To the north and east along the sea coast on the Bay of Bengal.
	2. Vizagapatam ...	18,344	
	3. Godavery	7,109	
	4. Kistna	8,036	
East Central ...	5. Nellore	8,462	
	6. Madras	27	
	7. Chingleput	2,753	
	8. South Arcot ...	4,873	
Ceded Districts.	9. North Arcot	7,139	In the centre of the penin-sula and mostly south and east of Mysore.
	10. Kurnool†	7,358	
	11. Bellary	11,007	
	12. Cuddapah	8,367	
West Central ...	13. Salem	7,483	
	14. Coimbatore	7,432	
	15. Nilgiris	749	
Southern ...	16. Tanjore	3,654‡	To the south, forming the south-eastern boundary of the peninsula.
	17. Trichinopoly ...	3,515	
	18. Madura	9,562	
	19. Tinnevelly	5,176	
West Coast ...	20. South Canara ...	3,902	On the Western Coast.
	21. Malabar	6,002	

Northern Circars.

The four districts at the head of the list are known as the "Northern Circars." Prior to 1859-60 these circars consisted of five districts, but in that year the three districts of Rajah-mundry, Masulipatam, and Guntoor were divided to form the present Godavery and Kistna Districts. The northern districts were formerly under the Nizam's Government, and in that time the divisions were as follows :—Guntoor, Condapilly, Ellore, Rajahmundry, and Chicacole. They came finally into British possession in the year 1823, by the payment to the Nizam's Government of Rupees 11,66,666 in lieu of an annual tribute. When these districts fell into the hands of the East India Company they consisted chiefly of large estates held by renters or zemindars ; of lands called "Hávelly," which were the old demesnes, or private estates, of former rulers ; and of tracts near the principal towns which had been resumed by the Mahomedan Governors of the districts, and appropriated for the support of their numerous bands of soldiers and public establishments. For some years prior to 1855-56 these Northern Circars were under the charge of a separate Commissioner, but each district

---

* Districts with a sea board are called "Maritime Districts."

† Kurnool is not strictly speaking one of the historical "Ceded Districts."

‡ Exclusive of Puducottah territory, the area of which is 1,380 square miles.

had then also its own revenue and judicial establishments. The appointment of Commissioner of the Northern Circars was abolished in June 1856.

The part of the Presidency usually known as the Carnatic **Carnatic.** appears to have been originally formed of three divisions, namely, Northern, extending from the River Pennar to the River Gundegama, and consisting of a portion of the Nellore District; Central, extending from the Coleroon to the Pennar River, and containing a portion of Trichinopoly, Chingleput, North Arcot, South Arcot, Madras, and Nellore Districts; and Southern, consisting of a portion of the Trichinopoly and the whole of Tanjore, Tinnevelly, and Madura Districts. These districts came into the possession of the British between the years 1799 and 1801.

In the year 1859-60 the two districts of Madras Town and **Chingleput** Chingleput were amalgamated into a single district, the collec- **and Madras.** tion of Sea Customs revenue being separately provided for. In the year 1870 the Chingleput District was again divided as before, leaving the administration of the Madras Town District in the hands of the Sea Customs Collector. The Chingleput District was obtained from the Nabob of Arcot in 1763 in return for services rendered to him and his father by the Company. The grant was confirmed by the Great Moghul in 1765, and for a long time the district was known as the " Jaghire " of the East India Company. The site of the town of Madras was obtained in the year 1640, by a grant from the descendants of the Vijianaggur rulers, subsequently confirmed by the Moghul Government.

The districts of Bellary and Cuddapah were ceded to the **Ceded** English by the Nizam in the year 1800 for the maintenance, in **Districts.** perpetuity, of a body of troops known as the Hyderabad Subsidiary Force, and as payment for troops furnished during the Mysore wars. The territories so made over are still known as the Ceded Districts.

In 1800 the rights of sovereignty exercised by the Nizam **Kurnool.** over the Kurnool country as Soubadar of the Deccan became vested in the East India Company. The Nizam, in the treaty of partition, gave over to the British all his possessions south of the Toombudra and Kistna rivers below their junction. At this time the ruler of the Kurnool country paid a yearly tribute of one lakh of Rupees to the Nizam. In 1839 the Kurnool District, through the rebellion of the then ruler of the country, was placed under British administration.

West centre Districts. Salem and Coimbatore. The districts of Salem and Coimbatore came into British possession, the former in 1792 by the treaty of Seringapatam, and the latter in 1799 after the final defeat of Tippoo and the partition of his territory between the British, the Nizam, and the legitimate successor to the Mysore Government, the late Maharajah of Mysore.

Neilgherries. The Neilgherry Hills, formerly a taluq of the Coimbatore District, was constituted a separate district under Act I of 1868.

West Coast Districts. Canara and Malabar. The two districts of Malabar and Canara, on the western side of the ghauts, fell into the possession of the British in 1792 and 1799 respectively. Canara was in 1859 divided into North and South Canara for administrative purposes, and in 1860 North Canara, with a population of 378,825, was transferred, for convenience of administration, from the Madras to the Bombay Presidency. The taluq of Kundapur, which formerly belonged to North Canara, is now attached to South Canara.

FORM OF ADMINISTRATION.

Government of the Presidency. The Administration of the Madras Presidency is vested in a Governor, with a Council of three Members, one of whom is the Commander-in-Chief for the time being, and the others Members of the Covenanted Civil Service. The Commander-in-Chief is Second in Council, but the Senior Civilian Member presides in the absence of the Governor. The appointment of the Ordinary Members of Council is made by the Queen in Council. Additional Members are added to the number for purposes of legislation only by the Governor; the particulars will be seen under Section III. The cabinet system of administration, under which each member of the Executive Council deals with separate subjects and refers special cases only to the whole Council, is carried out in a certain degree. It does not prevail however to the same extent as in the Supreme Council, still less to the same extent as in a European cabinet.

Secretariat. The different Secretariat Departments of the Government are given in a list below :—

Financial Department	...	⎫
Judicial	do.	...	
Public	do.	...	
Educational	do.	... ⎬ Under the Chief Secretary to
Political	do.	... Government.
Ecclesiastical	do.	...	
Marine	do.	...	
Legislative	do.	.. ⎭

Revenue do. ... ⎰ Under the Revenue Secretary
Pension do. ... ⎱ to Government.

Public Works do. ... ⎰ Under the Public Works
Secretary to Government
and the Joint Secretary to
Government for Irrigation.

Railways ... ... Under the Public Works
Secretary to Government.

Military Department ... Under the Military Secretary
to Government.

Attached to the Chief Secretary, Revenue Secretary, Public Works Secretary, and Joint Secretary for Irrigation, are four Under Secretaries. An Assistant Secretary is also attached to the Judicial and Legislative Departments.

The principal executive and other officers who are in direct communication with the Government, and the secretariat departments in which for the most part their communications are received, are shown in the list given below :—

Officers in direct communication with Government.

JUDICIAL.

The Judges of the High Court.
District and Sessions Judges.
District Magistrates.
Inspector-General of Police.
Inspector-General of Jails.
Magistrates of the Town Police Court.
    Do.   of the Egmore Police Court.
Judges of the Madras Court of Small Causes.
Advocate-General.
Government Solicitor.
Administrator-General.
Coroner of Madras.
Inspector-General of Registration.

PUBLIC.

Collectors of Districts.
Surgeon-General, Indian Medical Department.
Sanitary Commissioner.
Committee for the Examination of Assistants.
Private Secretary to His Excellency the Governor.
Government Astronomer.
Superintendent, Government Central Museum.
Chemical Examiner.
Superintendent of Stationery.
Supervisor of the Government Press.
Protector of Emigrants.
Translators to Government.
Examiner of Medical Accounts.

POLITICAL.

Resident in Travancore and Cochin.
Government Agent at Chepauk.
Government Agent at Tanjore.
Political Agent at Puducottah.
Collector in charge of the Special Agent's Department at
    Cuddalore.
Officer in charge of the Stipend Pay Office at Vellore.
British Consular Agents at Pondicherry and Karikal.
Receiver of Carnatic Property.

ECCLESIASTICAL.

The Right Reverend the Bishop of Madras.
Venerable the Archdeacon of Madras.
Senior Chaplain of the Church of Scotland.
Marriage Registrar for the Town of Madras.

MARINE.

Master Attendant, Madras.

FINANCIAL.

Trustees of the Civil Fund.
Accountant-General.
Commissioner of Paper Currency.
Presidents of Municipalities.
Superintendent of Stamps.

EDUCATIONAL.

Director of Public Instruction.
Commissioner for the Uncovenanted Civil Service
Examinations.

REVENUE.

Secretary to the Board of Revenue.
Conservator of Forests.
Director of Revenue Settlement.
Superintendent of Revenue Survey.

PUBLIC WORKS.

Chief Engineer, Public Works Department.
Chief Engineer for Irrigation.
Consulting Architect.
Consulting Engineer for Railways.
Examiner of Railway Accounts.
Examiner of Public Works Accounts.

MILITARY.

Adjutant-General.
Quartermaster-General.
Inspector-General of Ordnance.
Surgeon-General, British Medical Service.
Commissary-General.
Controller of Military Accounts.
Superintendent of Family Payments and Pensions.
Remount Agent.
Judge Advocate-General.
Superintendent of Army Clothing.

Apart from the Secretariat departments just mentioned, Administrative Departments. there are also the administrative " departments " into which the executive body is divided. Though the same term is used for each, the divisions are not identical in the two cases. The mode in which the work of these administrative departments, or different branches of the executive agency, is carried out, will be detailed hereafter under different sections.

The normal strength of the Covenanted Civil Service in Covenanted Civil Service. Madras, present and absent on leave, is usually taken to be about 160. The appointments in this Presidency reserved by law for Covenanted Civilians are the following :—2 Members of Council, 2 Judges of the High Court, 21 Judges, 3 Members of the Board of Revenue, 2 Secretaries to Government, 19 Collectors, 2 Secretaries to the Board of Revenue, 1 Collector of Customs and of Madras, 17 Sub-Collectors and Principal Assistants, 2 Under Secretaries to Government, 19 Head Assistants and Senior Assistants, 1 Special Assistant. The following appointments are held by Covenanted Civilians by usage though not by law :—1 Resident at Travancore, 1 Registrar of the High Court, 1 Commissioner of the Neilgherries, 1 Director of Revenue Settlement, and 1 Deputy Director of Revenue Settlement. A certain number of the Small Cause Court Judgeships have usually been held by Covenanted Civilians. The position occupied by a Junior Civilian as an Assistant, and until he acts in one of the posts detailed above, is not reckoned as an appointment. There are thus about 100 appointments ordinarily available to the service, and the service is kept at such a strength that, allowing for absentees, a Junior Civilian will get his first acting appointment in the lowest grade at about the close of his fourth year after arrival in the country. The ordinary annual recruitment calculated so as to ensure these results is about 7, giving an average of 28 Junior Civilians who will be at any one time not yet provided with an appointment. Recruitment in the Civil Service has not always been regular ; prior to 1861 there was a large under-recruitment, followed in the years 1862, 1863, and 1864 by a correspondingly large over-recruitment. A second under-recruitment followed the year 1869. These inequalities have produced some inconvenience. The Covenanted Civil Service is so called because each member of the service, before leaving England, enters into a covenant with the Secretary of State, wherein his privileges are recited, and in which he binds himself to certain conditions. The Covenanted Service have for leave and pension special rules attached to the Civil Leave and Civil Pension Codes.

Staff Corps. The Staff Corps, which provides officers for military duties, for duty in the civil branches of the Army, and for purely civil duties, numbers in this Presidency about 559 officers ; of these about 149 are employed in civil duties, that is to say, in the Political, Public Works, Police, Survey and Forest Departments, and 410, including unemployed officers, are in Military employment. The Staff Corps are under Military rules as regards leave and pension. The following table gives further particulars as to numbers :—

Major Generals.	Colonels with Colonel's allowances.	Brevet Colonel and Lieutenant Colonels.		Majors.		Captains.		Lieutenants.	
		Military Employ.	Civil Employ.	Military Employ.	Civil Employ.	Military Employ.	Civil Employ.	Military Employ.	Civil Employ.
8 unemployed.	33. 2 in Military employ ; rest unemployed.	164	40	104	60	74	42	27	7
Total 8	Total 33	Total 204		Total 164		Total 116		Total 34	

The Uncovenanted Civil Service comprises every person in the employ of Government, other than a Covenanted Civilian or an officer of the army, who is in receipt of 10 Rupees a month and upwards. No means are at present available for computing the exact number of Uncovenanted Civil Servants in the Presidency, but the number must be many thousands. A few of the superior posts are held by Europeans, but the service is for the most part composed of Eurasians and Natives. An Act of Parliament of 1793 (33 George III, cap. 52), in extending the East India Company's charter for another period of twenty years, provided among other things that no office, place, or appointment in the "Civil line" of the Company's India service should be filled up except by the appointment of a "Civil servant," that is a member of what is now the Covenanted Agency. This disability was removed in 1861 by Parliament in their Civil Service Act (24 and 25 Victoria, cap. 55) under which it was declared that with the exception of certain reserved appointments there detailed as belonging to the Covenanted Civil Service, all offices should be open. The Uncovenanted Service, though practically in existence for a very long time, dates then legally from the year 1861. The Uncovenanted Service is for pensionary purposes under the Civil Pension Code, and in that respect all its members are on the same footing. Some of its members, though not all, are provided with leave rules under the Civil Leave Code.

Uncovenanted Civil Service.

Below the Uncovenanted Civil Service is a large class of Government servants, with important duties, but whose salaries nevertheless do not place them in that class. The sub-division of the soil into so many independent interests necessitates in particular a large staff of Government officials in connection with revenue administration. Each village has its staff of officials, of whom the most important are the head of the village and

Other Civil agency.

magistrate, the accountant, the watchman, and the distributor
of water. These will be more particularly described hereafter.
If to these are added the large number of peons and other ministerial servants in Government employ, we shall obtain a total
under the present head of probably not less than half a lakh of
persons. Village servants have no pensions; the rest are
provided for under the Civil Pension Code. There are no
codified leave rules for this class of public servants.

ADMINISTRATION OF TRIBUTARY STATES.

TRAVANCORE.

History of
political
relations.

The English first settled in Travancore in 1684 at Anjengo,
when a Commercial Resident was appointed, whose functions soon
became political. In the war in Madura and Tinnevelly in 1756,
the Travancoreans, though not actual allies of the British, effected
diversions in their favor against the Mahomedans and Polygars
whose country they entered for the purpose of plunder through
the Ariencavoo or Puliaray and Aramboly passes. In the wars
with Hyder and Tippoo the Rajah of Travancore was an ally of
the British, and in the treaty concluded with the latter in 1784,
he was specially named as included in its provisions. In 1788
the Rajah seeing Tippoo establishing himself at Palghaut and
Calicut, and by his proximity threatening the lines of Travancore,
which connect the ghauts with Cranganore, applied to the
British Government for officers and sergeants to drill his troops,
but this being refused he accepted the offer of two of the
Company's battalions to be stationed on his frontiers at his
expense. Notwithstanding this, in the following year Tippoo
attacked the lines, and though at first he was unsuccessful and
had to retire wounded, yet in a second attempt he forced the
lines and ravaged the country. Up to this point the Governor-
General had been prevented by the restrictions placed on
his power by Act of Parliament from adopting measures to
counteract the danger existing from the scarcely concealed
hostile intentions of the Sultan of Mysore, but freed from this
restraint by the open aggression of Tippoo on an ally, Lord
Cornwallis at once decided on war as "a measure not less
necessary to vindicate the insulted honor of the nation, than to
provide for its future security by accomplishing at a favorable

moment the reduction of the power of Tippoo Sultan." The
result of this war was the treaty of 1792, which secured Travancore from further danger. In 1793 the Bombay Government
entered into a treaty with the Rajah, by which they bound him
to supply a large quantity of pepper for ten years in return for
arms and European goods. In 1795 a treaty was concluded
with the Rajah by which he agreed to pay an annual subsidy
equivalent to the cost of three battalions of sepoys, a company
of European Artillery, and two companies of lascars, and in
1805 a further treaty was entered into by which he engaged to
make such addition to the payment as should maintain one
more regiment of sepoys, and in case an additional force were
necessary to defend his territory against attack or invasion, he
agreed to contribute such a sum as was just and reasonable
in proportion to his revenue. This treaty gave the Governor
General power to interfere in the internal management of the
country, and even to assume the direct management of such parts
as seemed necessary to provide funds if there were grounds for
apprehending failure to defray the expense of the permanent
force and of any extraordinary force. The subsidy was finally
fixed at Rupees 8,00,000, at which sum it now stands. In 1808
an insurrection broke out, headed by the Dewan Vailoo Thumby
and his brother. The chief object was the assassination of the
Resident, Colonel Macaulay, and a party of Nairs endeavored to
surprise him in his house at Cochin, but he escaped on board a
vessel in the harbour. The Officer Commanding at Quilon was
at first unable to cope with the greatly superior numbers of the
rebels, but on being reinforced he marched out and utterly
defeated the Dewan who commanded a force of 30,000 men with
18 guns. A British force was then sent to invade Travancore
from the South, which, after forcing the Aramboly lines near
Cape Comorin and capturing the Forts of Oodiagherry and
Pulpanapuram, advanced on the capital and opened up communications with the Quilon force. The Rajah tendered his submission and disclaimed any sympathy with the insurgents. The
debts, however, into which the country was thrown by these
events prevented the punctual payment of the subsidy, and the
administration of the territory would have been assumed under
the terms of the treaty of 1805 had not the death of the Rajah
and the succession of a female led to the union in the person of
Colonel Munro of the combined functions of Resident and
Dewan. Under his administration tranquillity was restored, the
public services reorganized, debts discharged, and the financial

prosperity of the kingdom secured; and in 1829 the Rajah having attained his majority was formally installed, and thenceforth no political troubles affected the State. In 1862 a sunnud was issued by the Governor-General conveying to the Rajah the assurance that on failure of natural heirs the adoption of a successor according to Hindu law would be recognized. In 1865 a Customs Convention was entered into with Travancore by the British Government. According to this Travancore undertook—

First.—To raise the selling price of salt at the coast depôts to the British monopoly price, and at inland depôts to that price *plus* cost of carriage.

Secondly.—To abolish import duty on all British Indian produce imported by sea or land, and on goods of foreign origin exported through British Indian ports or by land from British territory, receiving as compensation Rupees 40,000 a year. Tobacco is not included.

Thirdly.—To levy the same import duty as the British Indian Government on foreign goods imported direct, except on cotton and metals, which were to pay 10 per cent. and tobacco which was to pay 120 Rupees per candy.

Fourthly.—Not to levy export duty of more than 5 per cent. except on timber, pepper, and betel-nut.

In consideration of this undertaking the British Government on its part agreed—

First.—To supply salt at Bombay on the same terms as to the Madras Government, namely, levying no duty, except three Pies per maund for petty local expenses.

Secondly.—To declare Travancore sea-ports to be British Indian ports within the meaning of Section 12, Act VI of 1863, and to levy no duty by sea or land on goods to and from Travancore. Opium is excepted.

Features of the country.

The mountains which separate Travancore on the east from the British provinces of the Coromandel Coast, and which at some points rise to an elevation of 8,000 feet above the sea, are covered with forest jungle; the flat country, which extends to an average distance of about ten miles from the sea inland, is distinguished by an almost unbroken mass of cocoanut and areca palm cultivation, this constituting the wealth of the country. The geological formation is peculiar. The whole country is undulating, and is traversed east to west by numerous rivers, the floods of which arrested by the peculiar action of the

Arabian Sea on the coast spread themselves out into numerous lakes or lagoons ; these connected by artificial canals, form an inland line of smooth-water communication, which extends nearly the whole length of the coast, and is of great value during the monsoon, when the coast itself is closed to navigation. According to the trigonometrical survey the area is 6,653½ square miles. The population has been given till recently at 1,280,000, but there are reasons for supposing that this number should be nearly doubled. The number of houses is supposed to be about 500,000, giving four or five souls to a house. The forests contain valuable timber, principally teak, anjelly, ebony, and blackwood. The borassus and other palms and the cotton tree are abundant. Elephants, tigers, cheetas, panther (including the black species), bear, bison, elk, deer, nilghau, and various species of monkeys are found in the forests. Pepper and cardamoms and nutmegs and cloves in a less degree, are characteristic productions of Travancore. The ordinary staple productions are the cocoanut, the areca nut, and the jack fruit, all grown in gardens ; various kinds of yams and other farinaceous roots are also grown. Rice is cultivated in the valleys and along the edges of the backwaters and in the tract of the flat country near Cape Comorin known as Nanjinad. Coffee has been introduced of late years by European planters, and is becoming a valuable article of export.

A census has recently been carried out in Travancore. The *Travancore Census.* rules and arrangements were nearly the same as those adopted in British India. There was first a registration of houses, and then a registration of shops, pagodas, churches, mosques, schools, and chuttrums. This was followed by a preliminary house-to-house enumeration occupying thirty days. Finally there was a synchronous enumeration of the population of the whole State in one day, the 18th May 1875. The result gave the population at 2,311,379 against 1,262,647, the result announced in 1854, and 906,587, the result announced in 1816. The cost of the operation was Rupees 32,000. The difference in accuracy between a census taken as the present one was on scientific principles and former censuses taken on a mere haphazard method is so great that no argument can be raised on the difference between the results. Taking the most important divisions of the community, the figures stand as follows :— Hindus, 1,700,317, or 73·64 per cent. ; Christians, 468,518, or 20·29 per cent. ; Mahomedans, 139,905, or 6·06 per cent. The feature that will probably cause most surprise in these figures is the large proportion of Christians, amounting to upwards of 20 per cent. of the population against $1\frac{1}{2}$ per cent. in the British portion of the Presidency. In Tinnevelly, where this element is strongest in the British Territory, the proportion does not rise above 6 per cent. In fact the total Christian population of the whole of the Madras Presidency is only 545,120 or but one-sixth more than that of Travancore. The Travancore Christians are thus classified :—Syrian Christians, 295,770 ; Roman Catholics, 109,820 ; Protestants, 61,284. The Hindus are separated in the census tables into 75 castes, but nearly 50 per cent. of the total are comprised in the two principal castes, Malayala Sudras and Eloovars ; the Nairs and Teers of Malabar. The Brahmins only number 38,434, of whom 27,672 are classed as foreign Brahmins. In the matter of education Brahmins, as might be expected, take the lead, 50 per cent. being returned as educated. Among the Nairs the proportion is 21 per cent. Taking the percentage throughout for educated persons it is 11·08 among the males and 46 among females compared with the figures 9·4 and ·16 in the Madras Presidency generally. Looking at the population of the country as now ascertained with respect to area it amounts to 343·4 per square mile. The average in British territory is 226, and the only districts in which the density of population exceeds Travancore are South Arcot, where it amounts to 360, Malabar, where it is 376, and Tanjore where it rises to 540. The great increase in the last-named district is evidently due to the fact that there is hardly any unoccupied area in it, whereas in Travancore as in Malabar large areas of primeval forest exist, much of which can never be inhabited.

Taxation in Travancore. The census shows that the total revenue raised in the State in that year amounted to $2\frac{1}{4}$ Rupees per head of the population, or almost the same as in the British territory. The average incidence of the land tax was 11 Annas per head as against 1 Rupee 6 Annas in British territory. This difference, however, is in part counterbalanced by the excess in customs, a great part of which is export duty on agricultural produce. The salt revenue amounted to $7\frac{1}{3}$ Annas per head, which is somewhat in excess of the average throughout the British territory. The salt consumed, however, is Bombay salt, the extra cost of carriage of which is now included in the selling price. Fish-curing is also largely carried on.

Zillah Courts were first established in Travancore in M. E. Growth of the Judicial system.
987. They were seven in number, and were placed under the
orders of the Dewan, who was then supreme head of all departments. The term regulation had not then come into use. All
measures of State were made known by royal proclamations
under Sign Manual, or by Sattavari-olais or Hookoonnamas.
The duty of these Courts was to inquire into all cases brought
before them, civil, criminal, or police, and to report to the
Dewan, whose approval in each was necessary to give effect to
their proceedings. This patriarchal system remained in force
till 990, when an Appellate Huzzur Court was formed for the
hearing of appeals from the decisions of the Zillah Courts.
This court still formed rather an appendage of the Dewan's
Cutcherry than an independent Court of Justice. In 993
Tahsildars, who were up to that time confined exclusively to
revenue duties, were for the first time invested with jurisdiction
in petty cases of police. The first experiment was tried in the
outlying taluq of Shencottah, adjoining British territory. In
1007 Munsiff Courts were created, vested with jurisdiction
in petty police cases and in civil suits not exceeding Rupees
100 in value. In 1010 a general scheme of judicial administration was conceived, founded on the arrangements obtaining in
the Madras Presidency, and was carried out by means of seven
regulations. Regulation I prescribed the general powers and
functions of Munsiffs, together with rules of general procedure
to be observed in the trial of civil suits. Regulation II
provided for the adjudication of suits by punchayets. Regulation III laid down the procedure for execution by Munsiffs of
decrees passed by all the courts. Regulation IV revised the
powers and constitution of Zillah Courts. Regulation V
created the Appeal Court subsequently called the Sudr. Regulation VI invested the Tahsildars with police powers. Regulation VII created Circuit Judges, and, in addition to defining
their powers, laid down the procedure to be observed in the
trial and commitment of criminal cases. These regulations,
though modified subsequently in some respects, form still the
groundwork of the present judicial machinery. In 1023 sub-
officers of police were appointed to exercise the powers of the
police officer or Tahsildar during his absence for the commitment
of cases only. In 1025 a regulation was passed reducing the
number of Munsiffs and relieving them of the duty of executing
decrees passed by the Appeal and Zillah Courts. In the same
year a law was passed to enable parties to sue *in formâ pauperis.*

In 1030 an important administrative change was made. Revenue
divisions were formed and the Dewan Peishcars, who were till
then doing duty in the Huzzur Cutcherry in charge of special
departments under the orders of the Dewan, were sent out to
take charge of them with powers of general control and supervision in all matters, revenue, magisterial, and police. They
were still subject to the orders of the Dewan as head of the
Administration and Chief Magistrate. In 1032 Circuit Courts
were abolished and Sessions Courts, three in number, were
constituted in their place. In 1036 Sessions Courts were in their
turn abolished, and the Zillah Judges were invested with the full
powers of the former Circuit Judges. This regulation provided
also for the adoption of the scale of punishments prescribed in
the Penal Code of British India. It also conferred on single
judges jurisdiction in causes up to Rupees 300, and in 1038
appeals in such cases were made inadmissible; but this was
rescinded and superseded by Regulation II of 1041, by which
small causes involving sums up to Rupees 10 before Munsiffs,
and up to Rupees 50 before Zillah Judges from the judgments of
Munsiffs, were determinable without appeal. This jurisdiction
still continues in force. In 1037 a very important reform was
introduced, a regulation being passed which virtually adopted
the British Civil Procedure Code. The present Sudr Court was
at the same time constituted under that title, the name of Appeal
Court being discarded. Regulation I of 1039 was passed for
the punishment of offences against the telegraph. Regulation
II of the same year created copyright in books. Breaches of
contract by artisans and workmen were made punishable by
Regulation I of 1040. In 1040 another regulation was passed,
defining the status of Vakils, their discipline and rights in
relation to the courts. A statute of limitation was also passed
in the same year. By Regulation I of 1041, single judges of
Zillah Courts were empowered to try and determine both
criminal and civil cases. In the same year a regulation raised
the jurisdiction of Munsiffs to suits of Rupees 200 value.
Regulation III of 1041 legalized admission of approvers in
criminal cases. Regulation I of 1042 introduced an amended
system of registration of assurances based upon that obtaining
in British India, but did not come into force till 1043. The use
of stamped cadjans and the then existing agency of registration
ceased from the date last named. Regulation I of 1043 legalized
the employment of Vakils in criminal cases. Regulation I of
1047 provided for the better conduct of business in the Sudr-

Court by giving a casting vote to the Chief Judge in certain cases. Another regulation was passed in the same year to relieve the Dewan of magisterial functions and appellate jurisdiction in criminal cases, and for redistribution of magisterial powers generally. In 1049 a Zillah Court was established at Alwaye presided over by a single judge.

Of revenue regulations not many have been passed. In 1035 and 1036 regulations were made for the levy of port dues at the port of Alleppey. Regulation II of 1040 provided for the adjudication of claims to waste lands, and rules for the sale of waste lands with special reference to the cultivation of coffee in the hill tracts of the State. In 1042 a royal proclamation was issued defining the rights and relations between Jenmies or landlords and their tenants. *Revenue Regulations.*

The present judicial machinery is thus the outcome of the legislation of more than half a century. It may be summarized as follows. First as to criminal jurisdiction. Sub-Magistrates are Magistrates of first instance in all cases, and have power to pass sentence of fine up to Rupees 10, imprisonment up to 30 days, and corporal punishment up to 6 lashes. The Magistrates have power of fining up to Rupees 50, imprisonment 3 months, and corporal punishment up to 1 dozen lashes. The Criminal Courts have power of fining up to Rupees 500, imprisonment 3 years, and corporal punishment up to 3 dozen lashes. All cases involving punishments higher than what is here mentioned must be referred to the Sudr Court for approval, whether the Criminal Court records a finding of conviction or acquittal. Appeals lie from Sub-Magistrates to Magistrates, from Magistrates to the Criminal Courts, and from the Criminal Courts to the Sudr, except in cases of disputed possession of lands, &c., wherein the order of the Magistrate is final as to present occupancy till a decision from a competent court of civil jurisdiction is obtained. The Sudr have also a general power of revision over all the decisions of the lower courts; for this purpose they peruse the calendars which are submitted to them in every case disposed of, in which the Zillah Court passes remarks. Next as to civil jurisdiction. Munsiffs have jurisdiction in suits up to Rupees 200, their decisions in suits up to Rupees 10 on the small cause side being final. The Zillah Courts have original jurisdiction without limit, and in suits up to Rupees 50 on the small cause side, in appeal from the decisions of Munsiffs their judgment is final. The Sudr have no original jurisdiction, but receive appellate regular *Present judicial machinery.*

appeals from the Zillah Courts and special appeals from decisions of Munsiffs, where points of law are involved. The Maharajah is the highest appellate authority in the State in all criminal and civil matters. All punishments exceeding 14 years of imprisonment or 36 stripes, all punishments involving imprisonment for life, and all sentences of capital punishment, must be confirmed by the Maharajah.

The Bar. There are Vakils attached to courts of all grades, Munsiffs, Zillah Courts, and the Sudr. Local examinations are held, and such candidates only as pass are allowed to practise in the courts, those passing high being selected for the Sudr, and those passing lower being permitted to plead in the Zillah and Munsiffs' Courts. Three Barristers of the High Court of Madras are also enrolled Pleaders of the Sudr. Several of the other pleaders have passed the British legal tests. The nominal roll of the Sudr Bar consists of 51 pleaders, and that of the Zillah Courts of 84 pleaders. Attached to the Sudr and to each of the Zillah Courts is a Sircar Vakil, who discharges the duties of a public prosecutor in criminal cases and those of a Government Vakil in civil suits where the Government is interested.

Criminal Courts. The Criminal Courts of First Instance are those of the Sub-Magistrate. Tahsildars are ex-officio Sub-Magistrates, as also are Police Amins. The former perform, in addition to their magisterial work, revenue and police duties; the latter similarly combine police with magisterial work. There are special Sub-Magistrates in a few places. Previous to 1048 there were altogether 57 officers exercising the functions of Sub-Magistrates. The Tahsildar Sub-Magistrates were divided into three classes in respect of their salaries, which were Rupees 100, 70, and 56, respectively. In the year 1049 the Maharajah abolished the last class altogether, making the salaries of all Rupees 70 and upwards. The Police Amin Magistrates were divided into two classes on salaries of Rupees 35 and 30. In their case the salaries were raised to Rupees 50 and 40 according to length of service. As to the standard of qualification of the Sub-Magistrates, it may be observed that they have had previous training for the most part in the various ministerial offices, Huzzur, Division, and Taluq. Some of them have passed the legal tests, and upwards of 20 are well acquainted with English. The Dewan Peishears who are in charge of the divisions are ex-officio Magistrates, and are four in number. The Commercial Agent at Alleppey, the Superintendent of the Cardamom Hills, and the

Conservator of Forests are also Magistrates. Thus there are in all 7 officers exercising the powers of a Magistrate. Regulation II of 1047, which was passed towards the close of the preceding year, which relieved the Dewan of direct magisterial functions, reserving to him as before full executive and administrative control, and which redistributed magisterial powers among the various grades, came into force from the beginning of 1048. Nearly all criminal cases come before the Sub-Magistrates in the first instance, few original cases being taken up and tried by the Magistrates. When cases are referred to the Magistrate by the Sub-Magistrate for higher punishment or other reasons, such cases are taken as original cases on the file of the Magistrate.

There is no distinct organized Police in Travancore, such as **Police.** has of late years been introduced into British India. That is to say, so far as the supervising and controlling agency is concerned, the Police has no separate establishment; the mass of the force however has always occupied a distinct footing and been employed exclusively for Police duties. The Dewan Peishcars or Divisional Officers, and the Tahsildars, combine revenue, magisterial and police functions, while Sub-Magistrates are Magistrates as well as Police Officers. There are however some purely Police Officers answering to the grade of Inspectors in the present British Police. There were eight of these including two newly appointed in the year under report. Their salaries, which varied much before, were raised during 1049 and fixed with reference to a scale by which the officers were graded into two classes according to their service and qualifications. Next come some ranks in the force which, known under various designations, Cutwalls, Police Naiks, Aminadars, Vicharipoos, Jemadar, Havildar, Duffadar, and the like, may be classed as answering to the grade of Head Constables. Their number is 56, and their pay ranges from Rs. 6 in the case of the Duffadar to Rs. 17 in the case of the Cutwall. The rest of the force may be termed " privates, " and are known as Naikens, Moodalpers, Peons, and the like; their pay ranges from Rs. $4\frac{1}{2}$ to 6, and they number about 1,900. The total strength of the force of all ranks in 1048 was 1,964, and has been augmenting considerably of late years, 31 being added in the year 1049. The whole force in 1040 was 1,043 and in 1045 was 1,667. The cost of the Police Force in 1048 was Rupees 8,960 per mensem, or for the year Rs. 1,07,520. The cost of the Police Magisterial

Officers and their establishments and Huzzur Central Office and establishment charged to Police amounted to Rs. 2,611 or 31,332. The entire cost was thus Rs. 1,38,852. All the principal ranks are stipendiary, and are paid exclusively by the State. The Desacavalgars or village watchmen, the remains of the ancient hereditary Police still found in Shencottah and Thovallay, are remunerated partly by the Sircar in money, and partly by the ryots in kind. The lowest class are required to render some kind of police duties, such as guarding public cutcherries and buildings in their own villages, but receive no remuneration.

Jails.

There are four jails in the State, are all under the general control of the Dewan. The Central Jail and another supplementary to it are at the capital; there is one at Quilon and another at Alleppey. The Durbar Physician, as Principal of the Medical Department, has chief medical charge, one or two subordinates having immediate charge of the hospitals attached to each jail. The charge of the jails themselves is vested in superintendents or jailors. No valuation has been attempted of the work done by the convicts as a body; a large number of them are employed in the making and repairing of roads at the capital and at Quilon. Others are told off in small parties, from day to day, for garden-work in the palaces, hospitals, Sircar buildings, and public gardens. Parties are told off to cart their own daily provisions, to cook their own meals, to wash their own clothes, to shave, to draw water for cooking and cleaning the jails and urinals, to make their own fetters, and to remove poudrette. Some are employed to saw timber in the Marhamut workshop, and a few are employed in ivory carving. By the custom of the country Brahmins and females of all classes are exempt from hard labor or labor of any kind; they are from the same cause free from capital punishment.

Registration of Assurances.

The old system of Registration of Assurances, which was superseded in 1042 by the regulation now in force, provided a regular agency of village notaries, who derived their appointments from, and acted under, the orders of the Sudr Court. Their number was unlimited. They were remunerated, not by salaries, but by fees levied upon the instruments which they registered, and which had to be drawn up by themselves and to be transcribed for registry. The stamped cadjans were supplied to them through the Munsiff Courts, and were sold at certain fixed rates, the proceeds being credited to the State. The Village Registrars (or Oorkanakens) had power to make summary inquiries into objections against the execution of the deeds, and to refuse registration in case they were deemed valid. They were also prohibited from registering whenever they found that the Sircar had liens on the property, such as for arrears of revenue, or had them already under attachment, or that they were Service or Personal Inam tenures. The revenues under the system did not average more than Rupees 1,200, as unstamped documents were not invalid but were only subjected to a penalty of 3 per cent. on value when produced before a Court. This unpaid agency did not work either to the profit of the State or to the satisfaction of the public, and the latter were subjected to much annoyance, delay, and extortion. A reform was effected by new legislation, which brought into existence the present system. Under this the Registrars are paid servants of the State, divided into four classes with reference to the quantity of work of the various districts. As a rule, there is a Registrar to each Revenue Taluq, and none is appointed who has not passed a public examination in the law and rules of Registration. Above the District Registrars are Inspectors, who are three in number, and whose duty it is to inspect every Registry Office within their ranges once in two months at least, examine the state of the registers, and report the result in their fortnightly diaries. The work of these District Registrars is checked and controlled by a Central Office, at the head of which is the Huzzur Registrar.

The broad distinctions in the tenures of land in Travancore **Tenures of** are Jenm, Madambimar and Sircar. **land.**

The Jenm lands may be sub-divided into Devasom, or those **Jenmum** held by pagodas, and Bramasum, or those held by Brahmins. **lands.** The normal condition of the Jenm tenure is absolute freedom from tax of any kind, and the tenure dates from that remote period of antiquity when, according to tradition, the " Kerala" country was reclaimed from the sea and parcelled out by Parsurama among a colony of Brahmins. The colony still remains, and is known as that of the sixty-four village communities. The tenure ceases the moment it passes into alien hands for a money consideration, whatever the nature of the transaction. The mere letting out of lands however for annual rent to a tenant does not vitiate the tenure. The moment an alienation or kanom takes place, the land becomes liable to a light tax called rajabogum, amounting in the case of gardens to one-sixth or one-eighth of the full rental (Venpauttom or Kundapauttom); in the

case of paddy lands the tax amounts to nearly the same proportion of the full grain-rent, that is, half, three-tenths, or one-
tenth of the quantity of seed required to sow the land, the
full grain-rent being represented by an average of three
times the quantity of seed. If the Kundapauttom of the
alienated garden was fanams 100, the rajabogum or karum or
tax would be nearly $16\frac{1}{2}$ or $12\frac{1}{4}$ fanams; in the case of paddy
lands, if the land was one parah khandum, that is, a block of
land which would require one parah of seed, the full grain-rent
would be 3 parahs. The light tax chargeable would be only $\frac{1}{2}$,
$\frac{3}{10}$, $\frac{1}{10}$ of one parah. Even if the mortgage is afterwards
redeemed by the Jenmi, the light tax continues on the land for
ever and at the same rate. The only variation is for worse;
for if the mortgagee dies heirless, the Sircar seizes the tenure,
transfers the land to the head Sircar, and pays to the Jenmi
or landlord the residue of rent or mitchavarom if any was
paid to him by the deceased. Again, if the land is abandoned
(Nirthul) by the kanom holder on account of its becoming unfit
for cultivation, from various causes, it is at once transferred
to Sircar and granted as a new Sircar pattom tenure if it is ever
reclaimed. A Jenmi, as a rule, never alienates absolutely
(Uttipare) except to other Jenmies, Brahmins or Davasoms
(pagodas).

Madambimar lands. The Madambimars are, in common parlance, also called Jenmies, though strictly speaking they are not so, because their
lands are subject to the rajabogum, whether in their own hands
or alienated to others. They are generally Nairs, or others not
Brahmins. These also seldom alienate by absolute sale; if they
do, the tenure is extinguished as with Jenm lands, the land is
transferred to Sircar, the purchase money, less a fine of 25 per
cent., is given credit for, and interest is allowed on the 75 per
cent. only, the remainder of interest being added to the existing
rajabogum karom, which will still be much short of full pattom
or rent of the land. At every alienation, however, this fine of
25 per cent. is levied, till sometimes the purchase money entirely
disappears, and interest, added to rajabogum which continues
unabated, may absorb all the rental and even exceed it.

Sircar lands. All other lands are known as Sircar that is liable to full assessment or pattom, whether actually paying it at the full or reduced
rates or not paying it at all, as when given away as Inams. The
Sircar, in fact, takes in respect of these lands the place of the
Jenmi or landlord. These may be broadly sub-divided into six
classes—(1), Kundukrishipattom; (2), Kuttagapattom; (3)

Vempattom ; (4), Otti ; (5), Anubogum, &c., or personal Inams ; and (6), Ulliam or service. It is not easy to state precisely how the proprietary right in such lands came to be vested in the Sircar or the governing power, the primeval tenure of all lands on the coast being pure Jenm according to accepted tradition. Probably, when the Rajahs were called in by election by the Numboory landlords, as they did once in twelve years for the purpose of government, some lands were granted to them. Accretion of escheated lands, unoccupied lands reclaimed in the course of years, annexed home farms of subjugated chiefs, and lands purchased for money from the Dutch, have also contributed to increase the roll of Sircar lands. The kandukrishi lands are literally the " home farms " of the sovereign. The lands are theoretically speaking cultivated by the sovereign himself. Seed and hire for cultivation, the latter being given in kind, used to be advanced to the actual tenants and recovered with interest out of the harvest, of which they got for their share generally a little more than half of the gross produce. Of late years this system has been discontinued, the grain-rent alone being recovered from the cultivators in kind. The tenants are really tenants at will. They cannot sell even the occupancy right, nor can they transfer it without the previous consent of the Sircar. As a matter of fact, however, the Sircar never interferes with their occupancy. The grain-rent is collected in kind, is stored in various granaries, and is spent according to the requirements of the large feeding-house at the capital. If there is any surplus, it is sold and the proceeds credited to the general exchequer. (2.) The few lands which now remain under the head of Kuttagapattom are the purchases from the Dutch (Paliport), from the Jenmi (Pooliendurti), and the jungle lands called Kudukaval, forming the frontier defences towards Cape Comorin. The bulk of such tenures have been sold in past years and converted into vempattom. The above are rented out to the highest bidder, who levies full rent and makes some profit himself. This system of farming out for short periods, which leads to oppression of the tenants, is now discouraged. (3.) The vempattom lands are lands liable to and paying full tax or assessment. In the case of gardens a general deduction of 25 per cent. is allowed as compensation to the owner for the cost and labor of growing the gardens. In the case of paddy lands 20 or 30 per cent. is allowed as a permanent deduction for adverse seasons, blights, and floods of ordinary kind. When an extraordinary drought or flood occurs, remissions on a larger

scale are allowed as a matter of grace. In the case of lands
lying on 'the borders of backwaters or rivers the assessment is
remitted on fallows of alternate years once in three years or once
in four years. These fallows having been determined originally
on the oath of the ryots, the remission is called Sathiakoravu.
In the Nanjanaud, where there is river irrigation which is sometimes deficient, remissions are allowed for blighted or withered
crop, though never for waste lands. Where the water-supply is
dependent on the falling rains and on rivers, both waste lands
and withered crop are allowed for. A deduction is also allowed
when dry crops are cultured on paddy lands. The lands falling
under this head were formerly unalienable by the occupant ryots,
the proprietary right being theoretically vested in the State. In
1401 rights of full property were conferred on them without
payment, but subject to a fine or fee of 2 per cent. on the money
consideration indicated in the conveyances. This fee yields an
annual sum of Rupees 30,000, representing a value of transactions in this description of land (before unsaleable and unmarket-
able) of Rupees 15,00,000. (4.) Otti, or as it is commonly
called Pandar Otti, denotes a mortgage, the parties to the transaction being the Sircar on one side as mortgagor and the ryot
holding the land on the other as mortgagee, the consideration
being either actual cash borrowed by the State or something
equivalent. It is, in fact, in no respect legally different from a
simple mortgage dealing, or kanom, between a jenmi who
borrows and a tenant who lends the money. One kind of consideration is actually money borrowed from the ryot to meet State
necessities. Another kind is an acknowledgment of money
invested in forming a garden, repairing tanks, making improvements or reclaiming lands, from all of which either new revenues
have been added or old revenues revived and secured. A third
kind consists of State debt which came with the various petty
kingdoms and principalities from time to time subdued and
annexed to Travancore. A fourth kind consists of similar debts
coming with escheats. Interest is allowed on these loans at rates
rising from 5 to 12 per cent. per annum according to the
circumstances and times when the obligations were contracted.
These transactions are in many cases several centuries old. The
interest is made payable by a deduction from the tax or pattom on
particular lands. Whatever remains after deducting the interest
and adding rajabogum on the full pattom becomes the next tax
payable on otti lands. These lands are alienable at will, but at
every alienation both the principal and interest are reduced 25

per cent. ; in other words, the Sircar repudiates the obligation to that extent by refusing to pay the full original interest. When the number of hands thus changed amount to 16, the debt is extinguished, and the land begins to pay full assessment. In some few places the fine is levied in cash in a lump, leaving the assessment on the lands as favorable as before. Economically and financially this plan is by far better, as the value of property remains the same to the ryot and the Sircar is benefited by the lump receipt and is saved the constant correction of accounts. In Nanjanaud no such fines are levied on alienations of otti lands, unless the family of the survey holder becomes extinct. In some few cases near the capital no fines are levied under any circumstances. (5) Anubogum lands are held on *bonâ fide* favorable or personal Inam tenures, and are liable to pay no assessment except the usual rajabogum at $\frac{1}{6}$ and $\frac{1}{4}$. In some cases they are liable to quit-rents in addition. They may be mortgaged and redeemed without fines, but when absolutely sold the tenure is resumed and the land transferred to " otti" and dealt with under the rules applicable to that head. (6) Oollium, or Vritti tenures constitute the Service Inams. They are held either for services actually performed at the present time, or for former services ; in the latter case they are of the nature of Inams held for personal benefit. As a general rule, the former are inalienable, and the latter, when alienated, become liable to fines or ottivilakum. But even in regard to the former a succession duty or addukuvathu is levied on every change of incumbency calculated at 50 per cent. of a year's rental (pattom) for gardens and $2\frac{1}{2}$ fanams per parah of paddy land. If the holder's family becomes extinct, the tenure is either transferred on payment of a high fine or premium (adiyara), or sold to the highest bidder at a public auction, when sometimes very high prices are realized. The bulk of these tenures are the Nair Vrittis, the holders of which are bound to supply at certain fixed prices vegetables and provisions for pagodas, for ootperas or charity feeding-houses, and for the royal birthday ; they are also bound to raise sheds, to thatch and guard public buildings, and to do occasional peon's duties. They receive advances from the public funds and settle accounts subsequently on producing vouchers for the due delivery of the provisions, supplies, or work done. The Nair Vrittis are held free of all assessment or pattom, but they are liable to the payment of the rajabogum quit-rents at $\frac{1}{5}$, &c., as already alluded to, plus a fee called " load-tax" (chumadupanam), which is about 2 fanams payable on the whole Vritti. This is supposed to represent the commuted value of a load of vegetables, &c., which each Vritti holder was bound by the tenure to bring without payment. When Vrittis have been found excessive in proportion to the service required, they have been charged with ½ pattom and left with the holders. Where lands were insufficient, they have been supplemented by grants of money from the State treasury without interest. Where there were no lands previously, money grants were made on the same condition for service. When the service is not rendered for a time, the full pattom on the lands is levied as a penalty if the holder refuses to render it, and the land itself becomes liable to be resumed and transferred to another. This, however, seldom happens. Where the money loans received from the State alone constitute the consideration for the service, it can be redeemed and enfranchised by the repayment of the original sum if the holder is inclined to relieve himself from the service. This measure was sanctioned recently. The Nair Vrittis consist of about 20,000 holders of 5,764 gardens and 220,000 parahs of paddy land ; the annual rental of the former being about Rupees 9,000 and that of the latter about Rupees 2,00,000. The State loans advanced for service amount to about Rupees 2,00,000, the interest on which is about Rupees 12,000 at 6 per cent. Thus, the total value of the tenures is about Rupees 2,21,000, and deducting from this quit-rent paid amounting to about Rupees 21,000, the net value may be given at Rupees 2,00,000. Other kinds of Service Inams are of a miscellaneous and local kind, such as those belonging to canoe services, elephant trapping, wrestlers, songsters, coppersmiths, potters, musicians, dancers, &c.

Assumed Pagoda lands. Of the Devasom Jenmi lands alluded to above, 378 pagodas were assumed and brought under the direct management of the Sircar in the year 987, during the administration of Colonel J. Munro. They consisted of 62,000 gardens and 548,000 parahs of paddy lands, the former yielding a rental of about Rupees 50,000, the latter Rupees 3,50,000, total Rupees 4,00,000. The annual expenditure out of this is only Rupees 2,50,000, leaving a surplus Rupees 1,50,000.

Large Jenm holdings. There are certain large Jenm holdings called Adhigara Oyevoo and Desa Oyevoo, consisting of compact blocks of territory. The largest of these is the Edapully Rajah, a Numboori Brahmin of the highest rank. He was and still is in some respects an independent chief, and is entitled to all sources of revenue,

whether actually levied by himself or administered by the State for
him ; compensation being settled and paid every year. He pays
no tribute excepting a sum of Rupees 1,000 per annum, which is
for police services rendered. He has, however, no police, civil or
criminal authority within the principality. The annual revenue
amounts to about Rupees 75,000. The Pooniat Rajah is another
chief whose tenure is peculiar. Attingul consists of two
Adhigaroms, and is the private property of the Ranees. The
annual rental is probably below Rupees 20,000. Killimanoor
is the estate of the Coil-Tumburans, who are generally allied by
marriage to the Ranees and, consequently, to the reigning
Sovereigns. There are other large holdings in which, besides
exemption from tax of any kind, the proprietors have power to
deal with their property without the interference of Government.

1. Mahadevaswami Pagoda (Kottarakarray).
2. Kavioor   do.   (Tiruvellah).
3. Kamooganicheri   do.   (Puthanapooram).
4. Elankonappen   do.
5. Pangotoo Krishnaswamy (Kottarakarray).
6. Mannadi Bagavathy (Koonatoor).
7. Paniannarkavoo (Tiruvellah).
8. Congrapully Numburipad's Sastha (Canjoripully).
9. Agherra Numbooripand (Kottarakarray).
10. Do. and Omanpalh   do.   (Quilon).
11. Vunchipelar Peruvauthanum Sastha.

The lands of the Sree Pudmanabha Swami temple extend over
the whole of Southern Travancore, and are for purposes of
account divided into three divisions, Madapaud, Neendakara
Sanketham, and Colatoor-Melanganom. The tenure, which is
pure Jenm, dates from every remote antiquity. The annual rental
of these lands is about Rupees 73,000, derived from 21,517
gardens and 92,960 parahs of paddy lands, the former yielding
Rupees 14,000, the latter Rupees 59,000. The funds belonging
to this pagoda are separately collected and accounted for, but
the State has a general control ; any surplus is credited to the
State, and deficits, when they occur, are made good by the State.

The earliest survey or ayacut remembered by the oldest living **Surveys and**
accountant in Travancore is that of the year 914, when Travan- **Assessment.**
core was within its ancient limits. There were several surveys
both anterior and subsequent. The surveys on which the present
revenue arrangements are based are those of the year 948 ; this
was a very comprehensive one, and embraced nearly the whole of

the lands, gardens and paddy fields now belonging to the State. There has however been subsequent surveys. No idea is afforded by the ayacut accounts of the whole extent of paddy lands, but those which come under assessment consist of 31,81,620 parahs of lands, or about 40,000 acres at 8 parahs per acre, assessed with a net revenue, after making all deductions, of Rupees 8,08,958, or 2 Rupees per acre. It is impossible to say that the ayacut rates of assessment on paddy lands have been fixed on a uniform plan or principle, but a very minute local appraisement by arbiters and Sircar officers seems to have preceded the operation of classification. Each field expressed by the quantity of seed it took to sow was rated at so many parahs of produce, and commonly expressed as double, treble, quadruple, &c. North of Trevandrum the average rate of rent was about double the seed. In the south it went up to beyond ten times, but the average was probably five times, and in recent years all excessive rates above ten were reduced to that level. The average gross produce in the north may be put at between 7 and 8 times, and that in the south at between 12 to 15 times the amount of seed. The Sircar share is thus about a fourth in the one case and a third in the other.

Extra cesses. The above are the standard pattom rates on the lands. There are however various other extra cesses, about 200 in number, corresponding to the abwabs of North India, collected over and above the standard rates. They amount to Rupees 60,000, and are met with in all taluqs.

Mode of collecting assessment. The taxes on gardens are collected in money with a few exceptions. The tax on paddy land is collected part in grain and part in money, according to the wants of the Sircar with reference to neighboring temples and charity feeding institutions. The proportion may be stated as a third in grain and two-thirds in money. All grain received in kind, but found in excess of Sircar wants, is commuted into a money payment at varying rates. For gardens 10 equal kists are required and for paddy 4 kists for each crop; only two instalments however are allowed for the portion payable in money.

Former customs duties. As in British India, there were inland and frontier and sea customs duties levied in Travancore up to the year 1012, when the inland transit duties were abolished, and the frontier and sea-board chowkeys alone were retained. There were import as well as export duties on almost every article up to the year 1040, when, by a convention with the British Government, import duty, except on articles brought direct from countries other than British India and Cochin, was abolished. The Government undertook to compensate Travancore by an annual cash payment. The export duty was retained, but it was in no case to exceed 5 per cent., except in the case of timber, which was subject to a duty of 10 per cent. The articles of Sircar monopoly, namely, salt, tobacco, pepper and opium, were exempted from the convention. The pepper monopoly was abolished in 1036, and superseded first by an excise duty of Rupees 15 per candy levied in the taluqs before the article left, and afterwards in 1044 by an export duty of 5 Rupees per candy ; this continues to the present day. The monopoly in the highest year has yielded a net revenue of Rupees 3,50,000 and in average years Rupees 1,50,000. Under the excise system it yielded a maximum of Rupees 95,000 and an average of Rupees 55,000 ; under the present arrangement the export duty gives Rupees 15,000 on an average. Tobacco, which was also a strict monopoly, was formerly imported by the Sircar from British India and Ceylon and sold in the Sircar's own bankshalls. This system was abolished in 1038 and superseded by an import duty, which has been successively reduced from Rupees 190 to Rupees 110 upon the best kind. Under the present arrangement merchants import tobacco on their own account, but by certain routes only, and not below a certain quantity ; and they are required to bond it in Sircar warehouses. In the time of the monopoly it yielded a maximum of Rupees 12,00,000 and an average of Rupees 10,00,000 ; under the excise arrangement it yielded at first nearly Rupees 8,00,000 and afterwards Rupees 9,00,000. The quantity of tobacco consumed has more than doubled itself between 1033 and 1049.

Salt was made a monopoly of the State in the last two months Salt monopoly. of the year 988. In the following year 989 the sales stood thus : home-made white salt 50,000 Indian maunds, black salt 81,000 Indian maunds, total 131,030 Indian maunds ; foreign salt imported 153,000 Indian maunds ; grand total 284,000 Indian maunds. The total revenue yielded to the Sircar was Rupees 1,85,149. The price was Rupee 1-1-0 per maund for the best quality, lower prices being put on inferior salt. At the end of the year the selling price was reduced to Annas 11¾ per maund. The amount of revenue and the prices remained with little variations till the year 1034, when the price of foreign salt was raised to Rupee 1-1-0 and the revenue indicated a corresponding increase. In the year 1037 the selling price of home-made white salt was raised and made equal to that of foreign salt. But this increase in the selling rate was then made applicable only to the districts north of the Wurkally barrier. In the following year the increase was extended to all white salt sold throughout the country. The revenue continued to increase from year to year until 1040, when it reached Rupees 5,48,659. At the close of this year, by an arrangement with the British Government, the price was assimilated to that of British India; that is to say, from Rupee 1-1-0 it became Rupee 1-8-0 per maund. In all the subsequent revisions made by this Government the Sircar has followed the example set. In 1041 the price was raised from Rupee 1-8-0 to 1-11-0, and in 1045 it was raised from Rupee 1-11-0 to Rupees 2, which latter is the price ruling at present. At the time when the price was first assimilated with the British rate, it became necessary to discontinue the production and sale of black salt; from its bad quality this could not be sold at the same price with the rest.

Present supply of salt.

The present supply is derived partly from the Sircar pans in South Travancore, four in number, and partly from Bombay. Occasionally salt from Tinnevelly or Tanjore is imported. The actual prime cost of home-made salt is 1 anna and 10 pies per Indian maund, or Rupees $13\frac{1}{4}$ per garce. Imported Bombay salt costs the Sircar Rupees 38 per garce when landed and delivered into the stores. Unlike the operations on the other coast, there are in Travancore two seasons of manufacture, one between September and November and the other between January and June. Salt is not taken over from the ryot as soon as made, but is buried in pits and allowed to season till the bitter taste has worn off. It is dug up and received into store as required, and then only payment of the kudiwarum is made. The interval between manufacture and payment is sometimes several years. This is the system of the country, but a concession was made in the year under report, by advancing 50 per cent. of the price on the estimated quantity as soon as it was removed from the pans.

Abkary.

The revenue from Abkary is managed much as it is in British India; that is to say, the monopoly of selling toddy and country liquor is farmed out, taluq by taluq, to the highest bidder. The contractors are forbidden from selling below certain rates; the Tahsildars recover the rents from the contractors in ten equal monthly instalments, the last two months of the year being left out. If the contractor chooses to register sub-contracts or sub-leases before the Tahsildar, this officer is authorized to help the contractor in enforcing recovery of his dues by summary process. Fifty-seven years ago the revenue from this source was Rupees 41,124, and continued fluctuating between that sum and Rupees 59,448 up to the end of the year 1033. Since then it has risen rapidly, and in 1047 had reached Rupees 1,06,591.

The opium monopoly includes also that in gunja, which is **Opium.** cultivated in the southern extremity of the State. Opium was made a source of revenue for the first time in 1037; it then yielded Rupees 14,774, but fell off in subsequent years owing to losses sustained by the contractors. It is again reviving at present, the rental for the last two years having been Rs. 9,161 and 10,178; the amounts were fully recovered within the close of each year. Opium is consumed chiefly by the Moplas, north of Quilon, and especially in Meenachel, a hilly taluq, where the drug is resorted to as a preventive of malarious fever. A single contractor usually holds the farm of this monopoly for the whole State.

The whole range of forests in the country is under the charge **Forests.** of the Conservator, excepting the Cardamom Hills, mostly included in the Thodupulay Taluq, and a small tract in South Travancore, both of which are separately administered. The forest tract in South Travancore is under the control of the Revenue Department. Timber is felled here at Government cost, and periodically sold by public auction at a depôt established in the Thovalay Taluq under the superintendence of an officer called Aminadar. Besides the general conservancy of the forests, the Conservator is charged with the duty of supervising the trapping of elephants, the collection of revenue from miscellaneous forest produce, the supplying of timber for Government requirements, and other items. The most valuable timber trees produced in the forests are teak, blackwood and ebony, in respect of which the Government has a monopoly. No permits are granted to private individuals for felling them. Timber of other kinds is allowed to be cut by private parties on payment of a fee, or kutticanom, at certain fixed rates. As a means of check, watch stations are provided at various places, and timber felled under permits is subject to inspection at these stations in the course of transit.

Cardamoms.   One item of miscellaneous forest produce is cardamom. In the forests under the Conservator this spice is not regularly cultivated, but grows wild. Of late, however, it would seem that attention has been directed towards bringing it under regular cultivation as in the Cardamom Hills. Cardamom gardens to the extent of some hundred acres have been marked out. The Cardamom Hills were under the supervision of the Conservator of Forests till the year 1044, when they were transferred to a special Superintendent. The undivided attention which the change has secured for the industry has produced increased efficiency in the working of the department.

Davasom.   The revenue of the lands belonging to the Sri Padmanatha-sawmi Pagoda, which have been acquired from remote times by gift, amount to Rupees 75,000 and go to defray the daily expenses of the institution ; surpluses are credited to the State treasury and deficits, which rarely occur, are made good from it. This temple is more or less independent of Government management. The State had no concern with the management of any temples before the year 987, when the landed property of 378 temples was assumed and the management taken over. Other minor temples, 1,171 in number, which had no property, were also assumed either before or at that date. The expenditure, establishments and rules for management, were settled on this occasion on a permanent basis. The lands thus assumed now yield a revenue of Rupees 4,30,000, while the annual expenditure on the 378 pagodas concerned with them amount to about Rupees 3,92,000. The annual grants for the other 1,171 temples amount to about Rupees 28,000. The interest of Government in respect of these institutions is for the most part that of a trustee, and as a church establishment they cannot be regarded as expensive.

Ootperas.   The ootperas or charitable feeding institutions are 45 in number, inclusive of 3 conjee-houses. The chief is at the capital, and is known as the agrasala. The others are distributed at convenient stages on the line of road commencing from the Aramboli Pass in the south and ending at Paravoor in the north. The former is intended to feed all comers, the latter to feed travellers only—Brahmins are the chief recipients of the charity. Of the conjee-houses one is at Thovallay close to the Aramboli Pass, where all classes and castes of travellers are fed ;

one is at Shencottah a little way beyond the Ariengavoo Pass, where also all classes are served; the third is at the capital, which is confined to the very poorest of all classes and creeds, and chiefly to the dumb, the lame, the sick and the blind.   The ootperas are primarily intended for the relief of the poor and wayworn traveller, but it cannot be denied that they have come in some cases to be regarded as feeding-houses for the poor of a resident population.   It may be remarked that 75 per cent. of the people fed at these charitable institutions come from the southern provinces of the Madras Presidency, and from Malabar, and form a kind of migratory population.   The reduction of expenditure on ootperas has been kept in view of late years.

The system of State vernacular education embraces— **Vernacular Schools.** (1) Proverti or Village Schools, (2) Taluq District Schools, and (3) Aided Schools receiving grants.   The third class is confined to the town of Trevandrum.   The department was organized in the year 1042.   The course of instruction in the village schools consists of reading, writing, both on paper and cadjan; arithmetic; geography, both general and of Travancore; and writing from dictation from the History of Travancore.   The course of instruction in the taluq schools is the same, but the standard is higher, and Indian History is also taught.   Sanscrit is taught in three and Tamil in all of the taluq schools in South Travancore.   At the central vernacular school at Trevandrum the standard embraces the first book of Euclid, Algebra (to simple equations), and the History of India and Travancore.   In the girls' schools the subjects are the same as in the taluq schools, with the addition of some vocal music.   Some of the teachers are females.   The class books used in all the vernacular schools have been translated or compiled by a committee who were brought into existence simultaneously with the system of State vernacular education.   Uniform fee is collected in every school, namely 2 annas, except at the central school, where it varies with each class from 2 annas to 4 annas.   The first masters of Proverti schools are paid Rupees 7 per mensem and the under-masters each Rupees 5.   But the pay is reduced when the fees realized fall short of 25 fanams, or the attendance falls short of 25 boys. Formerly, when this was not attained, pay used to be refused altogether.   In a recent year this rule was relaxed, and the masters were paid in proportion to the fees realized.   The buildings and furniture are provided by the villagers themselves.

Maps alone are at present supplied by the Government. In some schools the boys sit on the ground. The salaries of Taluq Schoolmasters range thus : 1st Master, Rupees 20; 2nd Master, Rupees 12; 3rd Master, Rupees 10; Monitors, Rupees 5. The head-master of the central school is allowed a salary of Rupees 60 and the under-masters from Rupees 30 to 10. The aided schools receive a grant of Rupees 60 per annum each on condition of their teaching the same subjects as are taught in the Government schools and of undergoing periodical inspections. There is nothing to prevent other subjects being taught. The village schools are inspected at least once in two months by Deputy Inspectors whose salaries range from Rupees 30 to 35. There were ten of them in 1049. The district or taluq schools are inspected once in three months by Inspectors whose salary is Rupees 85, inclusive of a travelling allowance of Rupees 15. The aided schools in the town of Trevandrum are visited every month and supervised by a special Inspector on a salary of Rupees 40 per mensem. The whole department is controlled by a Director, whose salary is Rupees 150.

Vernacular Schools belonging to Missionary Societies.   The educational operations of the various Missionary Societies have always been a very active widely influential agency in the education of the youth of the country, especially of the lower classes. The results of their labors may be summarized thus in a recent year :—

	No. of Schools.	No. of Pupils. Boys.	Girls.
The London Mission Society	137	4,040	1,036
The Church Mission Society	110	2,600	560
The Catholic Mission, Vicar Apostolic, Malabar.	258 (average 25 each)	6,000	1,500 (guessed)
Vicar Apostolic, Quilon	72	2,674	228
Bishopric, Cochin	28	589	197
Syrian Metropolitan See of Malabar	132	20,000	7,000 (deducting 2,000 for English schools).

It is under contemplation to introduce a system of grants-in-aid or of payment for results in respect of some of these schools.

Medical Department.   The total monthly cost of the Medical Establishment is Rs. 3,924, and of the Vaccination Establishment Rs. 882, giving a total monthly cost of Rs. 4,086, or Rs. 57,672 per annum. The medical institutions maintained at the capital are the Civil or General Hospital, the Charity Hospital to which is attached a Small-pox Hospital, the Lunatic Asylum, the Lying-in Hospital, and the Jail Hospital. There are subordinate dispensaries attached to the Rajah's Palace, to the First Prince's Palace, to the public offices, and to the Durbar Physician's residence. The medical institutions at out-stations consist of three at Alleppey, namely, a Civil Hospital, Charity Hospital, and Jail Hospital, and twelve at other places. The medicines and medical stores cost on an average Rs. 30,000 per annum. The total annual expenditure of the department amounts to nearly Rs. 1,08,000.

The Revenue Survey Department is attached to the Dewan's **Revenue** Cutcherry, and is directly under his orders. It was organized in **Survey.** the year 1040. The survey operations are mostly in connection with coffee estates.

The Sircar Press was organized about forty years back, at the **Press.** time when the Trevandrum English school came into existence. The scope of its operations was exceedingly limited for a long time, the demand for printing work being confined to the publication of the Trevandrum Almanac and the requirements of the English school and one or two more departments. Recently the department has undergone considerable improvement in strength and efficiency. The stock of printing machinery and types received valuable additions during the years 1040 to 1044. In 1045 a Lithographic Press was supplied with an establishment to work it. At the present time almost every department derives help from the Press, and the general introduction of paper recently effected is calculated to render the need for its assistance still greater.

The Unjel, in former days, was maintained for State service **Unjel or** only, but about 1036 it was thrown open to the public and the **Local Post.** system of levying postage introduced. In 1036 there were 44 stations or Post Offices, and 30 more have been added in subsequent years, making a total of 74 at the present day. The total cost was last year Rupees 21,847, or with contingencies Rupees 22,099. The distance traversed by runners every day is 620 miles. From the Central Post Office at Trevandrum one line runs south to Thovallay, another runs north as far as Pavoor, another to Shencottah by the new road *via* Needloovengaud. A branch line runs from Quilon to Shencottah, and another from Krishnapoorum to Thoduvellah; ten other branch lines start from the main ones and proceed into the interior and towards the coast. The average speed attained is between 3 and 4 miles per hour. The total number of private despatches in the year 1049 was 207,796, and was in excess of the number in the preceding year by 11,265. The income yielded from this source was Rupees 11,568. Owing to the substitution of paper for palm leaves, on which latter most of the correspondence of the country used to be carried on, the additional number of covers did not yield a corresponding increase in the receipts, the weight of the letters being considerably reduced. The Unjel carries also the letters, newspapers and books received into the country through the British Post Offices, of which there are about eight. By the extra charge levied on these it earned in 1049 Rupees 324.

Mint. With the exception of two stamping presses, an assaying furnace, and assay balances and weights, procured from the Madras Mint and from England, there is no machinery in the Travancore Mint, and the operations are carried on in the native style. For some years past the operations have been very limited. At present work is confined for the most part to copper coinage. The British Rupee is current in the State. The local coins are, therefore, only of lower denominations. A fanam is equal to 4 chuckroms (silver coin), and a chuckrom is equal to 16 cash, (copper coin). $28\frac{1}{2}$ chuckroms go to the rupee, a chuckrom being nearly 6 grains Troy. The copper coinage yielded Rupees 1,913 in 1048 and Rupees 2,539 in 1049, deducting cost of metal; allowing for charges of establishment, the result was a loss of Rupees 421 in the one year and Rupees 21 in the other.

Elephant Department. Elephants are taken in pits, partly by Government agency and partly by private individuals. In the latter case, the captor receives a reward from the Government of Rupees 150, the animal itself being royal. There are in all about 500 Sircar pits and 500 private pits. Each pit is 8 feet square, rounded off towards the bottom. They are scattered over the valleys frequented by the animal. When an elephant falls into a pit, a report is sent to the Aminadar of the range, who reports to the taluq, and a party with tame elephants is then immediately despatched to capture it. After capture the animal is taken to certain large stables or enclosures and there let loose. It then becomes the business of the Mahoot to tame it. When young, a few months suffice for taming; when old, it takes longer. A full grown elephant at work costs about Rupees 51 per mensem, inclusive of the Mahoot's salary. When out of work and left to graze in the forest, Rupees 7 per mensem are allowed.

The gross receipts from all sources indicated in the Financial **Financial**. Returns for five recent years are given below :—

—	1045.	1046.	1047.	1048.	1049.
	RS.	RS.	RS.	RS.	RS
1 Land Revenue ...	16,66,950	16,43,954	16,59,923	16,81,217	16,93,651
2 Miscellaneous ...	6,09,182	4,86,687	5,98,907	4,69,338	6,29,807
3 Judicial fees, &c. ...	1,17,418	1,20,813	1,28,501	1,31,641	1,44,258
4 Customs	3,63,822	3,55,244	4,55,811	4,13,027	3,87,994
5 Arrack and Opium ...	1,00,605	1,05,494	1,08,658	1,22,447	1,34,996
6 Tobacco	7,75,031	8,10,511	8,89,114	8,62,893	9,09,746
7 Salt	9,57,228	10,03,336	9,83,815	9,91,317	9,88,798
8 Cardamoms & other goods.	2,06,767	4,09,923	3,78,585	2,73,394	2,24,870
9 Timber	1,08,074	1,20,174	83,701	1,03,728	1,01,710
10 Interest on Government Securities.	1,73,393	1,59,079	47,035	1,98,066	1,06,637
11 Arrears of Revenue collected.	55,537	29,257	38,862	53,403	29,664
Total ...	51,34,007	52,44,472	53,72,372	53,00,471	53,46,131

The disbursements for the same period were as follows :—

—	1045.	1046.	1047.	1048.	1049.
	RS.	RS.	RS.	RS.	RS.
1 Dovasom	5,59,243	5,52,827	5,54,735	5,44,922	5,73,253
2 Ootporas	3,21,572	3,05,950	2,94,791	3,06,517	3,09,644
3 Palace	5,42,603	4,90,549	5,11,494	5,03,233	5,41,939
4 Huzur Cutcherry and other civil establishments.	5,62,219	5,65,867	5,83,781	5,92,721	5,64,045
5 Judicial Establishments.	1,54,969	1,57,415	1,48,668	1,54,114	1,69,105
6 Police	1,33,242	1,32,956	1,32,609	1,36,455	1,42,430
7 Nair Troops	1,53,631	1,77,597	1,59,364	1,49,620	1,54,905
8 Elephant and Horse establishment.	67,649	65,696	62,715	63,599	66,251
9 Education, Science and Art.	1,14,545	1,23,244	1,09,987	1,15,883	1,14,346
10 Medical	...	...	...	...	1,45,480
11 Pensions	1,21,912	1,21,517	1,26,706	1,34,654	1,35,029
12 Public Works... ...	9,67,801	11,68,728	13,20,967	10,58,617	10,15,913
13 Costs and charges of goods sold, &c.	3,52,902	4,13,969	4,08,021	3,71,170	3,78,008
14 Contingent charges ...	2,00,608	1,96,593	1,78,188	1,62,886	1,80,972
15 Subsidy	8,10,652	8,10,652	8,10,652	8,10,652	8,10,652
16 Moorajapom	1,94,752	...	...	...	...
17 Tulaburum	1,61,177	...	...	...	...
18 Tirumadampu ...	20,690	...	...	18,425	...
19 Pulmagarbhum ...	...	...	90,979	...	...
20 The Rajah's trip to Bombay and Benares.	...	...	...	1,54,592	...
21 Sankara Chariar Swamy's visit.					20,130
Total ...	54,40,167	52,92,560	54,93,657	52,78,060	53,21,292

COCHIN.

According to tradition the Rajahs of Cochin claim to hold the territory in right of descent from Cherman Perumal, who governed the whole country of Kerala, including Travancore and Malabar, as Viceroy of the Chola Kings about the beginning of the ninth century, and afterwards established himself as independent ruler. The genealogical table, showing the descent of the present ruler of Cochin cannot be traced beyond the last three centuries, and even for this period the information is untrustworthy. From the commencement of the present century the information becomes better defined, and the following names appear in regular succession :—Rama Vurmah, died at Trichoor, September 28th, 1805 ; Rama Vermah, died at Velarapully, January 14th, 1809 ; Veera Kerala, died at Tripoontorah, August 6th, 1828 ; Rama Vurmah, died at Tripoontorah, November 18th, 1837 ; Rama Vurmah, died at Irinjalacodah, May 31st, 1842 ; Rama Vurmah, died at Trichoor, July 10th, 1851 ; Veera Kerala, died at Benares, February 22nd, 1853 ; Revi Vermah, died at Tripoontorah, February 7th, 1864 ; and Rama Vermah, the present Rajah, who ascended the musnud March 28th, 1864. In 1776 Cochin was subjugated by, and became tributary to, Hyder Ali. In 1792 Tippoo ceded the sovereignty to the British, who left the country under the uncontrolled authority of the Rajah, subject to a tribute of 1,00,000 Rupees ; this undertaking was concluded with the Rajah in the previous year, when the Company restored to him the districts and forts taken from him by Tippoo. The Cochin State is in subsidiary alliance with the British Government under treaty of 17th October 1809. By this treaty, which was entered into on the suppression of an insurrection raised by Cochin jointly with Travancore against the British power, the Rajah agreed to pay the East India Company, in addition to the usual subsidy of one lakh of Rupees, an annual sum equal to the expense of one battalion of Native Infantry, or 1,76,037 Arcot Rupees, making an aggregate annual payment of Rupees 2,76,037, paid in six equal instalments. It was further stipulated that, should it become necessary to employ a larger force for the defence of these territories against foreign invasion, the Rajah should contribute towards the expense in proportion to his means. The Rajah engaged to be guided at all times by the advice of the English Government ; to hold no correspon-

dence with any foreign State without the knowledge and sanction of the Company ; and to admit no Europeans to his service,
and permit none to remain in his dominions, without the consent
and concurrence of the Company. Power was given to the
Company to dismantle or garrison any fortress in His Highness'
territory. On the other hand the Company undertook to defend
the integrity of the State territory against all enemies. Subsequently the annual subsidy to the British Government was
reduced to Rupees 2,40,000, being one-half of the estimated
amount of the revenue at that time ; and at a still later period
the payment was fixed at two lakhs only, which forms the pecuniary obligation of the State at the present day. There is a
British Resident for Cochin jointly with Travancore.

Cochin contains seven districts, namely, Cochin, Cannanore, **Features of the country.**
Mugundapuram, Trichoor, Tallapully, Chittoor, and Cranganore.
The total area is 1,361 square miles.

A census was recently taken of the population of this **Recent Census.**
State. The inhabitants have been enumerated five times
during the last 55 years, the figures presenting the total population being respectively 223,203 in 995 M.E. ; 288,176 in
1011 ; 356,802 in 1024 ; 399,056 in 1032 ; and 601,114 in 1050.
The augmentation in numbers appears to have been great and
continuous, though not always uniform, being 29 per cent. for an
interval of 16 years between the first and second censuses ; 27
per cent. for the second period of 13 years ; 11 per cent. for the
third period of 8 years ; 49 per cent. for the fourth period of
18 years ; and 170 per cent. for the whole interval of 55 years,
between the earliest and latest enumerations. The highest rate
of increase has obtained during the present administration,
which has been marked also by the rapid development of the
food resources of the country. In the following table is given
the present annual increase in each of the principal countries
of Europe, together with the number of years in which the
population would be doubled if the rates continued so :—

Countries.			Increase per Annum.	Years.
Russia ...	...	...	1·39	50
England...	...	...	1·29	54
Prussia ...	...		1·13	61½
Spain ...	...		0·89	78
Italy ...	...	...	0·70	99
France ...	...	...	0·35	198

The rate and years for Cochin are 1·86 and 39, respectively. The male population of the country has increased during the interval between 995 and 1050 from 109,669 to 302,030, or 175 per cent., and the female from 113,334 to 299,084, or 164 per cent. The subjects of the Cochin Government, excluding those whose domicile of origin is elsewhere as above shown, may be ethnically divided into 530,262 Malayalees, 31,325 Tamulians, and 30,849 other languages. The subjoined table shows the distribution of the Cochinites and foreigners according to the districts in which they reside :—

No.	Districts.	Malayalam.		Tamulian.		Other Races.		Total.		Grand Total.
		Cochinites.	Non-Cochinites.	Cochinites.	Non-Cochinites.	Cochinites.	Non-Cochinites.	Cochinites.	Non-Cochinites.	
1	Kanayannoor ...	86,245	1,341	1,341	294	4,337	125	91,923	1,760	93,683
2	Cochin	81,813	221	1,088	8	10,697	74	93,598	303	93,901
3	Kodungaloor ...	18,426	100	594	40	1,218	19	20,238	159	20,397
4	Mugundapuram	110,407	422	1,851	111	2,161	22	114,419	555	114,974
5	Trichoor ...	98,904	217	869	413	944	365	100,717	1,025	101,742
6	Tallapully ...	103,160	995	3,393	184	2,712	21	109,265	1,200	110,465
7	Chittoor ...	31,307	1,633	22,189	1,223	8,780	820	62,276	3,676	65,952
	Total ...	530,262	4,929	31,325	2,303	30,849	1,446	592,436	8,678	601,114

Taking the three principal caste divisions of the people the figures stand as follows :—Hindus, 426,922, or 71·02 per cent. ; Christians, 140,414, or 23·35 per cent. ; Mahomedans, 32,499, or 5·40 per cent. The proportion of Christians is 3 per cent. greater than in the adjoining State of Travancore, 21½ per cent. greater than in the Madras Presidency generally, and nearly four times as great as in Tinnevelly. The bulk of this population are Syrian Christians, though the report does not distinguish the different denominations. They are massed in the neighborhood of the seacoast back-waters and lagoons, and almost monopolize the boating and fishing industry. Of the Hindus 66·22 per cent. are classed as Malayala Sudras and Eloovars. The Brahmins number 22,342, or 3·6 of the total population, and 5·5 of the Hindu population. The density is 441 to the square mile, a result exceeded only in Tanjore. The luxuriant growth of the cocoa palm on the sea shore and back-waters is the chief support of this heavy population. Little labor being entailed by this cultivation, abundant opportunity exists for further earnings. Nearly the whole produce of the country consists of special articles for export, the collection of which at the port of Cochin by the endless net-work of canals affords ample employment to boatmen, imported rice being distributed in the shape of return cargo. The fact that a sufficient fish diet is available to the great bulk of the people at an almost nominal cost is not to be overlooked in drawing conclusions regarding the density of population.

The census shows the total revenue for that year as a little **Taxation in** over 2 Rupees a head, or quarter of a rupee less than in the **Cochin.** British territory and in the adjoining State of Travancore. The difference indeed is almost explained by the smaller revenue from salt already referred to. The average incidence of the land tax is Rupees 1-4-0 a head, or 2 Annas less than in British territory. The geographical formation of the country does not favor the Travancore system of indirectly taxing the land by export duties.

PUDUCOTTAH.

The Puducottah State is surrounded by the British Districts **Description.** of Tanjore, Trichinopoly, and Madura. Its gross revenue is about five lakhs of Rupees, of which three lakhs are Inam and Jaghire and two lakhs are payable to the Rajah. The British Government has no treaty with Puducottah, the Rajah of which is exempt from tribute, and has independent Courts of Justice. The Madras Government, however, receives petitions of complaints from his subjects and sends them for the report of the Political Agent, who is considered entitled to advise and remonstrate with the Rajah on all subjects of importance. The area of the State is about 1,046 square miles. The population, which is almost entirely agricultural, was 316,695 according to the census of 1874. The country is generally a flat plain, interspersed with a few small rocky hills, some of which are crowned by old forts. In the south-west hills and jungles are found, but elsewhere it is a well cultivated tract, and there are 3,000 tanks, some of considerable size. The alienations of land revenue are extensive. Members of the Rajah's family hold 110,000 acres, 95,627 acres are held by temples, and 9,584 acres are held by alms-houses. The Inams held by Brahmins, and on various tenures of service, amount to 100,000 acres. Further particulars will be found below.

History.   The first connexion of the British Government with this chieftain, then usually called Tondiman, was formed at the siege of Trichinopoly in 1753, when the British army greatly depended on his fidelity and exertions for provisions. Subsequently he was serviceable in the wars with Hyder Ali and in the Poligar war, the latter being the name given to the operations against the usurpers of the large zemindary of Shivagnnga in the Madura District after the cession of the Carnatic. In 1803 he solicited as a reward for his services the favorable consideration of his claim to the fort and district of Kilanelli, situated in the southern part of Tanjore; this claim was founded on a grant by Pratap Singh, Rajah of Tanjore, and on engagements which were afterwards entered into by Colonel Braithwaite, General Coote, and Lord Macartney. The Government of Madras ceded the fort and district of Kilanelli; and the cession was afterwards confirmed by the Court of Directors of the East India Company, but with the condition that the district should not be alienated, and that it should revert to the British Government upon proof being given at any time that the inhabitants labored under oppressive government. Kilanelli yields a revenue of about Rupees 30,000 a year. The grant was also made subject to the yearly tribute of an elephant; this tribute however was not insisted upon, and in 1836 it was formally excused. The Rajah Vijaya Raghunath Tondiman died on the 1st February 1807, leaving two sons, the elder of whom, aged eleven, succeeded. During the minority of the young chief the Resident at Tanjore exercised a strict superintendence over the affairs of the State, and procured various reforms of system in the revenue, police, and judicial departments. As the Rajah increased in age, the interference with his affairs was gradually lessened; and about the year 1817 he was placed in charge of the whole administration. Rajah Vijaya Raghunath Rai Tondiman Bahadoor died in 1825 and was succeeded by his younger brother Rajah Raghunath Tondiman, who died on the 13th July 1839. He left two sons, Rajah Ramachandra Tondiman Bahadoor, aged nine years, and Tirumalai Tondiman, aged eight years. The former succeeded eventually to the chieftainship. Until 1841 the administration was conducted by the widow assisted by two ministers, but in that year, in consequence of representations of injustice by relations of the Rajah, the Resident at Tanjore was directed to make Puducottah his occasional residence, and to take up the immediate superintendence and control of the business of the country, which was however to continue to be conducted by the ministers of the Rajah. The

Resident, on the receipt of these orders, laid down rules for the guidance of the ministers, which prohibited expenditure beyond certain limits, and forbade the ministers to make grants of land, to assign produce, to create offices, or to increase or decrease emoluments, without his sanction ; the rules prescribed also the mode in which public business was to be carried on. In the same year the Residency at Tanjore was abolished, and the charge of Puducottah was entrusted to the Collector of Madura. The administration of the State was prosperously conducted under the superintendence of this officer during the remainder of the minority ; all debts were paid off, and a surplus invested in the funds of the British Government. In 1854, owing to disturbances in the country, originating in part in the irregular conduct of public business by the present Rajah, who had then recently come of age, the Governor in Council decided upon the system of administration now in force. That system is 1*st*, that the acts of the Rajah, through the Minister or Sirkele, shall be subject to the revision of the Political Agent with regard to all appointments and dismissals of public officers ; 2*nd*, that, subject to the Political Agent's supervision, the Sirkele shall manage the finances, the Rajah being restricted to his privy purse allowances ; 3*rd*, that there shall be a full yearly report of affairs ; 4*th*, that the Political Agent shall expel from the territory all disorderly persons and evil counsellors. In 1865 the Political Agency was transferred from Madura to Tanjore, and in 1874 from Tanjore again to Trichinopoly.

There have been no regular treaties between the British **Treaties.** Government and the Rajah, but in 1803 the fort and district of Kilanelli were granted to him by Lord Clive, then Governor of Madras, as mentioned above, and in 1862 a sanad was granted to him by the Viceroy Lord Canning, assuring him that the British Government would recognize the right of adoption, and that nothing should disturb the arrangement so long as the House should remain faithful and loyal to the Crown.

BANGANAPALLI.

The Jaghire of Banganapalli situated in the Kurnool District **History.** was originally granted to Mahomed Beg Khan, eldest son of the Grand Vizier of Aurangzeb. It was afterwards confirmed by successive grants from Mysore and Hyderabad ; and at the treaty of 1800 was conferred on Muzafar Mulk and his heirs in perpetuity. In 1825, in consequence of the disorders which prevailed in the jaghire, its management was temporarily assumed by the Company, and the Collector of Cuddapah was directed to examine the accounts of the chief and settle the claims of his creditors, to whom three-fourths of the net revenue was allotted, and the dividends regularly paid by the officer placed in charge of the jaghire. In 1848, the accounts being closed, the jaghire was restored to Hussain Ali Khan, the eldest surviving heir. Hussain Ali Khan died before a sanad recognizing him could be issued. He was succeeded by his nephew Ghulam Ali Khan, the late chief, to whom in 1849 a sanad was granted renewing to him and to his heirs their former rights and privileges, with administration of civil and criminal justice except in cases involving capital punishment, and stipulating that no grant should be made without a written document distinctly specifying that each alienation should hold good during such period only as the jaghire should remain in the enjoyment of the grantor. All frontier duties were abolished. In 1862 a sanad was granted to Ghulam Ali Khan guaranteeing that the British Government would permit and confirm any succession to his State which might be legitimate according to Mahomedan law. In October 1868 Ghulam Ali Khan, c.s.i., died, and his nephew and son-in-law, Fatte Ali Khan Bahadoor, the present ruler, was recognized as his successor. Under the sanad granted to Ghulam Ali Khan and renewed in the name of the present chief, the jaghire is confirmed as an independent State free of peishcush and pecuniary demand, the chief being bound at all times to maintain faith and allegiance to the Paramount Power. The civil jurisdiction of the chief is unrestricted ; but in the administration of criminal justice he is debarred from mutilating criminals, and capital sentences must be sanctioned by the Madras Government before being carried out.

Statistics.   The area of the jaghire is estimated at 206½ square miles, or 132,191 acres. Of this 54,171 acres are held on full assessment, and 38,578 acres are held on favorable tenure. There are only 29 acres of fully assessed land unoccupied. The remaining area, amounting to acres 29,413, is unassessed, and comprises hills, streams, roads, village sites, &c. The population of the jaghire was returned at 45,065 in the census of 1871. The land revenue amounts to Rupees 2,24,841, and the miscellaneous revenue to Rupees 9,798, but considerably more than half the land revenue is assigned as maintenance to members of the family. The jaghire contains some of the finest gardens in this part of the country, the mangoes and oranges of Banganapalli being celebrated. The Collector of Kurnool acts as agent to the Madras Government; he does not however forward an administration report of the jaghire.

SUNDOOR.

The State of Sundoor is situated nearly in the centre of the General Bellary District. The area is roughly estimated at 140 square description. miles, of which more than a third is hill territory; it is also surrounded by a cordon of hills, which completely isolate it from the neighbouring country. The administration is in the hands of a European Agent, who is the chief executive officer, and whose decisions on both the revenue and judicial sides are final. The law in force is substantially that of British India. The population of the State, not including the hill sanitarium of Ramandroog, is according to the recent census somewhat over 14,000, showing an increase on the census of 1865 of more than 1,000 persons. The average revenue from all sources somewhat exceeds Rupees 45,000. Of this sum about Rupees 24,000 is realized from land, about Rupees 18,300 from contracts of different kinds, and the rest from miscellaneous sources. The land revenue includes grants of land to dependents and service lands, and these are generally estimated at the highest figure; the contracts also form a somewhat precarious and fluctuating source of income. The following Inams are enjoyed :—Bramadaya, Rupees 4,571; Komaraswami Pagoda, Rupees 2,045; other temples, Rupees 2,332; Fakirs and others, Rupees 1,298; and sundry small jaghires, Rupees 1,360. In all, lands to the value of Rupees 12,506 per annum are alienated. Since November 1863 nearly a lakh of Rupees has been paid towards the liquidation of debts; but, it is to be regretted, with less practical result than might reasonably be anticipated. The system of paying with one hand, and contracting fresh obligations with the other, has not yet been entirely abolished. Education is in a backward state, roads are still urgently required, and public buildings are wanted. The incubus of debt is a considerable check to efforts in these directions.

History.   The present chief of Sundoor is Siva Shan Mukha Row.   The
founder of the family was Malloji Row Ghorepura, an officer in
the army of the Bijapur State, whose son Biroji entered the
service of the Rajah of Sattara.   The Sundoor State had been
previously held by a Beder Poligar, but Biroji's son Siddoji took
Sundoor from the Beders, and his conquest was confirmed to him
and his heirs by Sambhaji, the successor of Sivaji.   Siddoji died
in 1715, and was succeeded in Sundoor by his second son
Gopal Row, whose fate is involved in obscurity.   All that is
known of the history of that time is that Sundoor was taken by
Hyder Ali some time after his capture of Gooty in 1779; that he
and his son Tippoo built the fort; and that Gopal Row's son,
Siva Row, was killed in action in 1785 in a vain attempt to
recover his patrimony.   In 1790 Siva Row's brother, Vencata
Row, acting on behalf of his nephew Siddoji, drove out Tippoo's
garrison, but did not attempt to occupy Sundoor till the fall of
Seringapatam.   The Peshwa then claimed the State as his own,
and presented it to Yeswant Row Ghorepura, a distinguished
officer of Scindia's army, who belonged to the same family.
Yeswant Row did not take possession, and the widow of
Siddoji, who died in 1796, adopted Siva Row, a son of Kandi
Row the younger brother of Yeswant Row.   The Peshwa made
an unsuccessful attempt upon Sundoor in 1815; at his request
in 1817 the British Government, in conformity with the provisions of the treaty of Bassein, sent a force under Sir Thomas
Munro to reduce it, and in October of that year the fort and
government were surrendered.   Siva Row was compensated, on
Sir Thomas Munro's recommendation, with a jaghire of Rupees
10,000.   In 1818, after the failure of the Peshwa's government,
Siva Row was restored to his State, and in 1826 received a
sanad from Government confirming the lands of Sundoor to him
and his heirs for ever free of peishcush and pecuniary demands.
Siva Row was succeeded in 1840 by a nephew named Venkat
Row, who died in 1861.   His eldest son, the present chief, being
then a minor, was not invested till 1863, when the sanad was
renewed.   The present chief has the entire management of the
revenue and police of his State, and the duty of administering
civil justice.   He is bound at all times to maintain allegiance to
the British Government, and to assist them against foreign or
domestic foes, maintaining a watch over public peace and deliver-
ing up offenders who escape into his territory from British
India.   In the administration of criminal justice he is required
to refer all cases calling for capital punishment for the orders

of the Madras Government. He is held responsible to the
British Government for the satisfactory administration of his
State, and in case of misgovernment the Governor in Council
has the power to take such measures as appear proper for the
establishment of order and security. The Collector of Bellary
acts as Government Agent, but does not submit an administration report.

Sundoor contains a very important hill sanitarium for Euro- Sanitarium of
peans in the plateau of Ramandroog. Permission was obtained Ramandroog,
from the Rajah in 1846 to establish a sanitarium there, and it
has since been utilized chiefly as a convalescent depôt for
the troops serving in the Ceded Districts. Ramandroog is
distant from Bellary 38 miles, and from Secunderabad 270
miles. The station is built on an elevated plateau 3,150 feet
above the sea-level, 1,825 above Bellary, and 1,200 feet above
the surrounding plains. The greatest extent of the plateau
is from north to south one and a half miles, and it varies in
breadth from half to three-quarters of a mile. The general
aspect of the surface is undulating, the eastern ridge of the
hill being more than 100 feet higher than the western ; the
ground gradually slopes down from the former to the latter,
where in many places the descent to the western plains is very
precipitous. Owing to this conformation no rain water lodges
on the hill. The soil on the plateau formed by the disintegrated
rock is scanty, but sufficient in some spots on the west and south
sides of the hill to admit of a certain amount of cultivation ; on
the eastern side the rock is generally bare. During the months
of January, February, and March the air is cool, dry, and
bracing, being generally 12° cooler than at Bellary during the
same period. April and May may be called the hot months,
when the mean of the thermometer is about 80°. The morn-
ings and evenings during these months are however cool and
pleasant, and towards sunset a fresh breeze sets in from the west.
Early in April and during May partial showers fall ; the air,
except in the early morning and evenings, is close and sultry ;
and the sky becomes cloudy. Towards the end of May
banks of clouds are seen forming in the west, and occasional
heavy showers of rain fall. This is soon followed by violent
storms bringing in the south-west monsoon. Rain continues with
occasional breaks till the middle of October, after which, to the
end of the year, the rainfall is inconsiderable. During the
south-west monsoon fogs cover the hills from sunset till 9 or
10 o'clock next morning, the thermometer in the early morning

falling to 62° Fahrenheit. The damp and chilly state of the
atmosphere at this period necessitates the use of fires in barracks
and houses. The north-east monsoon sets in about the middle
of October, and a cold wind prevails from the north-east quarter
till the end of February, when it gradually veers round to the
south-west. During the south-west monsoon the sides of the
hill and the ravines and nullahs at the base contain a large
amount of decaying vegetable matter. After the rains are over
the surface of the country rapidly dries up and the atmosphere
becomes full of impurities; this probably accounts for the not
unfrequent occurrence of malarious fever during the period of
the year just mentioned. The rainfall is greater than in the
plains, but seems to have fallen off in the last few years—a
fact which is probably due to the unlimited destruction of
trees and shrubs during the minority of the present Rajah.
The climate of Ramandroog is suitable for cases of general
debility, unattended by organic disease. Hepatic, cardiac,
rheumatic, pulmonic and bowel affections appear to be aggra-
vated by the climate, especially during the rains. All cases of
glandular affections derive great benefit, and children of a
scrofulous habit of body thrive remarkably. The depôt can
accommodate 60 single men and 10 families. There are three
good roads up to the Droog, one by Yettinhatti and Bavihalli,
which is the one used by travellers from Bellary; one from
Hospett; and the third, the steepest of all, from Narayan-
deverkerra. There are about fifteen houses on the Droog
belonging to Bellary residents. Two carriage roads run along
the whole platform, and many good bridle roads have been cut
along the sides of the hills to the north and south.

GANJAM AGENCY.

**Nature of
Hill tracts.**

The Maliah tract at present under the jurisdiction of the
Ganjam Agent occupies the western portion of the District of
Ganjam covering an area of about 3,500 square miles, or about
five-twelfths of the entire district. It is inhabited chiefly by
Khonds and Savarahs. The term Maliah or Malwah means
high lands, and is the name given by Khonds to the upland
regions of Orissa generally. The country is mountainous and
covered with dense forests of sàl, which however never attain

any great age, as they are periodically cleared by the Khonds
and Savarahs for cultivation purposes. Agriculture is practised
by the Khonds with a degree of skill and energy which is
perhaps nowhere surpassed in India, and the result is a high
degree of rural affluence.   The Maliah Khonds are extremely
rich in every species of agricultural stock. The Khonds
inhabit the northern and central portions of the Maliahs in
Ganjam and comprise many tribes speaking different dialects
and of various degrees of lawlessness.   Those on the Kalahundy
and Jeypore borders, known as the Kuttiah Khonds, are
perhaps the most fierce and warlike. The tribes occupying the
hills bordering on Ganjam, with the exception of the Simili
Khonds of Bodagadah, are somewhat more civilized ; and in the
Goomsur Maliahs, where many of them speak Uriya, there is not
much perceptible difference between the Khonds of the hills and
those living in the jungle villages at the foot of the ghauts.
The Savarahs occupy the Pedda Kimedy, Surangi, and Parla
Kimedy Maliahs to the south of the Khond tribes, with whom
they have little in common.   In agriculture they are on a par
with the Khonds.   The region occupied by this people extends
from the Kimedy Zemindari to the Godavery, or for 200 miles.
The principal means of access to the Maliahs from the plains
is by the Kalingia Ghaut Road from the foot of the hills at
Durgaprasad in the Goomsur Taluq to Kalingia on the summit,
a distance of seven miles.   It was originally constructed by the
Sappers and Miners, and is at present maintained by the
Department of Public Works.   It is accessible to carts.   There
are many other rough ghaut tracks connecting the Maliahs with
the low country available for foot passengers and cattle.   A
cart road is under construction from the Parla Kimedy plain
country to Gumma in the Parla Kimedy Maliahs.

In the year 1836 the Zemindari of Goomsur and the Maliahs **Government**
attached thereto were resumed by Government in consequence **jurisdiction.**
of the rebellious conduct of the Zemindar and were placed under
the control of the Collector.   During the war it came to the
notice of the Commissioner that meriah sacrifices were practised
in certain portions of the Maliahs, and in consequence a
Military Assistant with an armed force was specially entertained
with a view to their gradual suppression.   It was at the same time
considered necessary for the prevention of further disturbances
that the administration of criminal and civil justice in the Hill
Zemindaries should be removed from the jurisdiction of the
ordinary Courts and placed under the Collector, and Act XXIV

of 1839 was passed giving the Collector, or Agent to
the Governor of Fort St. George, the necessary powers.
During the time the Maliahs were under the control of the
Collector and Agent it was discovered by his Military Assistant
that the meriah sacrifices were not confined to the Maliahs of
this district alone, but extended to those of the neighboring
district of Vizagapatam as well as to those under the jurisdiction of the Bengal Presidency and Central Provinces, and that
female infanticide was also practised in some of them. The
Government of India therefore considered it proper to create a
separate Agency for the suppression of meriah sacrifices and
female infanticide in the Hill Tracts of Orissa in general, and
appointed an Agent under Act XXI of 1845, to whom all the
Maliahs then under the Collector and Agent were transferred.
This arrangement continued up to May 1862, when the Government having been satisfied that these rites had been completely
and successfully put down the Meriah Agency was done away
with, and the Maliahs were retransferred to the Collector and
Agent. In 1863 all the Agency tracts situated below the ghauts,
with the exception of Goomsur and Suradah, were retransferred
to the jurisdiction of the ordinary Courts, and in 1866 Goomsur
and Suradah also were removed from the jurisdiction of the
Agent. In 1869 the Chokapad Mutah of the Goomsur Taluq
and the petty Chieftainships of Koradah and Ronabah were
restored to the Agent. The Maliahs at present under the jurisdiction of the Collector and Agent are the following :—Goomsur,
Suradah, Chinna Kimedy, Pedda Kimedy, Bodagadah, Surangi,
Parla Kimedy, Mutahs of Koradah and Ronabah, Jaradah,
Jalantra, Mandasa, Budarasingi, and Kattingiah. Of these the
Goomsur Suradah and Chinna Kimedy Maliahs are under the
direct management of Government; the two former having been
forfeited to Government along with the Zemindari of Goomsur,
while the latter was taken by Government in consequence of
disturbances, towards the quelling of which the Zemindar,
who is a nominal proprietor, was unable to render assistance for
want of influence with the Khonds. The remaining Maliahs
are held on sanads by their respective Zemindars, who derive
more or less revenue therefrom. The Government derive
no revenue from the Maliahs under their own management.
The population of the Maliahs under the Agency is computed
at 185,957 according to the Census of 1871. In these Maliahs
the Agent exercises the powers of Civil and Sessions Judge,
though questions of disputed succession to landed estates are

decided by Government on the report of the Agent. The Penal and Criminal Procedure Codes are in force. These tracts are Scheduled Districts under Act XIV of 1874.

VIZAGAPATAM AGENCY.

In 1835 Sir Frederick Adam, Governor of Madras, visited the **History of** Circars, and recorded in a Minute his opinion as to the **the Agency.** expediency of exempting the Hill Zemindaries from the general regulations. Mr. Russel, Special Commissioner in the Northern Circars, after minute inquiries into the causes of disturbances then lately suppressed, and the policy needful for adoption in order that the recurrence of such outbreaks might be prevented, reported finally on this subject in 1836 and 1837. He observed that a system which was adapted to districts where the authority of Government is paramount could not fail to be inapplicable to mountainous tracts, where, up to that period and after a lapse of more than thirty years, the Government had in effect no police and no power. He proposed, as the course best calculated both to add to the weight and influence of the local authority, and to remove existing causes of irritation on the part of the Hill Zemindars arising from the unbending forms of regulation procedure, that those tributaries should be exempted from the jurisdiction of the ordinary Courts and placed exclusively under the Collector of the District, in whom should be vested the entire administration of civil and criminal justice, under such rules for his guidance as might be prescribed by orders in Council. This proposal was approved by the Government, and forms the basis of Act XXIV of 1839. It was further enacted that the Collector, as Agent to the Governor, should have the power of making commitments by warrant which is possessed by the Governor in Council by virtue of Regulation II of 1819, subject always to the orders of Government on each case. The present Agency embraces Jeypore, with those portions of the Zemindaries of Madgole, Pachipenta, Kurupain, and Merangi which lie within the hills and the hill mutas of Palcondah, those of Golgondah, and the Hill Zemindary of Kasipur. These tracts are Scheduled Districts in the same way as the Ganjam Maliahs.

CONSULS, &c.

Consuls and
Consular
agents.

At Madras the folloing Governments are represented by Consuls : America, Austria, Belgium, France, Germany, Italy Portugal, Spain, and Sweden and Norway. At Cocanada, America, Austria, Bremen, France, and Germany are represented. At Tellicherry France has a Consul. At Cochin, both France and Germany have Consuls. At Bimlipatam, Germany has a Consul. The French consuls act under the authority of the Consul-General of France at Calcutta. The Madras Government have Consular agents at the French settlements of Pondicherry and Karikal.

POLITICAL PENSIONS.

History of
Carnatic
Family.

The Musalmans first assumed the actual government of the Carnatic at the commencement of the last century, when the Emperor Aurengzebe, after conquering and annexing the independent Musalman kingdoms of the Dakhan, appointed Kasim Khan Nawab of the Carnatic. The Nawabs were subsequently appointed by the Viceroy of the Dakhan, subject to the confirmation of the Emperor at Delhi. Anwar ud Din Khan, the first Nawab of the present Arcot family, was the last Nawab appointed directly by the Viceroy, in the year 1744. In the general dissolution of the Mogul empire, numerous claimants to the dignities of the viceroys and nawabs started up; and Anwar ud Din Khan was killed in endevouring to suppress a rebellion fomented by the French. The English espoused the cause of his son Muhammad Ali Khan, who afterwards assumed the title of Walajah, and by their aid he succeeded his father as Nawab in 1749. In 1795 he died and was succeeded by his son Umdat Ulmara. The English had long been the virtual masters of the country, and the disadvantages of the double government being evident, thay resolved to end it; and on the death of Umdat-ul-Umara in 1801 the civil administration of the country was assumed with the collection of the revenues. The Nawab was permitted to retain his state and title with a pension of one-fifth of the revenues: but the heir to the dignity, Ali Husain, refusing to sign the treaty relinquishing his rights, he was set aside, and his cousin, the son of Amir ul Umara, Nawab Muhammad Ali Khan, Walajah's second son, was raised to the titular dignity under the style of Nawab Azim ud Daula; he on his part engaging to comply with all the demands of the English Government. Azim ud Daula had two sons, Azam Jah and Azim Jah. He died in 1819 and was succeeded as titular Nawab by Azam Jah, who, dying in 1825, was succeeded by his son Ghulam Muhammad Ghous Khan. On the death of the latter in 1855 the title and dignity of Nawab was abolished and the allowance of one-fifth of the revenues resumed. Azim Jah, the uncle of the last Nawab, long claimed, as the legal heir, the right to succeed to the musnud; and in 1867 the Government compromised his claim by creating him hereditary Prince of Arcot, with a perpetual stipend and other privileges and immunities. He died in 1874 and was succeeded as Prince of Arcot by his eldest son Zahir Dudula Bahadur.

The assumption of the internal administration of the **Carnatic Stipends of 1801.** Carnatic by the British Government in 1801, and the change in the succession, led to the grant of stipends to the different members of the families of the Nawabs Muhammad Ali Khan Walajah and Umdat ul Umara, and to some of their officers and dependents. The total annual amount of these stipends at first granted was seven lakhs. Many additional grants to various claimants, distant relatives, connexions, or servants and dependents of these Nawabs were made subsequently, the last grant on this account being made in the year 1840. The aggregate amount of these subsequent grants was three lakhs of rupees per annum. The amount now paid on account of these stipends to the descendants of the original grantees has been diminished by lapses to little more than one lakh per annum. The continuation of Carnatic stipends of 1801 to the heirs of the stipendiaries is made entirely at the discretion of the Governor in Council, and is regulated by precedent and by the rulings of the Court of Directors. Some of the stipends latterly granted were given in lieu of Jaghires or land assignments formerly given by the Nawabs but now resumed by the British; in these cases the stipendiaries retain the name of jaghiredars Others of the stipendiaries are called yeomiadárs, as their stipends are the equivalents of yeomiahs or daily allowances made to them by the nawabs. In all matters relating to their stipends these persons come under the same rules as the other stipendiaries of 1801.

Carnatic Stipends of 1855.

On the death of Nawab Ghulam Muhammad Ghous Khan in 1855, and the consequent resumption of the fifth of the revenues heretofore allowed to the titular nawabs, the Government granted stipends to all members of his immediate family and to all his chief officers servants and dependents. The total amount thus granted was upwards of five lakhs per annum, and the number of persons stipended was nearly five thousand, of whom less than one thousand now remain, the rest having died or having commuted their stipends. The continuations of the stipends of members of the immediate family are made, under rules laid down by the Government of India, for two or three lives only; the stipends of all others are life grants, and cease absolutely with the deaths of the holders. The total amount of the Carnatic stipends of 1855 now aggregates little more than three lakhs per annum.

Prince of Arcot Family Stipend.

The family of the late Prince Azim Jah of Arcot enjoy a perpetual stipend of a lakh and a half of rupees per annum, of which one lakh is divided among the members of the family, and the remaining 50,000 Rupees is set apart as an appanage of the title in addition to the personal share of its holder.

Carnatic Agency, &c.

The whole of these stipendiaries are mustered and paid by an officer called the Government Agent and Paymaster of Carnatic Stipends. It is the duty of this officer to report lapses, and to submit for the consideration of Government distribution rolls of those who claim continuations from the lapsed stipends. A Receiver of Carnatic Property was appointed under Act XXX of 1858 to administer to the estate of the late Nabob of the Carnatic. He was also to pay persons claiming to be creditors of the late Nabob, under the orders of the Supreme Court, with interest not exceeding six per cent. per annum. For the performance of these duties the Receiver was to receive a commission not exceeding five per cent. upon the value of the property collected by and distributed under the Act; by Act XXI of 1868 his duties were somewhat extended. From 1858 to 1875 the Receiver realized Rupees 20,29,700, and disbursed, under the orders of the Supreme and High Courts, Rupees 33,37,619. The subsequent transactions have been limited, and the Receiver's functions may, in point of fact, be said now to have ceased.

Other political pensions.

Other political pensions have arisen under various circumstances, as detailed in the following paragraphs. These are all paid by the revenue authorities of the districts in which the pensioners are permitted to reside.

On the assumption of the Kurnool territory by the British **Kurnool**
Government in 1800 pensions were granted to the Nabob's **pensioners.**
personal family and such of his relatives and dependants as
were in receipt of allowances from him and held jaghires resum
able at his pleasure. The pensions so granted were all declared
by the Government of India to be life-grants and amounted to
Rupees 2,22,651-4-0 per annum. By the death of most of the
recipients, and consequent lapse of their pensions to Government,
the total amount of these pensions was gradually reduced till,
on the 1st April 1875, it stood at Rupees 79,159-10-0, which was
still further reduced to Rupees 75,123-10-0 drawn by 127
persons on the 1st April 1876. Of the last amount Rupees 1,860
were transferred to Hyderabad in the course of the year.

The "Two-Lakh Fund" was a sum of two lakhs of Star **Two-Lakh**
Pagodas set apart by treaty for the maintenance of the families **Fund pensioners.**
and connexions of Hyder Ali and Tippoo Sultan, and their
dependants. There are at present 70 pensioners under this head,
drawing an aggregate pension of Rupees 9,624-10-0 annually,
with a clothing allowance of Rupees 1,255 per annum the
latter sum being enjoyed only by certain of the pensioners. The
pensioners principally consist of the descendants of the officers
of Hyder's and Tippoo's courts, whose present pensions have
devolved to them by gradual lapses. Some are the relatives,
and a few others the dependants of the widows of Hyder Ali
and Tippoo Sultan. Under this head is also paid a sum of
Rupees 1,251 per annum, intended for the ceremonies over
Padshaw Begum's tomb, the principal wife of Tippoo Sultan,
and for other religious ceremonies known as the Ashar Fateahs.

The Mysore pensioners also are the descendants of the officers **Mysore**
of Tippoo's court. They are so called in contradistinction to the **pensioners.**
Two-Lakh Fund pensioners, as their pensions are chargeable to the
Mysore State. There are at present seventeen pensioners under
this head, drawing an aggregate pension of Rupees 7,184-11-0
annually. A sum of Rupees 276 per annum is allowed for the
performance of fateah ceremonies over the tomb of Goolam Ally
Sadoor, one of the principal officers of Tippoo's court.

The Kandyan pensioners include the relatives and servants of **Kandyan**
the late King of Kandy, Vickrama Singah, who was deported **pensioners.**
to Madras in 1816 and died at Vellore in 1832. They reside
principally at Vellore. They are in receipt of pensions aggregat-
ing Rupees 3,068-12-0 per annum, which are paid by the Madras
authorities but are chargeable to the Ceylon Government.

Goomsur pensioners.

The late Goomsur pensioners were the members of the family of the late Zemindar of Goomsur, who had been implicated in disturbances raised in Goomsur and elsewhere in the Ganjam District. They were originally brought to Vellore in 1837, when they consisted of some twenty persons; the number has now been reduced by casualties, &c., to only one member, a concubine of the ex-zemindar.

Palcondah pensioners.

The Palcondah pensioners, of whom there are five in number, are the members of the family of the late Zemindar of Palcondah. They were banished to the North Arcot District in 1834, and placed under restraint there to prevent their entering into intrigues with the disaffected adherents of the family in Palcondah and elsewhere in the Vizagapatam District. They consist of the son, two daughters, and two widows of the Zemindar, and are in receipt of pensions amounting in the aggregate to Rupees 2,928 per annum. They reside in the mahals in the Fort at Vellore.

Cuttack pensioners.

The Cuttack pensioners are the members of the family of Rajah Pillay *alias* Lutchmee Narrain Bunge, a turbulent character who created disturbances in the Ganjam District. He was sent to Vellore in 1856 by desire of the Bengal Government, accompanied by his wife, a son, and two male relatives, and died in 1857. The present members of his family consist of his widow, his son, and his uncle. They are in receipt of a pension of Rupees 25 per mensem, or 300 Rupees per annum. They reside in a mahal in the Fort at Vellore, and are under surveillance.

NON-POLITICAL PENSIONS.

Nature of the pensions.

The following is a list of civil pensions other than political pensions classified for purposes of account. It will be seen that it includes both non-official and official pensions. In the Accountant-General's Office all these pensions are grouped under two major heads "Allowances and Assigments" and "Superannuation and Retired Allowances."

Compensation ... { Compensation in lieu of lands and privileges resumed.
Do.   to private persons.
Do.   to Pagodas and Mosques.
Salt and Toddy compensations.
Yeomindars.

Miscellaneous, *i.e.*, other pensions and charitable allowances chargeable on revenue.

Superannuation,
Revenue.
{ Revenue.
{ Abkáry.
{ Customs and Salt, &c.

Superannuation,
Civil.
{ Law and Justice.
{ Public Departments.
{ Post Office.

Do. Marine.

Superannuation, Public Works Department.

Compassionate
Allowances.
{ Pensioners of Native Pension Fund.
{ Lungerkhana.
{ Charitable Allowances of General Nature.

Gratuities.

The titles of the non-official pensions indicate generally the mode in which they have arisen. Compensation money paid to mosques and pagodas is here specified, but will be mentioned again under the section on Public Endowments. The alienation of pensionary allowances by persons holding them is prohibited; on the other hand Collectors are authorized to see that families which are entitled to a share or to maintenance obtain their dues, and, if necessary, to make a proper partition themselves. Whether a non-official pension is hereditary or not depends on the circumstances under which it was originally granted. In most cases of hereditary pensions, the hereditary line is not allowed to be continued by adopted children, but even this is permitted in cases where the pension took its rise in compensation for land charitably granted and then resumed. Pensions which are not hereditary are often gradually reduced on each occasion of a succession. There are certain rules for the commutation of non-official pensionary allowances into a lump sum fixed at so many years' purchase according to age or circumstances, of which pensioners frequently avail themselves; the Government exercise their discretion as to disallowing commutation when the object appears to be an improvident one. The adjudication of claims to these pensions rests entirely with Government in the Pension Department. non-official pensioners, unless specially exempted, are required to appear periodically before the Revenue authorities of the districts in which they are permitted to reside, for muster and inspection. Payment is made to pensioners at stated intervals by the same officers. The duty of reporting casualties among pensioners is imposed by Govern-

ment on various officials, and rewards are offered for information as to casualties which have not been brought to the
notice of these officials within three months after their occurrence.   Official civil pensions are regulated entirely by the Civil
Pension Code recently issued by the Financial Department of
the Government of India; the Code contains clear instructions
regarding the points mentioned above and several others.   Military pensions are administered in the Military Department, and
certain minor Police pensions are administersd under special
rules in the Police Department.   Covenanted Civil Servants,
Judges of the High Court, and Chaplains are specially provided
for in the Civil Pension Code.

PUBLIC ENDOWMENTS.

Nature of the endowments.   Since the year 1817 the Government have assumed the more or
less direct control of all endowments in land or money made by
the British or previous Governments, or by private persons, for
the support of religious or charitable institutions, or for public
buildings, such as bridges, choultries, &c.   By Regulation VII
of 1817, the Board of Revenue was appointed to control all
these endowments, subject to the general supervision of Government.   So far as endowments for religious purposes were
concerned, this control was transferred by Act XX of 1863 from
the Board to District Committees appointed by Government.
These have proved a failure, and the mismanagement and
malversation of public funds have been so great, that a revision
of the law is again under contemplation.   The supervision of
endowed charitable institutions still rests with the Board.   In
most cases the institutions are allowed by the Board to
remain under the immediate management of private individuals
appointed as trustees by the founders, and the Board do not
interfere so long as the object of the grant is duly fulfilled;
where there has been neglect or irregularity on the part of the
trustees, the institutions have been placed under the management of Collectors acting as agents to the Board.   Chuttrums
constructed and endowed by Government are managed similarly
by Collectors.   The policy has latterly been to transfer all such
charitable institutions as have been directly managed by Collectors, to Local Fund Boards, and it is under contemplation to
place these Boards in charge also of the privately managed

institutions; if this is done they will virtually take the place of
the Board under Regulation VII of 1817. The British Government in some cases keep up the endowments of pagodas and
mosques, the obligation to do so having been handed on to them
by previous Governments. In deference to certain objections,
efforts have from time to time been made to convert all ready-
money payments of this nature into assignments of land revenue.
The arrangement has however been only very partially carried out
owing to the general reluctance of landholders to have their
revenues so assigned. It has now been settled that money
allowances shall continue to be paid, but not from the Government Treasury. The payments are to be made in future direct
to the trustees by the villagers concerned; they will do this out
of the revenues due by them to Government by the system of
what is called Beriz deductions, the Government taking so much
off the demand. The annual value of the land revenue assigned
for religious and charitable institutions is about 29 lacs of rupees,
and the ready-money payments made by Government for the
same institutions amount to about five lacs; total 34 lacs of
rupees.

ESCHEATS, &c.

On a person dying intestate and without legal heirs his real **Escheats.**
property escheats to Government. Section 6, Regulation 7 of 1817
provides that such property shall be sold on the public account
or otherwise disposed of at the pleasure of Government.
Excheats of valuable property often occur in Malabar; in other
districts the instances are rare. Buildings are generally sold;
ordinary assessed land is sometimes sold, and sometimes given
to occupiers on condition of merely paying the assessment;
Inam land is resumed and fully assessed. In many cases the
property is assigned by Government to persons having a natural
though not a legal claim. The Board of Revenue are charged
with the duty of, bringing cases of escheat to the notice of
Government; when the property is valued at not more than
Rupees 50 they are authorized by Government to dispose of the
case themselves.

When intestates leave personal property to which no proper **Lapses of**
claim is made, the ownership vests in Government. Under **personal property.**
clause 7, Section 16, Regulation III of 1802 the Zillah Judges are
to take charge of such property pending the orders of

Government. In practice, when the value is small, the Collector takes charge and disposes of the property at his discretion.

PETITIONS.

The petition system.   The petition system, under which a person aggrieved with the action of any Government official appeals to the next higher authority by means of a petition, and receives back a reply endorsed on his petition, either refusing or promising redress, assumes an unusual importance in this Presidency owing to the number of small holdings of land under Ryotwari, and the consequent multiplication of details in administering the land revenue. Most of the petitions presented to Government officials relate to land revenue. An aggrieved person may appeal in succession to the officers representing each grade in the department concerned, and may finally address in turn the Local Government, the Government of India, and the Secretary of State. The three last named alone have prescribed certain rules checking the indiscriminate presentation of petitions; in all other cases there is no check beyond the discretion of the officer receiving them. In a few cases the quasi-judicial Regulations provide for appeals, and impose limits on their presentation. In a recent year the Board of Revenue received 3,330 petitions; called for reports, that is to say, took evidence, in 230 cases; gave redress in 15 cases without calling for evidence; and gave redress in 43 cases after calling for evidence. In the same year the corresponding figures for petitions dealt with by Government, in all departments other than the Military and Public Works, were 2443, 150, 53, and 49, respectively.

SECTION II.

ADMINISTRATION OF THE LAND.

GOVERNMENT AND ALIENATED LAND.

(a).—HISTORICAL SKETCH.

THE early movement of races in Southern India seems to show an indigenous and mostly pastoral population, superseded by an invasion from the north of one or more immigrations of Hindu agriculturalists, and these again superseded by a further invasion from the north of a more military class of the same general race. The aborigines of the south remain still in a distinct form in the hill tribes, but these may very possibly represent only the most degraded form of the early civilization. The aborigines were Mongolian by race, Dravidian in speech, demonolators by religion, and in their occupations chiefly pastoral. The first invaders were cultivating Brahmins and herdsmen of the Aryan stock, and an admixture of these with different tribes of the aborigines gave the present southern nations. The cause of the first migration was probably the displacement of the pure Hindus in the north by another kindred race of different political constitution, of which the Rajputs are now the best known type. This race followed agriculture as their proper calling and had fixed property in land, but simultaneously showed an aptitude for arms. In their turn they moved south and are traceable successively in Guzerat, the western coast, and the extreme south of the peninsula. The Nairs of Malabar and the southernmost part of Canara and the Vellalars of Tinnevelly are probably the most distinctive present specimen of the race. As far as the movement of races going to form a landed proprietary is concerned, the history ends with the Hindu migrations. Two Mahomedan and one British conquest have since taken place, and each has effected considerable change in the landed institutions of the country. But neither has affected the agricultural population

Movement of races.

itself. In speaking of Aryan immigrants superseding Dravidian occupants it is of course understood that they superseded them only in the sense of being successful in introducing their own institutions and vocabulary. Upon the inflectional grammar of the Dravidian language or languages they produced no effect whatever, a certain proof of the vitality of the Dravidian race. In fact there is no such thing in the south of India as an Aryan Hindu race; the Hindus here are but Arianized Dravidians.

Aboriginal landed institutions. Regarding the landed institutions of the aboriginal Dravidians little or nothing can be ascertained. They must have been chiefly a pastoral race, but the cairns belonging to this period, which are to be found all over Southern India, contain brass and iron implements of agriculture, and the old Tamil language contains words showing that agriculture was practised. The language also shows that they had kings occupying fortified habitations and ruling over defined districts. On the immigration of the Aryans forming the Pandyan and later dynasties they appear to have passed for the most part into the position of prædial slaves.

The most ancient Hindu village system. The presence of the Hindu immigration in Southern India is first traceable in the springing up of organized village communities of the type found among the ancient Teutons of the West. Tribal arrangements may have given place to village communities among the Dravidians themselves before the appearance of the Aryans; but the presence of the type just mentioned is conclusive as to Hindu influence. In the early Hindu village system, the village was governed by a headman, there was a highly concentrated system for regulating common affairs, and the division of labor was rigidly carried out in the practice of the different trades and professions by individuals receiving a regulated remuneration. Local taxes for common purposes were levied rateably. The ownership by the individual in the soil was at first weak, for the land being abundant was the property of him who liked to take it, and, there being more in reserve, occupation alone could give to the land but a slight marketable value. Ownership however gradually grew stronger as occupants closed in on the first settlers. The Government, as soon as any arose, limited its operations to taking from each individual cultivator a share of the produce. This primitive form of village corporation remains more or less intact in many places to this day, the only difference being that the lower orders have been to a considerable extent emancipated and that the Government have assumed the additional duty of assigning waste lands to new occupants. It will be noticed that the communistic principle is not fully developed in the village system here described. For instance there is no joint claim to the whole village area, including waste; and there is no combination to exclude strangers. If this form of village community corresponds, as there seems little doubt that it did, with the first Hindu immigration of Brahmins and herdsmen, it appears that those races were content with little, and easily amalgamated with the aborigines in their arrangements regarding landed property.

Another form of village community sprung up at a more recent date, instituted, it is supposed, by the quasi-military Hindus, who represented the second set of Hindu immigrants. This form was the result of an occupation by a body democratic among themselves, but forming an exclusive oligarchy as regards the aborigines and others whom they found before them. The distinctive features of this system of village corporation, as opposed to that already prevailing in Southern India, were that the dominant race claimed a strong proprietary right in the whole of the village area, whether cultivated or uncultivated; that they gave no franchise to aborigines or strangers; and that in their own internal administration they had a tendency to communism, and adopted government by panchayet or committee in preference to that by a single headman. In other respects the arrangements were the same as in the more ancient form. The details of their land administration will be mentioned hereafter. The government had no concern with the distribution of lands, and it is believed that they settled, not with the individual cultivator singly, but jointly with the village authorities. These communities also exist to this day, but their special characteristics have been much curtailed. The panchayets are of less importance than they were, and have generally given place to headmen. The rents to the dominant body survive in a few cases only of what are called Swatantrams in the Chingleput District, and the rights to the waste, though still asserted by Mirassidars and Karoikárar in the southern districts, are recognised by Government only as a preferential claim to be indulged under certain conditions and in common with other inhabitants of the village. *The more recent form.*

In the times of the early Hindu village communities proprietary rights, as defined by powers to alienate, existed to a very trifling extent. In the more ancient form of community, as has been said, tenures had no market value; and in the later and more democratic communities where rights were more decided, *Ancient proprietary rights.*

the land was not an individual but a common property, and one
man could not without the consent of the others sell to a stranger.
Still transactions occurred in the latter case among the members
of the community themselves, which showed an individual ownership within that limit.   Sales were not common, and mortgages
were usually not foreclosable for a very long period ; but the
latter existed in abundance, showing a certain value in individual
ownership of landed property.   Individual property in land sprung
up earlier than elsewhere in the districts on the Western Coast,
probably owing to the political circumstances which rendered the
Government authority weak, and the state demands light.   The
attitude of the Hindu rajahs with regard to the soil has been
much discussed. It probably varied entirely with the circumstances
of times and places. The object of Government is to obtain
revenues for Government purposes.   If it found communities so
organized as to able to farm the villages properly and to render
the proper state dues, the Government would not interfere in the
direction of the disposal of the lands claimed by the community.
If it found an imperfect organization it would be forced to
interfere in the disposal of the lands, especially of the waste lands,
with a view to the proper development of the country and
realization of the revenue.   The tendency probably was for the
villagers to lean more and more on the Government in these
matters, and hence in many parts of the country the state
interference became a regular institution.   Still there is no
evidence that any Hindu governments ever took the step of
ejecting an occupier ; even if they failed to obtain their dues
from him they limited their reprisals to personal torture or
sale of moveable property.   The sale law is not a native institution.   The discussion whether the Indian Governments are
"proprietors" of the soil or not, seems to be little more than a
dispute about words.

Slavery.   By far the greater part of the laboring classes of the people
must have been, during the early historical periods, in a state of
acknowledged slavery.   In Malabar and Canara where the land
became gradually the subject of distinct properties, the laborer
was the personal slave of the occupier of the soil, and was liable
to be sold and mortgaged by him independently of his lands.   In
the Tamil country the slave was considered rather as attached to
the soil.   In the Telugu country only does slavery seem to have
been weak. It must be noticed however that South Indian slavery
was always domestic, and never the subject of foreign traffic.   It
even appears that in the Tamil country the Pariahs or Pallers,

slaves attached to the Vellalars, and the Pullis, slaves attached
to the Brahmins; used to claim hereditary landed property as
the incident of their slavery. Slavery did not survive the
Hindu period, except to a very limited extent. As long as the
Government land-tax was moderately light, as it is believed
to have been in the Hindu period, the proprietor could afford to
maintain slaves and servants to cultivate for him. The Mahomedans are believed to have raised the land-tax, and rendered it
necessary for the landlord to work at the plough in his own
person or with the help of his family. This is the explanation
usually given, and there is probably some truth in it; it is by
some however denied that the land-dues of the Mahomedans were
higher than those which obtained before their time. It is at any
rate certain that slavery has gradually died out.

In the earliest times the land-revenue was the sole government impost, and the revenue system of the country may be said to
have been founded on the absence of taxation properly so called.
This principle has been brought down to the present day with no
very great modification, and has met with opponents. The
oriental theory, as now interpreted, is that the portion of the
produce of the land which is given by nature, as opposed to that
which is produced as the interest of invested capital, is the proper
source from which to draw revenue; and that if this be not
alienated to individuals, or appropriated by them by prescription,
the necessity of taxing labor or capital is obviated. This state of
things is not inconsistent with the creation of private property
in the occupation of land, in capital sunk in it, and in that
portion of the rent which is allowed to individuals to give them
an interest in the soil. The land-revenue was levied by all
Hindu governments in the shape of a proportion of the gross
produce fixed according to the capacity of different soils and
the value of different products, or the commuted money-value
of that proportion. There was no settlement for a succession of
years or seasons, but each crop was divided as it was produced.
The Metayer system of Italy and some other modern continental
countries is but a repetition of this plan. The Government share
was usually taken in kind under what is now called the Amany
system. In those times, when the boundaries of fields were ill-
defined and the holdings very small and intermixed, and where
it was the practice to thresh out grain at once after reaping, it
was easier, and gave less opportunity for abuse, to divide the
grain so threshed out than to calculate annual money payments

*Early system
of land
revenue.*

according to the quantity and quality of land actually cultivated. In certain cases, however, the value of the crop was estimated after reaping, and a portion of this value was paid in money to the State. This commutation system would naturally take the place of the other where joint settlements were made with villages. It was also considered more applicable to dry-land crops than to wet-land crops. The amount of the Government share in Hindu times was very fluctuating. The institutes of Menu would have it that the State should take of grain only "an eighth part, a tenth, or a twelfth, according to the difference of the soil, and the labor necessary to cultivate it." But it is quite certain that the average share under Hindu Governments considerably exceeded these theoretical limits. The Hindu share was, as first mentioned, probably less than the Mahomedan share, but it must have been very much above the share of Menu, or it will be impossible to account for the slow development of individual landed property. It is probable that in times of war the land demand was increased.

State of the country before the Mahomedan invasions.   Certain characteristics have been mentioned which are believed to have been broadly true of the whole of Southern India in ancient Hindu times. If a step forward is taken, and the approximately modern ante-Mahomedan period is considered, we find considerable variations in different parts of the country. For convenience sake we may roughly divide the country as existing at that period into three principal tracts, the Tamil Country, the West Coast, and the Telugu Country.

—The Tamil Country.   The Tamil Country lies between Nellore on the north and the most southern extremity of the East Coast, skirting the Mysore plateau on the eastern side. It was the scene of the three old Hindu dynasties of Pandya, Chola, and Chera. The exact limits of these kingdoms cannot now be traced, and without doubt was in a state of constant change. It is only known with certainty that they met near Caroor, about 40 miles west of Trichinopoly, a town which alternately passed into the hands of each of the rivals. Pandya is generally identified with Madura, Chola with Tanjore, and Chera with Salem. In the Tamil Country the republican form of village community above mentioned was especially prevalent. On the first establishment of a Tamil village the rights of occupancy of the whole land were divided into a number of equal shares or "ploughs," and apportioned to the different members of the settling community. At the earliest stage it is probable that there was common cultivation, and that the net produce after payment of taxes was divided according to the shares. Subsequently individual cultivation seems to have been carried on, but the land to be cultivated by each was re-apportioned by lot in the original proportions either annually or at every five, six, or ten years. In Tanjore, Tinnevelly, Madura, Dindigul, and the other Tamil provinces south of the Coleroon, individual occupancy seems to have arisen at an early date. The division of lands was then considered permanent, and as far as occupation and cultivation went the ancient collective tenure was converted into one of severalty. For all other purposes, however, the communistic principle still prevailed. A sharer could not sell his land without the consent of the community, and on the other hand the possession of a share, whether inherited or acquired by sale or mortgage, gave a proportionate claim to all incidents common to the village, as for instance the advantage arising out of mines or quarries, fisheries, forests, taking up of new waste, pasturage, &c. Gradually the shares became sub-divided; but in the accounts of the village the original partition always remained, the small holdings being represented in terms fractional of the original shares, and the possessor of a reduced share possessing a corresponding share of the communistic rights and duties. The name given to these communistic rights and duties was kaniachi among the Vellalars. When the property fell into the hands of the Brahmins it was called Swastium. The same property when found in the possession of Mahomedans or Native Christians was called Mirási, the name now most usually employed in all cases; Mirás is an Arabic word, meaning inheritance or patrimony. Pasangkarei in Tamil and Sarwadáyan in Sanscrit are also terms for the same thing. In some instances, principally in Tanjore, the whole Mirási of a village was vested, either by purchase or otherwise, in the hands of one individual; it was then called Ekabhogam. The duties of the individual Mirasidars, as such, consisted of paying certain small taxes or "merei" to the community for purposes of internal village administration. The following list taken from old accounts is illustrative of the nature of these taxes:—To feeding Brahmins on particular festivals, to lighting the village temples and gates; to expenses incurred on certain anniversaries; to feeding travellers and strangers, one meal to each; to repairing the village wall; to repairing the chief temple; to constructing a new gate for the village; paid to certain men for killing a tiger, &c., &c. The rights of the Mirasidars were more numerous than their duties,

the institution being one for the assertion rather of the former
than of the latter. Against the Government the Mirasidars
asserted freedom from all interference in the apportionment of
land within the village boundary, or in the management of village
affairs ; claiming the exclusive right to a hereditary possession and
usufruct of the former and a hereditary authority in the latter.
In Tondeimandalam lying between the south of Nellore and the
Coleroon, or the country now comprising Chingleput and North
and South Arcot, the Mirasidars claimed also as a perquisite a
portion of arable land, called Grama Manyam, free of all Government demands. Against non-Mirasidars the claims of the
Mirasidars were the same as those of any owner of landed property
against strangers, the latter having no part in the corporation and
being admitted to cultivate only on sufferance. Non-Mirasidars
paid village taxes to the Mirási corporation, and these contributions eventually no doubt removed the necessity for the Mirasidars
themselves making any contributions at all; at the present
day we find the Mirasidars in some localities claiming such
contributions from non-Mirasidars, in the form of a proportionate
deduction from the gross produce of lands paying tax to Government, and this merely as a perquisite and without making any
return for it. The village government was carried on by a
panchayet, or body of five, and the headman was only president in a
sort of council. The management of all internal details and the
realization of the government dues from the individual cultivator, vested with this body or their delegates, and public opinion
was no doubt the check on injustice. The collection of the
revenue cost the Government nothing. The demand was
a maximum demand liable to remissions on the report of the
village authorities. In early times each village was composed
of a number of families claiming to be of the same brotherhood
or class, and generally the villages in the same part of the
country were of one tribe or sub-division of a tribe. The principal caste was that of the Vellalar, the professional cultivator.
Non-Mirasidars were nearly always tenants of the Mirasidars
collectively or severally, and in that capacity they were called
Poyakaries. Besides the village mereis, they paid an ordinary
rent. The profit of the Mirasidar owner after paying Government dues was called Swamybhogum or landlord's profit.
In many cases one family of tenants rented the same farm at a
stipulated amount of share of produce for several generations,
and thus gradually acquired a prescriptive right to remain and
not to have their rents raised. They also gradually acquired

rights of alienation. This class of tenants were called Ul-kudi
or inside cultivator. Tenants who had not attained to
such a position were called Para-kudi, or foreign cultivator.
These tenancies resembled very closely those of the *coloni*
and *aratores* of the Roman empire. That the Mirasidars
enjoyed a clear landlord's rent, and that individual property
gradually arose, may be seen from deeds of sale belonging
to the period. The Mirási system flourished as long as the
Government demand was not excessive. The Mahomedan
rulers are generally supposed to have augmented the land-tax
to such a point as to have absorbed all landlords' rents, and
to have reduced the Mirasidars to much the same position as
an Ul kudi. Tanjore retained the Mirási system the longest,
and at the beginning of this century the landlord's rent was
still about 25 per cent. of the crop. At the same period the
Tinnevelly rent had sunk to $13\frac{1}{2}$ per cent. It should be
mentioned, to render the description of the Tamil system
complete, that Manyams or alienations of State demands on
certain lands were already prevalent in the Hindu period.
In these cases the alienation was either in favor of a village
servant in accordance with custom and under the authority of
the village register, when it was classed as Tarabadi; or in
favor of some independent person under special grant from the
ruling power, when it was called Sanad or Dumbala. The
Mirasidars paid the Government tax on Manyam lands to the
persons to whom the rights of Government were under these
arrangements transferred. Occasionally the payee would himself
get possession of the land, and pay the Government dues to
himself; whether this was done with the consent of the
Government, or only by accident and encroachment is a point
much debated.

The tract of country known to ancient Hindu geographers as —The West-
Kerala comprised the whole of the tract lying along the Western ern Coast.
Coast and under the mountains as far as Gokurna in North
Canara. Travancore and Cochin were from the first under
rajahs belonging to the land-owning class. Malabar was
similarly ruled, but broke up in the ninth century into a
number of petty principalities, among the chief of which was
that of the Zamorins at Calicut found still in authority by
Vasco di Gama at the end of the fifteenth century. Tuluva, or
Canara, as it has erroneously been called by the British, was
established as a separate Hindu dynasty held by the land-owning

class; but in the twelfth century this dynasty made way for that of the Pandyans, and a century later for that of the Telugu speaking kings of Vijayanagar, the representatives of the old Carnatic or Canara Empire. The characteristic of the whole of the Kerala country was the presence of a strongly developed personal and individual land-property, the absence of a Government tax on land, the absence of a concentrated village system such as obtained in the Carnatic, and the existence of a military tenure similar to the feudal system of Europe. The country was originally sub-divided between a race of Brahmins or priests called Namboories, and a military tribe called Nairs; these two holding in subjection the agriculturalists of the country consisting of persons called Teers and others. The Nairs paid no land-tax but attended the kings to the field with their retainers. The Namboories also paid no land-tax, but furnished the expenses for the support of the temples. In the ninth century a Zamorin of Calicut became a convert to Mahomedanism, and about this time a large colony of Mahomedan settlers of Arabian descent were allowed to occupy lands in Malabar. These Mahomedans, called Moplahs, were mostly merchants, and were equally exempted from payment of direct land-tax. In the absence of land-tax the kings of the country had considerable domains assigned to them, which were cultivated by slaves and yielded a sufficient revenue for household expenses. The subordinate chiefs maintained their own internal police arrangements, and excepting in time of war the personal expenses of the rajahs were not large. But they were not without other branches of revenue. A succession duty equal to 25 per cent. on the value of the estates was levied on Mahomedan subjects being landholders. There were also import and export duties, mint duties, fines, escheats, confiscations, protection, money received from persons of other states who claimed asylum, benevolences in the shape of offerings made to the crown at great festivals or on an occasion, and fees on marriages of important persons. There were also license-taxes, and royalties on gold ore, elephants, ivory, teak-trees, bamboos, and vessels wrecked on the coast. The inhabitants of the West Coast did not congregate together in villages, but resided in scattered habitations on their farms and in their gardens. For fiscal arrangements there were authorities in charge of defined tracts of country. The proprietary right in the land differed from Mirási right in being individual and not communistic. Whether enjoyed by the original Nairs and

Namboories, or by the more recent Moplahs, it was equally
called Jenum, or birth-right. The owners seldom cultivated
their own lands, but let them out on limited leases to tenants
called Patomkars. The crown ceased to recognize the immunity
from land-tax if an original Jenumdar once parted by sale
with his right. Hence mortgage was the rule of the country,
and sales scarcely ever occurred. The mortgagee again could
not acquire the Jenum right by simply foreclosing; the landlord
never losing the power of subsequently reclaiming his property
by paying the principal, and being always entitled to some
recognition of his ownership even if it were only given in
the shape of a sheaf of corn or a pound of butter. The
Malabar mortgages possessed another peculiarity in the principle
of self-redemption. On the death of the owner of mortgaged lands,
it was usual for the heir to furnish a new instrument recognizing
the act of his predecessor, but on this occasion he was entitled
to deduct 13 per cent. from the principal of the debt. Thus in
a few generations the lands reverted to the ancient family
proprietors. These were the primitive tenures of the West Coast,
and as long as they were recognized by the Governments, there
can be little surprise that landed property so carefully protected
should be strongly asserted by the holders. There is no trace
that up to the time of the Mahomedan invasions there was any
land-tax south of Tuluva, and in the southernmost part of
Tuluva it must have been even then a very light one. The
Tuluva country began to change its land-revenue features in
the thirteenth century when invaded by the Pandyan king.
On that occasion the original Nairs seemd to have been
dispossessed in favor of a race of cultivators called Hullers, and
in making the transfer of property the land-tax, such as it
was, suffered an increase. It is reported that the new Government required the grain to be husked before being delivered
into the public stores, thus adding 10 per cent. to the impost.
In A. D. 1336 when Tuluva came under the Rajah of
Vijayanagar, the system was still further adapted to that
prevailing in the north.

Regarding the Telugu country as it existed in the pre- —The Telugu
Mahomedan period there is much less to say than regarding the Country.
two other main divisions of the Presidency; partly because it
had less characteristic features, and partly because such special
features as it possessed have been almost entirely obliterated
by the subsequent Mahomedan and British occupations, and

information on the subject is therefore very meagre. As far as
can be ascertained, the village system in the Telugu country
was more of the ancient non-republican form than in the more
southern parts of the country. There are traces however, in
certain parts, of a right akin to mirasi right in the ancient
landholders whom the Mahomedans called kudeem. It is known
that a large proportion of the cultivators, if not all of them,
possessed under the old rajahs the privilege of hereditary
occupancy, and that their assessment was light. Hence the
land must have been saleable. Traces of landed proprietorship
are however by no means so clear as on the west coast, or even
as in Tondeimandalam. The hilly portions of the country seem
to have been from time immemorial parcelled out among chieftains
of the military class, who held hereditarily, exercised uncontrolled
territorial jurisdiction within their limits, and appropriated the
entire revenues subject to the condition of performing military
service or other offices at the court of their superior rajah, at
Cuttack or Vijayanagar for instance. In the plains were found
a number of petty non-military Hindu rajahs, forming an ordinary
landed aristocracy. These petty chieftainships obtained more
or less all over the Presidency, but are the more noteworthy in
the Telugu country because it is there that they have been
principally supported and incorporated into the revenue system
by subsequent Governments. The origin of these chieftainships
was no doubt various, and while some represented old families,
others were at the time of the Mahomedan invasions little more
than Government officers for the collection of revenue in large
tracts.

**Mahomedan
invasions.**   India has twice been subject to Mahomedan rule, once under the
Turks after the invasion of Mahommed of Ghuznee in the eleventh
century, and once under the Moguls after the invasion of Baber
in the sixteenth century. On each of these occasions the southern
part of the peninsula was overrun by the conquerors, though not
to the same extent as more northern provinces. About the year
1300 Allahoodeen formally completed the conquest of the Deccan;
and in the year 1347 we find direct Mahomedan authority
extending as far south as the Krishna river. There is no accurate
account of the mode in which the Turks raised supplies, but it
was probably through the local Hindu chiefs. The occupation was
strictly a military one, and the police and revenue administration
still remained for the most part in the hands of the local chiefs.
There is no distinct trace of any changes of land-revenue system.

The Mahomedans were well content to leave such institutions as they found them, and indeed the only information now available as to the rates of taxation peculiar to the Hindus is that given by the Mahomedan historian Ferishta. It is asserted that the Turkish invasion had the indirect effect on landed property of forcing up the land demand exacted by the Hindu chiefs, and so of weakening private property. In the interval between the Turkish and Mogul dynasties a number of the Hindu kingdoms of the south were absorbed by Mahomedan kingdoms, the result of incessant petty wars. This period saw the rise of the farming system, mere outside speculators taking the place in many cases of the old native rajahs. Where the Mahomedans found it inconvenient to deal with village communities, and native rajahs were not at hand, they appointed farmers of the land-revenue. Such men undertook the farm as a mere temporary speculation, without acquiring any local rights, claims or ties of any kind, and without interfering in any way with the existing rights of the cultivators. By the time that Akber succeeded to the throne in 1556, the conquest of the country was sufficiently confirmed to enable him to inaugurate measures of a more detailed nature for regulating the revenue system. Akber perfected the land settlement of his predecessor, Shir Khan ; and Malik Amber, an Abyssinian under the Mahomedan princes of the south, and Sevajee among the Mahrattas, carried out Akber's principles in a large portion of the south. The farming system had naturally led to abuses on the part of the farmers and to resistance on the part of the cultivators, and Akber was desirous of superseding it. He endeavoured to settle in all cases with village communities. With this object he surveyed and classified the lands in the villages, took the average produce of each class of land, ascertained the average price of produce for ten years past, and took one-third of the average gross produce paid in cash as the Government demand. In this way was calculated the amount to be paid by each village. At the same time a detailed statement was drawn up of the amount payable by each cultivator, for the guidance of the village authorities. The close similarity between these assessment arrangements and the assessment arrangements of the present day will be observed ; and at the same time this important distinction, that village settlements have been abandoned. The assessment obtained under Akber's system was less than former assessments, but it was anticipated that the difference would be made up by increased punctuality of payment, for the joint responsibility of the community was the condition on which the reduced rates and other advantages were accorded to the villagers. The community managed their own affairs and disposed of their own waste. Under this settlement lands exempted from revenue were registered and inquired into, and those that were improperly held were resumed. Remissions were given on the occurrence of great calamities, but not otherwise. Payment was enforced by personal restraint and seizure of goods, but not by sale of lands. On the other hand the Government reserved the right to take land from those who would not cultivate and give it to others. The Mahomedan arrangements of this period were probably in many respects rather theoretical than practical, for a very short time afterwards the former farming system is found again re-established all over the country.

Early measures of the British Government. When the administration of Southern India fell into the hands of the British, the state of things was briefly as follows. Large farms were held by large renters called Zemindars, or in a few cases by Native chiefs dating from the pre-Mahomedan period; certain single villages were farmed by the headmen; and in other villages the more perfect democratic communities made joint-bargains for lump payments. The part of the country first acquired, and where the first administrative steps had to be taken, was the Northern Circars, or the tract lying on the northern extremity of the present Madras Presidency between the sea-board and the Orissa hills. As little was known by the Company's servants about the tenures or settlements of the country, the detailed administration was at first left entirely in the hands of the natives, the European officials merely keeping the books. The farming system was carried out even further than before. This administration was not successful. The Circars were divided into Zemindary lands, or lands found in the hands of middlemen, and Havelly lands or lands not so found. At the outset the British put renters even into the Havelly lands. The Zemindars invariably sub-rented the lands to another middleman, and the speculators or renters put in by the British into the non-Zemindary lands had little regard for the welfare of the cultivators. In either case the actual cultivator retained a very small share of the produce. This state of things lasted but a few years however, and in 1769 the Fort St. George Government took the detailed administration into its own hands, and set about making improved settlements. The first step was to appoint Provincial Councils. They found the work too great, and did not effect much. The next step was the appointment by the Court of Directors of a special Commission, or Committee of Circuit as it was called, consisting of certain members of the Madras Council, with instructions to make tours in the districts and institute inquiries into rights and interests. The instructions of the Court of Directors were conceived in a liberal and enlightened spirit, and were clearly and emphatically expressed. But this Committee was also a failure. The Provincial Courts did not sufficiently support its operations, and the middlemen did their best to create impediments. No fixed system was introduced. Annual leases were granted in the first instance, then settlements for three and five years. The Havelly lands were let in some cases on the village joint-settlement system, but the settlements were imperfectly made. In 1786 a Board of Revenue was established at Madras, on the pattern of the Board already existing in Bengal, and about the same time individual Collectors took the place of the Provincial Councils in the Circars.

In the same year that the Madras Government entered on the *Contemporary measures in Bengal.* management of the Northern Circars, the Bengal Government assumed that of Bengal, Behar, and Orissa; and experiments were conducted in the latter case in very much the same way as in the former. The Bengal Government however came earlier to a decision, and when Lord Cornwallis came to India as Governor-General in 1786, the plan of the permanent settlement with the Bengal Zemindars had already been arranged. An experimental settlement of the whole of Bengal for a ten-year period was announced in 1789, and in 1792 the experiment of a permanent settlement was declared to be confirmed.

The permanent alienation of the land-revenue thus made to *Permanent settlement in Northern Circars.* the Bengal middlemen had some supporters in Madras, and pressure was brought to bear on Madras by the Bengal Government to adopt the same policy in this Presidency. The Court of Directors wrote out to the same effect in 1795. The Madras Board of Revenue however reported that they were hardly prepared to recommend the perpetuation of the settlement, and that they required time for the collection of further information. In 1799 positive orders were brought out from England that Lord Cornwallis' permanent system was to be adopted throughout the Madras Presidency. On this occasion the Governor-General proclaimed his resolution to remove from office any public servant who evinced a want of zeal in fulfilling the intentions of Government. Eventually the Madras Government

reported to the Supreme Government that they were possessed
of materials for a permanent zemindary settlement in certain
parts of the country. Lord Wellesley, who had by this time
succeeded to the Governor-Generalship, directed the commencement of operations in the lands on the East Coast. A special Commission was accordingly appointed, and between the years 1802
and 1804 the northern districts of Madras were permanently
assessed. The lands already in the hands of Zemindars were
confirmed to them in perpetuity, the assessment being fixed
according to local circumstances. The Havelly lands were parcelled
out into estates of a convenient size, yielding from 3,500 to
17,500 rupees annual rent, or in some cases more, and were sold
as Mootahs or perpetually settled revenue farms, to the highest
auction bidder. Regulation XXV of 1802 constituted both those
descriptions of landholders "proprietors," and detailed the terms
on which they held their property.

Settlements in the Jaghire. The country round Madras known as the Jaghire had
been obtained from the Nawab of Arcot, partly in 1750 and
partly in 1763, in return for services rendered to that State.
The history of its settlement at the period now under notice is
of special interest, inasmuch as it shows joint-village settlements made as late as the end of the last century, and only
superseded by the forcible imposition of the permanent settlement.
The Jaghire was placed in 1794 in the hands of Mr. Lionel
Place, and it is to this gentleman that we are indebted for the
first correct information as to landed tenures in Southern India.
The villages in the Jaghire were discovered by Mr. Place to be of
the class already described as democratic or mirasi. The villages,
that is to say, were corporate bodies, with an internal municipal
constitution, and with the land the property of the corporation.
The land was sub-divided into shares which were saleable, and
still retained all the value of real property. In each village
there were besides the corporate members, cultivators holding as
tenants of the corporation and having on their side prescriptive
rights according to ancient agreements. Again there was a
third class cultivating from year to year without other privileges
than that of doing so. The distinction between the shareholder
and the tenant consisted in the fact that the latter could not sell
his rights of occupancy, nor enjoy any of the various immunities
and advantages belonging to the former as a member of
the corporation. Mr. Place in making his settlements, dealt
with the whole communities and not with any particular

individual, and left it to the villagers to assess themselves individually. Each village chose its own representative or representatives. There is every reason to suppose that the joint village settlements of Mr. Place would have proved successful. They were not allowed however even a few years trial. Under the orders of the Court of Directors the Jaghire was permanently settled in 1802, the lands being divided into sixty-one estates bearing an assessment of from 7,000 to 17,500 rupees, and put up to public auction as Mootahs or Proprietary Estates.

Whilst these measures for the settlement of the more ancient territories of the Company were in progress, new territories were being added to the Presidency, and the question of land-assessment came up again for discussion in connexion with the parts of the country ceded to the English in the south. In 1792 the first war with Tippoo placed a considerable tract of country, comprising the Baramahl, or Salem as it is now called, Dindigul, and Malabar, in the hands of the English. The second war with Tippoo added Canara and Coimbatore. According to a treaty made with the Nizam of Hyderabad in 1800 the whole territory lying south of the Toongabudra and of the Krishna river after its junction with the former, was ceded in perpetuity, constituting what are now called the Ceded Districts. In 1801 all the possessions of the Nawab of Arcot in the Carnatic were made over to the British, thus carrying their possessions down to Cape Comorin. *Acquisition of other territories.*

In the lands thus newly acquired the same distinction was found as in the Northern Circars. That is to say, there were lands holding direct from Government, and lands holding through intermediary chiefs. The latter went in the south by the name of Poligars. They may be classed under three heads, as :— 1st, descendants of the royal families of Vijayanagar, Conjeveram, and Madura ; 2nd, the military feudal chieftains of those sovereignties who had resisted the conquest of the Mahomedans, and had either retained by force, or through indulgence and tolerance, the estates which they had enjoyed under their ancient governments ; 3rd, district Collectors who had contrived to elude the immediate control of the Mahomedans, and who had gradually usurped the sovereignty of the districts. These distinctions were not recognised by the Mahomedans. All the Poligars were made to pay tribute and not according to *Dealings with the Poligars.*

any fixed principle, but according to the power of the government
to enforce it. The management of their chiefships, and the
control of their subjects, were left entirely to the Poligars; but
they were almost always at war with their neighbours, or in
revolt against the State. Whenever the exactions of the
Mahomedans were considered exorbitant, they were resisted, and
even if the dues were eventually paid, the Poligar took the earliest
opportunity of reimbursing himself and of taking revenge, by an
attack on the villages holding direct of the Government. In
many cases the Government ryots were obliged to compromise
with the invaders by agreeing to pay a stipulated amount,
denominated kavel or protection-money. This was, in fact, a
sum paid to one Poligar to induce him to give protection against
the encroachment of others. Under the systematic control of
the British Government, it was highly necessary to check the
unbridled conduct of the Poligars; but having no knowledge
of their true rights the Government were not always successful
in dealing with them. Permanent settlements which left about
two-thirds or more of their estimated revenue were made in the
Chittoor, Kalastry, Venkataghirry, and Bomrauz Pollams; and
most of those chieftains or their descendants still retain their
hereditary estates. In the southern part of the Tamil country
there were thirty-three Poligars, for the realisation of whose
tribute it was found necessary to appoint a separate European
Collector. These Poligars fought desperately for what they conceived to be their rights, and their reduction forms a noteworthy
incident in the military history of the Presidency. Of those
chiefs who had held their patrimonial estates for several generations, we find in the year 1803 thirteen only still in possession;
the lands of fourteen others were under charge of the European
Collector, and six were forfeited, given away, or sold. In the
districts ceded by the Nizam in 1800, there were eighty Poligars.
These also resisted the Government, and had to be reduced to
subjection by force of arms. In 1807 they were found to have
been thus disposed of : Pensioned 2, holding a Jaghire 1, residing
on their estates deprived of authority 23, managing their own
estates 40, expelled by force 6, in confinement 8, total 80.

Settlement of Baramahl. Turning to the settlement of the lands not held by Poligars, the
first case calling for special notice is that of the operations
in Baramahl, showing the rise of the ryotwari system. In 1792
a Commission was appointed to take charge of the Baramahl,

with Captain Read at its head. Captain Read was assisted by three junior Military officers, Macleod, Graham, and Munro, and by Mr. Hardis, a Civilian. The military exactions of Tippoo are supposed to have disorganized the natural institutions of the country, and to have impaired the efficiency of the village corporations. However this may be, it is certain that the new Commission directed their attention rather to individuals than to communities. In the Tahsildars of the period they found mere receivers of the revenue, and as the idea of dealing with village communities was not favored, there was no alternative but to deal with the individual cultivator. A system of individual settlements involved a detailed survey of fields, and this work was at once undertaken. The settlement also aimed at making moderate assessments and at guaranteeing them for a short period of years. Though the assessment was to be fixed for a period, every man was to be able to add to or throw up his lands annually. No increases were to be made in the assessment on account of improvements made by the ryot, such as digging of wells, building tanks, or converting dry land into garden or rice-fields. By 1798 the Commission had completely surveyed the Baramahl and determined the rents which should be paid on the ryotwari system. The average assessment per acre was on the dry lands in the southern division 2 rupees, in the centre $1\frac{1}{2}$ rupee, and in the northern division 1 rupee. On wet lands, it was in the southern division 11 rupees, in the centre $6\frac{1}{2}$, and in the northern division $5\frac{1}{4}$. The average rent was little more than three shillings an acre on the common soils, and the average contribution of each cultivator was about 70 shillings a year. The ryotwar system, as thus propounded, was approved in theory by the Directors in England, but it was treated as an experimental measure and no practical steps were taken for confirming it. In 1799 orders were received, as already mentioned, for a permanent Zemindary or Mutahdary settlement throughout Madras. In pursuance of this decree the Baramahl was divided in the years 1803, 1804, and 1805, into 228 revenue farms, which were sold by auction to the highest bidders. The numerous bankruptcies which occurred showed that there was some flaw in the system. A great many of the farmers failed in the second year after having pillaged the villages placed under them. The system could not be carried out, and a return was almost immediately made to ryotwari. The supporters of the Zemindary system asserted that it failed in Baramahl only because

the assessments had already been fixed too high by Read's
Commission. On the side of the village-settlement system it is
said that no trial was made of it. The practical result however
was that ryotwari prevailed. What is said here of the
Baramahl, applies for the most part to the history of adjacent
parts during the same period, for instance of Dindigul and Coimbatore. The Ceded Districts were brought under the ryotwar
system by Colonel Munro a few years later.

Settlements in Malabar. The remainder of the Madras provinces consisted of Malabar
and Canara. The ancient feudal system which existed in
Malabar has already been mentioned. The country was in the
hands of a race of rajahs or military leaders, and their retainers
the Nairs ; holding in subjection the Teers, and other laborers, the
ancient inhabitants of the country. Instead of the districts in
Malabar being assessed at so many thousand pagodas, they were
rated at so many men liable to be called to the field. At the
peace of 1792, Malabar was ceded to the British Government
by Tippoo Sultan. It had been first invaded by the Mahomedans
under Hyder Ally thirty-four years previously ; its invasion
being invited in the first place by the Palghaut Rajah, to enable
him to repel the attack of the Zamorin of Calicut. The landlords
of Malabar did not yield readily, and in the struggles which
ensued between them and the Mysore Government most of the
ancient landed proprietors were either killed or expelled. In
the year 1783, Arshed Beg Khan was put in by Hyder as
governor of Malabar, and his administration appears to have
been more lenient and equitable than that of any of his
predecessors. The principles of his assessment are said to
have been as follows :—to the cultivator 5½ tenths, to the
proprietor 1½ tenths, to the government 3 tenths. Shortly
after the cession to the British a committee, consisting of
two Bengal and two Bombay servants, were deputed to
make a settlement of the country ; and their report, issued
in 1793, consisting of several volumes, furnishes a full account of
the district. In this province, where the landholders maintained
that not only were they the proprietors of their estates, but that
under the native princes they had never paid a land-tax at all, the
doctrine of State proprietary right to the land then prevailing
and a claim to half the produce assumed in other places, were not
likely to be acceptable. The Bengal and Bombay commissioners
found that in Malabar no such claims could be enforced, and
they proposed to regulate the future demand by the assessment
of Arshed Beg Khan. The first settlement, or rather realisation

of revenue, fell short of that amount by about twenty-five per cent., and an attempt to raise the rates caused an open rebellion, which lasted for some years, and cost a heavy expenditure of lives and money. In 1800, the province was transferred from the Bombay to the Madras Government, and its management was made over to Major Munro, the advocate of ryotwari, who in effect introduced the ryotwari system there. One of the earliest of this officer's measures was a survey and assessment. These led to urgent complaints, which were unattended to, and which ended in another rebellion more violent than the former. The second rebellion was suppressed, more by conciliation than coercion, and the result was the recognition on the part of Government of the proprietary right of the landholders to their estates. Peace being restored, the chief Brahmins and landed proprietors assembled at the Collector's invitation at his office, where they selected a committee from among themselves, to arrange matters for the future administration of the province. On this occasion the landholders agreed, after allowing fifty per cent. of the produce to the cultivator, to pay to Government a sum of money estimated at twenty per cent. of the gross produce, themselves retaining thirty per cent. as rent. It was decided that the assessment should be founded on the survey and assessment of 1800. Affairs remained thus for several years, but meanwhile many complaints were made as to the inequality of the assessment, the people not being satisfied with the arrangement of 1800. In 1817 Colonel Munro, who had been the principal agent in suppressing the last rebellion and in making the last settlement, was deputed to visit and report on the condition of the province ; the chief result of the visit was a reduction in the assessment. It should be mentioned that there are no compact villages in Malabar similar to those in the Carnatic. The taluqs in Malabar are divided into Amshoms, which are again sub-divided into Deshams. Over each Amshom is a headman called Adhigari, associated with an accountant called Menon. These officials are paid by fixed salaries. The Deshams are presided over by honorary headmen called Mukyastans. The houses are scattered, and there is therefore no village-site.

In Canara individual landed property was not so demonstra- **Settlements in Canara.** ble a fact as in Malabar. The primitive constitution of the district had been changed at its conquest in the 13th century by the Pandyan kings, and subsequently by the kings of Vijayanagar.

In later times it had been partially subdued by Hyder, whose
exactions are said to have impoverished the landlord class.
When the British Government obtained possession, the saleable
lands were few in number and limited in extent, and many of the
landlords were reduced to the situation of laborers on their own
estates. Still there could be no doubt with whom the Government
should settle ; proprietary rights were strong enough to render the
question of employing middlemen or of making joint-rent village
settlements quite unnecessary. Major Munro entered this district
for settlement in 1800, and at once established a ryotwar system
which was not subsequently modified. The extent of land in
Canara for purposes of assessment has always been measured
by the amount of seed it takes to sow it. The settlement for a
share of the produce has always been in the name of an individual
holder, against whose name in the public accounts is entered
every charge to which he is liable. This is the holder's " wurg "
or account, a word which has come to mean " holding " in the
Revenue system. Major Munro found this method of settlement
obtaining, and continued it without change. No alteration was
allowed in any man's wurg except on good cause being shown.
No general survey of the district was introduced, but partial
surveys were instituted for the purpose of obtaining general
data for assessment. A complete register, called the Bijawari
register, was formed of the extent, calculated by the seed, of
each holder's wurg. The only difficulty was with the amount
of the assessments. The settlement of Hurry Hur Roy, Rajah
of Vijayanagar, made in the 14th century, was for a long
time the standard assessment. Hurry Hur Roy took $2\frac{1}{2}$ katties
of seed as the basis of the calculation, and assuming the
proportion between seed and gross produce to be that of 1 to 12,
he apportioned the gross produce thus :—to the landlord $7\frac{1}{2}$
katties, to the cultivator 15 katties, to the Government $7\frac{1}{2}$
katties. The Bednore Government left this assessment as they
found it till 1618, when the Government share was increased by
50 per cent. The total jummah of Canara, at the close of the
Bednore Government, amounted to pagodas 3,20,827. Hyder
increased this to pagodas 5,33,202. Colonel Munro's settlement
in 1800 amounted to pagodas 4,65,148 ; of this pagodas 2,84,603
was composed of the ancient land-tax or Shist, and pagodas
1,80,545 stood for extra assessments imposed by the Bednore and
Mysore Governments, the extra imposts of the latter being
called Shamil. The inequalities caused by the new British

assessment were found in the course of a few years to be intolerable, and in 1817 a thorough investigation was instituted, ending eventually in the so-called Tharao assessment in 1819. The Tharao was a maximum assessment which the Collector could not exceed of his own authority, and was based on a detailed investigation of the collections on particular estates. The Tharao assessment was considered a moderate one when it was made, but it was a considerable time before the country attained even that standard, and constant remissions were necessary. The total amount of the Tharao assessment was Rupees 15,24,879 on 34,216 ryots as against Rupees 16,72,607 of the ancient Beriz comprising both Shist and Shamil. The village arrangements in South Canara are somewhat similar to those in Malabar, each wurg having its house situated upon it. The headmen of tracts are called Potails, and the curnams are called Shanbogues.

In the various experiments which were made during the first twenty years of the century in the mode of settlement for the land revenue, the Zemindary and Ryotwari systems played the most important part. The village joint-rent system was not however entirely overlooked. In 1808 this method was given a general trial in several districts on the authority of the Court of Directors. The Madras Board of Revenue were distinctly in favor of the system, and had not Colonel Munro been so much opposed to it, it is possible that it might have had a different fate. The plan was tried at first for a term of three years. The result was not entirely satisfactory. In many parts the head inhabitants, conceiving the assessment excessive, and finding themselves obliged to ask for remissions annually, refused to rent their villages. Speculators then came forward and out-bid each other, so that the villages were rented at a sum beyond what they could yield, and the contractors failed. Still the Government were satisfied on the whole, and in many cases made a further ten-year settlement on the same principle. It was even proposed by some to make a perpetual village settlement. The ten-year settlement was not approved by the Court of Directors, but their objections arrived too late to be acted on. A visit to England however made by Colonel Munro had probably not been without its effect upon the opinions of the Court of Directors and the Board of Control; and towards the close of 1817 instructions were received at Madras for the abolition of the village system, and the confirmation in all

Trial of village rent system.

practicable cases of the plan of ryotwar settlement with
individual holders. It was alleged that the village system
had been tried and had failed. The revenue authorities
declared that it had not been subjected to a fair trial, and
that it had not failed. They alleged too that the home authorities had decided hastily on insufficient evidence. " The
judgment," the Board of Revenue wrote, " which has been
pronounced in England against the village system, is founded
on a very partial and unfavorable view of its results; for it does
not appear that the authorities at home had, at the time when
that judgment was passed, any information before them
respecting any other portion of it than its commencement, the
triennial settlement." And they urged that the result of that
settlement was no test of the success or failure of the system,
inasmuch as the lands had been subjected to an over-
assesssment, "founded upon the fallacious data of the Ryotwar
collections."

**Final
establishment
of Ryotwari.** The Ryotwar system was however by this time in favor at
home, and orders were sent out for its reintroduction, in all
possible cases, under certain modifications prescribed by the
Court. At this period, in Ganjam, Vizagapatam, Rajahmundry,
Masulipatam, Guntoor, Salem, Chingleput, the Cuddalore
district, and the Western, Southern, and Chittoor Pollams, the
Permanent Zemindary system prevailed; in the Ceded Districts,
Nellore, the two divisions of Arcot, Palnad, Trichinopoly,
Tinnevelly, and Tanjore, the village system had been introduced;
and the ryotwar system was fully established only in Malabar,
Canara, Coimbatore, Madura, and Dindigul. The orders were
carried out; and all the necessary preliminaries having been
gone through, the village leases having expired, many of the new
Zemindaries or Mootahs having lapsed, or been bought in,
the improved ryotwar system was declared to be established
in Madras. Colonel Munro himself, who had been appointed to
the chief place in the government, took his seat in time to preside
over the act of final establishment in the spring of 1820. Since
1820 there has been a periodic revision of the rates of
assessment in ryotwari lands; a special Commission has dealt
with the whole question of Inam or rent-free lands; and
various legal enactments have been passed for the protection of
various landed interests or for the realization of the Government
dues. In the broad policy of Government however as to tenures
and settlements, there has been no change.

(b.)—Present Land Tenures

Whatever be the correct theory of law or political economy **Classification of tenures under Government.** as to the nature of the rights of Government in respect to land, an abstract question which has been much and perhaps uselessly discussed, it is quite evident that they must, as a Government representing the interests of the people at large, exercise a considerable amount of interference in affairs connected with the land. Whether this is called executive administration or exercise of a proprietary right is not of much importance. It is certain that a modern Government assumes large powers of interference under the unwritten traditional law of this and all other countries. The subject of land-tenures under Government will be classified here according to the extent to which the Government has parted with its own powers to control the disposal of, or the revenue demand on, the land; beginning with the cases of greatest alienation and ending with those of least. A classification according to either one or other of those two descriptions of control would have been preferable; but the subject is too complex to admit of such treatment. Following then this rough classification, the main cases to be considered will be those of:—(1.) Perpetual freeholds, with fixed tenure, a title-deed showing property as against Government, and no demands representing either a land-tax or the share of the produce. Cases will be (a) holdings under recent rules for redeeming the land-revenue, (b) holdings under the rules for redeeming building-site quit-rents, and (c) holdings under the rules for redeeming enfranchised Inam quit-rents. (2.) Holdings of enfranchised Inamdars, with a fixed tenure, a title-deed showing property as against Government, and a quit-rent fixed for ever, calculated at a beneficial rate. (3.) Zemindaries dating from earlier than 1802, with fixed tenure, a sannad showing proprietorship as against Government, and fixed land dues, with obligation for the Zemindar to enter into written engagements with his tenants, and subject to the law of primogeniture as to succession. (4.) Proprietary estates, that is to say Zemindaries created under the authority of the Regulations of 1802, with the same conditions, but no law of primogeniture. (5.) The so-called Unsettled Palliems without a sannad, but with land demand fixed for ever. (6.) Holdings of ryots under Ryotwari, with fixed tenure, but without a sannad expressly declaring proprietorship, and with a demand varying under certain special circumstances. (7.) Inam holdings, given by Government as emolument or in charity, with no title-deed showing unconditional property, with a tenure dependent on the fulfilment of certain conditions the decision as to which rests with the Government, and with a demand calculated as under Ryotwari but at highly favorable rates, the difference between these and normal rates constituting the emolument. (8.) Land held on special conditions, as (*a*) on cowles, and (*b*) under the tope rules. (9.) Unassigned lands still on the hands of Government, but to which, as part of village areas, certain persons have a preferential claim when application is made for their occupation. (10.) Unassigned lands still on the hands of Government without any such restriction.

Perpetual freeholds.

Absolute and perpetual freeholds have not existed in this Presidency until quite recently, and can now be acquired only by taking the benefit of the rules for redeeming the land-revenue, building-site quit-rents, and enfranchised Inam quit-rents. In regard to the first and second of these modes of redemption, it must be observed that inasmuch as land-tax is the main constituent of public revenue it is not allowed to be redeemed universally. It is only allowed in the case of lands occupied for building purposes or intended for gardens and plantations, of lands on the Nilgiris and the Pulny and Shevaroy hills, and of the coffee lands in the Wynaad. In all these cases, proprietors are allowed to redeem their land-tax, the rate of redemption being twenty-five times the sum annually paid on the land as assessment or quit-rent. The cost of survey and demarcation is borne by the person who redeems the assessment. In Zemindaries the Zemindar alone is given the right to redeem the land-revenue. In the case of ryotwari lands the proprietor holding directly from Government has alone the right. Applications for the redemption of land-revenue are disposed of by Collectors subject to an appeal to the Board of Revenue. On payment of the redemption money in full, with the cost of survey and demarcation, the party redeeming the assessment is furnished with a title deed in a certain prescribed form. The third mode of redemption shown above introduces the question of the Inam tenures of this Presidency, but as these are described in detail under the head "Inam Commission" it is only necessary here to mention that Inamdars holding lands enfranchised from service or from Government resumption, but subject nevertheless to a quit-rent, may redeem that quit-rent in perpetuity at twenty years' purchase. The class of holders mentioned in this paragraph have of course unlimited powers of alienating, devising, or disposing of their land. It will be observed that the freehold is absolute against that demand of the Government only which represents the Government right to share the produce, and gives no immunity from other Government demands, such as for artificial irrigation, education, or such matters; in all of which cases the land may be subjected to separate cesses or demands. The land also will always be liable to attachment, in the same way as any other land, in the event of its becoming obnoxious to any legal penalty which authorizes its attachment or sale. The redemption in no way affects sub-tenures, right of occupancy, or other similar rights; and the freedom conferred is absolute only as against Government.

In the case of Zemindaries the land has been perpetually **Zemindaries.** assigned by the Government, with a proprietary title, at any rate as against themselves. The land-dues however still remain as a charge on the land. The land-dues here are permanently paid, and may be taken therefore to be no longer a share of the produce but a tax. Zemindars hold under a " Sunnad-i-milkut Istimrar " and give in exchange a corresponding cabooleat or acceptance. Zemindars are at liberty to transfer, without the previous consent of Government, their proprietary right in the whole or part, however small, of their Zemindaries to any person they please by sale, gift, or otherwise; and such transfers are to be held valid and to be respected by the courts and officers of Government, provided they are not repugnant to the Mahomedan or Hindu law or to the regulations of the British Government. In order to be valid against Government, and in order to liberate the transferrer from his liability to Government dues, such transactions must be first registered in the Collector's office, and where there is a sub-division, the peishcush on the sub-divided portion must be adjusted by the Collector. The Government do not regulate the succession to Zemindaries. They sometimes interfere to recognize a *primâ facie* claimant in cases of demise and pending decision of the law-courts, but nothing more. The Zemindar is in most cases the owner of all waste land, or land not held by cultivators, within his estate, and he has certain powers of selling up cultivators for default of payment of land-tax which will be mentioned hereafter. The land being " permanently settled," that is to say, the land-revenue on it being fixed for ever, no increase of revenue accrues to the State as more and more land is brought under cultivation. Since the land-revenue on these estates was fixed, their value has doubled, but the benefit goes to the Zemindar alone. On the other hand the Zemindar's demand does not protect him from cesses for matters other than land-revenue proper. Zemindars have to keep up the regular establishment of village curnams or accountants ; they appoint these officials, but a civil court alone can remove them. About one-fifth of the whole Presidency is under Zemindary. The obligations laid upon Zemindars in their dealings with their tenants will be described hereafter in treating of tenancy.

—Ancient Zemindaries. The principal of the ancient Zemindaries found by the British Government on its assumption of the country may be said to have been Vizianagaram in the Vizagapatam District, Pittapur in the Godavery, Venkatagiri in the Nellore District, and Ramnad and Shivagunga in the Madura District ; but there were numerous other large estates of the same sort, especially in the north. These Zemindaries differ at the present moment from those subsequently created under Regulation XXV of 1802 in two respects only. In cases of succession by death the law of primogeniture obtains, the eldest son succeeding and the remainder of the family being entitled to no more than maintenance ; and the Zemindar cannot encumber or alienate the estate beyond his own lifetime.

—Other Zemindaries. The private estates conferred under Regulation XXV of 1802 go by various names, as Proprietary Estates, Zemindaries, Muttahs, &c. They must not be confounded with Jaghires, Shrotriems, and other classes of Inam holdings ; mere assignments of land-revenue already assessed by Government with no question of the Inamdars either farming the revenue or being proprietors of the land, and having no connexion with the Regulation just named. In the case of all estates which are not ancient Zemindaries, the ordinary Hindu rule of inheritance prevails. They are sub-divided and alienated freely like any other form of real property. The Government have no concern with regard to the succession.

—Extent and value of Zemindaries. The following table will show the extent and value of the Zemindary estates of this Presidency. The information is not perfectly true in detail, but is as accurate as can be obtained :—

Districts.	Name of the Zemindari.	Area paying Revenue to Government.			Revenue realized by Zemindars as given in the Land Cess Statements.	Peishcush payable to Government.
		Cultivated and Cultivable.	Uncultivable.	Total.		
		ACRES.	ACRES.	ACRES.	RS.	RS.
Ganjam ...	Parla Kimedy ...	255,040	68,640	323,680	4,66,000	82,139
Vizagapatam..	Vizianagram ...	217,328	94,784	312,112	17,00,000	4,96,686
	Bobbili	217,328	94,784	312,112	3,75,000	89,776
	Pittapur	174,080	32,640	206,720	8,28,000	2,50,160
Godavery ...	Nedavole and	120,320	17,920	138,240	2,82,000	1,19,468
	Baharzalli.					
Kistna ...	Wyyur	292,480	66,560	359,040	1,71,000	95,443
	Devarakota ...	79,360	35,200	114,560	1,89,000	81,397
Nellore	Venkatagherry...	Particulars not known ...		1,345,920	9,57,000	3,77,117
North Arcot...	Karvetnuggur ...	202,400	203,720	406,120	6,84,000	1,80,494
	Kalastry	130,560	254,720	385,280	4,53,000	1,76,816
		Particulars not known ...		334,080		
Madura ...	Ramnad	Particulars not available.		996,149	7,34,000	3,38,686
	Shivagunga ...	Do.	Do.	461,952	7,70,000	2,88,317
	Ettiapuram ...	301,730	36,020	337,750	2,04,000	89,387
Tinnevelly ...	All other Estates paying a peish-cush of less than Rupees 80,000—					
	Jeypore ...	Particulars not known ...		8,346,240	Not known...	16,000
	Other Estates.	4,192,734	2,065,892	6,258,626	61,57,000	24,52,184
		Particulars not known ...		94,080		
	Total ...	6,183,360	2,970,880	9,154,240	1,40,60,000	51,32,990
		Particulars not known ...		11,578,421	...	...
	Total Area ...	...	...	20,732,661	...	...

Inamdars who have accepted the terms of enfranchisement, **Inams enfranchised, but unredeemed.** but have not redeemed the quit-rent payable on their lands, call for notice here. They pay quit-rent, but their tenure, as regards security of occupation without conditions, and fixity of land demand, is superior to that of any class of landholders other than those who have redeemed. They have full powers of alienation, while they are protected from the periodic revision of the ryotwari rates contemplated by the Revenue Settlement Department.

Poligars hold in the southern and western portions of the Madras **Poligar estates.** Presidency very much the same position as the Zemindars of the northern districts. Originally Poligars were the descendants of officers of police and revenue agents of the Hindu sovereigns, who advanced themselves to the position of chiefs possessing military forces and strongholds. Gradually they reached the condition of tributary feudatories and proprietors of lands. Their historical relations with the British Government have already been described. All the Palliems have been assessed. Some have been granted permanent settlement under Regulation XXV of 1802, with sannads. The Palliems for which no sannads have been granted are called unsettled Palliems. Practically there is no difference between the settled and unsettled Palliems. The assessment is fixed and permanent in both cases and the succession is governed under the same principles. It was once considered

that the holder of an unsettled Palliem had but a life
interest in the Palliem, and that it was open to Government
to dispose of the Palliem as they pleased on his death, but this
view was not accepted by the Privy Council in a case recently
decided by them. The Government have directed the issue of
permanent sannads to the holders of all such unsettled Palliems
as may be willing to accept them on the condition of continuing
the tribute which they have been paying for upwards of 50 years.
Most of the Poligars have accepted the sannads, but there are a
few to whom they have not yet been issued. These latter then
have a demand perpetually settled but no permanent title, and
form a distinct class in the terms of the classification given above.
There were formerly also a few estates called Palliems held for
real or nominal police services to be rendered to Government
in the districts of Nellore, North Arcot and South Arcot. These
were settled by the Inam Commissioner and enfranchised as
Inams.

Ryotwari
tenure.

The ryotwari system of holding under Government has now
been the principal tenure of this Presidency for half a century.
It is difficult to define it in one or two words, but this only arises
from the inapplicability to oriental tenures of the phraseology of
European landed property. The terms of the engagement can
easily be enumerated, and these terms are sufficiently well
understood and practically acted on by the persons concerned.
No serious difficulty has as yet arisen owing to any difference of
opinion as to the interpretation of the ryotwari contract. In
ryotwari tenure the Government deals with an individual, who
is technically assumed to be acting on his own account and
not to be a middleman. As he is usually a very small holder,
this is often actually the case. The Government allow a
ryot who has once acquired possession to remain in possession as
long as he pays the Government dues. Even when he
becomes a defaulter, they merely sell such portion of his land
as is sufficient to cover the amount due, and under cover of a
special law for so doing; they do not dispossess him by any
form of eviction other than that provided by the legislature under
Madras Act II of 1864. If a ryot without authorization
takes possession of waste assessed land the Government do not
nevertheless evict him. In the particular case of a ryot taking
possession of unassessed waste land, the Government reserve the
right of putting on a prohibitory assessment ; for here the land
is very probably land which it is undesirable to cultivate. The

Government concede to the ryot complete power to alienate the land by lease, mortgage, or sale, and only stipulate that, unless he formally registers such alienation with the Collector, he will remain liable for all Government dues on the land however accruing. The trees on puttah lands are absolutely the property of the Puttadars, and nothing is charged for them except in the case of palmyras in the district of Tinnevelly. In Tinnevelly the tree-tax can be redeemed by the payment of twenty years' assessment. The most important item in the yearly demand, namely the normal land-tax, is fixed in advance and is liable to revision according to present arrangements only once in every thirty years from time of first settlement. Even when a revision takes place it has been guaranteed that no increase shall take place on account of improvements made by the cultivator himself. The normal rate of land-tax is fixed, but every year numerous questions arise of concessions made or extra demands for extra benefits conferred ; the settlement of these questions takes place at the annual Jummabandy. Moreover, the ryot has the power of yearly increasing, decreasing, or entirely abandoning his holdings ; this has also to be attended to at the Jummabandy. The law courts have recently declined to recognize the proprietary rights evidenced by the power to create an easement against Government, in ryotwari holders not claiming as hereditary mirasidars, and newly put in by the British Government ; but this is believed to be a new doctrine. The ryotwari system has taken the place in most localities of the Mahomedan system of renting whole villages to a single individual and leaving it to him to sub-rent to the villagers. It is popular with the people, and creates an elastic revenue which expands as increasing population and prosperity cause more land to be taken up. On the other hand it must be observed that the absence of middlemen causes an enormous amount of detailed labor on the part of the Government.

Though the State has a right to fix the land-tax at its discretion, it does so in accordance with certain principles. In ryotwari it is held that, with a few exceptions, its proper amount is half the value of the net produce of the land after the expenses of cultivation have been deducted from the gross produce. At the commencement of the ryotwari settlement the tax was determined in a somewhat rough and ready manner, which left many anomalies and inequalities to be afterwards —Principles of settlement of Ryotwary.

rectified. The worst of these have been amended from time to time, and at the present time there is a Survey Department which determines the exact area of villages and sub-divisions of villages (khandams) and fields, and a Settlement Department which calculates the rate of assessment for each in accordance with the "half net" principles. The calculation of produce and assessments thus revised are to be in force for thirty years. In Godavery, Kistna, and part of Kurnool an important deviation has been allowed from the "half net" principle in the case of land irrigated by channels led from the great anicuts across the Godavery, Kistna, and Tungabudra. The land-tax there has been calculated as if the land were not irrigated, and the irrigation is charged for at a uniform rate per acre. Further information regarding the Survey and Settlement Departments which underlie the whole ryotwari system will be found further on under the special sections allotted to those subjects.

—Ryotwari puttahs.

It has already been mentioned that the Government have in times past furnished a title-deed setting out what is there called proprietary right in the case of all Zemindars either ancient or created within this century, and that they still continue to furnish such title-deeds to persons who redeem the land-dues in perpetuity by a lump-sum payment. No such title-deed, however, is given to ryots holding under ryotwari, and they are left to make their own arrangements as to creating a title when they dispose of lands by private transaction. When first a ryot is put in possession of land he is furnished with a document called a puttah. But this is liable to revision at each annual Jumma-bandy, and is merely a document to show that, according to the Government register, the ryot for that year holds, without relinquishment, such and such survey fields, or parts of them, and that the Government looks to that ryot and no other for the Government land-dues until further notice. As long as the ryot actually holds the land according to the terms of the register, it is of service to him, as showing that the Government will not attempt to put any one else in possession and will not exercise any powers of attachment or resumption of the land without first dealing with him; and the attachment to landed property is a sufficient motive to make this a very important consideration. In the law-courts however a puttah is very weak evidence to prove possession, inasmuch as there is nothing to show that the arrangement therein indicated has not been superseded by some subsequent private transaction, and even at the outset the Revenue officials in issuing a puttah do not attempt to do more than give it to the person who has the best *primá facie* claim to possession. Regulation XXVI of 1802, Section 3, declares that the Courts shall not recognize transfers of land other than those shown in the register of landed property, and the register coincides with the puttahs issued ; but this provision is held to make unregistered transfers invalid only as against Government, and with reference to the Government dues. The puttah in fact, as has lately been expressed by legal authority, does not assume to be any muniment of title, a subject on which the Government is silent ; but is only a document indicating certain fiscal arrangements between the Government and the individual mentioned in it. The puttah given to the ryot is his surety against Government. No document of acceptance is received by Government from the ryot, as it is considered unnecessary, the law making the land and its produce liable to attachment for arrears in the land-dues in preference to any other claim and whoever be in occupation. A register however called a Chittah, showing the settlement of each individual, is maintained in each village ; ryots who are able to read are allowed to examine this register and can sign their names in it if they wish.

Occasions will often arise when persons wish to transfer their ryotwari puttahs to others. This the Government are always ready to do on production of agreements from both persons interested. In such cases the persons concerned prefer a joint application in the office of the Tahsildar of the taluq in which the land is situated. The Tahsildar publishes a notice thirty days in advance in the villages concerned, and, if no objections are raised, he himself orders the transfer. A puttah is then issued in the name of the transferee at the next Jumma-bandy. Meanwhile, as a rule, the new holder gets possession. In cases where transfer is sought under a decree from a Civil Court sanctioning the transfer, consent of the parties is of course unnecessary, nor is notice given to villagers. Looking to the fact that a transferee cannot obtain a puttah except the transferer is willing to enter with him into a joint agreement to that effect, it has been suggested that a law should be passed for the protection of the transferee making registration of transfers in the Collector's register compulsory. It has not

—Transfers of Ryotwary puttahs.

hitherto been thought, however, that the loss of the puttah is of
sufficient importance to the transferee to make it necessary to
legislate. In the event of the demise of a person whose name is
entered in the Government register, the Government themselves
take steps to ascertain who is the proper successor. On the
occasion of each demise the village curnam reports to the Tahsildar,
and the Tahsildar reports to the Collector. In one or other of
these reports, or in both of them, the name is given of the
person or persons who appear *primâ facie* to have the best claims
to succeed, under the Hindu or Mahomedan law of succession as
the case may be. The Collector, when satisfied, causes a puttah to
be issued in the name of the presumptive heir or heirs. The
transfer of puttahs is carried out as a departmental arrangement and under no legislative enactment. The most ordinary
cases are where the son or sons succeed the father. Among
Hindus property vesting in a person descends in the following
order :—Sons, sons' sons, sons' grandsons, wife, daughters,
mother, father, brother, brothers' sons, paternal grandmother,
paternal grandfather, paternal great grandfather, his sons,
his sons' sons, the other ascending ancestors, and their sons
and sons' sons in like order. The above is the ordinary line
of succession. But there are various complications of law ; for
instance if an undivided member of a family dies, leaving only
a widow and a brother, the latter succeeds in preference to the
former. The Mahomedan law of succession is still more
complicated. But the revenue authorities do not strictly go
into the details of law in issuing puttahs to the heirs of the
deceased individuals. The puttah is issued to the *primâ facie*
heir or heirs, leaving the question of possession and other rights
to be decided in Civil Courts. But when Courts pass their
decrees in regard to succession, puttahs are issued by the revenue
authorities according to these decisions. The Hindu law of
succession favors partition and creates very numerous sub-
divisions in the puttahs.

—Joint
puttahs and
divided
puttahs.

In both of the cases of transfer just named, whether that is to
say the transfer is effected before or after death, occasions will arise
when either two parties wish to be entered jointly and severally
in a joint puttah, or a person holding a puttah desires to split it
up and transfer part of it. The former case will arise occasionally when partition is inconvenient, as for instance when the heirs
to a single deceased holder are joint widows ; the State does not

encourage joint puttahs, but it raises no absolute objection if it suits the parties.   The Government will not separate a puttah once made joint without the consent of all the parties, even though one asserts a grievance.   The latter case where it is sought to subdivide a puttah is of course of constant occurrence. There were formerly certain regulations checking the splitting up of blocks or fields marked off by the peimash or survey department; but these were abolished in 1875, and there is now no limit to the smallness of a holding for which a Government puttah will be issued.

Assessed land will be vacant under various circumstances, as —**Application for instance, owing to its having never been occupied, or to for Ryotwari its having been just thrown up by a ryot, or to its having lapsed lands.** to Government on a demise or at a revenue sale.   When there are assessed lands in a village thus unoccupied, it is open to any individual, whether resident of the village or not, to apply for the land to be held by him under the terms of the ryotwari tenure.   All applications by strangers are invariably communicated to the Mirasidars and other resident villagers so that they may have the refusal, and it is only when the Mirasidars and residents do not agree to take up the lands that they are given to strangers.   When there are two or more applicants for the same land, preference is given to the ryot whose land adjoins, and when there is no such claimant, to the first among the applicants who is a ryot of the village in preference to a stranger. But no preferential claim on the ground of possession of the adjoining land, or of the residence in the village, is admitted in favor of a ryot by whose relinquishment the land becomes unoccupied and available for allotment.   In all cases Durkhasts for whole survey fields have preference over Durkhasts for portions only.   The applications are in the first instance disposed of by the Tahsildar.   From his decision an appeal lies to the Divisional officer if made within thirty days ; and from his decision again an appeal can be made to the Collector within thirty days.   The Collector's decision is usually final, but where a Collector has passed the decision on appeal from a Tahsildar within his own division a special appeal lies to the Board of Revenue if made within forty days.

Ryots are allowed to relinquish their lands provided they —**Relinquishapply for permission to relinquish sufficiently early in the ment of season to enable others to commence cultivation upon them. Ryotwari lands.**

15

The dates up to which ryots are permitted to relinquish their
lands in the several districts are shown below :—

South Canara Malabar	30th April of the fusly preceding for which relinquishment is made.
Ganjam Vizagapatam Godavery Krishna	31st May do.
Bellary Cuddapah Kurnool Nellore North Arcot Salem Coimbatore	15th July of the fusly for which relinquishment is made.
Madras South Arcot Trichinopoly Tanjore Madura Tinnevelly	15th August do.

The dates vary so as to follow those of the first rains in
each district. The lands relinquished must be accessible to
others, otherwise the relinquishment is not accepted. For
instance a ryot would not be permitted to retain all the fields in
his holding except the centre one, as this would not be an eligible
holding for another ryot.

—**Ryotwari
on the West-
ern Coast.**
The tenures and settlements as between Government and
the payer of the land-dues are in Malabar and Canara professedly a mere form of ryotwari. The special arrangements which
exist in those districts between the landlord and his tenants
do not as a rule affect the Government, and in dealing with the
occupant the Government ignore as much as possible the
existence of middlemen, or of interests other than their own.
Sometimes, for instance, the Government Puttahdar in Malabar
is a jenmi landholder with his tenants under him, and sometimes
he is a Patomkar tenant owing his separate rent to a superior
jenmi; but into this the Government do not go. Again in
Canara, though the landlord's right or mali sometimes falls to
Government by escheat, the Government are in the habit of
taking steps for divesting themselves of it and of handing it
over to the occupying ryot. In some respects, however, there
are considerable differences between this sort of ryotwar settlement and the ordinary ryotwary settlement, even from the

Government point of view. For instance there is no detailed survey in these districts, and the settlements are made not on fields but on holdings. Again, there are doubts whether there are any waste lands at the disposal of Government, all the waste being at present claimed as private property. Remissions again are never needed, owing to the certainty of the season and the lightness of the assessment. The ancient character of the proprietary rights enjoyed by West Coast landlords has already been seen from the historical sketch of land tenures. They are to the individual what the Mirási rights of the Eastern Coast are to the community.

The Ooloogoo Mottafysal and Amani systems of settlement —Ooloogoo. involve questions of demand rather than of tenure. In all cases Mottafysal, and Amani. where the Government apply them, they apply them to the individual ryot, and they are therefore different forms of ryotwari. Details of the demand will be given hereafter.

A cowle is an agreement to hand over land without payment Lands held on for a certain period, or on payment for a certain period of a Cowles, &c. diminished assessment gradually rising to full assessment. When the period is finished the holder becomes a ryotwari holder, but not before. In the meanwhile he is subject to the terms of the contract contained in the cowle. The cowle tenure is usually granted to induce cultivators to break up unpromising waste lands. Though much used between Zemindars, Inamdars, &c., and their tenants, cowles are not in frequent use by Government. Lands held under the tope rules hereafter to be described fall in reality, though not nominally, under this class of tenure. If the Government have good grounds under the contract for dispossessing the cowledar, they can do so and re-enter on the land. It will be noticed that this right is never claimed in the case of an ordinary Government ryot.

When the State has given up its right to the land-tax, or a Ordinary portion of it, in favor of an individual or an institution, or to Inam tenures of land. remunerate persons for performing certain duties, the grant is termed an Inam or Manyam. A very large number of such grants was made by former Governments, and it was a condition of most of them that they could not be alienated without the consent of the State, that they would escheat to Government on the failure of male heirs in the direct line, and that they might be cancelled on the occurrence of any lapse. In some cases the grants were to be resumed after a certain number of lives, that is to say after a certain number of successions by inheritance.

Other Inams depended on the execution of certain religions observances, or the performance of certain State services. In 1858 a Commission was established to examine the titles of the possessors of Inams, and to enfranchise them if they wished by commuting for a moderate quit-rent the right of Government to prevent alienation, to resume, or to demand service. There are still certain Inam lands the holders of which have not accepted the terms of enfranchisement offered by the Inam Commission. These remain on the old and very restricted tenure. They are subject to favorably calculated dues on account of land-tax, but on the other hand they have a tenure very inferior to that of enfranchised Inamdars or even to that of ordinary ryotwar holders. They cannot alienate their land. Succession is prescribed as above shown in a definite way. They hold only on the fulfilment of certain conditions, and Government claims an absolute right to adjudicate as to the proper fulfilment of those conditions. In the case of Village Service Inams the tenure may almost be said to be at the pleasure of Government. Full particulars regarding Inams will be given under the heading of Inam Commission.

Farming the Revenue. The principle of farming out the land-revenue in certain localities for a certain period has almost disappeared. Some rents, however, still remain. Thus in the Vizagapatam district the Hoongeram and Palcondah taluqs are rented out on a lease of years to a mercantile firm. Reckoning these taluqs and detached villages together there are throughout the Presidency 331 villages rented out, 87 in Vizagapatam, 231 in the Godavery, 12 in Chingleput, and 1 in North Arcot. A large number of these are hill-villages not surveyed and not touched by the Settlement Department. The old joint-rent system where the villagers themselves took up the lease and were jointly and severally responsible has now entirely disappeared. The last trace of it existed a few years ago in the hilly parts of the Godavery.

Mirasi rights. The rights which go by the name of mirasi must be mentioned here. They are not sufficiently strong to be classed as tenures or rights against Government, such as zemindary or ryotwari ; but they are something more than the mere preferential right to occupy new land hereafter to be mentioned, and they are recognized by the Government. The origin of mirasi rights in the Tamil country has been already described in the historical sketch of land tenures. Nearly all that remains now of the special rights of the communal oligarchies is the claim by certain hereditary mirasidars in the Chingleput District to fees upon waste which may hereafter be brought under cultivation, and upon lands now occupied by non-mirasidars which may hereafter be thrown up and again re-occupied under the darkhast rules. These fees, otherwise called swatantrams, were formerly taken from the gross produce before the division of the crop, and were then paid to the mirasidars both by the ryots and by the Government. They are now made payable entirely by the ryots, liberal allowance having been made with these on arriving at the money rates of assessment charged on their lands. The swatantram payable by the ryot under these circumstances is a yearly sum of two annas in each rupee of the Government assessment; this amount being held to represent the old average rate of 3 per cent. of the gross produce of the year. These fees are recorded by the Government in the land-revenue registers, and their collection is left to the mirasidars themselves. The total amount in the Chingleput District is very small, but the right is tenaciously held to, and represents what was in former days a highly important institution. There are some mirasi swatantrams in Tinnevelly, and possibly also in other districts, but Government has taken no steps to recognize them. It should be mentioned that the word mirasi means nothing beyond hereditary right, and that it is often applied to other rights besides the special right now under mention; it is applied, for instance, in the north to hereditary rights to village offices.

The unassigned land still in the possession of the State consists of all land which is not included in any Zemindary, ryot's holding, or other land already given out by Government for occupation. If it lies, however, within the boundaries of a village, certain prescriptive rights are conceded to the villagers of that particular village, probably as a relic of the old village communal system, in the way of preferential claim to occupy; and this distinguishes the case for the purposes of the present classification from that of unassigned land not so situated. Unassigned land within a village will be either of the assessed class or the unassessed class. The mode in which assessed lands are applied for and taken up in the first instance has already been described. The unassessed or poramboke land of a village is also at the disposal of the Government acting in trust for the interests of the village community. Subject to the instructions of the Government officers, certain portions are reserved for the gratuitous and communal use of the villagers,

Unassigned lands within villages.

as the tanks, streets, channels, threshing-floor, burial-ground, cattle-stand, &c. ; while in all cases except in the town of Madras and some places on the West Coast, a house-site and a back-yard with permission to cultivate garden produce in it, are provided gratuitously for each family. The addition to or subtraction from the area of village-site is provided for by fixed rules. The unassessed waste lands of a village, which are not yet assigned, and which are not reserved for these special purposes, are offered for sale in convenient lots free of assessment, and subject only to local taxes. In Tanjore and Madras there are no such lands to be sold, and on the Nilgiri and Shevaroy hills and in the Wynaad the arrangements in nearly all cases fall under the head next to be mentioned. The following are the upset prices fixed for each district and lands are made over to the highest bidder above that price :—

Districts.	Forest Land.	Open Land.
Ganjam	2½ Rs. an acre ..	5 Rs. an acre.
Vizagapatam	5 ,, do. ..	For all kinds.
Cuddapah	5 ,, do. ..	2½ Rupees.
Kurnool	10 ,, for black cotton soil.	5 Rs. for all qualities of soil.
Nullamallays	5 Rs. an acre ..	..
North Arcot	5 ,, do. ..	2½ Rs. an acre.
Trichinopoly	5 ,, do. ..	2½ ,, do.
Madura, Pulnis ..	10 ,, do. ..	5 ,, do.
Do. in the plains ..	5 ,, do. ..	2½ ,, do.
Tinnevelly, Hill ranges	10 ,, do. ..	5 ,, do.
Do. in the plains, all kinds	2½ ,, do. ..	..
Coimbatore (except Nilgiris) ..	5 ,, do. ..	2½ Rs. an acre.
Salem (except Shevaroys)	5 ,, do. ..	5 ,, do.
South Canara, Hill ranges	10 ,, do. ..	5 ,, do.
Do. plains ..	5 ,, do. ..	2½ ,, do.
Godavery * Kistna	2½ ,, do. ..	For all kinds.
Nellore ..	5 ,, do. ..	2½ Rs. per acre.
South Arcot	5 ,, do. ..	2½ ,, do.
Malabar	5 ,, per acre for Ponum land.	10 Rs. per acre for the more open and level lands, exclusive of Wynaad.

No lot within a village is allowed to exceed 10 acres except under orders of Government, but one person may bid for contiguous lots. The lots are as far as practicable in parallelograms. In selling the land the existing and customary rights of Government, of other proprietors, and of the public in existing roads and paths, and in streams running through or bounding the lands are carefully reserved, and when the sale is completed and money

* The Delta lands are excepted from the ordinary operation of the rules.

paid, a formally drawn up title-deed is granted to the purchaser by Government. The land is surveyed and demarcated before the sale, and its cost is borne out of the sale-money if there be any purchaser, and if there be no purchaser by the first applicant at whose instance the survey has been undertaken. The first applicant has in all cases to make a deposit covering the cost of survey. Due notice is given to the public before sale, and any claims put forward are disposed of on their merits. The Government can of course alienate the unassessed land, if they wish, by puttah or on cowle in the ordinary way, instead of selling the land in the manner just described. This is indeed in practice the most usual course as far as land in the plains is concerned.

Unassigned land outside the limits of any village as defined by custom or the Survey Department, is absolutely at the disposal of Government. Such portions of land are very limited on the plains, which are fully occupied by village communities, but they abound on the hill ranges where the indigenous tribes have established only a very partial occupation, and where general occupation is only just springing up. The alienation of lands lying outside villages will fall in a few cases under the rules described in the last paragraph. On the Nilgiris and Shervaroys, and in the Wynaad, however, there is a special provision that there shall be no upset price and that the lands shall be liable to assessment. Thus forest lands are free of assessment for 5 years on the Nilgiris and for 3 years in the Wynaad, after which they are assessed at Rupees 2 per acre. Grass land is liable to an assessment of 8 Annas per acre from the date of appropriation. On the Shervaroy hills all lands are liable to a uniform rate of 1 rupee per acre from the date they are taken up. In any of these cases the annual assessment may be redeemed at 25 years' purchase as already mentioned. *Other unassigned lands.*

In a ryotwari country the most important considerations connected with land tenures are those which concern the relations of Government with persons holding immediately from it. The system of tenancy under such land-holders is however fully developed, and is even a matter in which Government is concerned, the interference of the revenue officials between land-holder and tenant being often required under the law. In the districts on the east coast lands are rented out by the land-holders either for a fixed annual payment in money, or for a share in the produce, which is generally half. Ordinarily dry and garden lands are rented for money and irrigated lands *Tenures other than those under Government.*

for a share in the produce. Except in large zemindaries, where
rights have grown up from long possession, private tenants as a
rule are tenants at will, and the leases are from year to year.
On the west coast tenancies are more permanent and lands are
generally leased out for a number of years. In South Canara
tenants are of two kinds, Mulgueni and Chalgueni. The mulguenies are permanent tenants under the mulavargdar or landlord,
paying a fixed and invariable rent. These tenancy rights have
been for the most part obtained from the landlord as grants in
perpetuity on the payment of a fine and on condition of paying
annually a specified rent. Such tenants cannot be ousted except
for non-payment of rent, and even in this case not till they have
been fully recompensed by the landlord for the permanent
improvements they may have made on the lands. Subject to
payment of rent they are at liberty to sub-rent, mortgage, or sell
their interest, and are rather a description of subordinate landlords than mere tenants. On failure of heirs the title lapses to
the landlord. The chalguenies are temporary ryots under the
mulavargdars or mulguenies; their lease is for a limited term,
usually one year, or even at will. In the case of these tenants
the landlord has the right to raise the rent or oust the tenants
whenever he pleases, when no period is fixed, after however
re-imbursing him for all permanent improvements made by him.
Practically the tenants are seldom ousted. In some large estates
there is an intermediary tenancy, when the tenants have no
written leases but are in practice treated as mulguenies. The
rents of mulguenies and chalguenies are paid either in money or
a certain quantity of grain, and never by a share of the crop as
in other parts of the Presidency. In Malabar the tenants to
whom lands are leased out for cultivation are called patomkars.
The lands are generally leased for a period of between
three and six years, and the rent payable to the landlord
is fixed at two-thirds of the net produce of the land after
deducting the expenses of cultivation. When waste or jungle
lands are leased out the rent is one-fifth of the gross produce.
There are various kinds of leases. Where a simple rent is paid
annually the lease is known by the name of Verumpatom.
Where the proprietor receives from the tenant, in addition to
his rents, an advance of money, which may be considered either
as a loan or as a security for the due payment of the rent, it is
called Kanompatom. The tenant retains so much of the rent
as will discharge his claim of interest on the sum advanced, and
delivers over what remains to the proprietor. It is in fact

the same as the tenure acquired by a mortgagee, with the difference that the money advanced is generally small. In the case of kanompatom, if the patomkar gives up the land on the expiration of the lease, he loses 20 per cent. of the sum in deposit, being however re-imbursed for the permanent improvements which he has effected. The landlord can demand the land back from the tenant on paying the deposit amount with interest and the value of permanent improvements effected by the tenant. The tenant is liable to forfeit the whole of his kanom money should there be any loss in the originally estimated produce of the land. The proprietor can revoke a lease before the expiration of the lease on payment of double the value of improvements and the deposit money with interest. In some cases the rent for a series of years is paid in advance. The landlord is not then, however, at liberty to demand the land from the tenant before the expiration of the period, and if the tenant gives up the land the landlord must refund to him a deduction of 20 per cent. in the rent for the unexpired portion. This kind of lease is called Oodamtepatom. By another mode of renting lands termed Kaykanompatom, meaning tenure of labor or usufructuary tenure, the jenmkar conveys a piece of land to a person who undertakes to fence it with mud walls and plant it with productive trees, and the latter is ensured possession for a specified period, generally 12 years, free of all charges. At the expiration of the lease in this case the jenmkar has the right of resuming the land on paying the lessee for the buildings he may have erected, or the wells he may have dug, or the plantation he may have formed, according to a valuation; but the resumption of this tenure is rarely enforced by the jenmkar when the land has been properly cultivated, the tenant being commonly allowed to continue in possession at an easy rate of rent. The buildings and plantations are in fact the property of the tenant, and he can mortgage or sell them in the same manner as the jenmkar mortgages or sells his property in the land. The verumpatom and kaykanom-patom are the only leases for cultivation exclusively. The others partake partly of the nature of leases for cultivation and partly of that of mortgages. The death of either the tenant or the landlord generally puts an end to the lease. When a lease is renewed, it is customary for the tenant to pay the landlord certain fees at a fixed percentage of the deposit money. The Government tax is in some cases paid by the jenmkar, and in others by the tenants or mortgagees in possession.

Private
dealings in
land.

The Government are not concerned in any way in transactions connected with land other than those already mentioned. It may be observed, however, that private mortgages are exceedingly common. Sums of money are frequently advanced upon landed security, the condition being generally that the mortgagee shall enter and enjoy the land for a definite period, though sometimes it is arranged that the mortgager shall hold as a tenant of the mortgagee during the term, and sometimes the lands are hypothecated simply. Sub-mortgages are frequently made on the East Coast. It is not customary for an outgoing mortgager to claim compensation for improvements. Private sales of land again take place, but by no means so frequently. Mortgages are most numerous on the West Coast, especially in Malabar, for reasons already given. It is there considered disgraceful to sell absolutely the Jenm right, *i.e.*, birth-right or proprietorship. The Malabar mortgages are the most interesting. There are several kinds. One is called Kayividu Otti. In this land is pledged and delivered over to the mortgagee, the jenmkar receiving from the former two-thirds of the value of the estate and retaining a certain interest in the land itself. No rent is ordinarily paid by the mortgagee to the proprietor as it is generally equal to the interest at 5 per cent. on the sum lent. For instance, an estate yielding a rent of 50 fanams is valued at 1,500 fanams, and the land is mortgaged for 1,000 fanams. The proprietor cannot revoke the mortgage, but should the mortgagee be willing to restore the land and receive his money back, the proprietor is entitled to the first offer. If the proprietor wants to part with his entire rights, he must make the offer to the mortgagee, who must either accept or return the land to the proprietor that he may relieve himself by selling it to another and repay the sum advanced to the mortgagee. A second mode of mortgage is called Otti simply. This is nearly the same as Kayividu Otti, but the terms are less strictly expressed. It may be executed without the consent of the heir, nor are any witnesses necessary besides the parties and the writer of the document. If the pattam or landlord's share exceeds the interest on the sum lent, the excess belongs to the proprietor. If the mortgagee wishes to have the money back he must lose 10 per cent., but if the proprietor offers to return the money the mortgagee is not liable to any deduction. The mortgagee is entitled to compensation for his improvements on the land, and the proprietor to a deduction from the amount borrowed for any neglect on the part of the mortgagee and the consequent reduction in the produce of the land. A third kind is called Otti Kuli Kanam. This differs from Otti in that if the mortgagee desires to return the land, the proprietor is liable to pay 20 per cent. on the amount of improvements, whereas if the proprietor demands the land, the full value of improvements must be paid. A fourth kind is called Adima Jenm. The peculiarity of this mortgage is that the sum borrowed is not mentioned in the deed. The use of this form is confined to Rajas, Numburies and heads of villages. In other respects it appears to be nearly the same as the first kind. " Kettiadakam" is another species of mortgage. In this land is not delivered to the mortgagee. It is left in the possession of the proprietor until he fails in the regular payment of the interest, when the creditor seizes the land and retains it in his own possession. If the pattam or landlord's share exceeds the amount of interest the excess goes to the proprietor. These are the Malabar tenures. In South Canara, land and produce are separately mortgaged. If the land itself is mortgaged no interest is demanded. The mortgager is sometimes permitted to reside upon the estate and allowed to cultivate a small portion in the capacity of a tenant, but the mortgagee pays the Circar rent and transacts the whole business of the estate as if he were the proper owner. The mortgage bond always contains a clause that as soon as the sum borrowed is repaid the land is to be returned to the mortgager, the latter paying the expenses of all improvements. A certain portion of the produce of estates is frequently mortgaged for the discharge of interest on debts. In this case it is stipulated that a certain quantity of rice is to be paid annually, but that the person receiving the rice shall be allowed no interference with the estate. Should the mortgager fail in the payment, the land itself is to be made over to the mortgagee. The first of these Canara mortgages is termed Bogiadhy or living mortgage, the other Toradoovoo or dead mortgage.

The number of persons who own property, and who are independent of labor, as returned in the census schedules, is 176,580, or 1·1 per cent. of the male population. They are most numerous in the Tanjore district, where 7·7 per cent. of the males are so entered. In the Godavery district this class forms 3 per cent. of the population, while in Tinnevelly and Coimbatore only 0·04 and 0·02 per cent. are so returned. The Brahmins figure out of all proportion to any other class as

Number of landed proprietors.

holders of property; 64,545, or 11·7 per cent. of their numbers
being included under this head. The Kshatriyas have 3·1
per cent. The Chetties, who have their capital mostly
laid out in trade, have only 0·5 per cent. The Vellalers, or
cultivating castes, have only 1·6 per cent., but many of these are
wealthy, though they hold their lands only on ryotwari tenure.
The writer, or accountant castes are considerable holders of
property in the districts of Vizagapatam and Tanjore, where
22·4 and 31·4 per cent. respectively of their numbers are so
classed.

(c).—THE COLLECTION OF THE REVENUE.

Rates and amount of the Land Revenue.

It is impossible to exhibit, with any approach to accuracy, the
ratio of the Imperial Land Revenue to the actual gross produce
of the whole country and the net assets of land. No information
exists as to the actual gross produce of lands paying land revenue
to Government, nor is it possible to collect such information.
Though the Land-tax was imposed, theoretically at least, on a
share of the gross produce of the land, this share or its commuted
value has varied greatly in different districts and at different
times. The principle on which the Land-tax of ryotwary districts
is at present undergoing revision and re-settlement, preceded
by a scientific survey, is that it should in no case exceed 40 per
cent. of the gross produce in the case of lands for which irrigation is provided at Government cost, or one-third of the gross
produce in the case of lands not so irrigated. These proportions
are found to be nearly equal to half the net produce. If all the
land were ryotwary, it might be roughly assumed that the
revenues amounted to half the net produce, but much of it is
held at a favorable quit-rent or permanently settled, and in
these cases the sum paid to Government bears no fixed proportion
to the produce. The rate per acre of the Land-tax on ryotwary
land varies very widely in the different districts. In those where
the new survey and re-settlement have been introduced the rate
varies from 6d. to £1 4s., and the number of rates for a whole
district does not exceed 35. In districts where the land assessment is still imposed as at the beginning of the century, the rate
on irrigated land is occasionally as high as £3 10s. and that on
unirrigated land as high as 9s. The minimum rates on both kinds
of land in those districts are fractions of a shilling, and the total
number of rates in a district is as large as 885. Taking an
average of the whole Presidency, the rate per acre does not
exceed 2s. 3d. on unirrigated land or 9s. 6d. on irrigated land.

The following list shows the total collections of land revenue in this Presidency for the last fifteen official years, taking £1 to be equal to 10 Rupees. In 1866-67 there were only eleven months, because the date of commencement of the next year was altered from the 1st May to the 1st April :—

					£
1861-62	...	...	...	...	4,112,588
1862-63	...	...	...	...	4,206,498
1863-64	...	...	...	...	4,296,535
1864-65		...		...	4,181,162
1865-66	...		...	...	4,291,766
1866-67	...		...	...	3,635,509
1867-68	...		...	...	4,239,705
1868-69	...	...	...	...	4,058,757
1869-70	...	...	...	...	4,476,056
1870-71	...	...	...	...	4,393,351
1871-72	...	...	...	...	4,435,341
1872-73	...	...		...	4,688,448
1873-74	...	...	...	...	4,446,693
1874-75		...	...	...	4,632,063
1875-76	...	...	...	...	4,539,657

The land-revenue demand on all Zemindaries, Mootahs and other proprietary estates is fixed once for all, and no remissions are granted for loss of crop or other reasons. There is, therefore, no special yearly investigation and settlement as in the case of Ryotwari holdings. Slight variations, however, occasionally occur. For instance lands forming part of a Zemindary are sometimes taken up by Government for public works. Again the collection of Government quit-rents on Inams situated in the Zemindaries is sometimes transferred to the Zemindars, who add the amount to their peishcush less 10 per cent. for the trouble of collecting. In such cases the necessary adjustments are made by the Collectors and reported to the Board of Revenue. Water-rates are also charged on Zemindary lands, when water is used from sources of irrigation newly created by Government. The charge is made only on lands actually irrigated every year; but where the Zemindars consent, a composition is made with them for a term of years. Where existing works have been superseded by the new works, full allowance is made for the area previously irrigated by the former. For instance in the case of the Nedavole Zemindary in the Godavery, where the Government anicut works have obstructed the Zemindar's ancient sources of irrigation, the estate has been

The demand on permanently settled estates.

allowed to irrigate under the anicut channels free of charge 25,881 acres of land, which was formerly irrigated, or considered capable of being irrigated ; and for the excess cultivation an annual sum of Rupees 40,000 has been charged, with the condition that the amount is liable to be altered every five years with reference to the area irrigated. The charges for water-rate go under the general technical head " Miscellaneous Revenue." The jumma or peishcush paid by Zemindars has usually been fixed in the first instance at two-thirds of the gross estimated collections from the cultivator.

The demand on Inam lands. The whole question of the demand on Inam lands would naturally be treated here. Technically however, it is only the quit-rent on whole Inam villages, or " Shrotriems " as these are called, that is treated as a separate item, quit-rent on other or " Minor " Inams falling under the head Miscellaneous Land-revenue. The quit-rent on Inam villages is a fixed revenue, and no remissions, as a rule, are granted. Variations will however occur in the same way as in Zemindaries on account of lands being taken up by the Government for public purposes, or on account of water-rate, &c. ; or again in the event of the holder relinquishing land. The quit-rent on Inam lands is usually called jodi in cases where it represents the old quit-rent as opposed to that recently imposed by the Inam Commission.

Quit-rents on building sites. The quit-rents derived from building sites fall naturally for mention here. They are grouped, however, technically under Land-revenue Miscellaneous, and will be explained hereafter.

The demand in Ryotwari holdings. The actual rate at which the land is to be assessed under Ryotwari is fixed for a period of thirty years by the Revenue Settlement Department. But the ryot has the liberty, as already explained, of contracting or extending his holdings ; and the Government undertake to grant remissions of land-revenue, and assume the right to make extra charges, under certain circumstances. There are therefore considerable variations from year to year to be attended to at the yearly settlement of accounts. The ryotwari settlement is formed by adding to the assessment of the holdings (1) the charge on account of second crop cultivation, and (2) water-tax on ryotwari lands ; and deducting therefrom (1) the assessment of waste remitted, (2) occasional remissions, (3) fixed remissions, and (4) deductions on account of village establishments and sundry other purposes. Sundry items classed as Miscellaneous revenue are afterwards added to the demand.

The Jummabandy or yearly inquiry into the variations of ryotwari land-revenue generally takes place after December, by which time most of the important crops have been harvested. The different places where it is to be conducted are previously notified and the ryots of the villages concerned are invited to attend. The Tahsildar with his establishment and the Curnams and heads of the villages attend, and the Collector or his assistant making the Jummabandy sends in advance his Sheristadar or other head Native official to examine the accounts as prepared in the taluq. After the examination of the accounts is completed, the settling officer inquires into the claims of the several ryots in regard to remissions, hears any other statements they may have to make in regard to their lands, and issues a document to each individual called the puttah, showing the particulars of his holding, the amount payable by him, and the instalments in which it has to be paid. The puttahs are not necessarily renewed every year, alterations which occur in the holdings being often simply entered on the back of the puttah. Cultivation made after the Jummabandy, but appertaining to the fasli then in question, appears under Land-revenue Miscellaneous, and is treated as a separate item of revenue. Remissions granted after Jummabandy are similarly not shown in the accounts of the year, but the amounts involved are written off the accounts as irrecoverable with the sanction of Government in the following year. *—The annual Jumma-bandy.*

The standard rates of assessment are determined by the Revenue Settlement Department, as hereafter described. Briefly speaking, the lands are first classified according to their soils, and the grain values of each soil are determined by actual experiments taken over a large area and with the help of other extraneous information. From the grain value thus determined a deduction is made on account of unfavorable seasons and cultivation expenses, and the remainder, which represents the net produce, is halved. From this half a small deduction is again made on account of unprofitable areas, and the remainder is commuted into money at a fixed rate which represents the average value of the grain for a series of years sufficiently long to balance the ordinary fluctuations of seasons and other temporary causes. The money-rates thus obtained approximate as nearly as possible to half of the value of the net produce. *—Standard rates of assessment.*

In fixing the standard rates of assessment the irrigated lands are presumed to yield but one crop, and when a second crop is raised *—Second crop Culti-vation.*

on them with the aid of Government water half the standard
rate is charged in addition. In some cases however this charge
has already been commuted at the old Peimash or by the Settlement Department into a fixed payment consolidated with the
ordinary assessment, and this consolidated sum is then paid
whether the second crop is raised or not. The object of the
latter arrangement is to save Government the trouble of institut-
ing a scrutiny into the extent of second crop cultivation each
year, and to save the ryots from interference on the part of
petty revenue officials. To make the arrangement acceptable
to the ryot, the composition rates are somewhat lower than
those charged when the payment for second crop is left optional.
The ryots do not make any payment if the second crop in
question is raised without the aid of Government water. For
instance, a dry crop raised as second crop in land classed as
irrigated is not liable to any charge. It happens but seldom
that private irrigation is applied to wet lands. In the case
of unirrigated lands the ryot is competent to raise any number
of crops, for though the soil has been used more than once
in the year Government water has not been supplied to it. The
charge for second-crop cultivation is in fact a water-rate, though
not so called; it has really no reference to the more or less
frequent use of the soil. Irrigation under private wells is not
as a rule liable to any charge, but wells within the ayacut are
considered to draw water from the tank and a charge is therefore
made. It has already been mentioned that second-crop assessment
is charged where necessary on irrigated Inam lands.

—Water-
tax.

Water-tax technically so called is charged whenever lands
classed and assessed as unirrigated are irrigated by the aid of
Government water. The rates vary with reference to the usage of
the locality, to the character of the irrigation, to the time for
which the irrigation is required, and to the nature of the crop
raised; and run from 8 rupees to $1\frac{1}{2}$ rupees per acre. In the
delta taluqs of the Godavery and Kistna and in some of the
taluqs of Kurnool all the lands are assessed at dry rates, and the
whole charge for water appears therefore under water-tax.
Government water-tax imposed on Inam lands, or in Zemindaries, does not come technically under this head, but under
Land-revenue Miscellaneous.

—Waste
remitted.

Under the head of Waste Remitted are technically included
all deductions from the land-demand made on account of land
left absolutely waste; that is, in which no crop has been put

down. It is a remission of the full assessment, is made only where cultivation has been impossible on account of the usual supplies of Government water having been deficient or in flood, and is not given in the case of land classed as unirrigated. Any neglect to cultivate on the part of the holders invalidates the claim to remission.

Waste Remitted is in reality an "occasional" remission, inasmuch as it depends on the season. Being however usually a large item it is treated technically as a separate head. The occasional Remissions technically so-called include all remissions dependent on the nature of the season, other than that for absolute waste. They consist of the following items :—1. shavi or withered crops ; 2. panyboodthy, or payamali, that is to say land flooded and injured by water ; 3. palanastham or loss of produce ; 4. thirvakammy or difference between wet and dry assessment ; 5. fasalkammy or second crop not cultivated ; 6. remissions allowed on the introduction of new rates of assessment ; 7. miscellaneous remissions. Remissions under items 1 and 2 are as a rule granted on irrigated lands only when the crop is totally lost owing to either deficiency or excess of water, and provided only that such excess or deficiency has not been occasioned by any act or neglect of the person to whom the land belongs. Remissions for partial loss of crop under item 3 are only granted in districts which have not been settled by the Settlement Department ; these also are confined to irrigated lands. In granting the remissions last named no attempt is made to estimate individual losses, but the remission is granted in the form of a certain percentage taken off from the assessment of the lands in which the crop is lost, the percentage being determined with reference to the extent of the average loss sustained in the adjacent tracts. Remissions are not granted on unirrigated lands except in very exceptional years and under very exceptional circumstances and with the previous sanction of the Board of Revenue. The remission under item 4 is granted when a dry crop is put down on land classed and assessed as irrigated, but which otherwise would have been left waste. In such cases the dry crop assessment alone is levied, and the difference between that and the assessment chargeable on irrigated land is remitted. The remission under item 5 is granted where the land is assessed for two crops, but it has not been possible to raise a second crop for want of water. This remission occurs chiefly in districts not yet visited by the Settlement Department, where the rates are

—Occasional remissions.

high. In the districts which have been settled by that Department the collection of the whole assessment is enforced as a rule when the principal crop is raised, whether the second or inferior crop is raised or not. But if the principal crop fails or is not raised, and only an inferior crop is grown, then the second crop assessment is remitted. Remissions under item 6 are altogether of an exceptional character. They are granted with the special sanction of Government when any newly fixed rates of assessment are particularly high, and when their gradual introduction is considered desirable. The miscellaneous remissions consist of various sundry items, such as those granted on account of lands cultivated having been taken up for public works or for the Forest Department, on account of lands washed away by rivers, &c., &c.

—Fixed remissions.

" Fixed remissions " are remissions which are granted for reasons other than those relating to the season. They consist of the following items :—1. Remission granted for labor involved in reclaiming lands. This is mostly granted for lands situated on a high level in consideration of the difficulty of bringing them under wet cultivation. 2. Remission granted on the ground that the standard rates in unsettled districts are too heavy. The old pymash assessments having in some districts been heavy certain reductions were made in the rates of assessment. The difference between the old and reduced rates appears as remission. 3. Remission granted to privileged classes; that is to say remissions allowed to certain classes of persons who by custom or caste are prevented from cultivating lands themselves. These are fast disappearing with the introduction of the new rates of settlement, which do not recognize any class privileges. 4. Remission granted on account of irrigation by lift. This is granted for cultivation raised on high level wet lands by baling or other mechanical contrivances. 5. Remission granted under the topo rules. As an encouragement to the formation of topes or small woods, persons are allowed to plant trees under certain conditions free of assessment for 20 years. At the end of that period the land is assessed if retained in possession of the planter, but left unassessed if the tope is thrown open to the public. The assessment remitted during the 20 years is shown under remissions. As a rule, the land granted on these terms is one that has been waste for more than 10 years. If the trees are planted on land usually cultivated no remission is granted. 6. Remission granted for maintaining irrigation works. This is called technically " Dasbundum," and is an allowance made in the shape of remission of revenue in compensation for the construction of tanks, wells, and channels, and for the repairs of such works. 7. Remission on grass lands. Ryots in Coimbatore, and on a portion of the Nilgiris, are allowed to hold an extent equal to one-fourth of their holdings at one-fourth of the full assessment for purposes of pasture. The difference between the full and quarter assessment is treated as remission so long as the land is allowed to lie fallow and actually used as pasture. When once cultivated it is charged with full assessment and this is maintained whether the land is thenceforward cultivated or used for pasture again. No new lands are now granted under this tenure. 8. Cowle remissions. Lands which have been long lying waste or which require outlay of capital or labor to bring them under cultivation, are allowed to be taken on easy terms for a number of years; they are either free of tax or subject to a favorable assessment, and the difference between the standard assessment and the assessment actually charged is shown under remissions. 9. Remission granted on salt pans in South Canara. In this district salt pans are situated in lands forming parts of the private wurgs paying land assessment to Government. The land assessment payable on the pan-sites is remitted annually when they are used for salt manufacture, in accordance with the practice of the salt monopoly. 10. Remission granted on forest lands taken up for cultivation in the Nilgiris and in Malabar. Forest lands taken up in the Nilgiris and in Wynaad for coffee or other plantation are not charged with assessment for five and three years respectively in consideration of the preliminary expenses necessary for the plantations, and as a remunerative crop is rarely obtained until after the lapse of those periods. For the periods mentioned the assessment of the lands is shown under remissions. 11. Miscellaneous. This consists of various small items, such as landlord's share on escheated lands sold, remission of assessment in favor of pagodas, &c., &c.

Sundry Deductions, otherwise called Beriz Deductions, are —Sundry deductions.
in reality of two classes, though not so arranged technically. In the one case the principle is that the Government abandons a certain amount of the land-demand in consideration of the ryot discharging certain liabilities hitherto discharged by Government. Such are payments of fees or salaries to village servants, and of stipends to Inamdars. In the other case certain sums which are due from the ryot, and which have been hitherto consolidated with the land-demand, are now

separated from it, and the ryot is directed to pay them elsewhere. An example of the latter is the road-cess in the Kristna. The subtraction from the land-demand is a convenient way of adjusting accounts, and is an old practice in this Presidency. Sometimes a deduction will represent a transaction under both of the heads just mentioned ; as for instance where a deduction on account of village service represents partly the sum hitherto contributed by the ryot, and partly the sum granted by the Government. The amounts deducted are properly speaking paid by the ryots direct to the persons or authorities to whom they are due. But sometimes practically the village officers collect the amounts.

—The demand on the West Coast.

In speaking of west-coast tenures between Government and landholders it was mentioned that in form the agreement was a ryotwari agreement. The details of the demand made, however, show the peculiarity of the situation. Thus the average assessment, in Malabar, is Rupees 1-9-5 for dry land, and Rupees 3-0-3 for wet land, compared to an average for the whole Presidency of Rupees 1-1-0 for the former and Rupees 5-9-3 for the latter. The excess in the case of dry land is due to the fact that all the more valuable permanent garden produce is classed in Malabar under this head. The assessments, therefore, are very low and tacitly allow the existence of middlemen and of other interests besides those of Government. The wet cultivation exceeds that of any other district except Tanjore, and would, if assessed at the ordinary rates of other ryotwari districts, produce probably double the revenue. In Canara too ample provision is left for a landlord's share. The fiscal division of estates in Canara is noticeable. Bhurty means full or paying the entire Tharao demand. Kumbhurty means paying less than the full Tharao demand. The kumbhurty is again sub-divided into 1. Board Shifarish, or estates which owing to natural disadvantages never can be expected to pay the full demand, and are entered in the accounts as doubtful, but are practically treated as with reduced demand; 2. Káyam Kammi, estates in which the full assessment may be leviable in the future, but it is not certain when ; and 3. Waida, or estates which after a certain definite period will be able to pay the full demand, and will be required to do so. The settlement officer leaves Bhurty and Board Shifarish as he finds them, and settled in the lump; he deals with the Káyam Kammi at his discretion ; and in the case of waida there is usually an annual increment, to be decided by the settlement officer, by which

the estate is to be brought up to Bhurty and Kumbhurty.
Practically the same village agency is employed on the West
Coast as in other parts of the country. It should be mentioned
that the low assessments of Malabar have proved a serious
difficulty in levying cesses which are proportioned to the assessment. The important Local Fund Cess is a case in point and
yields a very poor revenue. In Zemindaries the Local Fund
Act has specially provided for assessing the cess on the rents
paid by ryots to Zemindars, and taking the amount from the
Zemindar, and the application of this to Malabar would give a
higher cess-revenue. But this has not hitherto been practicable
or even legal. One of the principal difficulties would be the
decision as to who is in such case the person to be dealt with
analogous to the Zemindar, land-ownership being on the West
Coast in a very confused state.

In some localities wet crops are still divided between the —The
Government and the ryot under the Amany system. The share demand
under Amany.
of Government in the produce varies according to usage, but in
the majority of cases it is 50 per cent. of the gross produce
minus fees paid to village servants. The crop is cut under the
personal inspection of Government officers, and the gross produce
is divided by actual measurement. After division the Government
share, which is called the Rajabhogam or Melvaram, is sold and
the proceeds are carried to the credit of Government. It will be
understood that the settlement in these cases is still with the
individual ryot, on the ryotwari system. The Amany method
of settlement and collection represents the traditional method
peculiar to the Hindus under their own rulers. Apart from the
machinery of collection, it will be seen that it differs from the
method of the English Government in that it settles on the
basis of dividing the gross instead of the net produce. Amany
is still a favorite system between Zemindars and their tenants,
and estates coming under the Court of Wards frequently bring
this mode of settlement with them. The British Government
have not encouraged it. It would be impossible at the present
day to keep in hand the large establishment that would be
necessary. Moreover the ryots are said to dislike Amany, as
the crops cannot be taken in until measured by the Government
official, and have often to lie on the ground till damaged. There
are at the present moment only eight Government villages in the
Presidency in which division of the produce takes place, namely,
5 in Madura, 2 in Chingleput, and 1 in the Kistna. The total
revenue of these is Rupees 6,000.

—The demand under Ooloogoo.

The demand under Ooloogoo differs from that under ordinary ryotwari in this that the Government dues vary to a certain extent with the current prices of grain. The grain is commuted for a money-value, but not for an absolutely fixed value. The commutation rate is founded on the price of past years, but all increase of price of over 10 per cent. above the standard is added to the demand, while all decrease of more than 5 per cent. under the standard is remitted to the ryot. If the ryots are dissatisfied with any year's settlement they can claim division of produce. There are therefore no remissions on account of the season. Ooloogoo holdings obtain now in only one small hamlet in Tanjore, the revenue of which is Rupees 3.

The demand in Estates rented out.

Revenue due to Government by renters of estates is collected in the same way as that due by any ordinary ryot under the ryotwari system, with the difference that the lands in the villages rented are not sold for arrears unless they are the property of the renters. The renter's right is saleable, but it is seldom sold as generally the sale of their personal property is sufficient to secure the revenue.

Land-Revenue Miscellaneous.

Under the head of Land-Revenue Miscellaneous are included all charges pertaining to lands other than those held by ryots under the ryotwari system, or lands held by Government ryots under certain peculiar circumstances. They consist of the following items : 1. Jodi on Sundry Inams. This is the quit-rent or favorable assessment charged on Inams smaller than a village at the time of the grant or by the Inam Commissioner. 2. Charge for water on Zemindari and Inam lands. This is a charge made for supplying irrigation to Zemindari and Inam lands from Government works. The charge is made only when the irrigation supplied is such as the landholders are not already entitled to in virtue of grants or original settlement. 3. Land cultivated but not included in the Jummabandy. This is the revenue brought to account after the annual settlement and issue of puttahs but belonging to the then current fasli. 4. Assessed land cultivated without Dhurkhast or permission. Assessed lands taken up without application and sanction are inquired into at the annual settlement and disposed of according to their merits. But if in any case inquiries cannot be completed within the year or if puttahs are delayed for any other cause such lands are shown under this item. 5. Fees for service of Revenue processes. This is the amount collected, in addition to the assessment, from revenue defaulters on whom processes are issued, to

meet the cost of the establishment entertained for the purpose.
6. Revenue from rented villages. This is mainly derived from
persons to whom villages have been rented out in consequence of
some difficulty in introducing a ryotwari settlement. 7. Graz-
ing-tax or grass-rent. This revenue is derived by the sale of
grazing farms in villages, principally in the districts of Nellore,
Kistna and Madura. The total amount in the Presidency is
about Rupees 1,41,000. 8. Rent of islands situated in rivers.
Lands in islands in rivers do not come under ryotwari settlement.
They are leased out and this is the amount of their rental.
9. Tax on trees on unassessed lands. This consists of rent of
palmyra trees, rent of fruit trees, and sale proceeds of trees.
The trees are the scattered trees standing on lands not held
under puttahs. Persons holding palmyra trees under such a
tax can only use or sell the fruit and leaf, the right to draw and
sell the toddy being the perquisite of the Abkarry contractor.
10. Quit-rent and ground-rent in the town of Madras. The
houses and lands in the town of Madras are subject to a quit-
rent. There is nothing similar in the districts. 11. Cultivation
of Poramboke lands. This is the revenue charged on unassessed
or reserved lands when improperly cultivated. 12. Rent of
garden and topes which have become the property of Government. 13. Sale proceeds of unassessed waste lands sold by
Government. 14. Revenue from hill villages. This revenue
is derived by the cultivation of lands on the slopes of hills. The
cultivation is not permanent and no puttahs are therefore
issued. 15. Revenue derived from coir the produce of Amendivi
Islands attached to South Canara. In these islands coconnut
is nearly the only product, and no land assessment is collected.
The islanders are compelled to sell all their coir to Government
at a fixed rate, lower than the market-rate. The Government
sell and realize a profit. The arrangement is similar to the salt
monopoly. 16. Excess collections over the demand. This is
overpayment erroneously made by the ryots and which is to
be eventually refunded. 17. Quit-rent on bungalows and
gardens. In some special cases lands are given on favorable
assessment for buildings, instead of being treated as ordinary
ryotwari lands. 18. Commission on private estates under the
management of Court of Wards. A commission of 1½ per cent.
is levied by Government on the revenue of the estates managed
by the Court of Wards. 19. Water-tax on summer crops
cultivated at the close of the preceding fasli, and not then
brought to account. 20. Revenue fines imposed on revenue

servants. 21. Revenue from sequestered Inams, or the assessment of Inam lands placed under attachment for various reasons, for instance the non-appearance of Inamdars for settlement. This item also includes the assessment of Service Inams kept under attachment pending the revision of village establishments. The assessment credited to Land-revenue Miscellaneous temporarily though eventually transferred to Village Service Fund. 22. Cultivation of jungle tracts newly cleared by burning in South Canara. The cultivation is not permanent and therefore puttahs are not issued annually. 23. Recoveries of cost of survey establishment lent to private estate under Court of Wards. 24. Russums or fees collected from Zemindaries, &c. These are payments made by certain Zemindars according to usage in addition to their peishcush. 25. Tax on house-sites and backyards exceeding the limit allowed. 26. Chunam shell-rent, or rent derived by farming out the right of collecting shells for making chunam. 27. Charge for water on miscellaneous Jeroyati lands, otherwise Ayan lands, otherwise non-Inam lands. This is the charge made for water on lands for which puttahs are not issued, but which are included under Miscellaneous Revenue. 28. Chank-shell farms. This is the license fee paid for fishing chanks. 29. Revenue deposits forfeited. Deposits are forfeited for various causes. For instance, a purchaser in a revenue sale deposits a certain amount, but if he fails to complete the sale by paying the full sum within the prescribed time, he forfeits his deposit. 30. Revenue from Amany villages. 31. Sundry items. These consist of various small items too numerous to mention.

Special cases of assessment.

A few special points remain for notice. On special products a special assessment was formerly levied ; this is now abandoned, and the land alone is taxed and not its products. Tank beds may not be cultivated ; if a ryot improperly occupies, remissions are refused, or prohibitory assessment is imposed, to compel him to relinquish. For river-bed cultivation the same remark applies ; there are no special rules. When wet land becomes no longer irrigable from one cause or another, the Collector has authority to class it as dry. When land is found on measurement to be in excess of what it was assumed to be in the register, 10 per cent. margin is allowed, but if it is over that the assessment is revised, and the amount exceeding the 10 per cent. is charged for. The same rule is followed in granting remissions ; when a deficiency is found to exist as compared with the register, that is to say, remission is granted only on such portion of land as is more than 10 per cent. below the registered amount. Lands under private tanks are charged at dry rates, and the Government take the amount from the ryots ; the tank-holder obtains his water-rate from the ryots under his own private arrangements. No additional charge is made on account of irrigation under jungle-streams and natural pools, provided that Government has incurred no expense in their improvement, and provided that the use of water does not interfere with the supply to any Government work.

Almost all the land revenue is derived from the lands elsewhere described as assessed lands. The following items however, and some others are realized from the unassessed waste :— Tax or rent of scattered trees; 2. Tax on firewood or timber removed for sale outside the village ; 3. Honey-rent ; 4. Chank-rent; 5. Chunam-rent; 6. Fish-rent; 7. Wax-rent ; 8. Rent for medicinal roots; 9. Rent on lime quarries ; 10. Quit-rent on land for houses in the town of Madras and the district of South Canara. These all fall under the technical head of Land Revenue Miscellaneous. *Land-revenue according to the land from which it is derived.*

Applications for mining are rare, and the question of assessment on lands so applied for is treated specially in each case. The question of the right of landholders to gold obtained from the soil is under discussion, and possibly resort will be had to legislation. *Assessment on lands containing minerals.*

In many cases the so-called irrigable ayacut under a work of irrigation is not really irrigable. In some cases on the other hand a larger extent of land is irrigated than is registered as irrigable. The Settlement Department in some districts and Collectors in others are now engaged in revising ayacuts with reference to the actual capacity of the tanks and the extent cultivated within the last five years. Particular cases are seldom dealt with in the ordinary course of the land administration. *Revision of Ayacut.*

The mode in which the sub-division of landed property is permitted has been already described, and it has been mentioned that the transactions are not valid against Government until the assessment on the sub-divided portions has been adjusted by the Collector. The principle observed in all cases is that the original peishcush or assessment is not to be disturbed, but is to be taken as a total and rateably subdivided according to the new subdivisions. In zemindaries and Inam lands the new proportions are based on the present estimated value of the *Sub-division of assessment.*

Payments of land-revenue.

lands, and in ryotwari holdings they are based on the assessment already fixed on such lands.

The peishcush of large zemindaries is generally paid into the Collector's treasury and that of small zemindaries and Inam villages into the taluq treasury. Other items of land-revenue are paid in the villages to the monigar. Payments are not collected, but brought by the parties. The curnam notes the payments in the accounts and the shroff examines the coin, after which a receipt is granted signed by the monigar and the curnam to the ryot paying the money. In the case of zemindaries the payments are made according to the varying instalments mentioned in the sannads, and in the case of all other revenue the following instalments are observed :—

Districts.	Proportion of Annual Tax payable by the 15th of each Month.								
	15th November.	15th December.	15th January.	15th February.	15th March.	15th April.	15th May.	15th June.	Total.
									ANNAS.
Ganjam ...	...	4	4	4	4	...	...	...	16
Vizagapatam	...	4	4	4	4	...	...	...	16
Godavery ...	...	4	4	4	4	...	...	...	16
Kistna ...	...	4	4	4	4	...	...	...	16
Nellore ...	...	2	2	2	4	4	2	...	16
Cuddapah ...	...	4	4	4	4	...	...	...	16
Kurnool ...	2	4	4	4	2	...	...	...	16
Chingleput	...	2	2	4	4	2	2	...	16
Bellary ...	...	2	2	4	2	2	2	...	16
North Arcot	2	2	4	4	2	2	...	...	16
South Arcot	2	2	2	4	4	2	...	...	16
Tanjore { Kar	3	6	7	...	...	...	...	...	16
{ Samba	...	...	...	2	3	5	4	2	16
Trichinopoly	...	4	4	4	4	...	...	...	16
Madura ...	...	2	2	2	2	4	4	...	16
Coimbatore	2	2	4	4	2	2	...	...	16
Nilgiris ...	2	2	4	4	2	2	...	...	16
Tinnevelly	...	2	2	4	4	4	...	...	16
Salem ...	2	2	4	4	2	2	...	...	16
South Canara	...	...	4	4	4	2	2	...	16
Malabar ...	2	2	4	4	2	2	...	...	16

Tuccavi.

Advances called tuccavi used to be made to Government ryots for mere cultivation expenses, but the system was found open to abuse and has now been given up. No advances to ryots are made at present except under the Land Improvement Act.

Land Improvement Act.

Under the Land Improvement Act, India No. XXVI of 1871, advances on interest at $6\frac{1}{4}$ per cent. per annum are made by Government to landlords and tenants desiring to make improvements in their lands. On application being made for an advance an inquiry is held as to the right of the parties to the land, and as to the character of the improvement. The proposed advance is made only in the event of the Collector being satisfied on these points. Collectors are competent to advance up to Rupees 500, the Board of Revenue up to 5,000, and the local Government up to 10,000. Advances of larger sums require the sanction of the Government of India. Either the value of the land itself must exceed the amount of the advance by one-fourth or other security must be given collaterally. Except with the special sanction of Government advances of 500 rupees and under must be repaid with interest within 7 years from the date fixed for the completion of the work and advances exceeding 500 rupees similarly within 12 years. If in any case the proposed period of repayment exceeds 20 years, the local Government cannot sanction, and the sanction of the Government of India has to be obtained. When advances made become payable, they are recoverable from the person to whom the advance was made, or from his security, as if they were arrears of land-revenue. But the interest of no person other than the person taking the advance is sold; that is to say, if a landlord takes a loan, the tenant's right is not sold, and if a tenant takes a loan, the landlord's right is not sold. Works for which advances are made and the accounts kept on the works are to be open for inspection by Government officers at all times. In cases of advances exceeding Rupees 5,000, the parties are bound to keep accounts in a certain form required by the Collector. In the case of works for which advances are made in a lump, the works must be inspected within one month of the date on which their completion is directed in the certificate, and in the case of works for which advances are made by instalments, the inspection must be made before each instalment subsequent to the first is paid. If the persons who receive the advance fail to perform the conditions under which it was granted, the Collector has power to recover under the Act the whole advance or such portion as has been granted. It is in contemplation to make revised rules simplifying the detailed procedure under the Act.

When land is needed for a public purpose or for the purposes of a company, it has been hitherto usual to take it by an amicable arrangement with the owners, the procedure laid down in the Land Acquisition Act being applied only in cases where the owners would not agree to reasonable terms, or where there

The acquisition of land for public purposes.

has been a doubt in regard to title. The Government of India
have recently directed that, with a view to securing an indefeasible title, lands required for public purposes shall always be
taken under the Act, though the amount of compensation may
be determined by a private settlement. The procedure to be
adopted under the law is briefly as follows. A declaration is first
made under the signature of the Secretary to Government or
other officer duly authorized that such and such land is
required for public purposes; the Collector then gives notice
to the public and to parties concerned, stating that the Government intends to take possession of the land and that claims to
compensation must be made to him on a date, and at a place
specified. On the date fixed the Collector inquires into the value
of the land and determines the amount and tenders it to the person
interested ; if the parties agree to the amount, the matter is at
once settled, and the Collector takes possession of the land. If
the offer is not accepted, and the Collector is unable to agree
with the parties, or if there is any question regarding the title
of the parties interested, the Collector refers the matter to the
Civil Court which, with the aid of assessors, determines the
amount of the compensation payable. In determining the compensation, the market-value at the time of awarding compensation, and the damage, if any, sustained by reason of severing
such land from the owners of other lands are taken into consideration, but not the urgency which has led to the acquisition,
nor the disinclination of the party interested to part with the
land acquired. An appeal is provided against the award made
by the Court. Payment is made to the owner by the Collector
according to the award, or if there has been an appeal according
to the decision on such appeal possession of the land is then
taken. If land is required only temporarily, the Government
directs the Collector to procure the occupation and use of the
land for such term as may be necessary not exceeding 3 years.
On the expiration of the term, the land is restored to the owner
with such compensation as may be necessary for any damage
done and not provided for by the original agreement. If the
land becomes permanently unfit for use, the Government takes
the land as if it was permanently required for a public purpose
or for a company. In case the Collector and the owner of the
land differ as to the condition of the land at the expiration of
the term, or to any matter connected with the agreement, the
Collector refers the matter for the orders of the Court.

When land-revenue due to Government falls into arrears it Coercive
measures. is recovered under Madras Act II of 1864 together with interest at 6 per cent. and costs of process, by the Collector or his deputy, by the sale of the defaulter's movable property including uncut crops or immoveable property including buildings on land, or by execution against the person of the defaulter. In the case of Zemindars holding under a Sannad Mulkyat Istimrar, the personal property must, under the terms of the sannad, first be sold, and the land only in the event of the first measure not proving sufficient. In the case of other defaulters, the Collector may at his discretion sell either the movable or immovable property or both. If there is any doubt as to ownership, the Collector will naturally attach the land in preference. Before any property is attached for arrears, due notice is given to the defaulter, and another notice is served previous to sale. Sometimes, though rarely, the arrear is realized by not selling the land, but by keeping it under Government management and appropriating the proceeds. Persons other than the defaulters who may be interested in the land can have the sale stopped by payment of the arrear. There is now no restriction as regards the distraint of implements of husbandry. The sale of land is at the discretion of the Collector and he is not bound to recognize any transfers, except such as have been registered in his office. The sale does not prevent the defaulter from collecting balances of rent due to him by under-tenants for periods anterior to the sale. Land may be purchased Benamee; that is, the defaulter himself or any of his friends may purchase it when put up for sale. The former law forbade this. The land-revenue has the first claim on landed property against all other creditors, and the crops of an under-tenant are not protected, except that the latter has subsequent redress. When a purchaser buys land at a revenue sale, he does so taking the land with all its encumbrances; these he must ascertain in advance from the Tahsildar or by local inquiry. Certificates of sale are issued to the purchaser, and the Board of Revenue receive a statement of sales; the sanction of the Board to sales is not now required, except in the case of zemindaries. There is provision for enforcing the certificate, and giving possession to the purchaser. In some cases Government buy the land for themselves. When the arrears cannot be liquidated by the sale of the property of the defaulter, and there is reason to believe that he is wilfully withholding payment of the arrears, or has been guilty of fraudulent conduct in withholding payment, the defaulter

is liable to be arrested and imprisoned for a period not exceeding
two years if the arrear exceeds 500 rupees, not exceeding
six months if it is at that amount or below, and not exceeding
three months if it is 50 rupees or below. Such imprisonment
does not extinguish the debt. When the revenue is paid in
kind the crop is not allowed to be removed until division has
been made. The above procedure is applicable not only to
arrears of land-revenue, but to all advances made by Government,
for cultivation or other purposes connected with the revenue,
to all fees due to village servants employed in Revenue and
Police duties, and to all cesses imposed upon the land. The
extent to which coercive process is employed in the collection of the land-revenue is, on the whole, not large. There
has certainly been a very large increase of late years in the
number of legal processes issued for this object, but the fact
is that formerly the law was not used while coercion took
place nevertheless. Moreover the provisions of the present law
are so lenient that it suits the convenience of ryots to allow
process to be issued though they intend ultimately to pay.
The interest charged on arrears has been reduced by Act II of
1864 from 12 per cent. to 6 per cent., and the ryot now gains
rather than loses pecuniarily by waiting for a better market, or
leaving his money out at interest, while the process is running.
Taking the absolute results, and without reference to the history
of the working of the law, there are no grounds for dissatisfac-
tion. In the recent Fusli 1282 recourse was had to coercive
process for recovering land-revenue arrears amounting to
£250,000. The ryotwari demand of that year was $4\frac{1}{2}$ millions,
so that the arrears were $5\frac{1}{2}$ per cent. on the revenue. Of the
£250,000 all were made good before sale except £45,000 or
1 per cent. of the demand. It may be said then that 95 per
cent. of the land-revenue is realized without trouble, and that
4 per cent. more can be recovered with only the trouble of
formally demanding it.

Recovery of   Zemindars, Shrotriemdars, Jaghiredars, Inamdars, and persons
private rents. farming lands or land-revenue under Government, are authorized
by Madras Act VIII of 1865 to recover their rents under a
summary process, provided that the landlord and the tenant
have exchanged Puttahs and Muchilikas or written agreements in
regard to the terms on which the land is to be held, and provided
the summary powers are sought to be exercised within one year
from the time when the rent becomes due. The Government,
that is to say, in these cases assists the landholder to recover from

his tenants. The landholders are allowed to exercise summary power even where no Puttahs and Muchilikas are executed if both parties have agreed to dispense with them. Landholders holding under ryotwary settlements, or in any other way subject to the payment of land-revenue direct to Government, and all other registered holders of land in proprietary rights who have not yet been mentioned, are given the benefit of the Act if [they have taken an agreement in writing from their tenants, but not otherwise. If the rent remains unpaid at the time when, according to any written agreement or the custom of the country, it ought to have been paid, the landholder is authorized to distrain, upon his own responsibility and with the aid of the Police if necessary, the crops and movable property of the tenants, after giving due notice; but he is bound to send within ten days a written notice to the Collector or other officer duly empowered in that behalf, showing the details of the property distrained, to enable the Collector to have the property appraised. Tenants are allowed to prefer an appeal to the Collector against wrongful distraint, but the appeal must be made within thirty days from the date of the distraint. If the appeal is established, the Collector orders the property to be restored, but if no appeal is made, or, if having been made it is rejected, the Collector on the application of the distrainer authorizes the public officer duly appointed in that behalf to cause the sale of the movable property, which is accordingly sold by him after due notice. Where the tenant has a saleable interest in the land, this also is sold under the rules laid down for the sale of the movable property. When there is no property or it is insufficient, the landholder can apply to the Collector for a warrant authorizing him to eject the tenant and to enter on the land; a warrant is accordingly granted and entrusted to a police officer. If no appeal is made to the Collector within fifteen days after the warrant is served, or if an appeal has been made and it is decided against the defaulter, the police officer places the landholder in possession of the land. The landholder is also competent to apply for a warrant for the personal arrest of the defaulter, which is granted if the Collector is satisfied that the defaulter is wilfully withholding payment or has been guilty of fraudulent conduct in order to evade payment; but no defaulter can be imprisoned for a longer period than two years, whatever the amount of arrear may be. It is open to the landholder either to exercise the summary powers above referred to, or to recover his rent in the ordinary Courts of law like any other debt.

(d).—ESTABLISHMENTS.

Village Officers.

The basis of the system of Revenue administration is found in the village corporations, which, as already stated, have existed from time immemorial, and in many respects still retain their vitality. In almost every Hindu village there are twelve village servants, called the Barabuloti or " twelve men," who perform all needful public offices. The following is the list. The first five only render service to Government, or are recognized as parts of the Revenue administration :—

1. Headman.	7. Smith.
2. Curnam, or Accountant.	8. Jeweller.
3. Shroff or Notagar.	9. Carpenter.
4. Nirganti.	10. Barber.
5. Toty or Taliary.	11. Washerman.
6. Potter.	12. Astrologer.

The headman, who goes by various names, such as monegar, potel, naidu, reddy, peddacapu, natamgar, &c., is an important officer; he represents the Government in the village, collects the revenue, and has also magisterial and judicial powers. As a Magistrate he punishes persons for petty assaults and affrays ; and as a Judge he tries suits for sums of money or other personal property up to Rupees 10 value, there being no appeal against his decision. If parties consent, he can summon a punchayet ; who will then adjudicate on suits without limit as to value, and also without appeal. The headman is generally one of the largest landholders in the village, and as a rule exercises much influence over the inhabitants. Acting as a Judge he is styled Munsif. In some cases the custom of the place separates the Munsifship from the Monegarship, and sometimes more than one Monegar is appointed for a village. The duties of the headman are defined in Regulation XI of 1816, but its interpretation in reference to his police duties has caused doubts. The curnam is the village accountant and is a very important ministerial officer. The accounts kept by him will be described hereafter. The shroff is found only in certain villages ; his duty is to test the money paid in by villagers to the headman on account of Government. The nirganti has charge of the irrigation of village lands where there is irrigation from tanks or channels. Some villages however have irrigation, but no nirganti, the work being done by the village peon or by the cultivators themselves. The village toty, otherwise taliary, vetty, or agrany, is simply a village peon acting under the orders of the headman. This office is generally held by the lower class of the community. The taliary is sometimes a separate official acting in the capacity of watchman. The remainder on the list are the artisans necessary to the internal conduct of a village community. In the revisions of Governmental village establishments which will shortly be mentioned, considerable changes have been made even in the assignment of duties and names of the officials.

When village offices are hereditary, as is the case in most localities, heirs succeed in the usual course, under the terms of the native law of inheritance, which is modified only to the extent of precluding partition. In the case of offices other than those of headman, curnam, nirganti, vettian and toty, the villagers manage their own affairs, the parties filing suits if they please before the Collector under Regulation VI of 1831. In the case of the offices just mentioned the succession is regulated by the Collector. With reference to the rights and fitness of the several claimants to office the native law of inheritance is attended to as far as is possible. Females and minors may in special cases succeed, appointing gumastahs or proxies with the sanction of the Collector. Adoption is recognized or not recognized in the usual way under the law. If any person having an interest desires a more formal inquiry, he may file a suit under Regulation VI of 1831 before the Collector. This officer will then issue process to parties and witnesses and hold a quasi-judicial inquiry. Disobedience to the summons can be punished under Sections 172 to 174 of the Penal Code. Act VIII of 1859, the Civil Procedure Act, does not apply to cases tried in this way, and there is no law for awarding costs. The Government of India have exempted these cases from the Court Fees Act except in certain minor matters ; stamps are therefore unnecessary. Section 3 of Regulation VII of 1828 gives Collectors power to revise the proceedings of their subordinates under this Regulation, without limit of time ; but three months has been fixed departmentally as the period for appeal. When a case is heard by a divisional officer, the parties may appeal to the Collector or to the Board direct, whichever they prefer. When the Collector has made a decision on appeal, this does not bar a further appeal to the Board of Revenue, or from them to the Government. There is no provision for enforcing orders passed

Succession to Village Offices.

under this Regulation, nor for ousting adverse occupants; but in practice the orders of the Tahsildar are not disobeyed. The procedure throughout is somewhat informal, but the Regulation proposes rather to be a measure of State administration than of adjudication of private claims. Collectors are instructed to respect possession extending over more than three years against any ordinary claim on grounds of hereditaryship; though there is no objection to their putting on record a statement of opinion that in the event of the demise of the present occupant, the claimant will have a right to secure a revision of the office. Collectors have the power of dismissing village officers for misconduct. The same questions then arise as in the case of succession by demise. An heir may succeed if no way concerned in the offence; or if this arrangement is not practicable a temporary appointment of a stranger may be made to last during the lifetime of the person dismissed. The Civil courts are forbidden by law to take cognizance of any questions of a nature provided for by Regulation VI of 1831. Curnams in zemindaries are provided for separately by Regulation XXIX of 1802, and placed under the jurisdiction of the Civil courts; they do not fall under Regulation VI of 1831 and the Collector does not regulate the succession to office.

Emoluments of Village Officers.   The non-Governmental village servants are almost wholly paid by fees from the villagers direct. In some cases, however, where the Government have in former days given Inam lands to such servants, these are continued. No new grants or allowances are made by Government to such servants. The Gevernmental village servants are paid in some cases by the enjoyment of Government land rent free or on a trifling assessment called jodi, in some cases by having assigned to them the State dues payable by some third person occupying land, in some cases by contributions of grain or money made by the villagers themselves irrespective of the land-revenue, and in some cases by salaries direct from Government. When land questions are involved in the emoluments of office, disputes are frequent, and are decided usually by suit before the Collector under Regulation VI of 1831. The most frequent cause of dispute is the question whether the village officer's case falls under the first or the second of the heads given above; that is to say whether he is to be put in possession of the land assigned to the office, or whether he is merely to be given the right to receive the Government assessment money from the hands of the occupant. This will depend very much on the terms of the original grant, which was often made before the Fysal or original settlement of the British Government, and is thus involved in obscurity. The general question, as to whether the land itself or the assessment only constitutes properly the emoluments of a village servant, has been much discussed; it has been decided in practice to adjudicate each case on its merits and with regard to its past history as far as this can be ascertained. Regulation VI of 1831 renders it illegal to make any formal alienation of Inam emoluments; until recently however the law was frequently evaded. The present cost of the village establishments in land and fees is about 47 lakhs of rupees.

The system of payment by Inams from Government or by **Revision of** Merahs from villagers has for some years been regarded as **Village Establishments.** objectionable, and the tendency has been to substitute salaries from Government in all cases. Act IV of 1864, which may be applied on occasion to different districts, was passed to enable the Government when they took over the entire charge of the village servants to recover from the villagers, in the form of a land-cess not exceeding one anna in the Rupee on their assessment, the amount of the fees which they originally contributed in private. The Inam rules, which may be applied from time to time, provide for raising the beneficial rate of assessment on lands hitherto Inam, while withdrawing some of the State claims on the lands and giving an absolute ownership in them to the present occupant. By a combination of these two measures the Government have had it in their power to make a complete revision of the village establishments in the direction of substituting stipends for other forms of emolument. The opportunity has been taken to revise the establishments as well as the emoluments, and to get rid of irregular claimants to the latter. The revision of village establishments is being carried out in a detached way in different localities; it has hitherto followed the operations of the Revenue Settlement Department, but in future it is to be carried out *pari passu* with the settlement. The salaries in the revised establishments are paid from a fund called the Village Service Fund. To this are credited all the new quit-rents which come in from the enfranchised lands, formerly Inam and paying little or nothing; the proceeds of the cess under Act IV of 1864, where imposed; and contributions made by Government in lieu of lands and fees formerly diverted to this purpose but since resumed by Government. The practical effect of the revision may be seen from the two following examples. A village servant is, we will suppose, in the

enjoyment of Government land; and his emolument consists in
his paying no assessment on it or only a nominal jodi. Under
the revision he will receive a salary instead of this emolument.
Special terms will be made with him as to the land. The
terms will be that Government will make him proprietor of the
land, which will thenceforward have no further connexion with
the office, and be an alienable piece of property belonging to the
individual; while the Government will thenceforward tax the
land with land-revenue, amounting however not to the full
amount, but only five-eighths of the amount. The special terms
are granted in consideration of the long period during which these
lands have been looked on by the people as quasi-private
property. A village servant again, we will suppose, derives his
emoluments from the payment to him by a third person of the
assessment properly payable to Government; that is to say, the
village servant is paid by what is called Tirvei-manyam and
not by what is called Nila-manyam. In this case, if enfranchisement is applied, the occupying ryot or third person continues to
pay to the village servant in whose name the Inam has been
enfranchised the full assessment, and the Inamdar pays to
Government five-eighths assessment, keeping three-eighths;
the ryot neither loses nor gains. Owing to illegal alienation,
and to irregular applications of the Hindu law of partition of
property on demise, many superfluous claimants to village service
emoluments have arisen. In some localities a number of persons
divide the emoluments in this way, one of the number only being
the actual working officer. When such persons can show a long
prescriptive enjoyment of their emoluments, however erroneously
acquired in the first instance, they are allowed to enfranchise on
five-eighths assessment. The rules indeed have been very
liberally interpreted, and in many cases even a single year's
possession has been respected and the possessor allowed to
enfranchise. The fees from villagers are, as has already been
said, no longer paid in these cases; the Government make good
the fees to the officers in the salaries which they give them, and
take from the villagers a one-anna cess to recoup themselves. In
revising village establishments small villages are clubbed together
in order to reduce the establishments where necessary with reference to the assets available for payment, but care is taken
that the clubbing is not carried too far, so as to cause inconvenience to the communities concerned. A resident munsif is
provided for each village, and the wishes of the villagers
are as far as possible consulted in carrying out the clubbing.
In the revision. the number of servants is generally reduced,

but their remuneration is, as a rule, improved. When revision has fully taken place it is evident that there will remain of the numerous land disputes now occurring under Regulation VI of 1831 only a few in connexion with the artizan non-Government village offices. Offices will however still remain hereditary where they are so at present, and cases of succession will still be triable under the Regulation. The districts in which the revision has been already carried out, or in which it is now being introduced, are the Godavery, Kurnool, Tinnevelly, Salem, Chingleput, and Trichinopoly. Revision will shortly be carried out in Nellore and the Kistna. In Tanjore the village establishments were to a certain extent revised in 1867, but the Village Cess Act, No. IV of 1864, was not brought into force, the existing assets of the district being sufficient. In the remaining districts the old system still continues. The rates of salary allowed in the revision are variable, but the following for Kurnool, the Godavery, and Trichinopoly, may be taken as specimens :—

Description of Servants.	Kurnool.			Godavery.			Trichinopoly.		
	Revenue.	Number of Men for each Village.	Rate per Annum.	Revenue.	Number of Men for each Village.	Rate per Annum.	Revenue.	Number of Men for each Village.	Rate per Annum.
Vettians.	RS. Up to 750 „ 1,500 „ 4,000 Above 4,000	1 2 3 4	48 rupees for each Vettian.	RS. Up to 1,000 „ 3,000 „ 6,000 „ 9,000 Above 9,000	1 2 3 4 5	48 rupees for each Vettian.	No scale.	It is not known how many Vettians were allowed for each village.	36 rupees for each Vettian.
Neerguntas.	None.	..	..	No scale.	Not known.	48 rupees per annum.	None.	..	..
Taliaries.	No scale.	Not known	48 rupees each for 2,470 Taliaries and 60 rupees for 22 Taliaries.	No scale.	For 714 villages at one Taliari each, and for 29 villages at 2 Taliaries for each were allowed.	Rupees 48 per annum.	No scale.	The number given for each village is not known.	36 rupees per annum.

Description of Servants.	Kurnool. Scale with reference to the Revenue of each Village.	Rate per Annum.	Godavery. Scale with reference to the Revenue of each Village.	Rate per Annum.	Trichinopoly. Scale with reference to the Revenue of each Village.	Rate per Annum.
Munsifs or Monigars.	RS. Up to .. 5,000 ..	RS. 60	RS. Up to 600 ..	RS. 18		
	" .. 7,000 ..	84	" 1,000 ..	24		
	" .. 9,000 and upwards.	96 / 120 / 144	" 1,500 ..	36	No scale.	42 rupees for each Monigar without reference to the revenue of the village.
			" 3,000 ..	48		
			" 5,000 ..	60		
	1 Reddy for Nundial Village.	240	" 7,000 ..	72		
			" 9,000 ..	96		
	1 Town Munsif ..	300	Above 9,000 ..	120		
			" 22,000 ..	144		
Curnams.	RS. Up to 1,000 ..	RS. 60	RS. Up to 1,500	RS. 60	RS. Up to 1,000	RS. 72
	" 1,500 ..	72	" 2,000	84	" 2,000	84
	" 2,000 ..	84	" 3,000	96	" 4,000	96
	" 3,000 ..	96	" 4,000	108	Above 4,000	108
	" 4,000 ..	108	" 5,000	120		
	" 5,000 ..	120	" 6,000	132		
	" 6,000 ..	132	" 7,000	144		
	" 7,000 ..	144	" 8,000	156		
	" 8,000 ..	156	" 9,000	168		
	" 9,000 ..	168	Above 9,000	216		
	Above 9,000 ..	180	" 22,000	240		

Taluqs.

There are in all 27,181 villages excluding those in permanently-settled estates, and these are distributed into 157 taluqs, each of which is controlled by a Tahsildar. The following statement shows the average area, number of villages, population, and land-revenue of the taluqs in each district according to a recent computation :—

Districts.	Number of Government Taluqs.	Average Area of each Taluq.	Average Number of Villages in each Taluq.	Average Population of each Taluq.	Average Land Revenue of each Taluq.
		SQ. MILES			RS.
Ganjam	3	647	460	190,366	3,98,416
Vizagapatam	2	1,541	63	114,848	1,09,100
Godavery	10	760	99	139,041	3,87,076
Kistna	11	608	118	117,204	3,37,740
Nellore	9	505	66	126,402	2,04,084
Cuddapah	11	834	94	122,836	1,79,942
Bellary	15	766	153	111,200	1,74,322
Kurnool	8	934	87	114,304	1,88,932
Madras	1	27	21	397,552	77,704
Chingleput	6	464	261	156,361	2,99,178
North Arcot	9	440	326	150,141	2,33,443
South Arcot	8	597	376	219,177	4,32,816
Tanjore	9	415	268	219,303	4,70,375
Trichinopoly	5	713	251	240,081	3,02,416

Districts.	Number of Government Taluqs.	Average Area of each Taluq.	Average Number of Villages in each Taluq.	Average Population of each Taluq.	Average Land Revenue of each Taluq.
		SQ. MILES			RS.
Madura	6	814	131	221,372	3,05,881
Tinnevelly	9	572	101	188,217	3,37,650
Coimbatore	10	799	152	176,327	2,61,996
Nilgiris	1	479	17	49,501	46,049
Salem	9	815	282	218,555	2,51,200
South Canara ...	5	841	256	183,672	2,57,515
Malabar	10	626	43	226,125	1,81,638

Excluding the three exceptional taluqs of Madras, the Nilgiris, and Cochin, each taluq has thus on the average 176 villages, a population of 166,772, a land-revenue of Rupees 2,78,482, and an extent of 694 square miles.

Taluqs are divided into five grades according to their **Taluq** importance. The Tahsildar's establishment consists of a **Officers.** Sheristadar, Clerks, Revenue Inspectors, and Servants. The Sheristadar is in immediate charge of the Taluq Treasury; as also of accounts, abstracts, registers, and periodical returns. The Clerks, of whom there are eight or nine, prepare the accounts, bills, abstracts, cultivation statements, season and other returns, village abstracts of demand, collection, and balance, settlement accounts, registers, &c., attend to correspondence, aid in Magisterial work, and have charge of the office records which under the ryotwary system are voluminous. The Revenue Inspectors, of whom there are three or four, are in charge of portions of taluqs and itinerate constantly from village to village seeing that the work of the village officers is properly performed, and conducting such local inquiries as may be considered necessary by the Tahsildar. Every Tahsildar is also a Sub-Magistrate. In this capacity, and also to a limited extent in his Revenue work, he is assisted by officers styled "Deputy Tahsildar and Sub-Magistrate," who are established in important towns and outlying portions of taluqs. Some of these officers are also placed in charge of large estates which do not fall within the jurisdiction of any Tahsildar. Each has a small establishment. The actual cost of all these establishments according to a recent computation was Rupees 14,64,732.

The 157 taluqs are distributed amongst twenty-one districts, **Districts.** two of which, namely Madras and the Nilgiris, being of an exceptional character, contain only one taluq each. The extent and revenue of each is shown in the following statement:—

Districts.	Extent.	Population.	Collection from all Sources in last Revenue Year.
	SQ. MILES.		RS.
Ganjam ...	8,313	1,520,088	33,01,554
Vizagapatam	18,344	2,159,199	24,11,916
Godavery	7,109	1,620,634	54,51,537
Kistna ...	8,086	1,452,374	56,74,860
Nellore ...	8,462	1,376,811	37,60,770
Cuddapah	8,367	1,351,194	23,74,878
Bellary ...	11,007	1,668,006	34,34,599
Kurnool ...	7,358	959,640	19,43,937
Madras ...	27	397,552	34,15,747
Chingleput	2,753	938,184	50,06,304
North Arcot	7,139	2,015,278	31,48,400
South Arcot	4,873	1,755,817	45,90,021
Tanjore ...	3,654	1,973,731	74,86,496
Trichinopoly	3,515	1,200,408	18,30,510
Madura ...	9,502	2,266,615	40,12,993
Tinnevelly	5,176	1,693,959	48,69,326
Coimbatore	7,432	1,763,274	30,29,273
Nilgiris ...	749	49,501	1,38,708
Salem ...	7,483	1,966,995	28,12,210
South Canara	3,902	918,362	22,04,630
Malabar ...	6,002	2,261,250	40,35,616

Each district contains on the average, excluding Madras and the Nilgiris, 7,285 square miles and 1,624,306 inhabitants, and has a revenue of Rupees 37,56,828. The revenue from all sources, instead of from land-revenue alone, is shown in this statement, because the establishments are required to administer all.

District Officers.

The districts were controlled on the 31st March 1876 by twenty Collectors and a Commissioner,* sixteen Sub-Collectors (called in two cases† Principal Assistants), eighteen Head Assistant Collectors (called in two cases Senior Assistants), three Special Assistants, eight Passed Assistants, and eight Unpassed Assistants (all of whom, with the exception of two Special Assistants, belong to the Covenanted Civil Service), assisted by fifty-four Uncovenanted Deputy Collectors. The number of Deputy Collectors is stated below, dividing them according to their class and according to their duties :—

Class.	Number.	Duties.	Number.
1 ...	6	Treasuries... ...	19
2 ...	12	General Duties ...	19
3 ...	13	Salt Department ...	12
4 ...	24	Exceptional ...	4

* Of the Nilgiris.
† Ganjam and Vizagapatam.

There are nineteen District Treasuries; and the average revenue being Rupees 37,56,828 as already shown, and the average disbursements considerable, a Deputy Collector is required for each. A Deputy Collector is in charge of the Salt Department in each of the twelve Maritime Districts. The Deputy Collectors on General Duties assist the Collectors and their Assistants in Revenue administration and Magisterial work except the Deputy Collector of Madras who is not a Magistrate. When an Assistant Collector has passed a certain examination in law and languages he is said to be a Passed Assistant, and may be placed in charge of one or two taluqs. Until he passes he is attached to some superior officer to learn his work. The Special Assistants, of whom one is a Covenanted Civilian and the other an Officer of the Staff Corps, assist the Agents to the Governor in Vizagapatam and Ganjam. The Head Assistant Collectors hold independent charge of two or three taluqs, but are subject to the complete control of their Collectors. The Sub-Collectors who are also Magistrates have larger charges, and are more independent. Their establishment consists of a Sheristadar or Manager, and Clerks and servants. The Collectors, who are also Magistrates, have each a territorial charge immediately under them, and exercise a general control over their Sub-Collectors, Assistants, and Deputy Collectors. They superintend and control all persons engaged in the administration of the revenue ; they are responsible for the Treasury to which the taluq collections are sent, and which keeps and dispenses a large stock of stamps ; they see that the revenues are punctually realized, and that when arrears accrue, the proper processes are resorted to for recovering them ; they manage estates of Minors under Regulation V of 1804; they determine boundary disputes under Regulation XII of 1816 ; they try cases of malversation under Regulation IX of 1822, and claims to village offices under Regulation VI of 1831 ; they decide rent cases between landlords and their tenants under Madras Act VIII of 1865 ; they take a chief part in the administration of Municipalities under Madras Act III of 1871, and of Local Funds raised for roads and communications, primary education, hospitals, and sanitation under Madras Act IV of 1871; as Agents to the Board of Revenue under Regulation VII of 1817 they are responsible for the due appropriation of endowments ; in Maritime Districts they manage the salt monopoly and control the Sea Customs ; finally, they are expected to be thoroughly acquainted with the state of Native feeling in their districts in regard to the policy and measures of Government, and to be the advisers of Government with respect to police, public works, education, sanitation, and the miscellaneous matters which conduce to the welfare of their districts. A Collector's establishment consists of (1) a Sheristadar managing the Native Correspondence Department; (2) the English Correspondence and General Account Department; (3) the Treasury and Stamp Department; (4) the Press Department; (5) Miscellaneous Office Servants. The Deputy Collector in charge of the Treasury supervises the second, third, and fourth departments, and a Head Clerk is in immediate charge of the second department. One-fifth of the costs of all the establishments which have been described is considered chargeable to Law and Justice on account of the Magisterial work performed by them, and the rest to Land Revenue. Collectors of districts are competent on their own authority to suspend from office or dismiss any servant of inferior grade to that of Deputy Tahsildar, Tahsildar, Sub-division Sheristadar, or Head Sheristadar. The nomination to the offices just specified vests in the Collector. The Board's sanction however is required for the appointment of Head Sheristadar and Sub-division Sheristadar, and that of Government for the appointment of Tahsildar and Deputy Tahsildar. In the case of Tahsildars, transfers involving a reduction of salary or suspension can only be made under the orders of the Board; in the case of Deputy Tahsildars, reference to the Board is not necessary. Tahsildars and Deputy Tahsildars can be dismissed only under the orders of Government. Collectors may dismiss Taluq Sheristadars on their own authority, reporting that they have done so to Government in order that the sanction given to their employment as Magistrates may be revoked. Collectors may suspend Tahsildars for grave offences, but a report must then be made to the Board within twenty-four hours. Collectors are competent to inflict fines upon any of their subordinates, but the amount cannot exceed Rupees 10 without the previous sanction of the Board. An appendix statement at the end of this volume shows in detail the charges of different divisional officers throughout the Presidency with their head-quarters, &c.

Board of Revenue. The whole of the machinery just described is controlled by a Board of Revenue, consisting of three Members, a Secretary, a Sub-Secretary, a Sheristadar, two Assistants, a Manager, Clerks and servants. The first duty of the Board is to secure the punctual collection of the revenues; to manipulate and record all statistics with regard to population, agriculture, exports and imports, health and the condition and advancement of the country ; to manage the expenditure of Local and Special Funds ; to take charge of the estates of Minors as a Court of Wards ; to secure the proper application of endowments ; and to decide the frequent appeals which result from a system in which the Government is concerned directly with peasant proprietors. To compare the Board of Revenue with departments of Government in England, it may be said that it performs the duties undertaken there by the Board of Customs, the Board of Inland Revenue, and the Commissioner of Woods, Forests and Land Revenue, as well as much of the work that devolves upon the Treasury. In communication with the Survey and Settlement Departments, which are subordinate to it, it carries on work similar to that of the Copyhold Enclosure and Tithe Commission in England. It takes the place in many respects of the Board of Trade, the Commission of Fisheries, the Registrar-General and Record Office so far as regards the census and life statistics, and the Warden of the Standards in stamping weights and measures. Under Regulation VII of 1817 it acts the part of the English Charity Commissioners In auditing charges connected with the administration of the revenue and the smaller local funds it does the duty of the London Audit Office. In four-fifths of the Presidency where the land is held direct from Government by peasant proprietors it does the work which is done on a smaller scale by the Duchy of Cornwall Office for the estates of His Royal Highness the Prince of Wales in the County of Cornwall. In its capacity as Court of Wards under Regulation V of 1804 and as a guardian of endowments under Regulation VII of 1828 it does work which in England devolves upon the Court of Chancery.

(c)—ACCOUNTS.

The old system of accounts in Government villages was **Village Accounts.** extremely complicated and cumbrous, and a thorough revision was made in 1855 by Jeyaram Chetty then Head Sheristadar to the Board of Revenue under the orders of Government. A complete uniform system of accounts was then prescribed, but since that date there have been various changes in the Revenue administration, such as the introduction of the survey and settlement in several districts, the settlement of Inam lands, the abolition of moturpha or profession-tax, the discontinuance of the Ooloogoo renting system in Tanjore and Tinnevelly, the abolition of garden rates, the creation of Local Fund Circles, and the like, these seem to call for a further revision of the accounts, and the matter is now under consideration. The village accounts at present kept are divided into permanent, daily and monthly, annual and quinquennial. The most important of the permanent accounts is the register of fields showing their size, description, assessment, and other particulars, as decided by traditional records or by the new Survey and Settlement Departments in districts in which they have worked. This is in fact the topographical map of the village reduced to the form of a statement. The other permanent accounts are abstracts of the field register and registers intended to show in one view the revenue and other particulars of the village for a series of years. The daily and monthly accounts show the progress of cultivation, and the progress made in collecting the state dues. They also include a rain register and a register of births and deaths in the village. The object of the annual accounts is to adjust the yearly demands between the State and the ryot. Owing to the nature of the ryotwari system the demand necessarily varies each year. The kurnam has to note down all the lands newly occupied by the ryot, and those given up, to record the extent actually cultivated and that left waste, to notice the claims of the ryots to remissions for loss of crops or waste from causes beyond his control, and to register the extent of second crop raised on single crop lands, and of Government water used for lands classed as unirrigated in the accounts. All this information is exhibited in the annual accounts which are checked by the taluq officials, chiefly by an officer called a Revenue Inspector, and with reference to these accounts and such other inquiry as is held by the Collector or his assistant at the annual Jammahbundy or settlement, the revenue demand payable by each ryot is determined. The quinquennial accounts are purely statistical. They show the rent-roll, the population, the number of ploughs and live-stock, and the number of irrigation works in repair in the village. All these accounts which are twenty-four in number with twelve enclosures are prepared on paper and are written in the vernacular of the district, the figures however being in English. Some of the registers are kept in the village, and others are sent to the taluq periodically for deposit.

Taluq Accounts.   The accounts kept at the taluqs or head-quarter stations of Tahsildars are prepared for the most part on the same principle as the village accounts substituting items of whole villages for those of individual holdings. The only accounts of importance in regard to which individual particulars are kept at the taluq head-quarters are the statements showing arrears outstanding against each ryot at the time of the yearly settlement, these being prepared with a view to decide whether the arrears should be recovered in the ordinary course, or remitted and written off as irrecoverable for any special reason.   Accounts are kept relating to stamps and progress of revenue work which do not appear in the village set of forms.   The taluq accounts were last revised in 1858 when a manual was prepared.   A further revision is in contemplation for the reasons given with regard to village accounts.

Collectors furnish accounts to the Accountant-General and **Huzur** Board of Revenue according to forms which have been prescribed **Accounts.** from time to time.   There is no manual.   The accounts sent to the Accountant-General are almost all monthly and relate to actual receipts and disbursements in the district.   Those sent to the Board are monthly, annual, and quinquennial.   Monthly the Collector sends to the Board a statement showing the area cultivated, the demand, collection, and balance statement of all sources of revenue and a report on season and prices.   Annually he furnishes a report on the settlement of the year called the Jammahbundy report accompanied with detailed statements showing the area occupied, the area actually cultivated and irrigated, the gross demand payable, the remissions granted with particulars, the amount and particulars of miscellaneous revenue, the actual collections, the extent of coercive processes used, and the arrears and the amount of arrears requiring to be written off the accounts.   He also furnishes the Board annually with separate statements showing the several crops raised and the extent under each crop, the revenue raised under each important work of irrigation, and the works of irrigation requiring repairs; quinquennially statistical information is given in regard to the number of ryots and agricultural stocks, rent-roll, population, sources of irrigation, and the extent of the cultivable lands available for cultivation.   There are various other statements sent by Collectors to the Board but they are not of sufficient importance to require mention.   Collection of statistical information on a still more comprehensive scale is under contemplation.

SURVEYS.

Before the year 1853 no regular Revenue Survey had been
attempted in the Madras Presidency, and the only maps were
those prepared by the Military Institution between the years 1805
and 1820. As regards field measurements, the Land Revenue
demand was either based on Curnams' unchecked statements,
or on measurements made in haste and with imperfect machinery. In the year 1853 an experimental survey of villages in
the South Arcot District was instituted. During the two
succeeding years the subject of a general survey of the Presidency was fully discussed, and in December 1856 the Court of
Directors sanctioned a definite scheme. In 1858 a Superintendent of Revenue Survey was appointed, an establishment
sanctioned, and work commenced. The original scheme has
since been considerably extended, and the settlement and demarcation of boundaries, as well as the topographical survey of all
zamindary and hill tracts, are now part of the duties of the
department.

Nature of
work.
The survey as now organized is conducted on the accurate
English method, and is, as far as is known, the only Indian
revenue survey, except those in progress in certain districts of
the North-West Provinces, which is based on rigorous principles
in every detail. It combines the operations of a revenue or
cadastral survey with those of a perfect topographical survey on
a trigonometrical basis. The revenue survey proper, with few
exceptions, is confined to villages in which land-tax is paid to
Government on the ryotwary system. Villages other than these
ranges of hills, and tracts of waste land or forest of inferior value
are excluded from the minute detailed field survey, and are
topographically surveyed on a scale of 4 inches to the mile for
detached Zamindaries and Agraharams, 2 inches and 1 inch to
the mile for large zamindaries and excluded tracts, and $\frac{1}{2}$ inch to
the mile in the case of the Nellumullei Hills. The operations in
Government lands are as follows. The village boundaries are
first settled, every turn of the line being permanently marked
with stone ; then disputes are disposed of, irregular boundaries
are adjusted, very small villages are amalgamated, and very large
villages are sub-divided. After these preliminaries, then the field
is pointed out by the curnam and is demarcated in accordance
with his puttah accounts and revenue records. The field

boundaries are permanently marked with stone and every holding
is registered. The law regarding boundary marks is contained
in Act XXVIII of 1860. Main circuits of from 50 to 100
square miles are carried out by the theodolite, the angular
work being checked by observations for azimuth at about
every 50 stations. Village boundaries are also surveyed by
theodolite, and check lines within the village forming minor
circuits of from 100 to 200 acres are run. While the boundary
work is being set up by traverse and plotted, the fields are
measured by chain in triangles, so that when the measurement
books are received in office, the map is ready to receive the fields.
After correction of any errors that may be found to exist, the
area of each field is taken by computing scale, and the sum of the
area so obtained is compared with the traverse area. In
zamindary and hill tracts, the details are put in by Plane Table.
The village map is then sent out for insertion of topographical
details. It shows eventually, the limits and area of every field,
with a record of the nature of tenure, cultivation, present
assessment, name of ryot and source of water-supply if irrigated.
The village maps are compiled into taluq maps, on a scale of
1 inch to a mile, and these form the materials for district
maps. The district and taluq maps are compiled in the
Central Survey Office at Madras. At the request of the Surveyor-General of India, the results of the Madras Survey are
being recast in such a form as to be available for the revision of
the Atlas of India. Village maps are reproduced by lithography
for the use of the Settlement Department. Taluq and District
maps are also lithographed; photo-lithography has been in use
in the survey office since 1873. The following scales for the
preparation of maps are in use :—Village maps, 5 chains to 1
inch, or 1 mile to 16 inches. Taluq maps, 1 mile to 1 inch, and
District maps, 2 miles to 1 inch.

The Presidency contains approximately 125,886 square miles, **Progress to
date.**
and up to the close of the official year 1875-76 the following
total progress had been made. The average size of a field is
about 2 acres. The average error in the village maps, shown
by the test of comparing the work with that of the great trigonometrical survey is 7·61 per mile. The measuring work of the
survey is followed by the equally important operation of classing
the fields with reference to the productiveness of their soils.
This is the work of the Revenue Settlement Department next
to be described.

Revenue Survey.

	Square Miles.
Villages mapped on 16-inch scale ...	40,407
Do. do. in progress ...	3,655
	44,062

Topographical Survey.

	Square Miles.
Zamindary and hilly tracts mapped on 4, 2, and 1 inch scale	17,393
Zamindary and hilly tracts in progress...	1,480
Topographically surveyed by a party from Bengal	3,000
Total surveyed ...	65,935
Remaining to be { Revenue ...	15,553
surveyed ... { Topographical ...	44,398

Maps.

Village maps published	13,420
Taluq maps published	75
District maps published	7

REVENUE SETTLEMENT.

History and nature of the deyartment. The principle adopted in this Presidency in the settlement of holdings other than those already permanently settled under the Regulation of 1802 is to fix a money-assessment founded upon due consideration of all the circumstances of the district, and to declare this assessment liable to revision after 30 years. A period is named as the Government reserve the right to derive benefit in the future from a share of the increased value conferred on the land by improved administration, the construction of public works, especially works of irrigation and railways, and the improved price of agricultural produce. The settlement is effected from time to time in different parts of the country. A revision of the land assessment of the Madras Presidency was undertaken in 1858 by Mr. Newill, who was then appointed Director of Revenue Settlement. This revision commenced in the South Arcot and Godavery Districts, and was shortly afterwards

extended to the Kistna District. In South Arcot only the
Chedambaram taluq and part of the Cuddalore taluq were
completed in 1861, but the whole of the Godavery and Kistna
Districts were settled in 1866-73, the settlement of the
Trichinopoly, Salem, and Nellore Districts was made in 1865,
1873, and 1874, and Kurnool proper, excluding two taluqs lately
transferred from Cuddapah, was settled in 1872. Operations
were further extended to the Tinnevelly, Chingleput, Cuddapah,
Coimbatore, and Ganjam Districts, and these are now far
advanced towards completion. The Settlement Department
at first consisted of three parties under Deputy Directors,
who were required to demarcate the village and field boundaries
in advance of the Survey, and to ascertain the value of
the lands as a preliminary to revising the assessment.
The former was a tedious process, involving much arbi-
tration and the investigation of many disputes. A patch of
waste land in the plains, or a few acres of barren hill side, were
disputed by rival villagers with a tenacity fostered by years of
factious contention; and though the possession, when gained,
could often be of no possible use, the claim of either party had to
be carefully considered, and the work in that spot delayed until
the matter was finally settled. The requirements of the Survey,
too, were not sufficiently known, and the marks erected, in many
cases, were temporary and destructible, and had frequently to be
renewed by others of a more permanent nature. This unsatis-
factory work continued to occupy much time and attention until
the Godavery, Kistna, Kurnool, Nellore, Salem, Trichinopoly,
and Tinnevelly Districts were demarcated and surveyed, when
the demarcation of boundaries was made over to the Survey
Department. This was in 1864. When freed from demarcation the Settlement Establishment was able to turn full
attention to its legitimate work of revising the land assessment. To do this it was necessary to obtain a general view
of the characteristics of each district about to be settled; to
ascertain particulars of the climate, rainfall, and physical
features of such tracts or divisions as might differ from each
other distinctly; to search the Collector's records for information
relative to the past history of the districts, their years of plenty
or famine, their lands, tenures, mode of taxation, and the cause of
their gradual progress; to study the relative values of such sources
of irrigation as they might possess; to determine how different
tracts were affected by roads, canals, market towns, hill ranges or
seaboard; and to acquire a general idea of the prevailing soils in

21

each tract, and the relative value of such black or red loam, sand, or clay as might be found to exist. Each taluq was next visited, and the Revenue officers and leading ryots assembled, and their opinion asked regarding the relative values of villages under such and such irrigation, or in such and such a position ; information was also recorded as to the payment of labor, the method of cultivation pursued, the crops grown, the mode of disposal of surplus grain, and the markets mostly frequented. The villages were next formed into groups, with reference to their several advantages of irrigation, climate, soil, situation, &c., and a series of experiments was made to ascertain the yield of the staple grains. When this was determined a table was framed showing the yield of each class of soil, and this yield was converted into money by an average struck on twenty years' market prices, with some abatement for traders' profits and for the distance that the grain usually had to be carried. From the value of the gross produce thus determined, the cost of cultivation was deducted, and the remainder or net value of the produce was then divided, and one-half taken as the Government demand on the land. The work so far was done by the officer at the head of each party, but in the mean time his native establishment had been employed in going over the villages and classifying the lands according to soil and circumstance. This operation was carefully watched and checked by the head of the party who eventually prepared a scheme for the settlement of the whole, or part of a district, and submitted it for the sanction of Government. In the manner just described 17 schemes, or estimates of financial results, have been submitted up to date, and on sanction accorded by Government the settlement has been introduced in the whole or part of nine of the twenty-two districts of the Presidency. This settlement is not only an acreage charge on the lands in each ryot's holding, but it fixes the charge on each acre of waste likely to be cultivated hereafter, and as an average district contains 100,000 ryots and some 10 lacs of fields the work of introducing the settlement by issuing puttahs, hearing appeals, and affording relief where needed is one of the most important parts of the process. In the districts first settled it was thought sufficient to accept existing entries in the Government account, and to issue the puttahs in the names in which they then stood, but latterly more has been done, and the opportunity of making the settlement has been taken advantage of to divide the common lands, to allot necessary grazing grounds, to transfer lands improperly assessed as wet to dry, or *vice versâ*, and to change many thousands of puttahs from the names of deceased ryots or vendors to those of the actual occupants of the land exhibited in these puttahs. When this has been done, a register showing the number, area, assessment, soil, irrigation, and name of the puttahdar of each field has been prepared for every village, and 30 copies of each register have been printed and distributed, one-third for sale to the ryots, one-third for official use, and one-third for reserve in store. The cost of settlement has been from the commencement to date Rupees 23¾ lakhs, or about 5 lakhs for each finished district, or Rupees 1,375 per village, or 4 Annas per acre. The work is necessarily slow; the average district of 1,500 villages and 100,000 puttahdars has occupied nine years to settle, but the work has been complete, and the figures furnished in the registers admit of revision, should such be necessary, on the expiration of the term of this 30 years' settlement without again going through the processes on which these figures are based. On the whole there is an increase in the revenue derived from increased rates, and the taking up of the waste. The additional revenue drawn from the finished districts is now 5⅓ lakhs of Rupees above the assessment of the year preceding that in which they were settled ; this is equivalent to a present return of 24 per cent. on the outlay, and this return is likely to increase as more waste land is brought under cultivation.

INAM COMMISSION.

The origin of Inam tenure can be traced to a very remote **Origin of** antiquity in Southern India. The gift of land is enjoined by **Inams.** the Hindu Shastras as the most meritorious of charities, and every Hindu Sovereign was therefore ambitious of distinguishing his reign by the extent and value of the lands he alienated in Inam to the religious classes of the community. Inam grants were generally made in a solemn and impressive manner. They were engraved on copper-plates or slabs of stone and were declared to be irrevocable " so long as the sun and moon endure ;" a heavy curse was invoked on those who disturbed the tenure, while great merit was ascribed to those who maintained and confirmed it. The grants made by the Hindu Sovereigns of Bijayanagar, the rulers of the Pandian dynasty whose seat was Madura, the Mahratta princes who latterly ruled at Tanjore, and the chieftains of Orissa who for many centuries ruled over the greater part of the Northern Circars were of this religious nature. During the period of anarchy which followed the over-throw of the Native dynasties and which continued, though in a less degree, after the establishment of the Mohammadan rule in Southern India, the power of granting Inams for numerous miscellaneous purposes was assumed by various petty chiefs, officers of Government, and others, who alienated the revenues to a considerable extent. Numerous Minor Inams of this description were granted by Zamindars, by Faujdars, and even by renters in the Northern Circars; while the Poligars of the Ceded Districts and the southern provinces of the Presidency were even more liberal. Though it was not the principle of the Mohammadan rulers to regard alienations of revenue as perma-nent and binding, their policy with regard to Inam tenures was practically lenient and they generally respected the more ancient grants held by Brahmins and on account of temples. They also made liberal fresh grants, not only to their own immediate relatives and followers, the higher ranks of their Civil and Military Officers and the religious classes of their own faith, but also to the Hindus and their religious institutions. Thus the effect of the Mohammadan rule was to add greatly to the already existing large extent of land exempt from the payment of revenue. Another period of political confusion ensued during the latter part of the last century when the supremacy in Southern India was contested between the British, the French, and the various local powers, which did not subside until the different treaties between the years 1750 and 1801 brought into the possession of the East India Company the whole of the present Madras Presidency. There is good reason to suppose that a large extent of land was granted as Inam during this interme-aidry period by parties who had not the least authority to make such alienations. During the earlier years of British rule the Government of the day, following the custom of the country, adopted the practice of rewarding meritorious services by grants of Jaghires, and thus many villages were alienated either in perpetuity or for a stated number of lives. This practice however gradually fell into disuse after the receipt of the despatches from the Court of Directors, dated 2nd January 1822 and 27th May 1829, in which they expressed their opinion of the superior propriety of money pensions to grants of land on all ordinary

occasions, and directed that grants of land should be restricted
to special cases. It was not unusual for the earlier Collectors to
grant Inams of their own authority for various purposes, but the
extent of land so alienated was comparatively trifling.

The enormous sacrifice of State revenue involved in these **Early**
arrangements attracted the attention of the British admini- **measures by**
British.
stration at a very early period, and caused a recognition
of the importance of a general inquiry into titles to rent-free
lands. The enactment of certain laws followed, and several
orders were issued on the subject; these however led to
no practical results. Steps were certainly taken to prevent the
diversion of Inams from the purposes for which they were
granted in 1831, but it was not until 1845 that active measures
were adopted to assert the reversionary rights of Government
in property of this description. A prohibition was then issued
against the devolution of Inam property by adoption, unless due
notice to Government was given, and it was further proposed to
limit the continuance of charitable grants to the lives of
existing holders, on the ground that it was objectionable in
principle that a portion of the land revenue should be set apart
for the maintenance of a class of persons who had no legitimate
claim on the State. The more liberal policy, which was afterwards adopted in dealing with these tenures, may be ascribed to
the discussion regarding the inadvisability of disturbing long
existing rights in landed property, which arose out of the insurrection of one Nursimha Reddi in the Cuddapah District. The
rules at first laid down for dealing with claims to succeed to Inam
lands resulted in charging the district officers with numerous
investigations of a complex and difficult character, which they
found it difficult to deal with concurrently with their regular
duties; the state of uncertainty in which this description of
property was placed gave rise to a feeling of irritation and
insecurity on the part of the holders, and the initiation of the general
survey and revision of the assessment eventually led to definite
proposals being made to the Home Government for the appointment of a special commission to deal with all tenures of this
description.

The Madras Inam Commission was accordingly established on **Institution**
the 16th November 1858 during the administration of Lord Harris, **of Inam**
Commission.
and Mr. G. N. Taylor, who was appointed Commissioner, shortly
after proceeded to Bombay to learn, by personal conference with
the authorities there, the details connected with the working of the

Inam Commission in that Presidency and with the proposed plan of
treating Inam tenures for the future. In his reports Mr. Taylor
proposed certain modes of procedure the object of which was
to carry on the necessary registration through the District
Revenue agency either under the orders of the Inam Commissioner or of a Member of the Board of Revenue. While the
subject was under consideration, Sir Charles Trevelyan arrived
and assumed the Government of Madras. The first question
which engaged his attention was the settlement of the Inams of
the Presidency, and in his Minute of the 13th May 1859 he
propounded certain rules by which the principles enunciated by
the Court of Directors were to be practically applied by the Inam
Commissioner in the investigation upon which he was about to
enter. His scheme was of a more liberal nature than that already
proposed by the Madras Government. The basis of his proposals
was that when it should be proved that land had for fifty years
been in the possession of a person, or of those through whom he
claimed, without the payment of land-tax, such length of possession should be held to be a good title to that land as Inam, whatever might have been the origin of the possession. The entries
in the Revenue Accounts were to be considered as sufficient
evidence of possession without the production of other proofs, and
where the failure of proof of fifty years' possession was owing
only to lapse of time, the Inamdar was to be allowed the same
advantage as if possession had been proved for the full term.
When the title to an Inam based on length of possession was
once established, it was then to be open to the owner of an Inam
held for personal benefit either to retain the Inam according
to his actual tenure subject to the liability of lapse and without
the power of alienation; or to enfranchise it by payment of a
moderately substantial annual quit-rent or a single fixed sum
equal to so many years' purchase of the quit-rent. The quit-rent
was to be estimated in terms particularly favorable to the
Inamdars in order to induce them to take advantage of the
arrangement afforded. With regard to Service Inams, those that
were attached to services still required were to be continued
intact; but where the services were such that they could not be
made available for any useful public purpose the holder was to
be enfranchised, and the land was to be fully assessed, still
giving the holder the opportunity of commuting as above.
As regards lands forming endowments of Temples and Mosques
held in remuneration for services to be rendered therein, these

were to be confirmed on their existing tenures, and to be resumable only when the object for which they were held had ceased to exist. All questions of disputed right between individuals relating to Inams were to be settled according to the established forms in the ordinary Courts of Justice. The claims of Government upon Inams previously to enfranchisement were to be determined by the officers of Government ; but after enfranchisement the Inams were to be in every respect under the protection of the Courts of Justice.

The operations of the late Inam Commission were conducted on these principles. Full information was prepared regarding the Inams of each village by the taluq and village officers, and the Deputy Collectors of the Commission inspected documents and took such further evidence as seemed proper, recording details in an English register in which the rate for enfranchisement was calculated and the acceptance or refusal of the Inamdar recorded. These registers were subsequently forwarded to the Commissioner for review and confirmation and for the issue of a title-deed. The progress of the work was at first somewhat impeded by the ignorance and mistrust of the people, as the imposition of the additional quit-rent was viewed as merely a step in the direction of the full assessment of all Inam property; but when the really liberal character of the settlement became generally known opposition ceased, and the operations of the Commission proceeded with a rapidity hitherto unknown in the investigation of Inam titles. *Work of the Commission.*

The Inam tenures of this Presidency may be divided into nine classes :—I—Those held for the support of religious institutions and for services connected therewith ; II—Those held for purposes of public utility ; III—Those held for the support of works of irrigation yielding public revenue ; IV—Those held by Brahmans and other religious classes for their personal benefit ; V—Those held by the families of Poligars and those who filled hereditary offices of trust under former Governments ; VI—Those held by the kinsmen, dependents and followers of former Poligars and Zamindars ; VII—Those connected with the former general police of the country ; VIII—Those held for ordinary Village Revenue and Police Service ; IX—Those held by various descriptions of artisans for services due to village communities. Each class will be noticed in the above order. *Classification of Inams.*

A considerable portion of the Inam tenures in the Presidency belongs to the religious institutions of the country, both Mohammadan and Hindu. A recent computation gives the *Class I.*

extent at acres 1,458,081 and the Government value or assessment at Rupees 24,22,467. They are held either directly for the support of the institutions or for various services to be rendered therein. There is hardly a village of any importance in the country which does not possess its two temples, one to Vishnu and the other to Siva, and which has not also its tutelary village deity known under a variety of names. The Inams of this description are therefore by far the most numerous, though the value of each taken by itself is often inconsiderable. With the exception of the Pagoda of Jagannath, which though not within this Presidency enjoys extensive Inams in the District of Ganjam, there are very few temples of note in the Northern Circars, nor are there any of much celebrity in the Ceded Districts excepting the temples at Hampi and Sandur. By far the larger portion of the Inams belongs to the Pagodas in the Southern Districts, such as Tripati, Conjiveram, Srirangam, Ráméswaram, and Madura. The valuable endowments attached to the different Mathams, or spiritual headships of the three leading sects of Brahmins are also included under this head, and are to be met with in nearly all the districts of the Presidency. There are besides throughout the country minor religious institutions not presided over by Brahmans, which enjoy Inams of more or less value. These belong to Bairagis and Pandarams or religious mendicants, and Jangams or priests of the Lingait sect. The Mohammadan Institutions are of a less varied character, and are generally in a decaying condition throughout the country. They consist chiefly of Mosques or places of public worship, Takyas or residences of Fakirs, and Dargahs or shrines of Mohammadan saints. The endowments attached to Christian Churches are very few and occur only in the Districts of Tinnovelly and Tanjore.

Class II.   A great variety of Inams falls under Class II, which embraces those held for the support of Chattrams, Water-pandals, Topes, Nandavanams or Flower-gardens, Wells, Ponds, Tanks, Bridges, Village Schools, and Veda Patasalas or Schools for teaching the Vedas. The extent was recently computed at acres 156,949 and the assessment at Rupees 3,07,912. The object of the greater part of these grants is the provision of water and shade, both wants of the first importance in a tropical country. Bridges and Village Schools endowed with Inams are few in number. Schools for teaching the Vedas are also not numerous and may be said to be falling into disuse.

The Inams of the third class usually known as Dasabhandams Class III. are confined chiefly to the Ceded Districts, the western portions of Guntoor, Nellore, North Arcot and Salem. The extent has been computed at acres 24,824 and the assessment at Rs. 1,40,715. They were granted as a recompense to private individuals who constructed tanks, wells, and river channels by means of which the revenue of the State was augmented. The extent and value of the Inam were in proportion to the capital expended on the work and the outturn in revenue. These grants are of two descriptions, " Khanda Dasabhandams " or Inams given in specific localities, and " Shamilat Dasabhandams" or the allowance as Inam of a certain proportion of each year's cultivation under the work in question. Inams of the latter description have not been brought on the Inam registers as they had no locality. In all ordinary cases Dasabhandamdars are under the obligation of maintaining the works of irrigation in due repair. In some cases such a condition was either not attached to Dasabhandam Inams or it had not been enforced for a long time. Such Inams have been treated and enfranchised as personal grants. In the Ceded Districts certain Wudders or tank-diggers held Inams for the service of executing the ordinary repairs of large Government tanks. Under the present organization of the Public Works Department the Wudders occupied an anomalous position, and the services attached to their tenures were reported to be very inefficiently rendered. Their Inams have consequently been enfranchised under the rules.

The Bhatta-vritti and Khairati Inams held respectively by Classes IV. Brahmans and Mohammadans for subsistence form nearly one- and V. half of the Inams of the Presidency. The extent has been given at acres 3,964,394 and the assessment at Rupees 54,89,928. As has been already remarked, the grant of Inams to Brahmans is of very great antiquity. The Mohammadan rulers also freely alienated lands to the religious classes of their own faith. These grants may be said to represent the accumulated charities of the sovereigns and chiefs of the country from the most remote times. The Inams held by the families of dispossessed Poligars in the Ceded Districts and the Baramahal, and of the ancient Kanungos, Despandyas, and Desmukhs, who have been permitted to enjoy certain lands free of all conditions of service to Government, have been all now treated as personal. When the Polliems were reduced at the cession of the territories to the East India Company, certain pensions and Inam lands were granted to the ex-Poligars for their subsistence. Although a vague impression appears to have prevailed at the time that they were liable to be called out for police service during emergencies, the occasion for such services very seldom arose, and the Inams have been practically enjoyed as personal. The Kanungos were the provincial, and the Despandyas the district, Registrars or Revenue Accountants. The Desmukhs were chief officers of police and revenue, corresponding generally to Zemindars. Their offices were abolished at a very early stage of the British administration, and the Inams granted to or allowed to be held by them being of a personal character have been enfranchised like ordinary Inams.

Class VI.   The Inams held under Class VI. are considerable in number and value chiefly in the Northern Circars and the Southern Palciyams of Madura. Before their cession to the British these countries were mostly held by Zemindars or Poligars who exercised the powers of sovereignty within their limited estates. They alienated lands not only for the maintenance of Brahmans and of their own relatives and dependents, but also to a large number of their household servants and to numerous men of rank of their own caste. Whole villages were held on conditions of service, which was neither rendered nor called for under the British administration. Of this character were the Bissois and Doratanams in the hill tracts of Ganjam and Vizagapatam, the Mukhasas of the Kistna District, the Amarams of North Arcot, the Umligas of Salem, and the Jivitams of Madura. All these tenures have been now enfranchised, a higher rate of quit-rent being charged on those which were held on the condition of actual service. Several miscellaneous Inams, such as those held by Desayis, Nattars, Settis, and other heads of castes, and by certain classes of servants known as Tambalas, Anakalas, Matapatis, and Jirars in the Ceded Districts, the services connected with which have long ceased to be required, have been also enfranchised and converted into private property.

Class VII   The seventh class comprises the Inams held by the Kattubadis, a class of peons who discharged police, military, and not unfrequently revenue duties. They were called into existence by the Poligars, who remunerated them by assignments of land and paid them batta also while on actual service; they were chiefly employed in the hilly and inaccessible parts of the country. On the introduction of the British rule they were generally left in quiet possession of their Inams and were but seldom called out for duty. The Inams of this class have now been all enfranchised. The Kattubadis are found in the greatest numbers in the Ceded Districts and North Arcot.

The Inams embraced in the eighth and ninth classes are those of the village servants, revenue and police, and of the village artisans. These were simply recorded by the officers of the late Inam Commission, as no steps could be taken in regard to the former until some decision was come to as to the principles on which the Village Establishments of the Presidency were to be revised and remodelled. The operations which have since taken place have been fully described in a previous division of this Section. *Classes VIII. and IX.*

In addition to dealing with Inams proper, the Commission investigated and disposed of a large number of anomalies which had for some time disfigured the revenue system of the Presidency. These latter measures have greatly tended to simplify the revenue administration of the several districts, and the discussion and final decision of may long-disputed rights between the Government and Zemindars, between Zemindars and Inamdars and their tenants, have facilitated the revenue procedure of district officers in no small degree. *Miscellaneous operations of Commission.*

The Inam Commission continued as a separate department up to November 1869, when, the bulk of the work having been completed, and under a pressing necessity for the reduction of Imperial expenditure, it was resolved to abolish the department, and the Inam Commissioner was ordered to submit his general report. The work which remained to be done was entrusted to a Member of the Board of Revenue, who was appointed Inam Commissioner *pro formâ* and to satisfy legal requirements. By the 1st July 1870 some 28,000 further cases were disposed of, and the work which remained at the time of transfer was got through; but it was found necessary to continue the appointment of a Member of the Board as Inam Commissioner. References are still continually made by Collectors in Inam matters, scattered cases still occur which have remained undisposed of owing to the absence of parties or other causes, and title-deeds for Village Service Inams enfranchised on the revision of the establishments coincident with new settlement have to be issued. *Close of the Commission.*

The total number of Inams confirmed, the quit-rent charged by the Inam Commission, and the cost of the Commission from its commencement to the present date are shown below :— *General results.*

—	Total Number of Inams.	Area.	Assessment.	Old Jodi.	Quit-rent newly charged.	Cost.
		ACRES.	RS.	RS.	RS.	RS.
From the commencement up to 30th June 1866.	367,427	5,977,305	90,90,881	8,42,765	10,62,767	
From 1st July 1866 to 31st March 1875.	36,384	256,681	6,28,663	56,181	1,79,723	13,23,901
1875-76 ...	166	6,825	9,464	510	1,938	
Total ...	403,977	6,240,811	97,29,008	8,99,456	12,44,428	13,23,901
Assessment of Inams fully assessed up to 1866.					1,13,962	
Do. do. since ...					Not known.	
Total ...					13,58,390	

Of the above-mentioned amount of quit-rent newly charged, Rupees 3,45,692* represent the sum charged on Village Service Inams enfranchised. The general success which has attended the proceedings of the Commission can best be judged by the very large proportion of those interested who accepted the terms proffered by Government. It appears from the figures given down to 1866 by which time the bulk of the work had been completed, that these terms were declined in only 6,588 cases, and that the rejections involved the temporary annual loss to Government of not more than Rupees 35,885; this sum was the quit-rent fixed for enfranchisement, and represents a little less than $3\frac{1}{3}$ per cent. on the whole amount of additional quit-rent imposed. The provisions in the rules authorizing the conversion of the absolute tenure on enfranchisement into a freehold by the redemption of quit-rent at twenty years' purchase was taken advantage of to a very trifling extent, only Rupees 666 of quit-rent having been redeemed in this way down to 1866. No other result was to be expected as twelve per cent. may be viewed as the ordinary rate of interest procurable among Natives of the country for money lent on undoubted security. They would hardly, therefore, be likely to invest largely in redemption of quit-rent which would return but five per cent. on the capital sunk. It will be seen that the total cost of the Commission since its

		RS.
* Godavery	...	1,25,257
Kurnool	...	2,11,612
Trichinopoly		8,823
Total ...		3,45,692

formation has scarcely exceeded thirteen lakhs of Rupees; a sum the reverse of excessive when the highly satisfactory results attained are considered. Landed property in which not less than two and a half million persons are in some measure interested, and extending to nearly 6¼ millions of acres in area, which was lately held on defective and doubtful titles, and which paid to the revenue less than one-tenth of the regulated land assessment, has now been confirmed to the holders on indefeasible Government titles; and the measure has resulted in a clear gain to the revenue of about 4½ lakhs of Rupees per annum. The alienation of State revenue has been considerably reduced, and at the same time contentment has been diffused throughout the whole body of the Inamdars.

WARDS' ESTATES.

Under Regulation V of 1804, the Members of the Board of Revenue are constituted a Court of Wards with authority to take charge of property devolving by succession on heirs incapacitated by minority, sex, or infirmity, from administering their own affairs, provided that the heirs concerned be persons paying revenue or rent direct to Government. In cases where lunacy may occur at some time other than that of succession, the Collector of the district is empowered by Act XXXV of 1858, Section 3, Clause 2, to move the Civil Court to put the estate under charge of the Court of Wards. Property under the Court has this special advantage that it cannot be attached or sold for arrears of public revenue; if one year shows a loss in the collections, the deficiency to the public purse has to be made good by the surplus collections of other years. The first step in assuming charge must be sanctioned by Government, but subsequently to that the Court of Wards administers the estates on its own responsibility. The estates are restored at the discretion of the Court. The estates are managed through Collectors, who employ special establishments at the cost of the estates. A paid Manager appointed under the Act to take charge of the property forms part of every establishment. There is also in most cases a Guardian, paid or otherwise, whose duty it is to attend to the private affairs of the work and to administer that part of the income which is set apart for the ward's private use. A commission of 1½ per cent.

Court of Wards.

on the revenues, deducting from these all establishment and maramut charges, is paid into the public funds as consideration for general supervision. Important public works which require execution on the estate have been hitherto carried out, under sanction of the Government, by the Public Works Department, the Public Works executive staff up to the grade of Overseers being provided for in the estimate, and the supervision being gratuitous. In minor cases the Collectors have carried out the works themselves with special and sometimes temporary engineering establishments. It is in contemplation that the Court should employ its own public works establishments hereafter in all cases. On the Ramnad estate the special establishment under the Collector already comprises an Assistant Engineer transferred by Government for that purpose from the Public Works establishment. Each estate sends up an annual budget to the Court, to be dealt with separately. The funds as raised from the estate are paid into the Government treasury, and accounts are there kept for each estate. The public funds cannot be indented on by an estate except by special loan. When the accounts show a large deposit for any one estate at any treasury the amount is remitted to the Bank of Madras through the Court. The Court keep a separate account for each estate, but the Bank of Madras keep only one account in the name of the Court. Surplus funds are invested in Government paper. In the management of the funds of an estate under the Court, the object held in view is rather to improve the estate, than to attempt to accumulate savings so as to make a purse for a ward on his succeeding to the estate in person. Under Act XXI of 1855 the Court have also control of the education of every male minor whose property has been taken under their management with that of such minor's younger brother or brothers. The wards are generally educated, either by a tutor or by attending school, at the head-quarters of districts, where they can be under the eye of the Collector. There is a penalty for aiding and abetting the marriage of a minor made without the consent of the Court. Disqualified proprietors cannot adopt children without the Court's consent. An appendix statement at the end of this volume shows the estates under management at the end of Fasli 1285, with the names, age and sex of the wards, the date of assuming management, date when they will probably be restored, and the rent-roll according to the best information.

SECTION III.

PROTECTION.

LEGISLATING AUTHORITY AND GOVERNMENT LAW OFFICERS.

UNDER the Indian Councils Act of 1861 (24 & 25 Victoria, Cap. 67), the local legislating authority for the Presidency of Madras is vested in the Governor in Council; the Council, at meetings held for the purpose of making laws and regulations, consisting of the Ordinary Members with the addition of the Advocate-General and such other persons, not less than four or more than eight in number, as the Governor may nominate. Not less than one-half of the persons so nominated are non-officials. At a meeting of the Council for this special purpose, the Governor, or in his absence the Senior Civil Ordinary Member of Council, presides, and business can only be transacted if the Governor or some Ordinary Member of Council and at least four other Members are present. In the case of a difference of opinion the President has if necessary a casting vote. The business of the meeting is confined to the consideration of measures already introduced into the Council, or to granting sanction for the introduction of new measures. No measure affecting the public revenues can be introduced without the previous sanction of the Governor. Every law or regulation made by the Council must, before it comes into force, receive the assent of the Governor in the first instance, and subsequently that of the Governor-General, and is eventually subject to be disallowed by the Crown. *Council for making laws and regulations.*

Except with the sanction of the Governor-General previously, obtained, no measure can be introduced, (1), Affecting the public debt of India, or the customs duties, or any other tax or duty now in force and imposed by the authority of the Govern- *—Limits of its jurisdiction.*

ment of India for the general purposes of such Government; (2), Regulating any of the current coin, or the issue of any bills, notes, or other paper currency; (3), Regulating the conveyance of letters by the Post Office or messages by the electric telegraph within the Presidency; (4), Altering in any way the Penal Code of India as established by Act of the Governor-General in Council, No. XLV of 1860; (5), Affecting the religion or religious rites and usages of any class of Her Majesty's subjects in India; (6), Affecting the discipline or maintenance of any part of Her Majesty's Military or Naval Forces; (7), Regulating patents or copyrights; (8), Affecting the relations of the Government with Foreign Princes or States.

—Rules of the Council. Rules for the conduct of business at the meetings of Council have been made under the provisions of Section 37 of the Act. The most important of these relate to the introduction of Bills. When leave has been obtained for the introduction of a Bill either from the Council when sitting or from the Governor during the adjournment, the Bill is printed, together with a Statement of Objects and Reasons, and a copy is furnished to each Member of the Council. On the day fixed for the introduction of a Bill, or on any subsequent day, the principles of the Bill and its general provisions may be discussed, and if necessary it may be referred to a Select Committee for report. All reports of Select Committees, as well as the Bill and the Statement of Objects and Reasons, must be published in the Official Gazette, and copies furnished to all the Members of the Council before the measure is brought up for final consideration.

Advocate-General. The principal law-officer of the Government is the Advocate-General. His duties, briefly put, are—(1), to advise the Government upon legal matters refered to him; (2), to appear for the Government in legal proceedings on the Original Side of the High Court in which the Government is interested; and (3), to appear at the Madras Sessions and prosecute in cases of murder, counterfeiting coin, and offences by Government servants against the Government.

Government Pleader. The duties of the Government Pleader as at present constituted are—(1), to appear before the High Court, Appellate Side, when instructed to do so by Government in all appeals in suits in which Government or officers of Government are parties; (2), to appear before the same tribunal in support of convictions in criminal appeals when directed to do so by Magistrates or by the High Court; (3), to appear for Government in civil or criminal cases in mofussil Courts when instructed to do so; (4), to advise Government or the Board of Revenue on legal questions arising out of suits, &c., in the mofussil.

The Crown Prosecutor is Standing Counsel to Government in **Crown Prosecutor.** criminal cases arising within the original jurisdiction of the High Court. It is his duty to appear for the prosecution on behalf of Government and conduct all the cases at the High Court Sessions; except that in cases of murder, and certain other serious offences, in which the Advocate-General is required to appear on behalf of Government, he acts as the Advocate-General's junior. It is also the duty of the Crown Prosecutor to appear as Counsel for Government and conduct Government prosecutions before the Presidency Town Magistrates; the Government Solicitor furnishing him with the necessary briefs. The Crown Prosecutor is the officer to whom commitments for trial before the High Court are made by the committing Magistrates. The Crown Prosecutor is also ex-officio Public Prosecutor for the purposes of the Presidency Magistrates' Act, 1877, and, as such, when directed by the Government to do so, presents appeals to the High Court from orders of acquittal, or dismissal, or discharge, made by Presidency Town Magistrates.

To each District Court is attached a Government vakeel, **Government Vakeels.** who is a member of the Local Bar. He is required to appear and act in all Government suits in the Courts of the District Judges' stations. Besides the regulated fees in each suit he receives a salary of Rupees 21 a month.

The functions and duties of the Government Solicitor are **Government Solicitor.** shortly these—To advise the different departments and officers of Government in matters on which the opinion of the Advocate-General may not be required; in cases where that officer's opinion is required, to lay the papers before him, and on receipt of his opinion to forward a copy of it to Government; to prepare contracts for the several departments of Government, and all deeds and conveyances to Government; to furnish the Crown Prosecutor with the necessary briefs in Police cases in which that officer has to appear, i.e., all cases in which the prosecution is instituted or carried on by or under the orders or with the sanction of Government; to appear at the Police Courts and instruct the Crown Prosecutor in such cases; to send the necessary briefs to the Advocate-General for the quarterly Sessions of the High Court in all cases of murder, coining and other cases in which the Crown is immediately interested and to appear in Court on the trial of such cases; and to institute, defend and conduct all civil suits and proceedings by or against Government, and where the sanction of Government has been obtained by or against its officers.

Clerk of the Crown.

The duties of Clerk of the Crown are—(1), to draw up indictments against prisoners committed to stand their trial at the High Court Sessions; (2), to make copies of all depositions, exhibits, &c., for prosecuting and defending counsel, or others employed in prosecution or defence; (3), to draw up warrants, and sentences passed on prisoners during the Sessions; (4), to prepare lists of special and petty jurors, and settle all doubtful cases arising under the lists; (5), to draw up and issue jury rules; (6), to take recognizances of witnesses, and bail bonds of prisoners; (7), to issue subpœnas for all witnesses on behalf of prisoners in jail, prosecutors, and the Crown; and (8), to register the proceedings of Courtsmartial.

Administrator-General.

The Administrator-General is appointed by the local Government, and must be a member of the Bar of England or Ireland or of the Faculty of Advocates in Scotland. He is not an officer of the High Court, but obtains from that Court letters of administration authorizing him to deal with and dispose of estates committed to his custody. He gives general security to the Secretary of State for the due execution of his office, and no special security is required to be given by him to the High Court when administrations are granted by that Court to him. The duties of the office are detailed in Government of India Act II of 1874. Under Section 15 the Administrator-General is entitled generally to letters of administration unless they are granted to the next of kin of the deceased. By Section 16 he is required within a reasonable time after he shall have had notice that a person has died, (other than a Hindu, Mahomedan or Buddhist, or a person exempted under the Indian Succession Act, 1865, Section 332, from the operation of that Act) and that the deceased has left assets within the Presidency, to take steps to apply for letters of administration, and this whether the deceased has left a will or not provided that the assets are of greater value than Rupees 1,000, and provided that no person shall within a month after the death have applied within the Presidency for probate of a will or for letters of administration of the estate. If the assets do not exceed 1,000 rupees in value in the whole, the Administrator-General is not bound to act, but he may either grant a certificate of administration to some person entitled to a share of the

effects of the deceased or take charge of the estate himself
without letters of administration. In certain cases such as
where danger is to be apprehended of misappropriation, deterio-
ration or waste of an estate, the Administrator-General may be
directed by the Court to apply for letters of administration
to the effects of any person whether Hindu, Mahomedan,
Buddhist or not, and power is also given to the Administrator-
General to collect and hold all such assets until the right of
succession or administration is ascertained; and if no person
appears according to the practice of the Court and entitles
himself to probate of the will, or grant of administration as
next of kin of deceased, or if the person obtaining the order of
administration neglects to give the security required of him, the
Court is bound to grant letters of administration to the
Administrator-General. Any private executor or administrator
may, with the consent of the Administrator-General, by an
instrument in writing, under his hand, transfer all estates,
effects and interests vested in him by virtue of such probate
or letters to the Administrator-General, and the Administrator-
General shall have the rights and be subject to the liabilities
which he would have had and to which he would have been
subject if probate or letters of administration had been originally
granted to him. As soon as the Administrator-General takes
charge of the estate, the fact is advertised in the Gazette and in
the public papers, and creditors are called upon to prove
their claims. They are required to state the amounts and other
particulars, and to support their claims by such evidence as, under
the circumstances of the case, the Administrator-General is
reasonably entitled to require. If a claimant fail to do this
within one month of the date of the institution of any suit
he is liable to pay the cost of the suit, and if in any suit
judgment is pronounced in favor of the plaintiff, he is
nevertheless entitled only to payment out of the assets
equally and rateably with the other creditors. The Administrator-General like any other executor or administrator
keeps the assets for a reasonable time to answer the claims of
creditors. This time is fixed at one year, but where the case
permits of it, the account is closed earlier. Like any other
executor or administrator he is bound to pay all creditors
rateably or preferentially according to the law governing the
distribution. No claim can be made upon him, in respect of
any assets paid or delivered by him, to any legatee or to any
person entitled on distribution without notice of the claim. The

following are preferential payments:—(1), Funeral expenses; (2), death-bed charges; (3), fee for medical attendance; (4), board and lodging for one month prior to death; (5), expenses for obtaining probate or letters of administration; and (6), wages for services rendered to deceased within three months of his death by any laborer, artizan, or domestic servant. After this comes payment of other debts, which are on an equal footing. The Administrator-General is bound to keep the accounts prescribed by the Act and to allow persons entitled so to do to inspect them. He is bound to furnish half-yearly schedules of estates under his charge in form prescribed by the Act, and these schedules are published in the *Fort St. George Gazette.* Three copies are sent to Government for transmission to the Secretary of State for India for the information of persons in England who are interested in the matter. The remittances made by the Administrator-General to England are made through the India Office, at the rate of exchange annually fixed by Government, for the repayment of advances made in India. The Administrator-General of Madras is entitled to a commission of 5 per cent. (except in the case of officers and soldiers when the commission is 3 per cent.) on the assets, and no person other than the Administrator-General acting officially is entitled to charge any commission or agency charges for any thing done as executor or administrator under any probate or letters of administration granted by the Supreme or High Court in Madras since the passing of Act II of 1850, or by any Court under the Indian Succession Act, 1865.

Sheriff of Madras. The Sheriff of Madras executes the process of the High Court. He executes warrants of execution, warrants of arrest, warrants of attachment and sale of moveable and immoveable property, and warrants of possession of immoveable property. Where parties appear in person, that is to say without the intervention of a vakeel or an attorney, the Sheriff serves summonses to defendants, summonses to witnesses, citations, notices and all other process. He forwards to the mofussil Courts for service, summonses to defendants, notices, &c., issued by the High Court against parties residing in the mofussil. He also serves summonses to witnesses and executes attachments and other process issued by the Court for the relief of insolvent debtors. Also summonses to witnesses and executes all other process issued by the Crown side of the Court. The Sheriff presides over the preparation of the annual lists of persons liable to serve on juries, and summons the jurors who are to serve at each quarterly Sessions of the High Court. The Sheriff attends personally in

Court during the continuance of the Sessions. The Sheriff convenes public meetings under Act XXIII of 1840. At present he serves and executes within his jurisdiction process issued by Courts in the mofussil. This duty however he will cease to perform from the 1st October 1877 as all process issued by the mofussil Courts will have to be executed by the Presidency Courts of Small Causes under Act X of 1877.

The office of Coroner of Madras was first created about the year 1800. The duties are now regulated by the Coroner's Act, No. IV of 1871, under which the Coroner has to inquire into cases of death occasioned by accident, homicide, suicide, or suddenly by means unknown, and into the cause of the death of any person being a prisoner dying in jail. The Police authorities bring to his notice all cases of death occasioned in the way just mentioned, and he thereupon orders a jury to be assembled at the spot where the body is and holds an inquest on view of the body. Madras is divided into four Medical districts, and the Surgeon in charge of the district in which an inquest is to be held is generally summoned by the Coroner to give professional evidence. The Coroner's jurisdiction extends over an area of 28 miles and is conterminous with the Presidency Police and Municipal limits. Murders in the Presidency Town are rare, for during the eleven years, 1866 to 1876, only 35 cases have occurred in which the Coroner has been called upon to hold inquest. Drowning seems to be the mode most resorted to by suicides; since the year 1868 to the end of 1876 there have been 212 cases. During the same period there have been 26 cases of suicide by hanging, and only 8 by cutting the throat. Suicide by poison shows only 13 cases during this period. During the first twenty years after the creation of the office 413 inquests were held or an average of about 20 a year. For the twelve years from 1840 to 1852 there was a total of 1,217 or an average of 101 a year. For the twenty years from 1853 to 1872 the number had reached 3,403 or an average of 170 a year. For the four years from 1873 to 1876 the total number of inquests was 707 or an average of 176 a year.

Coroner of Madras.

POLICE.

Nature of the department.
The present Police organization in the Madras Presidency has been in existence for a little less than twenty years. The report of the Torture Commission in 1855 made certain what had for some time previously been a matter of inquiry and discussion, namely, that there was urgent necessity for Police reform in this Presidency. The Mofussil Police then existing were described by the Commission in very disparaging terms and a reform was at once projected. The Court of Directors in 1856 concurred in the views put forward by the Local Government, and the establishment of a Chief Commissioner with 20 District Superintendents and 20 Assistant Superintendents was sanctioned in December 1857. Mr. William Robinson of the Madras Civil Service, who had minutely studied the question of police organization in England and elsewhere, was appointed Chief Commissioner in 1858 and subsequently took the designation of Inspector-General of Police. The new constabulary was introduced in the District of North Arcot in 1859, and early in 1860 the work of reorganization was extended to all districts except those of the Northern Circars, where the measure was postponed till 1861. The force as now constituted consists of—

Inspector-General and Supervising Staff (3 Deputy Inspectors-General and 1 Assistant Inspector-General) ...	5
Commissioner and Deputy Commissioners, Madras Town	3
Superintendents	20
Assistant Superintendents	20
Inspectors	388
Sub-Inspectors	31
Constabulary of all ranks	22,691
Office Establishments and other servants (not Police Officers)	246
Total ...	23,404

Of the above the following are employed on purely State services :—

Salt Preventive Force	1,897
Land Customs Force	170
Jail Guards	1,143
Total ...	3,210

In addition to the above, 179 Policemen are supplied to banks, public companies, and private individuals on payment. Besides the prevention and detection of crime and maintenance of public peace and order, the Police undertake the guarding of jails, the guarding and escort of treasure, the escort of convicts, the guarding of salt-pans and platforms, the prevention of smuggling on foreign frontiers, the guarding of distilleries under the Excise Act, the protection of marine traffic in the harbour of Madras, the working of the Municipal, Cantonment, and Contagious Diseases Acts, and the serving of processes in criminal cases. The duties formerly performed by the Meriah agency in Ganjam are now performed by the Police, who occupy all the hill tracts in the Northern Circars. The Police also hold all the frontier posts formerly held by detachments of Madras troops.

CRIMINAL JUSTICE.

In former years there was a Supreme Court, presided over by Barrister Judges consisting of a Chief Justice and one or more puisne Judges appointed by the Crown, which exercised jurisdiction within the limits of the city of Madras. For the supervision of criminal justice administered in the Mofussil by the Company's Judges and Magistrates, there was again a Superior Court called the Foujdary Adalut which sat at the Presidency town. This latter Court was presided over by a chief and four other Judges, being covenanted civilians of experience taken from the judicial branch of the service. The Chief Judge was practically honorary President of the Foujdary Adalut, being one of the two Civilian members of Council. Appeals from the mofussil lay to the Foujdary Adalut. On the direct assumption of the Government of the country by the Queen, these two Courts were abolished as such, and were, by 24 and 25 Vic., Cap. 104, merged in one High Court of Judicature, with original and appellate jurisdiction, and presided over by a Barrister Chief Justice and four puisne Judges, one of whom is a Barrister and all of whom hold their appointments direct from the Queen. *Old Sudder Courts.*

The High Court exercises ordinary original criminal jurisdiction within the limits of the city of Madras, and tries all cases committed to it by the City Magistrates. Its procedure, in *High Court, Criminal Side.*

the exercise of its original criminal jurisdiction, is now
governed by Act X of 1875, entitled the High Court's
Criminal Procedure Act. By this Act it is empowered to hold
sittings on such days and at such convenient intervals as the
Chief Justice from time to time may appoint. These sittings are
presided over by a single Judge and are known as sessions, usually
held once a quarter. All prisoners committed to take their trial
before the High Court are arraigned at these sessions, and the
trial is held before a jury consisting, under the new procedure, of
nine persons, three of whom are usually Europeans. The relations between the Judge and the jury are the same as in English
law. Juries are of two kinds, common and special. All ordinary cases are tried before a common jury; but capital cases
and special cases usually those in which the Crown is directly
interested, and for which it prosecutes through the Advocate-
General, are tried before a special jury. Under Section 50 of the
High Court's Criminal Procedure Act the High Court has power
to sit at any place outside the Presidency town, and in any such
case juries have to be empannelled under special arrangements.
There is no appeal from a criminal trial before the High Court.
By its Letters Patent the High Court may exercise extraordinary
original criminal jurisdiction over all persons within the jurisdiction of any Court subject to its superintendence, and may, at its
discretion, try any such persons brought before it on charges
preferred by the Advocate-General, or by any Magistrate, or by any
other officer specially empowered by Government in that behalf.
European British subjects are committed by Justices of the
Peace to take their trial before the High Court. The High
Court has now no power to issue a writ of *habeas corpus*, but it
has somewhat analogous powers under Section 148 of the High
Court's Criminal Procedure Act; under this provision the High
Court may direct a prisoner to be brought before it to be bailed or
examined as a witness, or for other purposes. By its Letters Patent
the High Court is also invested with Admiralty and Vice-Admi-
ralty jurisdiction. As a Court of Appeal and Revision, the powers
of the High Court are prescribed by the Criminal Procedure Code,
Act X of 1872, as amended by Act XI of 1874. Appeals from the
Session Courts in the districts lie to the High Court and are heard
and determined by two Judges; but in case they differ in opinion,
the difference of opinion must be settled by adding one or more
Judges to the bench to hear and determine the appeal. All
sentences of death must be confirmed by the High Court. There
is no appeal from a judgment of acquittal; but the Local Govern-

ment are empowered by Section 272 of the Code of Criminal Procedure to direct an appeal to the High Court from such a judgment. There is also no appeal from convictions in summary trials of certain offences held by 1st-class Magistrates or benches of Magistrates with 1st-class powers, where the sentence does not exceed two months' imprisonment, or fine of 200 Rupees, or whipping only, nor from sentences passed by such Magistrates or by Session Judges in which the imprisonment awarded does not exceed one month, or the fine inflicted does not exceed 50 Rupees, or where the sentence is for whipping only. Under Chapter XXII of the Code of Criminal Procedure, the High Court exercises powers of superintendence and revision over all the Criminal Courts of the Presidency, in the matter of framing rules for their guidance, of revising their calendars and sentences, of calling for their records, and of annulling, suspending, or modifying their sentences.

In each of the districts of the Presidency, except in Malabar where there are two Courts, there is a single Sessions Court presided over by the District Judge who, in the exercise of his criminal jurisdiction, is styled the Sessions Judge. Sessions Judges are appointed and removed by the Governor in Council by virtue of the powers vested in him by Section 9 of the Code of Criminal Procedure. In the Nilgiris the Commissioner is the Sessions Judge. The Sessions Court cannot take cognizance of any offence as a court of original jurisdiction unless the accused person has been committed to it by a competent Magistrate, except when the offence has been committed before itself or under its own cognizance. Trials before a Court of Session are usually held with the aid of two or three Assessors, whose verdict however the Judge is empowered to set aside. Trials by jury also may be held before a Sessions Court, but only in those districts to which the jury system has been extended by the Government. As yet the jury system has not been extended beyond the five districts of North Arcot, Cuddapah, Godavery, Tanjore, and Vizagapatam, as it is difficult to procure the services of a sufficient number of qualified persons in the other districts. The crimes tried by juries are theft, robbery, and gang robbery, house-breaking, and receiving or concealing stolen property ; and it is to this careful selection of offences that the measure of success hitherto attained is chiefly attributable. The Sessions Court has power to pass the maximum punishment prescribed for each offence by the Penal Code, and, except in the case of death, its sentences are effectual without further reference, subject only to appeal

District Sessions Courts.

to the High Court. All capital sentences must be confirmed by
the High Court. The Sessions Court is also an Appellate Court,
as to it lie all appeals from the decisions of the District Magistrates or other Magistrates of the 1st class.

**Magisterial
Courts.**   Below the Courts of Session there are three grades of Criminal
Courts, presided over by Magistrates of the 1st, 2nd, or 3rd class.
At the head of each district is the District Magistrate, who is
also the Collector of the district. This officer is a Magistrate of
the 1st class, his Magisterial jurisdiction extends throughout the
district, all the other Magistrates in the district are subject to
his control, and he has the power of allotting the criminal work
of the district among the different Magistrates subordinate to him
and of defining their local jurisdiction. A district is divided into
divisions, consisting each of so many taluqs. At the head of each
division is one of the Covenanted Assistants of the Collector and
District Magistrate, who is invested with first-class powers, is
styled the Division Magistrate, and has control over the subordinate Magistrates within his division. The Sub-Collector of the
district, however, although a Divisional Magistrate, is styled the
Joint Magistrate. The Deputy Collector on general duty, an
Uncovenanted officer, is also a 1st-class Magistrate, and is usually
in charge of a division. Each taluq is under the Magisterial
control of the Tahsildar, who, for that purpose, is usually vested
with the powers of a 2nd-class Magistrate. He is assisted by
his Sheristadar who has third-class powers. In larger taluqs the
Deputy Tahsildar is likewise vested with the powers of a Magistrate of the 3rd class ; and in large towns there is a special Town
Magistrate with second or third-class powers as the case may call
for. All these Magistrates have various powers of ordering search,
commitment, taking of bail, &c. ; but their punitive powers
are limited as follows. A Magistrate of the 1st class may pass
sentence of imprisonment not exceeding two years, fine to the
extent of 1,000 Rupees, and whipping. A Magistrate of the
2nd class may pass sentence of imprisonment not exceeding
six months, fine not exceeding 200 Rupees, and whipping.
A Magistrate of the 3rd class may pass sentence of imprisonment not exceeding one month and fine not exceeding 50
Rupees. In addition to his other powers, a 1st-class Magistrate
may hear appeals from the decisions of Magistrates of the 2nd
and 3rd classes when so empowered by the Government.
All European Magistrates are invested with the powers of a
Justice of the Peace to enable them to deal with European British
subjects. Except in the Presidency town, no Justice of the Peace

can, under Section 72 of the Code of Criminal Procedure, inquire into a complaint or try a charge against a European British subject unless he is himself a European British subject. Justices of the Peace are appointed by the Governor in Council under Act II of 1869; and by Section 5 of this Act they have power to commit for trial European British subjects to the High Court or Court prescribed in that behalf by the law in force, and to do all other acts appertaining to the office of a Justice of the Peace. In the Presidency town the Magistrates now sit and exercise jurisdiction under a special Act called the Presidency Magistrate's Act IV of 1877. Their powers are co-extensive with those of a 1st-class or District Magistrate under the Code of Criminal Procedure. They are all Justices of the Peace, and one of them is styled the Chief Magistrate with power to regulate the conduct and distribution of business, to appoint the time of sittings, and otherwise to control the business of the Magistrates. They are not now called Magistrates of Police but Presidency Magistrates. The Commissioner of Police who, with two Deputies, administers the police of the town of Madras subject to the authority of the Inspector-General of Police, is invested with the powers of a Magistrate and Justice of the Peace under the provisions of Madras Act VIII of 1867. He does not, however, ordinarily exercise Magisterial powers. He may do so on emergency, but ordinarily his powers are limited to preserving the peace, preventing crimes, detecting, apprehending, and detaining prisoners with a view to their being brought before a Magistrate. Military Cantonments are administered by Cantonment Magistrates. These are, as a rule, Officers of the Army, and are invested with the powers of a Magistrate of a Division of a District within the meaning and for the purposes of the Code of Criminal Procedure. They are appointed by Government under Madras Act I of 1866. The Government have recently appointed certain persons in different towns to be Honorary Magistrates; these sit as Benches with the Stipendiary Magistrate as their President for the trial of certain offences. All Magistrates are appointed by the Governor in Council under Section 9 of the Code of Criminal Procedure. The lowest class of officers vested with criminal powers are the heads of villages called Village Munsifs, who, under Regulation XI of 1816, are empowered to take cognizance of petty offences of assault and abusive language, and to punish the offenders by imprisonment in the village choultry for twelve hours; or if the offenders are of the lower castes, by putting them in the stocks for not more than six hours.

Mode of collecting Criminal Statistics.

Criminal statistics are collected by the Police in the Madras Presidency in the following manner. Village Munsifs are compelled to report all crimes as they occur to their superior Magistrate and to the nearest Police Station. Beat Constables also obtain information of crimes, thus forming a check on Village Munsifs, and inspecting officers exercise a superintendence over the returns. Station House Officers report all crimes to the District Office, where the information is tested and recorded. Each Magistrate sends in to the District Police Office a monthly statement (termed Form B) of all cases dealt with or reported. These Forms B are collated with the Police reports, and discrepancies or inaccuracies form the subject of reference and investigation. Finally the annual statements compiled in District Police Offices are subjected to scrutiny in the Statistical Department of the Chief Office at Madras, and every discrepancy or apparent inaccuracy is referred back to the district for explanation.

PRISONS.

Jail accommodation.

The prison accommodation in this Presidency consists of 7 Central Jails, including the Penitentiary at Madras; 25 District Jails, including the European Prison at Ootacamund; 302 Subsidiary Jails; and 1 Jail for civil debtors at Madras. Central Jails are divided into two classes: the first class to contain 1,000 convicts and upwards; and the second class to contain less than 1,000 convicts. There are four first-class and three second-class Central Jails. The first-class Central Jails are Rajahmundry, Vellore, Trichinopoly, and Coimbatore. The second-class Central Jails are Salem, Cannanore, and the Penitentiary. Two abstract statements are appended showing the number of persons the different jails in this Presidency are constructed to contain. In the case of subsidiary jails the information is given by districts :—

STATEMENT I.—*Accommodation in each Central and District Jail.*

Jails.	Capacity of the Jail Barracks at 36 Superficial Feet per Head.			Daily Average Number of Prisoners of all Classes.		
	M.	F.	Total.	M.	F.	Total.
Russelcondah	127	3	130	107·77	3·88	111·65
Berhampore	160	32	192	172·18	13·63	185·81
Vizagapatam	282	18	300	300·40	30·53	330·93
Rajahmundry, Central ...	958	44	1,002	918·14	32·37	950·51
Do. District ...	88	18	106	89·60	12·56	102·16
Masulipatam	106	4	110	36·00	·90	36·90
Guntoor	105	15	120	92·02	9·42	101·44
Nellore	245	27	272	176·23	20·50	196·73
Kurnool	98	5	103	111·77	5·12	116·89
Bellary	388	27	415	346·26	21·47	367·73
Cuddapah	153	22	175	208·35	8·34	216·69
Chittoor	254	22	276	153·17	10·37	163·54
Vellore, Central	943	88	1,031	888·45	41·68	930·13
Salem do.	518	30	548	500·41	27·11	527·52
Guindy	87	...	87	65·25	...	65·25
Chingleput	130	29	159	149·54	9·20	158·74
Cuddalore	345	13	358	357·36	12·17	369·53
Tranquebar	116	8	124	126·70	11·84	138·54
Tanjore	169	28	197	159·35	10·87	170·22
Trichinopoly, Central ...	938	86	1,024	921·60	33·88	955·48
Do. District ...	180	18	198	147·12	·21	147·33
Madura	224	12	236	374·19	9·94	384·13
Tinnevelly	366	23	389	236·75	15·21	251·96
Cochin	29	8	37	·10	...	·10
Calicut	221	9	230	189·55	4·67	194·22
Tellicherry	161	5	166	82·49	3·26	85·75
Cannanore, Central	829	30	859	687·45	...	687·45
Mangalore	223	15	238	111·94	9·60	121·54
Coimbatore, Central ...	966	52	1,018	944·76	25·46	970·22
Do. District ...	180	...	180	195·37	·45	195·82
Ootacamund, District ...	201	12	213	155·65	2·27	157·92
European Prison ...	35	...	35	27·72	...	27·72
Penitentiary	436	45	481	398·35	50·32	448·67
Debtors' Prison, Madras ...	40	6	46	19·85	3·29	23·14
Total ...	10,301	754	11,055	9451·84	440·52	9892·36

Jails.	Total Population (all classes of Prisoners included).			Maximum Population on any one day.		
	M.	F.	Total.	M.	F.	Total.
Russelcondah	339	14	353	133	9	142
Berhampore	822	68	890	240	27	267
Vizagapatam	1,562	268	1,830	348	47	395
Rajahmundry, Central	1,395	57	1,452	1,005	36	1,041
Do. District	653	78	731	114	13	127
Masulipatam	152	6	158	49	1	50
Guntoor	499	41	540	119	16	135
Nellore	743	108	851	220	21	241
Kurnool	576	31	607	155	10	165
Bellary	1,370	87	1,457	434	22	456
Cuddapah	969	45	1,014	257	11	268
Chittoor	872	77	949	191	13	204
Vellore, Central	1,240	68	1,308	949	51	1,000
Salem do.	1,399	103	1,502	563	29	592
Guindy	228	...	228	81	...	81
Chingleput	797	44	841	179	10	189
Cuddalore	1,272	60	1,332	407	23	430
Tranquebar	621	67	688	166	21	187
Tanjore	758	52	810	193	12	215
Trichinopoly, Central	1,270	99	1,369	963	40	1,003
Do. District ...	610	3	613	167	1	168
Madura	1,777	45	1,822	482	16	498
Tinnevelly	1,148	67	1,215	280	21	301
Cochin	3	...	3	3	...	3
Calicut	1,082	34	1,116	263	5	268
Tellicherry	551	10	561	119	5	124
Cannanore, Central	933	...	933	708	...	708
Mangalore	563	46	609	137	13	150
Coimbatore, Central	1,239	58	1,297	999	26	1,025
Do. District	814	14	828	214	1	215
Ootacamund, District	388	34	422	189	3	192
European Prison	46	...	46	31	...	31
Penitentiary	2,385	379	2,764	558	92	650
Debtors' Prison, Madras	533	77	610	35	4	39
Total ...	29,609	2,140	31,749		...	

STATEMENT II.—*Subsidiary Jail Accommodation in each District.*

Districts.	Number the Jails will hold.			Average Daily Number of Prisoners in all the Jails put together.		
	Males.	Females.	Total.	Males.	Females.	Total.
Ganjam ...	437	269	706	85·73	24·20	109·93
Vizagapatam ...	194	147	341	138·71	27·67	166·38
Godavery ...	147	111	258	71·64	16·73	88·37
Kistna ...	137	75	212	66·19	25·09	91·28
Nelloro ...	98	49	147	33·05	16·34	49·39
Kurnool ...	141	85	226	57·32	17·23	74·55
Bellary ...	130	50	180	22·00	1·98	23·98
Cuddapah ...	107	42	149	50·82	3·54	54·66
North Arcot ...	206	93	299	89·98	12·10	102·08
Salem ...	214	120	334	76·07	7·14	83·21
Chinglepnt ...	376	200	576	48·80	3·91	52·71
South Arcot ...	274	108	382	79·20	13·82	93·02
Tanjore ...	225	80	305	74·29	14·44	88·73
Trichinopoly ...	185	89	274	36·64	6·84	43·48
Madura ...	137	72	209	92·02	20·25	112·27
Tinnevelly ...	232	77	309	81·11	11·14	92·25
Malabar ...	322	155	477	69·72	2·84	72·56
South Canara ...	126	50	176	39·25	9·17	48·42
Coimbatore ...	157	74	231	78·94	12·84	91·78
Nilgiri Hills ...	4	4	8	·24	·08	·32
Grand Total ...	3,849	1,950	5,799	1255·08	240·81	1495·89

CIVIL JUSTICE.

The administration of Civil Justice is under the exclusive **High Court,** superintendence of the High Court, constituted by 24 & 25 **Civil Side.** Vic., Cap. 104, and by Letters Patent. The High Court consists of a Chief Justice and four Puisne Judges ; the Chief Justice and one of the Puisne Judges being Barristers appointed by the Queen from the Bar of the United Kingdom, and the other Judges being members of the Civil Service appointed by Her Majesty on the nomination of the Local Government. The High Court exercises ordinary original jurisdiction over all suits the cause of action in which has arisen within the limits of the city of Madras, and it exercises appellate jurisdiction over all Civil Courts established throughout the Presidency. Original cases in the High Court are decided by a single Judge, from whose decision there is an appeal which is ordinarily heard and determined by a division bench consisting of two Judges. In the

same manner appeals from the Mofussil Courts are heard and
determined by a division bench of two Judges ; but in any case in
which the two Judges differ in opinion, the appeal is re-heard
and finally determined by a full bench consisting of three or
more Judges. By its Letters Patent the High Court possesses
powers of extraordinary original jurisdiction, in the exercise of
which it can call up and determine any suit within the jurisdiction of any Court subject to its superintendence. By
paragraph 17 of its Letters Patent (1862) it has power to hold
sittings under a single Judge for the relief of insolvent debtors
at Madras ; such Judge exercising, within and without the city
of Madras, such powers and authorities with respect to original
and appellate jurisdiction and otherwise as are constituted by the
laws relating to insolvent debtors in India. By its Letters Patent
the High Court also possesses Admiralty, Testamentary, and
Matrimonial jurisdiction.

Madras Small Cause Court.
All small suits of 1,000 Rupees and below that value within the
Presidency town are cognizable, and may be summarily determined
by the Madras Court of Small Causes sitting under Act IX of
1850, and consisting of a First Judge who is a Barrister, and
three other Judges who are as a rule appointed from the ranks of
the Uncovenanted Service. Questions of title cannot however be
decided by the Small Cause Court ; and all suits involving
title or affecting landed property in any way are carried into the
High Court, irrespective of the value in litigation.

District Courts.
In each of the districts into which the Presidency is divided
there is a chief Court styled the District Court, which is presided
over by a District Judge appointed from the Covenanted Civil
Service. In Malabar there are two Courts of this class, styled
respectively the District Court of North Malabar and the
District Court of South Malabar ; and in the Nilgiris the chief
Court is that of the Commissioner who sits as the District
Judge under a special enactment. The District Court is both
an Original Court and an Appellate Court, and by Section 27
of the Madras Civil Courts Act III of 1873 the District Judge
is vested with general control over all the Civil Courts of whatever grade established in his district, subject however to rules
prescribed for the purpose by the High Court. All appeals in
suits decided by the inferior Courts in which the amount litigated
is 5,000 Rupees and less, lie to the District Court ; but where
the amount or value of the subject-matter of the suit exceeds
5,000 Rupees, the appeal lies to the High Court direct under
Section 13 of the Act above mentioned.

The Court next in importance to that of the District Judge is Subordinate
the Court of the Subordinate Judge, formerly styled a Principal Courts.
Sadr Amin, who is usually a native officer belonging to the
Uncovenanted Service. The pecuniary jurisdiction of this officer
is co-extensive with that of the District Judge, whose Assistant he
really is in the disposal of original and appellate work. Subordinate Judges are appointed to districts in which the civil work is
unusually heavy. There is one Subordinate Judge in Bellary,
South Canara, Madura, and Salem, two in each of the districts
of Godavery, Tanjore, and Tinnevelly, and three in Malabar ; or
13 Subordinate Judges in all. Although the jurisdiction of a
Subordinate Judge is as large as that of the District Judge, the
latter is empowered by law to remove to his own Court any suit
or appeal which he may for any reason see fit to dispose of
himself ; and in the same manner the District Judge is
empowered to refer to the Subordinate Judge for disposal any
suit or appeal filed in the District Court. By Section 28 of the
Civil Courts Act the Government may invest any or all of these
Subordinate Judges with the jurisdiction of a Judge of a Court
of Small Causes for the summary trial of suits up to the amount
of 500 Rupees ; as a fact most of the Subordinate Judges are
invested with such powers.

At the five stations of Cuddalore, Vellore, Madura, Comba- Up-country
conum, and Masulipatam there is a Court of Small Causes held Courts.
under Act XI of 1865, with ordinary jurisdiction over small
suits up to 500 Rupees in value, but which jurisdiction the
Government may extend to 1,000 Rupees. These Judges are also
invested with the powers of a Subordinate Judge for the trial of
suits of any value by regular procedure, the decisions in which
are accordingly open to appeal. The Judges at Cuddalore,
Vellore, and Madura are at the present moment members of the
Covenanted Service, and the other two Judges are Uncovenanted. In Military Cantonments the Cantonment Magistrate
is generally invested by Government, under Madras Act I of
1866, with the powers of a Court of Small Causes with a
pecuniary jurisdiction not exceeding 500 Rupees.

As a Court proper, with all the functions of a regular judicial District
tribunal, the Court of the District Munsif is the lowest in Courts.
grade, but it is at the same time the most important to the
country, as it is widely distributed, and is thus the chief Court
of first instance open to the people. There is generally one such
Court at the head-quarters of every taluq of a district, and the
District Munsif's territorial jurisdiction is as a rule conterminous

with the taluq. The District Munsif is usually a native officer
of experience who has risen in the subordinate ranks of the
Judicial Department; but of late years he has been appointed
in many instances from the ranks of the native bar, having
previously undergone a "special test" examination as prescribed
for the grade. The District Munsif's jurisdiction extends to
suits, the value of which does not exceed 2,500 Rupees; and in
most cases he is invested with a Small Cause jurisdiction over
suits up to 50 Rupees in value. There are at present 113 such
officers located at different stations in the districts.

Village Munsifs' Courts and Punchayets. A still lower Court is that of the Village Munsif, established
by Regulation IV of 1816, to meet the simple requirements of
a village community. The head of the village is under the
Regulation *ex-officio* Village Munsif; local custom however
sometimes has it otherwise. The Village Munsif's judicial
powers extend to suits for personal property up to 10 Rupees,
his decisions not being open to appeal; if the parties consent, he
may try and determine similar suits up to 100 Rupees in value in
the character of an arbitrator, and when the litigant villagers
wish such a course, he has power under Regulation V of 1816
to summon a punchayet, generally of five persons, to decide suits
for personal property without limitation as to value. Under
Regulation XII of 1816 Collectors of Districts may summon
punchayets through the Village Munsifs, and may, with the
consent of parties, refer to such punchayets the settlement of suits
respecting the occupying, cultivating, and irrigating of land
between proprietors or renters and their ryots; as well as
claims to crops and lands and cases of disputed boundary.

Revenue Courts. Collectors, Sub-Collectors, and Assistant and Deputy
Collectors in charge of a Division sit as Revenue Courts and
exercise judicial powers under the following Regulations:—(a),
Regulation IX of 1822, on charges against native servants of
the Collector's public establishment, heads of villages, curnams
and their gumastahs and other village officers and servants, for
exacting or corruptly receiving money for the performance of
official acts, levying unauthorized cesses or extra collections for
their private use, embezzling public money, falsifying, destroying,
or concealing public accounts or other documents relating to the
receipt or expenditure of public money; (b), Regulation VI
of 1831, regarding claims to hereditary village offices in the
Revenue and Police departments, and to the emoluments attached
to these offices. The ordinary Courts have no jurisdiction in
regard to such claims; (c), Act VIII of 1865, Madras, regard-

ing disputes between landlord and tenant in which no question
of title is involved.   The Revenue Courts have power under the
latter Act to enforce the terms of a tenancy to compel the
exchange of puttahs and muchilkas, to settle the rates of assessment or rent, to order sales under distraint, to award compensation for damages in such distraint, to arrest defaulters, and to
eject tenants.   These Courts, however, do not possess jurisdiction
when any question of title to the land itself is raised in the course
of such a suit.

When a suit is instituted against Government, or against
Collectors or their subordinates for acts done in their official
capacity, a report containing the facts of the case, for the
accuracy of which the Collector is responsible, is submitted to
the Board of Revenue with copy of the plaint and of the draft
answer which it is proposed to file.   When the Board consider
the suit defensible they are empowered to sanction its defence
at the public cost unless the value of the suit exceeds Rupees
1,000, or unless there is some important principle involved, in
which cases the matter is submitted for the orders of Government.   Difficult and doubtful cases are referred for the advice
of the Government law officers.   In simple suits between
Government ryots for the transfer of puttah in which the
Collector is made a defendant *pro formâ* in view to registration,
the defence may be undertaken by him without reference to
higher authority.   When a suit is decided the result must be
reported to the Board and copy of the decree and judgment
submitted, and when the decision is adverse to Government the
report must be submitted in time to admit of orders being
passed as regards an appeal in such course is deemed advisable.
No formal application is required for sanction to defend suits
regarding claims to waste lands under Act XXIII of 1863, but a
report of the institution of the suit is submitted for the information of Government.   Suits against Government and Collectors
are chiefly of the following description : (*a*), for the cancellation
of sales for arrears of revenue under Madras Act II of 1864;
(*b*), for transfer of puttahs and registration of lands ; (*c*), disputes
regarding irrigation rights ; (*d*), claims to waste land assigned
by Government to parties under the rules for the disposal of
assessed waste ; (*e*), claims to house sites in the gramanattam or
village site.   In the great majority of cases the decision is in
favor of Government.

Suits against Government and Government Officers in the Revenue Department.

REGISTRATION.

In the year 1834 the Court of Directors of the East India Company proposed the enactment of a law making registration of deeds relating to immovable property compulsory under such penalties and safeguards as might be deemed requisite. Legislative proposals were accordingly made, and the subject was referred from time to time to various Committees, until in 1864 a Bill containing the main substance of the present law on the subject was passed as Act XVI of 1864. This Act has since undergone several modifications (*vide* Acts IX of 1865, XX of 1866, XXVII of 1868, and VII of 1871), and the law as at present administered is contained in Act III of 1877.

The Act just mentioned provides the machinery necessary for registration, lays down the duties and powers of the different classes of officers, declares what are registrable documents and the effects of registration and non-registration, and prescribes the mode, time and place of presentation and registration. The principle of the Act is the same as that of the law previously in force, No. VIII of 1871, but the new enactment has effected several detailed alterations. The main feature in the Registration law is the distinction of registrable documents into those which must be registered in order to obtain validity or what are called compulsory documents, and those which it is in the option of the parties to register or not as they think fit. Documents under the first head lose all validity if not registered. In the case of documents falling under the second head it is provided that a registered document of the same class shall take priority over a non-registered one. To remove a technical doubt the present Act also provides that all registered documents, whether compulsory or not, shall take priority over non-registered documents.

For registration purposes the Presidency is divided into 22 districts and 276 sub-districts. With the exception of Malabar, which is divided into two registration districts, Calicut and Tellicherry, the districts are conterminous with the limits of the Revenue Collectorates. The sub-districts are also, as a rule, co-extensive with the taluqs and the divisions of Deputy Tahsildars and Sub-Magistrates. The Government were originally in favor of employing the existing Judicial Agency, wherever practicable, in performing the work of registration, but the idea after due consideration was abandoned. The department is now administered by 22 Registrars and 276 Sub-Registrars under the control and supervision of an officer styled the Inspector-General of Registration. Fourteen of the Registrars are Deputy Collectors in charge of the District Treasuries, while the remaining eight are officers specially appointed. Of the Sub-Registry offices 200 are presided over by Taluq Tahsildars and Sub-Magistrates, and 76 by persons specially appointed. Originally all Registering officers and their establishments were paid by a commission on the fees collected, but this mode of remuneration is being gradually superseded by a system of fixed salaries and commission. The fourteen official Registrars are divided into three grades and remunerated by certain fixed allowances in addition to the salaries they draw as Deputy Collectors. The Special Registrars, who are Sub-Registrars as well at the head-quarters of the districts to which they are appointed, are divided under a scheme recently sanctioned into six grades and paid by fixed salaries varying from 50 to 500 Rupees and by a commission of 20 per cent. on the amount of fees collected by them after the first 30 Rupees. The Special Sub-Registrars also are distributed into six classes and remunerated partly by a fixed salary and partly by commission ; the former ranging from 30 to 100 Rupees and the latter being at the same rate as that allowed to the Special Registrars. The official Sub-Registrars receive a commission of 20 per cent. as personal remuneration on the fees they collect and 25 per cent. for their establishments and contingencies. The special Registering officers are, as a rule, chosen from among the graduates and under-graduates of the Madras University, and they are required to acquire a practical knowledge of their duties in the central office before taking up their appointments.

MILITARY.

The constitution of the Madras Army is as follows :—

General constitution of the Army.

2 Regiments of British Cavalry ;

2 Batteries of Royal Horse Artillery ;

11 Batteries Field Artillery ;

8 Batteries Garrison Artillery ;

A Heavy Battery is stationed at Secunderabad and a mounted Battery at Tonghoo ;

9 Regiments British Infantry ;

> The Queen's Own Sappers and Miners consisting of 10
>   companies;
> 4 Regiments Native Cavalry;
> 40 Regiments of Native Infantry of the above Force ;
> 5 Batteries of Artillery ;
> 2 Regiments of European Infantry ;
> 1 Company of Sappers and Miners ; and
> 5 Regiments of Native Infantry are serving in British
>   Burma ; and
> 1 Regiment of Native Cavalry and
> 5 Regiments of Native Infantry in the Bengal Presidency.

The Army is divided into 3 Divisions and 6 Brigades as under.
The commands of 1 Division and 2 First-class Brigades are held
by officers of the British service, and those of 2 Divisions, 2
First-class, and 2 Second-class Brigades by officers of the
Indian service.

Divisions.

Hyderabad Subsidiary Force.
Mysore Division.
British Burma Division.

First-class Brigades.

Centre District.
Nagpore Force.
Ceded District.
Northern District.

Second-class Brigades.

Southern District.
Malabar and Canara.

Commissariat. The executive of the Commissariat Department consists of
1 Commissary-General, 1 Deputy Commissary-General, 5 Assistant, 6 Deputy Assistant, and 11 Sub-Assistant Commissaries-
General. The head-quarters and the principal office and stores
are at Madras. The Amrut Mahal, or Government Cattle
Breeding Establishment, at Hoonsoor in Mysore is under the
control of this department, and supplies draught bullocks for
the army, the herds maintained averaging about 10,000 head of
cattle.

Ordnance. The head-quarters of the Ordnance Department is also at
Madras and is under the administration of the Inspector-General
of Ordnance and Magazines, 1 Deputy Inspector-General, and
7 Commissaries of Ordnance. The Gun Powder and Gun Carriage

Factories, each under a Superintendent, are at Madras. A Bullet Factory is attached to the Gun Carriage Factory, and a Laboratory and Percussion Cap Factory are maintained at St. Thomas' Mount. The Camp Equipage Depôt is at Madras. The Grand Arsenal is at Fort St. George; there is an Arsenal at Secunderabad, Magazines at Bangalore, Rangoon, and Nagpore, and Ordnance Depôts at St. Thomas' Mount, Trichinopoly, Bellary, and Cannanore.

The Army Clothing Department is located in Madras, and supplies the whole of the Madras Army, European and Native. The material is obtained from England and is made up under contract by native workmen. The sewing machine is now largely used. **Army Clothing.**

The Remount Depôt at Oossoor, about 30 miles from Bangalore, is under the superintendence of an Agent, assisted by a Veterinary Surgeon and a small European staff. It contains accommodation for 1,000 horses. The average number of horses purchased annually is about 600, a large proportion of which are Australians, which are principally required for Artillery and British Cavalry. The Northern and Persian horse is generally allotted to the Native Cavalry. The average price paid to dealers per horse is about Rupees 530, and, on transfer to the ranks, their assumed value is Rupees 700. **Remount.**

The Medical Department consists of two branches, the British and Indian. The former has 1 Surgeon-General, 4 Deputy Surgeons-General, 26 Surgeons-Major, and 49 Surgeons. The duties of this branch are connected solely with the medical care of the European troops. The Indian Medical Department has 1 Surgeon-General, 6 Deputy Surgeons-General, 82 Surgeons-Major, and 92 Surgeons. A large proportion of the officers and subordinates of the Indian Medical Department are employed on civil duties, and the medical care of the Native troops is also provided for by this department. The Government are kept informed of the state of the health of the army by periodical returns furnished by the Surgeons-General of both departments, and by the reports of the Sanitary Commissioner. Further particulars on these heads will be found in Chapter VI. **Medical.**

The army schools, which are maintained for both European and Native troops, are under the management of a Commissioned Superintendent, one Assistant Superintendent, and two Sub-Inspectors. **Educational.**

The head office for the payment of pensions and family payments is at Madras. The number of pensioners throughout **Pensions, &c.**

the Presidency is about 32,000, and the number of families receiving remittances from the troops in Burma and beyond the frontier is about 3,000.   They are all paid monthly.

MARINE.

Marine Department.
The Marine Department of the Presidency is presided over by the Master Attendant of the Port of Madras.   The local executive duties in connection with the conservancy of the port, as well as those of Shipping Master, are performed by the Deputy Master Attendant.   The Head of the Marine Department is the adviser of Government on all marine matters, and is vested with the control and audit of the marine expenditure pertaining to his own department, or incurred on account of freight and passage in connection with the Military and Civil offices.   It is his duty to arrange the programme of yearly reliefs by sea; and to exercise a general superintendence over vessels engaged for the conveyance of Government troops, passengers, stores, specie, or mails.   He is also Registrar-General of Shipping for the Presidency, and Superintendent of Marine for the whole seaboard.   The duties of out-port Masters Attendant and Conservators are similar to those of the Deputy Master Attendant at Madras.   They are required to enforce obedience to all port rules, and see that the provisions of the Conservancy, Passenger and Merchant Shipping Acts, Imperial and Indian, are properly observed.   They enforce quarantine regulations, and by virtue of their office are Government Surveyors of Shipping.   They sit also as nautical assessors in Courts of Inquiry held with reference to shipwrecks, and are Landing and Shipping Agents for Government consignments.   Some of these officers are Magistrates of the 1st or 2nd class and Justices of the Peace, their functions in this respect being confined to the trial or adjudication of offences against maritime law.

Eastern Group.

Ganjam.	Madras.
Gopaulpore.	Cuddalore.
Calingapatam.	Porto Novo.
Bimlipatam.	Tranquebar.
Vizagapatam.	Negapatam and Nagore.
Cocanada and Coringa.	Tuticorin.
Masulipatam.	

Western Group.

Cochin.	Cannanore.
Calicut and Beypore.	Mangalore.
Tellicherry.	

The pearl and chank fisheries in this Presidency are connected **Tinnevelly** with the Marine Department inasmuch as they are under the **Chank and** superintendence at present of the Master Attendant of Tuticorin; **Fisheries.** they are treated however as a branch of Revenue and are administered by the Revenue Board. The Tinnevelly chank or conch-shell fishery was some years ago carried on under Government management, the shells being sold to private persons who exported them to Bengal. About eighteen years ago a change was made in the management and the right of fishery was sold for a term of years. This plan was found to be undesirable, and in 1864 a system of licenses was introduced, which has been continued up to date. It is in contemplation to revert to the plan of Government management. The value of this fishery to Government is from 4,800 to 6,000 Rupees per annum. There is no outlay for establishment and no expenditure of any sort. The price paid for the right of fishing has been Rupees 20 per 1,000 shells, but this is probably a very low figure. The pearl banks on the Tinnevelly coast are of very ancient origin. The old head-quarters were at the Ramnad promontory, but for the last two centuries the head-quarters have been at Tuticorin, ninety miles north-east of Cape Comorin. In 1822 the Tuticorin pearl fishery contributed about Rupees 1,30,000 to the revenue, and in 1830 the yield was worth about Rupees 1,00,000. Between this and 1861 there were no fisheries, as the beds seemed to be exhausted. The causes assigned were the widening of the Paumben channel which increased the current and the interference of the chank divers. In 1856 an examination was made, the results of which showed the possibility of a fishery in 1861. Two fisheries actually took place in 1861 and 1862, the total amount realized being Rupees 3,78,581; since then, although oyster spat has on several occasions fallen on the banks, there has been no oysters. There is a prospect however of a fishery in 1880. These pearl fisheries are conducted entirely on account of Government. The divers employed being given one-third of all oysters they bring up subject to certain rules. The Government share of the oysters is sold by auction at so much per 1,000. The steamer *Margaret Northcote* and the boats *Pearl* and *Edith* form a guard establishment at the pearl

PROTECTION.

banks, the steamer being used for other duties when not required for inspection there. No crews are at present entertained for the *Pearl* and *Edith*, and the latter boat has been lent to the Marine Department at Paumben until her services are again needed.

AGRICULTURAL.

Wild Animals.

The Government offer rewards for killing elephants, tigers, cheetahs, bears, wolves and hyænas. Collectors pay the rewards on production of the skin, or other satisfactory evidence. Cheetahs and hyænas form the most frequent cases.

Road Avenues.

Road avenues are in most cases under the charge of the Local Fund Boards, nearly all the roads in the country being undertaken by them. Where this is not the case Collectors take charge of the avenues.

LOCAL FUNDS ADMINISTRATION.

Nature of Circles and provisions of Act.

In the Madras Presidency the Local Funds properly so called are constituted and administered under Madras Act IV of 1871. The whole of the Presidency outside the limits of municipal towns, and with the exception of the Jeypore Zemindary in Vizagapatam, and the Hill Maliahs in Ganjam, was brought under the operation of the Act immediately on its passing. The country was under the Act divided into circles, in each of which a Local Fund Board was constituted. The Collector of the district is under the Act ex-officio President of each Board situated within his jurisdiction, and the members of the Board are appointed by Government under the restriction that non-official members must be appointed in numbers at least equal to those holding Government appointments. The circles at first constituted were thirty-six in number; the districts of Nellore, Kurnool, Trichinopoly, the Nilgiris, and South Canara formed each one circle; the district of Bellary had three; and the remaining fourteen districts two each. In 1872-73 the two circles in Coimbatore were amalgamated, and the division

of the Godavery District was revised so as to make the
river the boundary between the circles. From the beginning
of 1875-76 the two circles in Vizagapatam have been amalgamated, so that the number now in existence is thirty-four.
The Madras Local Funds Act repealed the District Road Cess
Act III of 1866 and the Education Act VI of 1863. The
former imposed a cess not exceeding half an anna in the rupee
on the rent-value of occupied land to constitute a fund for
the construction and maintenance of local roads. The latter
enabled the inhabitants of a locality to tax themselves for the
upkeep of schools. On the repeal of these Acts the existing
funds and the charges appertaining to local roads and to
schools were transferred to the newly-constituted Local Funds.
The new Local Funds Act provided for the imposition of a cess
similar to the District Road Cess, but with a maximum of
1 Anna; for the establishment of tolls upon roads; and for the levy
of a house-tax. Two-thirds of the cess and the whole of the tolls
were made applicable exclusively to roads and communications,
and the house-tax was declared available for schools only, and was
to be imposed only in villages or groups of villages in which
schools existed or were about to be established. The objects
to which local funds were made applicable were described in
the Act to be—(I), the construction, repair, and maintenance
of roads and communications; (II), the diffusion of education,
and with this object in view the construction and repair of
school-houses, the maintenance of schools either wholly or by
means of grants-in-aid, the inspection of schools and the training
of teachers; (III), the construction and repair of hospitals,
lunatic asylums, choultries, markets, tanks and wells; the
payment of all charges connected with the objects for which such
buildings have been constructed; the training and employment of
vaccinators and medical practitioners; the sanitary inspection of
towns and villages; the cleansing of the roads, streets and
tanks; and any other local works of public utility calculated
to promote the health, comfort, and convenience of the people.
The Act also provided for the transfer to Local Fund Boards
of public dispensaries, choultries, tanks, &c., endowed and
unendowed; for vesting the endowments in the Boards; and for
enabling the Board of Revenue to transfer to them the powers of
control of charitable endowments conferred by Regulation VII
of 1817.

Immediately upon Act IV of 1871 being passed, the land cess **Assets of**
was levied at the maximum rate in all districts except Godavery, **Circles.**

Kistna, Kurnool, Chingleput, North Arcot, Tanjore, Madura,
and Tinnevelly, where it was fixed at 9 Pies. In 1873-74 the
rate was raised to 1 Anna in the Chittoor Circle, and in 1874-75
to the same rate in Vellore: both in the North Arcot District.
The house-tax under the same Act was imposed at first in those
areas in which taxes had been levied and schools maintained
under Act VI of 1863, but was discontinued under the orders of
Government from the beginning of 1873-74, since which date the
Union Funds referred to in the Act have been abolished. In the
first year only 9 new toll-gates were established, but the number
has since been considerably increased. The figures below show
the total number of tolls maintained in each year for the last
five years, including those which in Malabar and Canara are
kept up otherwise than under Act IV of 1871:—

1871-72	47 tolls.
1872-73	51 „
1873-74	55 „
1874-75	65 „
1875-76	72 „

In addition to the sources of revenue just mentioned, the Local
Fund Circles have hitherto received an annual grant from
Provincial Funds for the special relief of the funds devoted to
the construction and maintenance of Imperial Roads. They
possess also the endowment funds pertaining to the trusts of the
endowed institutions handed over to them under the Act; and
there are certain other assets, such as a share in surplus pound
receipts, ferry rents, fishery and grass rents, &c., which have
been made over to them by the Government under conditions.
The Provincial grants for the last four years are shown below,
and side by side the outlay made by the circles in the same
years on the roads in question:—

Year.	Provincial Grants for Roads.*	Outlay on Imperial Roads.†
	RS.	RS.
1872-73	11,52,115	13,58,591
1873-74	11,74,402	13,06,916
1874-75	11,57,527	13,51,546
1875-76	11,52,624	12,75,213

Charges on Circles. The passing of the Local Funds Act was, though not consequent on, yet coincident with, the decentralization scheme of

---

* Including establishment grant.   † Excluding establishment charges.

Provincial finance described further on under Chapter V. The
grants made on that occasion towards the control of certain services
being less than the past expenditure on those services, the
Madras Government was compelled to transfer a considerable
burden of charge from Provincial Funds to the Local Funds
constituted under Act IV of 1871. Upon what is technically
known as the Road Fund was laid the cost of the construction
and maintenance of all roads, &c., formerly provided for from
the Imperial grant under Communications, with a corresponding
charge for Public Works Department Establishment. The
charges provided for in the original Public Works Budget of
1871-72 for Communications and so transferred amounted to
Rupees 11,27,996. The old District Road Fund paid 10 per
cent. on outlay as a contribution for Public Works Department
Establishment; but in 1871-72 the charge, which was arbitrarily
fixed, was Rupees 5,59,083 and at the rate of 18·96 per cent. on
the outlay. In 1872-73 and 1873-74 a system was in force under
which the cost of the Public Works Department Establishment
was rateably distributed amongst the several funds from which
outlay was incurred after deduction of certain portions of the
cost of establishments maintained for special purposes, these being
charged in full to the funds concerned. The percentage charged
to Road Fund was in 1872-73 28·97 per cent., and in 1873-74
24·70. In 1874-75 a fixed rate of 25 per cent. on the outlay
effected through the Public Works Department was introduced
and has since been enforced. These arrangements regulated also
the charge for Public Works Department Establishment on
account of outlay from the other branches of the Local Fund.
Under education it was resolved to lay upon Local Funds the
whole charges incurred within Local Fund Circles in connection
with elementary education; and in pursuance of this decision,
the cost of Inspecting Schoolmasters, two-thirds of the cost of
Deputy Inspectors and certain contributions towards the cost of
Normal Schools were at first imposed on Local Funds. The last
two classes of charge were resumed as Provincial in 1874-75.
Local Funds bear all grants, salary and results, made to
schools of the lower class; but grants paid by Government to
schools established under Act VI of 1863 and transferred to
Local Boards continue to be credited to Local Funds. The
institution of Local Funds has given a great stimulus to primary
instruction, and the sums expended upon it are yearly increasing.
A modification of the results-grant system has been introduced,
whereby the permanence of the school is secured by the grant
of a small salary to the master, which is supplemented by results

grants, so that the master's remuneration still depends to a great extent upon his exertions. Further particulars on this head will be found under Chapter VII. Various charges in connection with medical services were transferred to Local Funds in 1871-72. The whole charges for vaccination, and for the salaries of medical subordinates, cost of medicines, &c., borne by Government in dispensaries endowed and unendowed are now transferred to Local and Municipal Funds. Local Funds contribute also in aid of dispensaries situated in Municipalities. When the medical subordinate in charge of Local Fund Dispensaries is the only one in the station, the Government have been in the habit since 1872-73 of contributing one-fourth of his salary, on condition that his services are available for Government employés at the station. The number of endowed dispensaries is ten only, but the number of Local Fund Dispensaries has increased to a very great extent. In the statement given below are noted the number of dispensaries under Local Fund Boards in each year, and also the total number and income of endowed institutions transferred to them in accordance with the provisions of the Act :—

	Dispensaries endowed and unendowed.	Endowed Institutions.	Endowment Revenue.
			Rs.
1871-72 ...	20	139	45,420
1872-73 ...	34	135	74,842
1873-74 ...	45	196	2,42,806
1874-75 ...	60	208	2,30,585
1875-76 ...	75	202	2,80,454

The travellers' bungalows and choultries throughout the country were, with one or two exceptions, transferred to the local boards in 1872-73 and 1873-74. The administration of the Vaccination Department was in 1874 handed over to such local boards as were willing to receive it, and payment by results as well as other schemes for stimulating operations have since been adopted. The accounts of Local Fund Boards are audited by the Examiner, Public Works Accounts, for Public Works, and by the Accountant-General for other charges. Each Local Fund Circle has its budget, which is reviewed in detail by the Revenue Board and Government. The financial control rests with the latter.

MUNICIPAL ADMINISTRATION—MOFUSSIL.

Municipal action in the rural parts of this Presidency may be said to date originally from the passing of Act XXVI of 1850, which authorized inhabitants of towns to raise voluntary taxes for sanitary and other public purposes. Little use was made of this enactment. The next Act of a municipal nature was the Towns Improvement Act X of 1865. The Government had for some time had under consideration the expediency of requiring the inhabitants of towns, who under the fiscal arrangements in force up to that time contributed a far smaller proportion to the general revenues than the inhabitants of the rural districts, to defray a portion of the cost of the Town Police, with the view both of reducing the charge which its maintenance entailed upon the State and so increasing the sum available for the general Police, and of providing funds for placing the Police in towns upon a more efficient footing than had hitherto been practicable. It was pointed out at the time that the moneyed and trading classes who resided and carried on their business in towns did not pay their fair share of taxation, and that at the same time, owing to the number of persons congregated in a small space, and the increased facilities for crime which were thereby occasioned, the expense of Police protection was greater in town than in country. The original intention was to make compulsory only that part of the taxation which was required to defray Police charges, while the raising of a rate for the purposes of conservancy or other purposes of local improvement was to be left optional with the rate-payers, the consent of a majority of whom should in each case be requisite. It was eventually decided however to include among the purposes for which the funds raised under the Act must necessarily be appropriated, the construction, repair, and maintenance of roads, drains, tanks, &c., and the carrying out of all measures necessary for the preservation of the public health. The Commissioners were provided with means of taxation, and the Government were held liable to pay a contribution amounting to 25 per cent. of the sum spent by the Commissioners on the objects above named. In addition to the funds raised for the purposes so specified, the committees were empowered to raise and expend with the previous sanction of Government such additional amounts as might appear to them necessary for

Marginal note: Historical Survey— Former acts.

other municipal purposes, for instance, the lighting of the town, the prevention or extinction of fire, the supply of water, &c.

—Act of 1871. The Act of 1865 was gradually introduced into all the more important towns, and in 1869-70 was in successful operation in 44 cases. In 1871 it was considered that the Act needed revision, and in Act III of 1871 certain changes were made of considerable importance. The introduction of the financial system known as the " decentralization scheme," which will be found described further on under Chapter V, operated to accelerate the passing of Act III of 1871, but did not materially influence its contents. The Act of 1865 contained a restriction which prevented the appointment as Municipal Commissioners of persons not residing within the limits of the Municipality. Experience had shown that the occasional presence of a European officer as a working member of the Commission was essential to the efficient working of the Act, and it was therefore considered advisable that the Government should have the power of appointing any officer they might think proper, subject to a limitation as to the proportion of official persons who should be members of these Commissions. It was also thought right to substitute the Revenue Officer in charge of the division of the district in which the town was situated for the Executive Engineer as an ex-officio Commissioner. It was considered important that Revenue Officers of all grades as the administrative agents of the Government should identify themselves with the successful working of municipal institutions within their respective ranges, and that they should regard the duty as forming an essential part of their official functions. The qualification for appointment to the office of Municipal Commissioner was also made more elastic, and provision was made for introducing the system of appointment by election whenever the Government might deem it proper to apply that system to a particular Municipality. The particular rules under which the latter arrangement is to be carried out are still under consideration. One of the most important provisions of the new Act was the application of municipal funds to certain educational and other purposes, which, though essentially of a local character and such as might properly be met by local taxation, did not come under the provisions of the Towns Improvement Act of 1865. Such for instance was the construction and maintenance of hospitals, the training and employment of medical practitioners, sanitary inspection and the collection of statistics of births and deaths. It was

considered of great importance that larger funds than were then
available should be provided for all these objects, and it was held
to be essential that these funds should be raised by local taxation.
The inclusion of education among the purposes to which municipal
taxation was to be applied had the effect of making compulsory
that which had previously been done in some towns by the voluntary action of a majority of the inhabitants under the provisions
of Madras Act III of 1863; the working of this Act had shown that
nothing short of a system of compulsory taxation would suffice for
any considerable extension of primary education among the people.
The Act of 1871 where introduced supersedes the Act of 1863.
Since the passing of the Act of 1871 it has been made a rule of
practice that the education undertaken by Municipalities shall
be of the " primary " description, that is to say, that it shall not
proceed farther than the third of the four standards laid down by
Government in the " Results Grant-in-aid " Rules. In addition to
the above, vaccination and the registration of births and deaths
within the limits of the town devolved on the Municipalities
constituted under the new Act. Another important change was
the withdrawal of the 25 per cent. grant which under the Towns
Improvement Act of 1865 the Government was bound to contribute in aid of the charges for Police and Conservancy. It was
at first designed that the Municipalities should be required to pay
the whole of the charges for conservancy and other municipal
purposes excluding Police, and 60 per cent. of the Police charges.
The system in force in Provincial Municipalities would thus have
been very nearly assimilated to that in the Presidency town,
where the Municipality contributed 50 per cent. of the Police
charges. These considerations did not however ultimately prevail,
and it was finally decided to withdraw the State aid altogether, to
relieve Municipalities from all Police charges, and to leave the
municipal powers of taxation in much the same condition as
they were before. The motive for withdrawing the grants-in-aid
was chiefly a financial one. The measure effected a net annual
saving to Imperial or Provincial Funds of about one lakh and
a half of Rupees. Moreover it would have been impossible
to extend the system of State grants to the new system of
taxation for local purposes, which was at the same time inaugurated in the rural districts, and there was no valid reason for
retaining the grant-in-aid system in the one case and discarding
it in the other.

To sum up the present situation of the Mofussil Municipalities, **Present**
Act III of 1871 has superseded Act X of 1865. By the change **situation.**

27

the Municipalities have gained in the direction of having no longer
to contribute 75 per cent. to public charges; they have lost
however in having had thrown on them four new charges, namely,
those for hospitals and dispensaries, for schools, for birth and
death registration, and for vaccination.   Each Municipality has
a Board or Commission presided over by the Collector of the
District, and this Board administers the Act under the supervision of the Government.   The Board is composed of official and
non-official members, the former being not more than one-half of
the whole number.   The Revenue Officers in charge of recognized
divisions of districts are ex-officio members of the Commissions
situated within those limits.   The members are appointed for a
term of three years subject to removal for misconduct or neglect
of duty.   Provision is also made for election by the rate-payers.
The Vice-President may either be appointed by Government or
elected by the Commissioners.   The taxes authorized by the Act
are—(1), rates on houses, buildings, and lands not exceeding $7\frac{1}{2}$
per cent. on the annual rent value ; (2), a tax on arts, professions,
trades, and callings varying from Rupee 1 to Rupees 100 ;
(3), a tax on carriages, horses, and other animals varying from
Annas 4 to Rupees 9 half-yearly ; (4), a fee not exceeding Rupees 2
half-yearly for the registration of carts ; and (5), tolls on carriages,
carts, and animals entering the municipal limits varying from
1 Anna to 1 Rupee.   In addition to the above, fees are leviable
for the use of markets, slaughter-houses, and cart-stands and
for the exercise under license of offensive or dangerous trades.
Rates on houses, lands, or buildings and tolls may be recovered
by distress and sale of the movable property of the defaulter or
the movable property on the premises, but in the case of the
other taxes payment can only be enforced by prosecution before
a Magistrate.   Since the passing of Act III of 1871 three
additional Municipalities have been constituted, making the total
number of towns at the end of 1875-76 forty-seven.

Statistics.   The following tables give statistics regarding the forty-seven
Mofussil Municipalities for a recent average year :—

TABLE I.—*Taxation and Incidence.*

Municipalities.	Census Population.	Income from Taxation.	Incidence of Taxation including Tolls.			Incidence of Taxation excluding Tolls.		
		RS.	RS.	A.	P.	RS.	A.	P.
Adoni	22,723	11,712	0	8	3	0	6	1
Anantapore	4,918	5,119	1	0	7	0	5	6
Bellary	51,766	47,338	0	14	7	0	9	0
Berhampore	21,670	13,058	0	10	1	0	5	0
Bimlipatam	8,744	10,698	1	3	7	0	2	10
Calicut	47,962	25,279	0	8	5	0	7	5
Cannanore	31,358	17,069	0	8	9	0	8	0
Caroor	7,945	8,056	1	0	2	0	7	1
Chellumbrum	15,519	11,438	0	11	9	0	5	6
Chicacole	15,587	7,639	0	7	10	0	2	5
Cocanada	17,839	19,053	1	1	1	0	9	10
Cochin	13,840	6,833	0	7	10	0	7	10
Coimbatore	35,310	22,098	0	10	0	0	6	1
Combaconum	44,444	34,958	0	12	7	0	5	11
Conjeveram	37,327	17,555	0	7	6	0	5	4
Coonoor	3,058	4,086	1	5	4	1	5	4
Cuddalore	40,290	25,354	0	10	1	0	5	1
Cuddapah	16,275	13,191	0	12	11	0	6	8
Cumbum	7,295	3,234	0	7	1	0	3	7
Dindigul	12,865	7,501	0	9	4	0	3	5
Ellore	25,487	7,476	0	4	8	0	1	10
Erode	7,817	5,789	0	11	10	0	8	11
Ghooty	6,730	4,800	0	11	5	0	4	10
Guntur	18,033	17,652	0	15	8	0	8	11
Kurnool	25,579	14,189	0	8	10	0	4	9
Madura	51,987	39,621	0	12	2	0	5	2
Manargudi	17,703	12,336	0	11	1	0	3	10
Mangalore	29,712	16,867	0	9	1	0	8	0
Masulipatam	36,188	19,347	0	8	6	0	5	1
Mayaveram	21,165	14,399	0	10	10	0	6	2
Negapatam	48,525	39,381	0	13	0	0	9	0
Nellore	29,922	15,483	0	8	3	0	5	11
Ootacamund	9,982	15,313	1	8	7	1	8	7
Palamcottah	17,945	10,983	0	9	10	0	3	11
Palgaut	30,752	16,496	0	8	7	0	2	5
Rajahmundry	19,738	11,040	0	8	11	0	6	0
Salem	50,012	29,288	0	9	4	0	6	2
Srirangam	11,271	8,871	0	12	7	0	12	7
Tanjore	52,175	35,329	0	10	10	0	4	10
Tellicherry	20,501	11,594	0	9	1	0	6	10
Tinnevelly	21,014	11,838	0	9	0	0	3	7
Trichinopoly	76,530	47,657	0	9	11	0	7	10
Tuticorin	10,565	15,879	1	8	0	0	11	10
Vellore	38,022	30,320	0	12	9	0	4	7
Vizagapatam	32,191	21,071	0	10	6	0	4	8
Vizianagram	20,169	11,800	0	9	4	0	3	2
Wallajapett	12,103	7,354	0	9	9	0	4	0

TABLE II.—*Proportion to* 100 *of different outlays.*

Municipalities.	Outlay on Grant I—New Works and Repairs.	Outlay on Grant II—Education.	Outlay on Grant III—Sanitation and Medical Services.	Outlay on Grant IV—Lighting, Markets, and Miscellaneous Public Improvements.	Outlay on Grant V—Executive.	Advances and Refunds.	Closing Balance.
Adoni ...	15	5	30	5	7	...	38
Anantapore ...	13	11	50	11	12	...	3
Bellary ..	29	5	46	10	9	...	1
Ghooty ...	19	7	49	8	13	...	4
Conjeveram ...	18	7	43	9	8	5	10
Caroor ...	36	3	41	7	8	...	5
Coimbatore ...	14	2	35	10	7	23	9
Erode ...	21	3	47	12	7	5	5
Cuddapah ...	21	5	44	10	11	3	6
Berhampore ...	22	11	36	7	11	...	13
Chicacole ...	24	9	43	3	9	...	12
Cocanada ...	35	3	36	11	13	...	2
Ellore ...	33	3	32	3	12	...	17
Rajahmundry...	27	2	42	6	5	6	12
Guntoor ...	16	7	46	9	8	1	13
Masulipatam ...	18	6	49	16	8	2	1
Cumbum ...	9	10	56	3	16	...	6
Kurnool ...	17	1	47	23	8	...	4
Dindigul ...	38	5	25	14	9	...	9
Madura ...	19	1	37	14	3	1	25
Calicut ...	18	4	62	6	8	1	1
Cannanore ...	17	4	52	11	11	...	5
Cochin ...	17	19	43	9	11	...	1
Palghaut ...	55	7	14	3	6	...	15
Tellicherry ...	27	14	38	2	11	...	8
Coonoor ...	21	1	37	11	12	7	11
Ootacamund ...	45	3	16	15	6	2	13
Nellore ...	15	10	47	14	8	...	6
Vellore ...	34	3	31	15	5	...	12
Wallajapett ...	30	9	35	12	14	...	...
Salem ...	25	8	54	5	7	3	−2
Cuddalore ...	34	2	41	11	7	...	5
Chellumbrum ...	15	2	36	6	16	1	24
Mangalore ...	41	2	26	11	7	1	12
Combaconum ...	28	6	35	5	6	...	20
Mayaveram ...	29	12	29	10	7	...	13
Manargudi ...	28	2	39	11	7	...	13
Negapatam ...	39	1	30	7	5	...	18
Tanjore ...	37	6	25	13	8	...	11
Palamcottah ...	15	4	47	18	9	...	7
Tinnevelly ...	12	7	46	13	21	...	1
Tuticorin ...	42	1	40	11	6	...	...
Srirungam ...	35	3	40	9	6	...	7
Trichinopoly ...	37	2	35	17	5	1	3
Bimlipatam ...	28	2	47	11	7	...	5
Vizagapatam ...	19	9	43	7	12	...	10
Vizianagrum ...	39	5	36	3	17	...	...
Average ...	28	5	38	10	8	1	10

MUNICIPAL ADMINISTRATION—MADRAS TOWN.

The Municipality of the Town of Madras dates its origin from **History and** the passing of Statute 33, George III, Chapter 52, Section 158, **constitution.** and may therefore be said to be an old-established institution, though it was only in 1856 that the public functionaries administering the funds were first styled Municipal Commissioners. The Act of 1856 was superseded by Act IX of 1865, and this in its turn gave way to Act IX of 1867, which, with a slight amendment effected by Act V of 1871, is still in force. The Municipality is divided into eight divisions. Four persons residing within the limits of each division are appointed by Government to be Commissioners for that division. The Commissioners hold office for three years, subject to removal for misconduct or neglect of duty. Provision exists for election by the rate-payers, but has not yet been carried out in practice. The entire executive power is vested in the President who is appointed by Government and paid from Municipal funds. An Executive Engineer, a Sanitary Inspector, an Assessor, and a Collector of Municipal Taxes also hold their appointments direct from Government and are removable at their pleasure. All other paid officials are appointed by the President, subject to the approval of the Municipal Commissioners when the salary exceeds Rupees 150 per mensem.

The taxes leviable under the Madras Municipal Act are— **Nature of** (1), a tax on carriages, horses, and other animals varying from 4 **taxation, &c.** Annas to 12 Rupees half-yearly ; (2), fees not exceeding 2 Rupees half-yearly for the registration of carts and other vehicles without springs ; (3), tolls on carriages, carts, and animals entering the municipal limits varying from 6 Pies to 4 Annas ; (4), a tax on arts, professions, trades, and callings classified as follows :—

Class I.—Persons with incomes ranging from
Rs. 150 to Rs. 350 yearly.

Do.	II.—	Do.	do.	„	100 do.
Do.	III.—	Do.	do.	„	50 do.
Do.	IV.—	Do.	do.	„	25 do.
Do.	V.—	Do.	do.	„	12 do.
Do.	VI.—	Do.	do.	„	4 do.

(5), licenses for the sale of spirituous liquors varying from Rupees 12 to Rupees 75; (6), sea tolls on boats or rafts calculated on the tonnage at the rate of 4 Annas per ton ; and (7), rates on houses, buildings, and lands not exceeding 10 per cent. on the estimated gross annual rent at which they might reasonably be expected to let from year to year. The above rates and taxes are all in force with the exception of sea tolls, the house rate being levied at 7½ per cent. Rates and taxes may be recovered by distress and sale of the goods and chattels of the defaulter, and any person carrying on his profession or trade without registration is liable, on conviction before two Magistrates, to a penalty not exceeding three times the amount payable for a registration certificate. Appeals against assessments are heard and determined by two Magistrates, who are empowered to state a case for final decision by the High Court. Under Act IX of 1867 the Town Police were paid from Municipal funds, but they were relieved of this charge by Act V of 1871, which, at the same time, extended the application of the Municipal funds to purposes of education, the establishment of hospitals, vaccination, and other works of local public utility. The population of nearly 400,000 inhabitants among whom the taxation is distributed are scattered over an area of 27 square miles.

Income and Expenditure for eight years. The following statements show for the past eight years the income, incidence of taxation, expenditure, and other particulars for this Municipality. Previous to 1871-72 the municipal accounts were kept for the calendar year. Column 7 in Statement I refers to the taxation authorized by the Act and not to all sources of income:—

TABLE I.

Years.	Population.	Number of Members of Committee.			Total Income from all Sources.	Incidence of Taxation per Head of Population.			Amount of Debt.
		Official.	Nominated.	Total.					
1	2	3	4	5	6	7			8
					RS.	RS.	A.	P.	RS.
1868 ...		13	19	32	7,35,077	1	4	6¾	...
1869 ...		9	23	32	7,05,063	1	0	9¾	50,000
1870 ...		9	23	32	6,13,371	1	2	6⅜	1,25,000
1871-72 ...	397,552	9	23	32	5,71,346	1	1	8¾	10,19,571
1872-73 ...		10	22	32	5,22,407	1	0	6¹⁄₁₆	12,60,000
1873-74 ...		9	23	32	5,91,343	1	0	0	14,28,000
1874-75 ...		12	20	32	5,36,292	1	0	2	14,30,000
1875-76 ...		12	20	32	6,08,218	1	2	3¼	14,30,000

TABLE II.

Years.	Total Expenditure.	Sinking Fund for reduction of Debt for Water-supply Project.
1	2	3
	RS.	RS.
1868	5,17,283	...
1869	6,52,921	...
1870	5,44,663	1,011
1871-72 ...	5,62,406	13,457
1872-73 ...	5,19,794	10,292
1873-74 ...	5,21,684	13,144
1874-75 ...	5,16,573	19,098
1875-76 ...	5,93,885	27,278

SECTION IV.

PRODUCTION AND DISTRIBUTION.

AGRICULTURE.

Description of Cultivable lands. THE land in every Government village, as plotted out by the old original Peimash or Survey, or by the operations of the recent Revenue Survey and Settlement, falls into two main divisions, the uncultivable portion and the cultivable. The former goes by the general name of poramboke, and consists of various classes of land which from one cause or another are uncultivable or not likely to be cultivated, such as hills, rocks, jungles, and other lands not naturally cultivable; and of lands reserved for public purposes, viz., village sites, roads, beds of tanks, channels, cattle stands, burial grounds, &c. As has already been explained in Section II no revenue is realized from poramboke lands, except a few miscellaneous items; it is not classified or assessed by the Revenue Settlement Department, and it is only surveyed by the Survey Department when it consists of small blocks interspersed in cultivable lands. In the case of all portions of a village area which are considered to be in any way likely to be cultivated, whether on the irrigated or unirrigated system, the land is surveyed and marked off into distinct numbers or fields by the Survey Department, each field is examined and classified by the Revenue Settlement Department, and the amount of Government due or assessment chargeable thereon is fixed and placed on record. Any one taking up this land knows in advance that he will have to pay so much and no more in the form of Government assessment upon it; this land is consequently called the assessed land, or sometimes the ayacut or cultivable area of the village. Assessed land will, of course, include Inam lands, though the terms made with the Inamdar are for the moment special, and full assessment is not levied. It is not often that the whole of the assessed land in the village has already been taken up by cultivators. In each village there may be said therefore to be a portion of assessed land

which is offered but has not yet been taken up, and which forms
the margin of cultivation, being always of poorer soil than the
rest of the ayacut ; this is otherwise called assessed waste.
Villages have communal rights of grazing over assessed waste.
Deducting this portion, the remainder of the ayacut consists of
lands in the occupation of cultivators, and for the most part
actually cultivated by them ; this is called the cultivated area.
In some cases the lands will from one cause or another be left
temporarily waste by the occupiers, who will not nevertheless
resign them. These occasional waste portions are ascertainable
from the cultivation accounts ; they can therefore be deducted and
the remainder will represent the area actually under crops. The
following figures show to a certain extent the proportion of
acreage belonging at a recent date to each of these four main
classes of lands for an area of, say, 65,664,000 acres. The whole
area of the Presidency is 88,523,520 acres, but the balance consists
of lands for which particulars of cultivable or uncultivable lands
are not known, lands lying outside villages, forest lands, &c.
The four classes of lands are of course locally interspersed, and
the division is merely a paper division :—

		ACRES.
1. Poramboke or uncultivable	... ...	23,964,160
2. Assessed waste not occupied	... ... }	
3. Assessed land occupied but not cultivated }		14,183,329
4. Assessed lands under crops	... ...	27,516,511
	Total ...	65,664,000

The word "ayacut" is most usually employed in the phrase
"wet ayacut," when speaking of the area irrigable by a
particular tank.

The greater part of the Madras Presidency is covered with Distribution
soils that were originally formed by the disintegration of rocks of of soils, as
the metamorphic and igneous systems. The soils derived from agriculture.
the rocks of the first-mentioned system, gneiss, mica, quartz, &c.,
which prevail the most widely, are very inferior ; especially when,
as is the case in many parts of Southern India, they occur as
sedentary soils, that is to say, when they rest on the rock from
which they were originally formed. The extensive ranges of
mountains known as the Pulneys, Anamallais, and Neilgherries
are composed of granitic rocks, the decomposition of which,
especially where the felspar occurs as orthoclase, affords a
productive soil in situations where the rainfall is not excessive.
The minor ranges of hills, of which there are many scattered

over the Presidency, consist chiefly of syenite and quartz rocks ; the former yields on decomposition a productive soil, but the soils derived from the latter are always inferior, and sometimes perfectly sterile.   Stretching across the country in a north-east direction from Trichinopoly there is a wide belt of green sand, which affords a highly productive soil.   The area of sedentary soil derived from inferior rocks is very considerable, but it fortunately happens that, owing to the gigantic scale on which the forces of nature have operated in Southern India, there is a wide extent of transported soils, formed of the disintegrated portions of the rocks of other formations.   Of this class is the black cotton soil, an alluvial soil met with all over the Presidency, sometimes in isolated patches of only a few acres in area, and sometimes in large plains of hundreds of square miles.   The depth of this soil varies from 12 inches to from 12 to 15 feet.   It is closely allied to the black earth of Southern Russia, and evidently occupies the sites of dried-up lakes.   From its unusual power of absorbing and retaining moisture, is in great request.   Another characteristic soil met with in all parts of the Presidency is the red soil, so called from its peculiar red appearance, derived from a large admixture of the peroxide of iron.   This soil differs very considerably in its character ; in some places forming extensive plains with a hard crusted surface almost incapable of producing even indigenous vegetation, and in other places being friable, open, easily worked, very hygroscopic from the oxide of iron it contains, and generally fertile.   As a rule, the most fertile tracts of land occupy low situations ; most of them are of alluvial origin, and from the facilities they afford for irrigation, they generally form the irrigated area.   The land most in need of irrigation from its extreme dryness and the natural poverty of its original constituents, is obviously the most difficult to provide with irrigation water, but such land constitutes three-fourths of the food-producing area of the country.

The seasons with reference to cultivation.   The most important cultivating season of the year in the greater part of the Presidency begins with the first rains that inaugurate the north-east monsoon ; this is generally about the end of September, the sowing month being October and the harvest month February.   Over the other portions of the Presidency the crops are raised under the influence of the rains accompanying the south-west monsoon, and in this case the sowing is performed in the months of April and May, while the crops are harvested in August and September.   All cultivation, whether artificially irrigated or not, depends more or less on the monsoon seasons. Land irrigated from wells is naturally the least so, and land irrigated from tanks, which do not in all cases get their supply from the immediate rainfall, are more independent than unirrigated land. The unirrigated land is absolutely dependent on the falling rain. Irrigated land, especially that under wells, has sometimes two crops in the year. Two crops can be got off unirrigated land only in certain highly favored localities.

Irrigated land forms about 15 per cent. of the area under occupation. It is watered exclusively from rivers, river channels, and tanks, and in most instances the water flows upon the land by gravitation. The area of land irrigated directly from rivers is extremely small compared with the area watered from river-channels. The reason of this is that the beds of most of the rivers on the plains are so frequently changed, or are situated in such deep valleys that it is difficult to get the water thence to the cultivated land. Hence the practice of putting dams or anicuts across rivers. Dams are constructed where there is space for the storage of water, and where the water can be raised to a height sufficient to command a suitable area of arable land. From the dams the water passes along channels to the cultivated land; the beds of these channels being kept so high that the water will flow by gravitation through sluices into the minor distributing channels. In many instances the irrigation water cannot be secured at a sufficient height, and the water is then raised from the channel by a picottah or similar means. Tanks are always placed in situations where the surface drainage of a more or less considerable area of country naturally flows or collects. Sometimes they are natural and form shallow lakes; but as a rule they are artificial and occupy a situation on land having a slight slope. In selecting the position for a tank the object is to secure for the upper slope a large collecting area and to command on the lower slope a sufficient area of arable land for watering by gravitation. Artificial tanks are always more efficacious than natural tanks equally supplied with water, because the land irrigated from the artificial tank is from its position generally well drained, while that irrigated from the natural tank is frequently altogether without drainage, being but a portion of the bed of some original lake. The only crop grown on this description of land is paddy. Where an abundance of water is available throughout the year, two crops are grown annually, but most of the land as already said produces

Treatment of irrigated land.

only one crop. The irrigation water is usually supplied
on each occasion to a depth of from 1 to 2 inches, and the
supply is made according to its abundance on every day,
every other day, or every third day, during the growth of
the crop. In many parts of the Presidency the practice
is to sow the paddy broadcast on a semi-liquid soil
which is brought into this state by frequent waterings and
stirrings. The practice is also common of transplanting
young seedling paddy plants from nursery beds into the field.
Beyond weeding and watering, the paddy land receives no
attention while under crop. Some varieties of paddy are six
months on the ground, others only four months. The crop is
cut when dead ripe, and is thrashed by striking the sheaves
on a log of wood or by the treading of cattle. The agricultural
practice in dealing with irrigated land is said to be capable
of improvement in the direction of a more economical use of
the water; as long however as the ryot is unable to apply
manure to his irrigated land he is under the necessity of using
a large quantity of irrigation water in order to secure silt in
its places. There are many practical difficulties in the way of
procuring manure; there is also a deficiency of capital to
invest in it.

Treatment of unirrigated land. Eighty per cent. of the food-producing area of the Presidency
consists of dry land. A very large area of these tracts is
covered by soils of the lowest value; there are however
considerable areas of really good soil. The dry lands are in
the hands of poorer cultivators than the wet lands, and it is
probable that their cultivation is more susceptible of
improvement than that of the wet lands. The black soils are
usually cropped with cotton and cholum. The red soils are
variously cropped; in some districts they constitute the chief
cotton-producing areas, but when good they are cropped with
the different cereals. The grey soils produce varagoo, korraloo,
and inferior cumboo, cholum, &c. Sometimes two or even
three crops are sown simultaneously on the same ground, so
that if one fails the other may succeed; choice being made
of crops that do not all bear at one time. The crops
grown on the unirrigated land are sown both broadcast and
in lines, but the former is more usual. The tillage consists
usually of ploughing in various directions; the native plough
stirs but does not turn over the soil and seldom penetrates
to a greater depth than three inches. The seeding is always
heavy, and there is probably a waste of seed. The actual

operation of sowing is either performed by broadcasting the
seed over the land by the hand, or by the aid of a drill formed
of three or four bamboo tubes connected at the top to a fixed
hopper into which the seed is placed and from which it passes
through the bamboo tubes into the soil.   During the growth of
the crop but little is done in cultivations or hoeings.   The crops
are all harvested by the hand, the work being paid for in kind.

Grass is encouraged to grow spontaneously in all parts of **Treatment of**
the village area where it will not interfere with other crops, but **pasture land.**
special grass-crops raised from seed, or developed by irrigation,
are as yet very rare in this Presidency, the remuneration not
proving sufficient.   Ryots will frequently leave permanently
uncultivated the least productive portions of their holdings
for the sake of giving a better pasture to the live-stock
required for farm labor than is to be got in the poramboke
land.   Or they will leave the land temporarily fallow in the
same way, with a view to combining pasture with fertilization
of the soil.   With the exception however of certain cases,
yearly diminishing, where a light assessment is placed on
arable land reserved for pasture, the ryots have to do this
at their own expense, paying full assessment for the lands thus
employed.   The principle of deriving remuneration from grass
and fodder crops in the form of farm manure will doubtless be
more acted upon as capital increases.   There is no want of
intelligence on the part of the cultivator.

Garden land is land irrigated with water artificially raised from **Treatment of**
wells, tanks, or other sources.   The crops usually grown are **garden lands.**
those that will mature satisfactorily with from five to eight
waterings in a month.   The water is raised by cattle-power and
manual-power only, horse-power or steam-power being not yet
in use.   For very low lifts a bale is used, that is to say, a bucket
suspended by two ropes, one of which on either side is held
by a man.   In baling the bucket is allowed to drop into the
water and when full swung up to the height needed, where a
third man who stands in the water catches and capsizes it.   For
higher lifts, up to about 12 or 13 feet, the picottah is used.   This
is a horizontal pole balanced on an upright post of a height regulated by the length of the horizontal pole.   The arrangement
is something like that of the ordinary weighing balance.   At
the end of the horizontal pole which projects over the water, an
upright rod is attached, generally of bamboo, and to the lower end
of this the bucket is fastened.   In working the picottah, an
alternate up-and-down motion is given to the arms of the

horizontal pole, a bucket being brought up each time the pole dips and rises. The motion is generally produced by the backward and forward walk of a man along the pole ; as he advances along the pole towards the water the bucket dips and fills, and as he walks back in the contrary direction, it rises to the required elevation, and is there guided and capsized by another laborer. Where the lift is great two and sometimes three men are employed on the horizontal pole. In cases where the lift is moderate a man on the pole is frequently dispensed with, a heavy ball of clay only being attached to the end of the pole opposite to that at which the bucket rod is attached. In this case a single man stands over the well, pushes down the bucket, guides it, and capsizes it at the point of discharge. For low lifts the picottah works at a very moderate cost, especially when worked by the cultivator himself. In well lifts, which are too high for the picottah, that is to say, for depths from 12 to 40 feet, the " Kavalay " is usually employed worked by cattle. This arrangement consists of a horizontal roller fixed over the well on uprights of three or four feet in height while a rope travels over the roller ; at one end of the rope a skin bucket is attached, and the other end is fastened to the yoke of a pair of cattle. At the place where the water is to be discharged from the bucket there is a cistern, and in front of the cistern an inclined path of 20 or 30 feet in length according to the depth of the water. When raising the water the cattle walk down the slope, and when the bucket descends to the water they are backed up again. In this way, the cattle alternately ascending and descending the slope, the bucket is filled and brought to the surface. The arrangement is very simple, but is rude and probably cruel to the cattle, the backward journey being often up a very steep slope. The cost of raising the water by this method is high. An improved lift has lately been introduced, by the aid of which it is anticipated that the water will be raised at one-half the cost. It is very desirable that garden cultivation should be extended, as a check on disastrous consequences of long continued droughts. At present about two per cent. of the occupied area of the Presidency is what is called " garden land." The crops grown are tobacco, sugar-cane, chillies, wheat, the ordinary cereals, &c.

Rotation of crops and fallows.

There is no established system of rotatory crops, but the principle of not overstraining the resources of the soil is fully understood by the ryots. A crop requiring little nourishment generally succeeds an exhausting crop, and fallows are common in the case of inferior soils. The liberty allowed to the ryots of relinquishing and taking up lands frequently brings the principle of leaving lands fallow into imperceptible play. Rotation and fallows are practised mainly in regard to unirrigated lands, and irrigated lands planted with sugar-cane ; in the ordinary irrigated lands, which generally consist of small holdings, manuring is more frequent and is considered sufficient to secure a good crop without rotation. Considerable care is bestowed on manuring garden lands under wells. Lands near villages are better manured than those at a distance, for obvious reasons.

The following statement shows the proportion existing between **Extent of** different species of crops throughout the Presidency at a recent **cultivation.** date :—

Food-grains	84·0
Seeds	5·2
Green and garden crops	1·8
Topes and orchards	2·2
Special crops, such as cotton and indigo, &c.	6·8
	100

The following statement giving the acreage under cotton in **Cotton** each district during a recent average year will show the cotton- **cultivation.** producing powers of the different parts of the Presidency :—

Districts.	Acres.
Ganjam	3,302
Vizagapatam	13,107
Godavery	10,348
Kistna	219,267
Nellore	18,378
Cuddapah	76,074
Bellary	385,596
Kurnool	243,637
Madras	...
Chinglepat	3
North Arcot	263
South Arcot	16,303
Tanjore	4,061
Trichinopoly	6,731*
Madura	95,101
Tinnevelly	281,569

* Does not include area of cotton cultivated with other crops.

Districts.				Acres.
Coimbatore			...	184,517
Nilgiris	...	...	...	...
Salem	..	...	...	12,630
South Canara	...	...		164
Malabar	...	...	...	... ...

Total   ... 1,571,587

—Cotton experiments.

During the last few years several experiments have been made with cotton of different varieties on the Farm at Sydapet. The soils of the Farm are very sandy, insoluble silica constituting nearly 90 per cent. of their entire weight, while the percentage of plant-food they contain naturally is extremely small. These soils are therefore much inferior to the "cotton" soils of Southern India, which are alluvial in their character and contain a moderately large percentage of clay and organic matter. It was only by the judicious use of manure that fair results were obtained in cotton culture at Sydapet. The following varieties of cotton were experimentally grown with the results noted :— WESTERN.—A 5-acre field sown with this variety of cotton and maize in alternate lines yielded 1,766 lbs. of seed cotton equal to 353 lbs. per acre, and this was in addition to a fair crop of grain and straw from the maize plants that grew in alternate lines with the cotton plants. HINGINGHAUT AND BUNIE.—These varieties are grown largely in Bombay, where they are said to be highly appreciated. At Sydapet the results obtained with them differed but little from those yielded by ordinary "Western" seed. YEA VALLEY.—This valuable species of cotton grows well at Sydapet and produces a lint that is long, white and silky, resembling very much the cotton lint imported into England from the Fiji Islands. But unfortunately the Yea Valley cotton plant has almost died out at Sydapet from the repeated attacks of a borer which confined its depredations to this species of cotton. Arrangements are, it is believed, in operation for obtaining a fresh supply of seed from Brazil. NEW ORLEANS.—This species of cotton has been grown with considerable success at the Farm, a return per acre of from 100 to 180 lbs. of clean lint in addition to a fair crop of maize having been frequently obtained. This species of cotton is probably peculiarly adapted for cultivation under an improved system of farming; indigenous varieties are very liable to run to stem and leaf under the influences of manure while the returns from this species of cotton are always large when manure is liberally used. The plant seems however to have two or three objectionable characteristics; it bears at very uncertain intervals, and produces gatherings that vary greatly in amount, while the harvest is spread over several months, thus necessitating a considerable expenditure in gathering the crop and in keeping down the weeds, which from the open shade the cotton affords grow very freely amongst it; but these defects also, to a certain extent, characterize indigenous varieties of cotton. Crops sown in September do not begin to bear until the following March, and the plants must remain on the ground until the end of August or the beginning of September to admit of a fair return being obtained. As in the Cotton States of America the sowings are made in April and May, and the whole of the harvest is over before the end of December, it is probably desirable that a supply of fresh seed should be obtained from the Southern States, preference being given to the Mexican variety, from which the true New Orleans variety is said to have originated. It is said that the ordinary black-seed New Orleans cotton was introduced into America from India. It appears desirable that a maize or cholum crop should always be sown with the cotton crop in alternate lines; in this way the food-producing area of the country is not lessened by a larger area of land under cotton, nor will the returns from the area under cotton be materially diminished if the cultivation is properly conducted. The cholum and maize plants grow upright and do not interfere with the early growth of the cotton plants, and before the cotton plants begin to throw out lateral branches, the maize or cholum will be ready for harvesting. The New Orleans plant was treated as a biennial, but the results were not satisfactory, the cotton of the second year being much less in quantity while its fibre was harsh and short. EGYPTIAN.—This species of cotton has yielded very fair results at Sydapet, though as yet it has been cultivated there only on a very limited scale. Its cultivation is somewhat costly, as the plant throws out many lateral branches, thus preventing the use of cattle in weeding the land; but it is hoped that by sowing only the seed of the most upright-growing plants this habit may in time be overcome. The lint produced is soft and silky, and it separates readily from the seed. The experiments above described afford ground for thinking that with due care and a judicious use of manure the cultivation of foreign cotton of finer quality than the indigenous cotton of local origin can be successfully introduced into this country. It is desirable, however, that further experiments should be tried on a larger scale both on the Government Farm at Sydapet and on the District Farms when established, and the matter engages attention.

Indigo cultivation.   The following is a statement for indigo similar to that given above for cotton :—

Districts.					Acres.
Ganjam ...				...	986
Vizagapatam	...				3,803
Godavery	...			...	1,730
Kistna ...	...	...	...	...	42,975
Nellore ...	...	...	...	...	57,519
Cuddapah	...		...	...	62,824
Bellary	...		...	...	10,358
Kurnool ...	...	...	...	...	40,556
Madras ...	...	...	...	...	...
Chingleput	...	...	...	...	5,157
North Arcot	...	...	...	...	13,728
South Arcot	...	...	...	...	61,318
Tanjore ...	...			...	472
Trichinopoly	...		...	...	837
Madura ...	...	...	...	...	72
Tinnevelly	...	...	...	...	245
Coimbatore	...	...	...	...	...
Nilgiris ...	...	...		...	...
Salem ...	...	...		...	2,087
South Canara				...	...
Malabar ...				...	...
Total				...	304,676

Wheat cultivation.   The cultivation of wheat in this Presidency is very limited, and is chiefly confined to six districts as shown below :—

Districts.					Acres.
Kistna ...	...		...	...	2,145
Cuddapah	...	...	...	...	2,283
Bellary ...	...	...	...	...	3,387
Kurnool ...	...	...	...	...	5,557
Coimbatore	...	...	...	...	2,108
Nilgiris ...	...	...	...	...	3,199
All other districts		...	...	...	667
Total				...	19,346

The quantity of wheat exported to Foreign Ports and British Ports beyond the Presidency during 1875-76 was 8,764 cwt., value Rupees 36,292.

The principal coffee tract of Southern India is along the **Coffee planting.** Western Coast, and coffee estates extend in nearly an unbroken line along the summits and slopes of the Western Ghauts from the northern limits of Mysore down to Cape Comorin. The only portions of the area within the limits of the Madras Government are the Wynaad tract and the Nilgiri Hills. Coffee plants were introduced as a curiosity into the Wynaad about fifty years ago by Major Bevan; the first regular plantation was opened out by Mr. Glasson in 1840 on a hill at Manantoddy, and was soon followed by others. Nearly all the land taken up at this period was what is known as grass or bamboo land, and in consequence most of the estates proved unprofitable. Of many of them not a trace except the ruins of bungalows remains at the present day. After the first attempts coffee cultivation was transferred to South Wynaad. For ten or fifteen years it made little progress. In 1855 and 1856 a number of new estates were opened out, some too hastily and consequently with little success. In 1862 the returns showed 9,932 acres under cultivation. In 1865 there were 200 estates covering 14,613 acres. An official inquiry was made on the subject of Wynaad coffee in the year 1868, and according to the returns then made the average was 29,909·08, of which 21,479·54 acres were held by Europeans and 8,429·54 acres were held by natives. Subsequent returns have shown no increase in the acreage until quite recently when high prices have stimulated cultivation. The following table showing the quantities of Wynaad coffee shipped on the Malabar Coast during a period of twelve years indicates nearly all the crops, as very little passes out by Mysore or Coimbatore :—

Years.					Cwts.
1856-57	...	...	...	...	32,658
1857-58	...	...	...	...	20,416
1858-59	...	...	...	...	36,934
1859-60	...		...	...	49,680
1860-61	...			...	...	48,742
1861-62	...	...	...	...	...	91,080
1862-63	...	...	...	...	...	43,907
1863-64	...	...	...	...	...	91,947
1864-65	...	...	...	...	...	110,548
1865-66	...		...	...	125,891
1866-67	...	...	...	...	...	66,552
1867-68	...	...	...	...	...	128,011

Coffee cultivation on the Nilgiris was reported on in 1872. A large area of land on the Nilgiris has proved to be admirably suited for the cultivation of the coffee shrub. Not less than 13,000 acres are now under coffee plantations, whereas twenty years ago the area under this crop did not much exceed 500 acres. This great increase is entirely the result of private enterprise, and has added much to the prosperity of the Nilgiris, while at the same benefiting the districts immediately adjoining. In the establishment of these coffee estates a property has been created worth about five millions of Rupees, on which the annual expenditure cannot be less than two millions of Rupees. Of the total expenditure about one-third is for the payment of wages to coolies; and most of this is carried into the low country, either in payment for food grains consumed by plantation coolies, or as cash carried by the coolies themselves when they return to their homes. Estimating that the sum sent into the low country in this way represents annually Rupees 6,00,000, this will support about 14,000 families of laboring people. Moreover in carrying coffee to the coast, and in sorting, packing, &c., a large amount of other labor is employed. Until a few years previous to 1850 the coffee plantations in this district were found only on the eastern slopes, but they have now been extended to the southern, northern, and north-western slopes; there are also some extensive plantations in the Ouchterlony Valley and in the neighbourhood of Coonoor. Coffee cultivation has also been commenced on the Shevaroy Hills in the Salem District, and on the Pulney Hills in Madura. An official investigation is about to be made into the whole question of coffee cultivation in this Presidency.

Tea planting.   Tea cultivation has not the same interest in Southern India as coffee cultivation, and there are few plantations except on the Nilgiris. The tea plant was introduced on these hills nearly forty years ago, but it is only during the last ten years that any real progress has been made in the cultivation. The experiments made between 1835 and 1840 were useful in proving that the tea plant would thrive on the hills, but little else resulted from them, though the opinions frequently expressed by Mr. John Sullivan and Monsieur Perrottet, and founded on these experiments that the greater part of the district was well suited for tea culture, have now been proved to be accurate. It is difficult to account for the little interest that was taken in tea cultivation previous to 1865, for there was evidence that the plant would succeed well. At the present time the area under tea cannot be much less than 2,000 acres. The oldest estates are planted with tea of the China variety; those that have recently been opened, on situations not too exposed, are generally planted with the Assam variety, or with plants produced from a cross between the China and Assam varieties. The China variety is the most hardy and best adapted for high and exposed positions, but grows slowly, and produces very little leaf. The Assam variety is suited only for sheltered situations on rich fertile soil; when so circumstanced it grows rapidly, and is a large producer of leaf. The hybrid is the most generally useful, combining the leaf-producing quality of the Assam with the hardihood of the China variety. Most of the tea estates on the Nilgiris are on land which was formerly under grass; such land especially, if heavily covered by ferns, gives good results, but shola land is preferred when it can be obtained equally well situated, as on such land the shrub grows with much greater rapidity, and gives earlier and heavier flushes of leaf. The plantations are generally small, ranging from 50 to 80 acres in extent, and besides these there are numerous gardens varying from plots of a single acre up to 15 or 20 acres. The bulk of the plantations appear to have been started as experimental plots, and gradually increased until they have reached their present area. They are generally not well arranged, and are ill-provided with buildings; many are altogether without buildings, being worked in connection with some other estate.

Tobacco cultivation in this Presidency has recently been the subject of an official inquiry. Tobacco is grown more or less *Tobacco cultivation.* throughout the Presidency, with the exception of Malabar and the Hill Ranges; but the chief localities of production are the alluvial lands of the Godavery District where is grown the well known "Lunka" tobacco (so named from the lunkas or river islands on which it is cultivated) and parts of the Coimbatore and Madura Districts from which the Trichinopoly cheroot manufacturers draw their supplies of raw material. The plant is grown on almost every description of soil, from black loam to sand, and from irrigated land to high arid sites. Alluvial lands are preferred; then high ground, and such places as deserted village sites, and backyards of houses, the latter on account of the salts impregnating the soil, and also probably for convenience of position as regards manuring and watching and curing the produce. Of the more esteemed tobaccos used for European consumption; the best of the Godavery produce is grown on these alluvial lands which receive rich deposits of silt in

the river floods and are out of the influence of the sea-freshes;
while the Dindigul tobacco is produced on a carefully cultivated
red loam to which an alluvial character has been artificially
imparted. Some of the highest priced tobacco is grown on rich
dry land under irrigation, but this while suited for chewing, is too
coarse in texture of leaf and too pungent in flavour for smoking.
In some parts irrigation is practised and in others it is dispensed
with ; only a small quantity of water is supplied to the plant, and
as a rule not by gravitation, but by mechanical appliances, and
preferably from wells of brackish water containing potassic salts.
Excessive damp is prejudicial, and the seed-beds and soil
generally are superficially drained or stand high. The crop
while young is gently watered by hand, and heavy rains
detract from the quality of the tobacco, the tobacco grown on
ordinary irrigable lands being generally inferior. The manures
used are the droppings of sheep and goats penned on the land
previously to cultivation, cattle-dung and urine, ashes and
sweepings. In Nellore salt-earth is used. The manures are
very plentifully applied to all soils except alluvial lands. The
seed is invariably sown in seed-beds. The seasons of cultivation
vary according to local climatic considerations. As a rule,
sowing commences after the local rains from July to October,
though tobacco is sometimes grown as a second crop commencing
in January. The site of cultivation is thoroughly ploughed and
manured, the seed germinates in some eight days after sowing,
and the seedlings are transplanted in the course of some six
weeks, on attaining a height of five or six inches, into holes
a foot to a yard apart, sometimes in ridges, sometimes on the
flat surface of the field. In some localities the seed-beds and
young plants are protected from the extreme heat of the sun by
means of mats, etc., and all leaves except ten or twelve are
nipped off to strengthen those left ; the flowers are also
promptly nipped off with the exception of those purposely left
for seed. The leaves begin to ripen in the course of some two
months from transplantation, and as soon as one or two turn
colour, the whole crop is collected. This is effected generally
by cutting the stem with a knife, though in Ganjam and the
alluvial lands of Vizagapatam the leaves are nipped off
separately, and in part of Tanjore some leaves are first plucked
in January and the stem and remaining leaves cut down in May
or June. As a rule no second crop is gathered, and where the
after sprouts are collected at all they are of very inferior quality.
The process of gradually drying and fermenting is effected by

modes slightly differing in detail. In Nellore, for instance, the
cut leaves are hung in the sun for two days, put in heaps,
turned every two days, and ranged in layers for twenty days,
during which time they are frequently turned. They are then
tied in bundles, dipped in water, sweetened with date jaggery,
and are then ready for sale. In other parts, as in the Salem
District, the plants are left a day or two in the field, then
exposed to the sun and dew alternately for a week, then
wrapped in straw and buried in the ground for a week, after
which the leaves are stripped from the stems, made into bundles,
placed in straw, and put under heavy weights, with their ends
exposed for six weeks, the piles in which they are laid being
opened and turned every other day. In other localities the
leaves, after drying in the fields for a day or two, are hung over
poles or ropes, preferably in the shade, in regular drying sheds or
in the cultivators' houses, and subsequently stacked in heaps
which are opened out and pressed together again at stated
intervals until the requisite curing is effected. Occasionally
the leaves are sprinkled with jaggery water or an infusion of
the cassia auriculata while drying, and in Coimbatore the
festoons of leaves after being strung are hung up on the
milk hedge (euphorbia tirucalli) to acquire thence a flavour.
State interference has been suggested in the case of this
industry, but the Government have decided otherwise. Such
interference has not been found necessary with indigo or coffee,
and it was relinquished in the case of tea when that industry
had made much less progress than tobacco has at the present
time. The tobacco grown in this Presidency is at present
inferior; but it seems clear that this is mainly due to the fact
that there is a great demand for the coarse article, and that it is
found to pay better to grow a large quantity of inferior leaf
than to grow a smaller quantity of superior leaf. European
capital would, however, doubtless improve the curing processes.
The statistics of the tobacco industry lately obtained are too
voluminous to be here inserted.

Nearly one half of the whole number of persons shown by the last census as in employment, that is to say, 4,878,890 persons, are given as cultivators. These are peasant proprietors holding land either under Government directly or under Zemindars, &c. The number of holders of Government puttahs was at the last census 2,392,064 only, but one puttah often includes several members of the same family. Every section of the community, from the Brahmin to the Pariah, and Hindu or Mahomedan, is

Agricultural condition of ryots.

represented in the list of cultivators. The desire for holding land is as strong as in any other part of the world. Of late years and consequent on the gradual abolition of domestic slavery, the lower orders of the Hindus have become farmers on their own account to a larger extent than before, and their position has improved. The direct taxes to which an agriculturalist in this Presidency is now liable are very numerous, but though the multiplicity of the present taxation is no doubt an unwelcome substitute for the simplicity of the old taxation, all the present taxes and imposts put together amount to no more than the old land assessment. The rise in prices of late years has improved the position of the agriculturalist, and it may be hoped that with increasing resources more capital may be invested in the development of the soil. The most needy cultivators are those who hold the dry lands.

Agricultural condition of farm laborers. In addition to the great body of small farmers upwards of two millions of adult males are returned by the Census as "laborers," and probably more than three-fourths of these are employed in connection with the cultivation of the land. These represent for the most part the classes of the community who were formerly prædial slaves. The principal caste engaged in inferior agricultural labor is that of the Vannians. Throughout the greater part of the Presidency the agricultural laborer receives his wages in the form of farm produce ; and it is only near large towns that money wages are paid. The rate of hire varies from one to two Madras measures of grain per day, the higher rate being that usually given for occasional labor and the lower rate that for long engagements. These two classes of laborers differ very much in their circumstances. The latter have little liberty, being usually in debt to their employers on account of the advance made to them on first taking service. The casual laborer, on the other hand, finds living precarious ; he meets with regular employment only at the busy seasons of the year, and during the remainder of the year has to depend upon such work as he can secure on the roads, and other public works, or upon the small earnings to be made by selling fuel, grass, &c., in the large villages and towns. It is usual for the wife and other members of the laborer's family to contribute their earnings. The following statement shows the rate of wages of agricultural laborers obtaining in June and December of a recent average year. Wages of certain other laborers have been added for illustration : —

Districts.	Average Wages per Month.					
	Prevailing at the end of June 1875.			At the end of December 1875.		
	Able-bodied Agricultural Laborer.	Syce or Horse-keeper.	Common Mason, Carpenter, or Black-smith.	Able-bodied Agricultural Laborer.	Syce or Horse-keeper.	Common Mason, Carpenter, or Black-smith.
	RS. A. P.	RS. A. P.	RS A. P.	RS. A. P.	RS. A. P.	RS. A. P.
1. Ganjam ...	3 0 0	6 0 0	7 8 0	3 0 0	6 0 0	7 8 0
2. Vizagapatam.	4 8 0	6 0 0	9 12 0	4 8 0	6 0 0	9 12 0
3. Godavery ...	6 0 0	6 0 0	12 0 0	6 0 0	7 0 0	12 0 0
4. Kistna ...	7 8 0	7 0 0	12 8 0	7 8 0	7 0 0	12 8 0
5. Nellore ...	6 0 0	6 0 0	15 0 0	3 8 0	6 0 0	12 8 0
6. Cuddapah ..	7 8 0	6 0 0	22 8 0	7 8 0	6 0 0	22 8 0
7. Bellary ...	4 0 0	6 0 0	15 0 0	4 0 0	6 0 0	11 4 0
8. Kurnool ...	4 0 0	6 0 0	11 0 0	4 0 0	6 0 0	12 0 0
9. Madras ...	6 8 0	5 8 0	9 6 0	6 0 0	5 8 0	13 12 0
10. Chingleput...	3 12 0	5 0 0	10 5 4	3 0 0	6 0 0	13 10 8
11. North Arcot.	4 0 0	7 0 0	15 0 0	4 0 0	7 0 0	14 0 0
12. South Arcot.	4 0 0	5 0 0	11 4 0	4 11 0	5 0 0	11 4 0
13. Tanjore ...	4 11 0	6 0 0	11 13 4	4 8 0	6 0 0	11 13 4
14. Trichinopoly.	4 8 0	6 8 0	9 11 0	4 0 0	6 8 0	10 0 0
15. Madura ...	6 0 0	7 0 0	20 0 0	6 0 0	7 0 0	20 0 0
16. Tinnevelly ...	6 0 0	6 0 0	14 6 0	6 4 0	6 0 0	14 6 0
17. Coimbatore...	4 0 0	6 0 0	15 0 0	5 8 0	6 0 0	16 0 0
18. Nilgiris ...	7 0 0	8 0 0	25 0 0	7 0 0	8 0 0	25 0 0
19. Salem ...	2 8 0	5 4 0	16 14 0	2 8 0	5 4 0	15 0 0
20. South Canara.	7 8 0	6 0 0	20 10 0	7 8 0	7 0 0	20 10 0
21. Malabar ...	7 8 0	7 0 0	15 0 0	7 8 0	7 0 0	15 0 0

The wages of agricultural labor have increased during the last quarter of a century, though not in proportion to prices. Where wages are paid in grain it is evidently difficult to secure progressive rates.

The agricultural live-stock of this Presidency consists of cattle, sheep, and goats, horses being almost entirely unrepresented. The cattle are small in stature, the average live weight not being much more than 350 lbs. In one or two localities the breed of cattle is superior; as in Nellore and the surrounding districts and in the districts bordering the Mysore frontier. Cattle are kept for draught, for the dairy, for breeding, and for manure purposes; they are hardly ever fed or fattened for slaughter as in other countries, the meat market being supplied chiefly by the slaughter of worn-out draught cattle, old or barren cows, &c. The sheep are light-framed animals with long legs, yielding on the average about 25 lbs. of mutton per head. The yield of wool, which is always largely mixed with hair, is usually not more than 1 lb. in the year per head. The large losses of cattle from the occurrence of preventible diseases have

Live-stock, treatment and present condition.

attracted the attention of Government, and the provisions of the Cattle Diseases' Act have been applied to some districts. At present however there is no agency for enforcing its provisions other than the ordinary Revenue establishment. Attempts are at the present moment being made in Europe to secure the services of a competent Veterinarian to fill the post of Inspector of Cattle Disease.

Fairs and Markets.

Fairs and markets are held periodically throughout the Presidency, the latter generally weekly or bi-weekly, and the former on the occasion of different festivals. At the fairs, in addition to the usual sale of agricultural produce, considerable numbers of farm-stock are brought together, especially in the breeding districts. The markets are on a very much smaller scale, and grain and petty articles of domestic use constitute the chief articles of trade. The produce brought for sale to a market is in most instances of no greater bulk than a cooly-load ; and live stock is seldom offered.

Food prices.

The prices of food-grains are ascertained by local inquiry at the head-quarters of Tahsildars and Deputy Tahsildars and reported to the Board of Revenue once a month. The number of local measures of capacity per rupee is given in these reports. The measures are converted in the Board's Office into seers' weight of 80 tolas, and a general statement is then published in the *Fort St. George Gazette*. Once a fortnight a statement is sent to the Government of India showing the prices prevailing at the head-quarters of each collectorate; this is published in the *Gazette of India*. The grain markets are now much steadier than they were some years back. The years 1874-75 and 1875-76 may be taken to have been average years; the retail prices of the principal articles of food in those years is shown below :—

Items.				1874-75.	1875-76.
				RS.	RS.
Price of rice, 2nd sort, seers of 80 tolas per rupee...				15·2	16·0
Do. paddy,	do.	do.	...	27·2	28·6
Do. cholum,	do.	do.	...	25·7	26·6
Do. cumboo,	do.	do.	...	26·0	26·4
Do. ragi,	do.	do.	...	27·9	27·9
Do. varagu,	do.	do.	...	37·0	39·6
Do. wheat,	do.	do.	...	10·7	11·4
Do. salt,	do.	do.	...	15·7	15·8
Do. cotton, per candy	...	...	...	111	104

General agricultural statistics.

General statistical information regarding agriculture is now available to Government on the following subjects:—(1) Area cultivated and uncultivated : (2) Crops cultivated and area under crops ; (3) Prices of food grains, and (4) Price of labor. This information is not quite sufficient. and the question of collecting agricultural statistics on a more extended scale is under consideration. The village agency is perhaps sufficient for what would be wanted, but additional establishments, estimated to cost $2\frac{1}{2}$ lakhs of rupees, would be required to secure proper supervision and for tabulation of results. Little or no information is at present available for Zemindari or Inam villages.

The Government Agricultural Department in this Presidency is confined at present in great measure to the operations connected with the Government Farms already established or hereafter to be established. The officers of the department are however available for making tours, for answering references from districts, and for many miscellaneous duties in connection with agricultural questions. The proposed extension of agricultural education in connection with the department will be mentioned in the next paragraph. The department is now under the control of a Superintendent, who is placed immediately under the orders of the Board of Revenue. He has two Assistants who have received an agricultural training in Europe, and also certain office establishments; the cost of this establishment and of such experiments as are made from time to time is met partly by a Government grant and partly from receipts in the Farm and certain Local Funds. At present there are only two Government farms in operation, both situated at Sydapet close to the Presidency town, and in fact forming practically but one farm. It is intended gradually to open similar farms in other districts. Four have actually been sanctioned, but from the impossibility of obtaining properly qualified native superintendents and other causes, neither of them has yet been opened. The idea of establishing Government Farms in this Presidency originated in 1864, and a small farm was established in 1865 at Sydapet under the management of a committee. The success which attended the experiment induced the Government to take it under their direct management, and to extend its operation ; hence the present Sydapet Farms. These institutions have been concerned with too many tentative measures to be capable of showing a commercial success, but many important agricultural experiments have been made, and some have produced encouraging results, in indicating the general direction in which improvements can be effected in the agricultural practice of this Presidency. Attention has been given to subsoil

(marginal note) Direct Government operations.

drainage, improved tillage, the restoration of exhausted soils, economy, and the proper utilization of irrigation water; the fertilization of arable soils by the use of lime, saltpetre, oil-cake, poudrette and other manures available in Southern India, but now unused by the ryot; the introduction of new crops, suited to the climate of India and adapted for cultivation under an improving agricultural practice, such as maize, Sorghum Saccharatum, Carolina paddy, Guinea grass and other grasses, New Orleans cotton and other superior varieties of cotton, tobacco of sorts, &c.; the production of live fences, in view to affording protection, shelter and fuel; the introduction of water-lifts, barn machines, carts, ploughs, cultivators, cattle-hoes, reaping knives, &c., of improved construction, and the improvement of similar kinds of machines and implements now in use in this country; improvement of the live-stock of the country by careful breeding and feeding, and by introducing and acclimatizing new breeds; with other matters.

—Agricultural education.

Between the first opening of the Experimental Farm and the end of the year 1875 several apprentices joined the institution, an apprentice meaning here a student drawing from the institution a small stipend. These apprentices were either Eurasians or Hindus, the former generally the sons of old soldiers resident at Palaveram or St. Thomas' Mount. In establishing this class, the intention was merely to afford an opportunity to a few young men to make themselves acquainted with the routine out-of-door duties of the farmer. In 1871, in order to provide the necessary agency for carrying on the District Farms, another apprentice class was established. This second class was better paid and was established in view to training Superintendents for the District Farms. The young men of both classes came to the Farm ignorant of agriculture, and as the training was entirely out-of-door and mechanical, they made but little progress towards gaining a real knowledge of this subject. It appears to be established that youths trained under such a system cannot be usefully employed in the districts in spreading agricultural knowledge, or in conducting agricultural operations of any complexity, and it has been recently decided to establish a School of Agriculture at Sydapet. Suitable educational buildings, a Veterinary Hospital, a Chemical Laboratory, and an Agricultural Museum will be erected. The institution will be attached to the Educational Department and will be placed under the direct management of the Superintendent of Government Farms, who will be assisted in lecturing by officers of the Madras Medical College and others. The instruction will extend over three years, and will embrace a thorough study of agriculture and of such portions of Chemistry, Geology, Zoology, Botany, and the Veterinary Art as bear on the theory and practice of Agriculture, Farm Book-keeping, Land Surveying, Mensuration and Drawing. The students, before admission, must have passed the Matriculation Examination or the General Test Examination, or the special Entrance Examination of the Institution. Candidates must be above 16 and below 24 years of age. The course is entirely free. A considerable number of Stipendiaryships and a few Scholarships have also been established, and the regulations provide for the gratuitous admission of school teachers and others to certain special courses of lectures. Those who obtain no stipendiaryship or scholarship, pay their own expenses, but no fee is demanded from them. Judging from the number of applicants and the qualifications of the present students there are grounds for believing that it will amply fulfil the object for which it has been established. Some of the present students intend to settle on the Nilgiris as farmers, others similarly on the plains in the ordinary course. Some hope to get employment as agricultural teachers under the Government or under Zemindars or in Native States. The estimated annual cost of the institution is Rupees 15,000, not including the salary of the Superintendent or his Assistants.

Under Native Governments and for a long time after the British —**Public** took possession of the country, no expenditure appears to have **Exhibitions.** been incurred on account of Cattle Shows. Public exhibitions however of cattle and useful productions of all kinds in agriculture, manufacture, minerals, and arts were held in several districts of this Presidency in 1855, 1856, 1857, and 1859, at an annual expense varying from Rupees 13,000 to Rupees 35,000. Since then the exhibitions have been continued with more or less regularity year by year.

HORTICULTURE—CINCHONA.

The object of the Government Cinchona Plantations is the **Government** provision of an abundant and cheap supply of the febrifuge **Cinchona** **Plantations.** for the use of hospitals and troops in India, and the spread of Cinchona cultivation throughout the Hill Districts. In

1859 Her Majesty's Government engaged the services of Mr. Clement R. Markham for the special duty of introducing the Cinchonas into India. He started on an expedition to South America in the early part of 1860 and arrived in India at the end of the same year with the first instalment of Cinchona plants. These plants were in an unhealthy state when they arrived at Ootacamund. In July 1861 the experiment was entrusted to Mr. McIvor and ever since the plantations have made satisfactory progress and proved a decided success. There are three Plantations at Neddivuttum, the *Denison*, the *Kilgraston*, and the *Napier*; two at Pykara, the *Wood* and the *Hooker*; one at Ootacamund, the *Dodabetta*; and one at Mailkoondah, the *Stanley* Estate. The last-named was abandoned in 1871 with a view to ascertain whether the Cinchona could be left to mature. The experiment has proved a failure and the *Stanley* Estate is exterminated. The seven estates cover upwards of 1,200 acres, surface measurement. The number of Cinchona plants permanently established on the 31st March 1876 was 1,190,458, of which the Officinalis and Succirubra number half a million each. Operations of late years have been restricted in a great measure to conservancy, and the experimental cultivation of the rarer and more valuable varieties of Cinchona. The first yield of the plantations was in 1872, when the trees planted at the commencement of the enterprize were twelve years' old. The outturn was 7,294½ pounds of dry bark which realized Rupees 7,294-8-0. The prices varied from 2s. 3d. per pound to 2s. 10d., or an average price of 2s. 6¼d., which must be considered satisfactory. A second consignment of 23,646 pounds of dry bark was made in the spring of 1873, which sold for Rupees 34,900. The average price realized was 3s. 2¼d. per pound. The third consignment went to England in 1875. The quantity despatched was 28,659 pounds, and sold for Rupees 28,659; the average price per pound was 2s. 1d. The next consignment of 63,600 pounds was remitted last January and realized Rupees 96,039-2-8. In addition to the above the plantations furnished the Quinologist with 362,050 pounds of green or 111,481½ pounds dry bark, valued at 95,500 Rupees. The entire return on the estates accordingly during the five years to 31st March 1876 aggregated Rupees 2,35,000 or about 28½ per cent. on the total outlay. The outlay to 31st March 1876 including the cost of convict labor was Rupees 8,25,350.

Quinologist.   When Mr. Markham visited Ootacamund in January 1866 he suggested the appointment of a Quinologist to investigate on the spot various questions connected with the elaboration of alkaloids, the harvesting of the bark, the most economical and efficacious mode of preparing the febrifuge, &c. The services of the same officer were also to be turned to profitable account in utilizing the medicinal plants of India generally. This was carried out, and the office continued in existence to the end of 1875, when it was abolished. The Quinologist's Department has cost the State Rupees 1,28,684 made up of the following items :—Salary Rupees 77,366, Plant, materials, and building Rupees 33,193, and Establishment Rupees 18,125. The returns from this department have been 922 pounds of "Amorphous Quinine," manufactured out of 362,050 pounds of Cinchona green bark and valued at Rupees 59,930 or at the rate of 130 shillings a pound.

HORTICULTURE—GOVERNMENT GARDENS.

The Ootacamund Botanical Gardens were opened during the Governorship of the late Marquis of Tweedale, and cover an area of 51·45 acres. The professed object of the gardens is 1st—The improvement of horticulture in this Presidency by the dissemination of information ; 2nd—The introduction and acclimatization of vegetable productions of Europe and other parts of the world hitherto unknown in India ; and 3rd—The distribution of good seeds and plants. In 1871 these gardens which had hitherto formed a part of the charge of the Superintendent of the Cinchona Plantations were placed under a separate officer, and their importance was further recognized by a more liberal allotment of funds. *Ootacamund Botanical Gardens.*

The Kulhutty Garden is maintained as a branch of the Ootacamund Gardens. It is adapted for the ripening of vegetable and flower seeds as it enjoys a drier and a warmer climate than that at Ootacamund. *Kulhutty Garden.*

The Burliar branch garden was purchased by Government in 1871 for the sum of Rupees 2,000. The garden is in charge of the Superintendent of the garden at Ootacamund, and is worked out of funds provided in the budget for the latter. It is situated at an elevation of 2,500 feet above sea-level, and the extent is 8 acres. The object of its acquisition was to extend the culture of the Ipecacuanha plant which was found not to flourish at Ootacamund The locality was believed to be *The Burliar Garden.*

specially adapted for the growth of West India plants, as well as those from the Straits and the Eastern Archipelago. The experience of the past five years has proved that the garden is well adapted for the purpose contemplated.

Coonoor Gardens.

In the early part of 1874 the Government opened a pleasure ground at Coonoor. The plot is about 30 acres. The outlay to the 31st March 1876 has been Rupees 8,931-13-5 provided exclusively by Government.

Agri-Horticultural Society.

A donation of Rupees 250 per mensem is paid to the Agri-Horticultural Society at Madras and an annual contribution of Rupees 500 is made for prizes for agricultural and other products, such as cotton, tea, cereals, forage, gums, resins, dyes, shade and avenue trees, &c. ; special payments are also occasionally made.

MINERAL RESOURCES.

Government operations.

The development of the mineral resources of this presidency is at present in its infancy, and there is no special Government agency. Inquiries and investigations have however been made on several occasions. The Government of India have expressed an opinion that when waste land is sold actually for cultivation no special reservation of a Government right to a share in its mineral wealth should be made, but that land known or strongly believed to contain mineral wealth should be removed from the category of cultivable land and be granted to applicants on special agreements only. The Government have acted on this principle, and no land answering the above description has as yet been alienated at all.

Gold.

An examination was recently made of the gold-bearing rocks in part of the Wynaad District. Gold has long been known and worked in the Wynaad, but the amount obtained has always been small, and the gold-dust generally found so minute in size as to necessitate its being secured by amalgamation. In the vein-stone the gold is generally so finely distributed through the matrix as to be scarcely visible even with the assistance of a magnifier; occasionally it appears in the form of particles or strings, but always in minute quantities. There is no instance of the metal appearing in any abundance in the quartz. With regard to the alluvial deposits it appears certain that there is at

present no probability of their being worked with any profit on
a large scale. The quantity of gold known to exist in them is
always small, and the serious difficulties necessarily incident on
a new undertaking are such as to make the profitableness of
explorations doubtful. Quartz-mining however presents more
favorable indications, the number of quartz-reefs and veins
being large, and their extent by no means insignificant. Most
of the reefs are more or less auriferous, particularly in
Nambalicode and Moonad. Preliminary experiments on the
southern ends of six reefs have given an average proportion of
7 cwts. of gold to the ton of quartz, and it is calculated that
this will allow of a profit on the extraction. In one reef the
proportion given was 11 dwts., and in two others the proportion was 10 dwts. The best assay of reef-gold showed a fineness
of 20 carat 3⅔ carat-grains ; but it is anticipated that a purer
alloy than this will be found in some reefs, owing to the
generally high standard exhibited in the alluvial gold from
Wynaad and the Malabar low country. Several applications
have recently been made for land in the Wynaad ostensibly
for coffee-planting but really for gold-mining. A small quantity
of gold is washed from stream gravels in the Godavery valley ;
the profits are very trifling.

In 1870-71 the Government of India Geological Survey **Coal.**
carried on the general mapping of the sandstone area in the
eastern portion of the territory of the Nizam of Hyderabad,
and southwards into this Presidency as far as Ellore in the
Godavery District. On this occasion the coal-bearing rocks of
the Godavery were mapped, and a series of borings for coal
were taken near Dumagudem the head-quarters of the navigation
works at the first barrier of the river. The coal was found to
be of an inferior quality. The sandstones of this part of the
country seem to belong to the true coal-bearing rocks, but to
be for the most part devoid of coal.

Some remarkable deposits of magnetic iron ores are found in **Iron.**
the Salem District. The ores occur in large beds of from 50 to
100 feet in thickness, and the outcrop may be traced for miles.
On one hill, six miles from Salem, there are five bands of
magnetic iron from 20 to 50 feet thick. In 1825, Mr. Heath, of
the Civil Service, obtained a Government advance and formed
a company to establish iron works at Porto Novo near Cuddalore,
at Palampatty near Salem, and at Beypore on the West Coast.
At the last place the iron was to be obtained from laterite. The
Porto Novo works were begun in 1833, and those at Beypore

some years later. The Government gave their aid, but the
experiments failed. The causes assigned were the distance of
the works from the source of supply, scarcity of charcoal, and
various other practical difficulties. Several companies took up
the matter, but with no final success. The little information
that is available regarding native working in iron will be found
under the head of Manufactures.

FORESTS.

History of the department. The Forest Department in this Presidency had no existence
before 1847. Up to that year the forests were nominally in
charge of Collectors, and no special arrangements were made for
their conservancy. In 1847 the Executive Engineer of Malabar
brought to the notice of Government that the forests in Malabar
and Coimbatore were being denuded of timber by the Malabar
merchants who supplied the Bombay market, and that some
arrangements were necessary to preserve them. On this a special
officer was appointed to explore, conserve, and work the Government forests in those districts, and this arrangement continued
in connection with the Public Works Department for seven
years. The importance of forest conservancy had then become
apparent and an officer was appointed in 1856 as Conservator of
Forests of the Madras Presidency. Up to 1871-72 the department was directly responsible to Government, but in 1872-73 it
was reorganized. The district officers were placed under the
orders of the Collectors, the account department was transferred
to the Board, and the office of Conservator was abolished and
converted into that of Inspector of Forests, with the duty of
visiting them and offering advice to Collectors. This arrangement, however, was found inconvenient, and the organization was
again altered in 1875, when the department was placed on a
footing somewhat on the plan adopted in Bombay.

Present constitution. The following are the rules under which the department is
worked at present. The relative position of the District Forest
Officers to the District Collector is analogous to that of the
District Police Officers to the District Magistrate. In all forest
matters the District Forest Officer is subordinate to the Collector
subject to the following restrictions. All orders of a professional
character relating, for example, to felling, planting, and such

operations emanate from the Conservator, but reach the District
Forest Officer through the Collector. If the latter sees any
reason to object to them he can do so, and differences of opinion
between him and the Conservator, which cannot be otherwise
settled, are referred to the Revenue Board, and if necessary to
Government. The Conservator is specially responsible for the
economical working of the department. The Conservator is at
liberty to communicate direct with District Forest Officers for
the collection and dissemination of scientific or professional
knowledge. In like manner all correspondence between District
Forest Officers and the Conservator, including bills for travelling
allowances, periodical reports, estimates, &c., are sent through the
Collector, who makes such comments as he may deem advisable.
The Collector cannot as a rule issue orders to District Forest
Officers direct, but in the event of his deeming it necessary to
order him to proceed to a particular locality, or to take special
action in any forest matter, he may do so, taking care to
send a copy of such order for the information of the Conservator.
The Conservator is the controlling authority in all matters of
promotion in the subordinate branches and in all matters of
departmental discipline. The control of forest expenditure rests
with the Conservator subject to the approval of the Revenue
Board and Government. The Conservator has power to sanction
expenditure on any one work up to Rupees 500 and the Revenue
Board up to 5,000 Rupees, provided that funds are available
in the budget grant. An annual plan of forest operations is
prepared by each District Forest Officer and forwarded through
the Collector to the Conservator. The Conservator in like
manner submits through the Revenue Board sketch of proposed
operations in the several forest divisions or districts for the
information or orders of Government. The Conservator submits
" notes " or "inspection reports " on the forests visited by him.
These tour notes are transmitted to the Secretary to Government, Revenue Department, through the District Collector and
Revenue Board, for any remarks or suggestions which they may
have to offer. The cost of the establishment in 1856, when the
department was first formally organized, was Rupees 4,530, but
now, according to the revision in 1875, it costs Rupees 2,24,616,
exclusive of contingencies, mileage, &c.

The object of the department is to prevent denudation of **Object and**
forests and to meet a rapidly increasing demand throughout the **duties.**
country for timber and fuel, but a not less important object is
the preservation of the natural influence of trees on the climate

and drainage of the country and supply of water. Forests are divided into local and imperial. The former, which are generally close to the villages where agricultural communities live, are placed in charge of Collectors entirely for local purposes, the remaining forests alone being in charge of the Conservator. In the latter no one is allowed to remove timber or firewood without a license, which is granted on payment of a fixed seigniorage, or free of duty when the timber or firewood is required by the people for their domestic use. Certain tracts and trees are reserved for railway fuel and departmental felling for supply to Government and for sale to the public.

Progress made.

The area of the forests conserved is not known, but it must be more than 5,000 square miles. The question of surveying the State forests is now under consideration. The area of reserves and plantations for railway fuel is about 6,200 acres, estimated to yield 67,000 tons of firewood annually, and the area of teak, sandalwood, &c., plantations is about 2,500 acres.

Receipts and charges.

The receipts and charges of the department have been as shown below for fifteen years down to 1874-75 :—

Years.				Receipts.	Charges.	Balance.
				RS.	RS.	RS.
1860-61	...	...	...	3,52,449	1,68,716	+ 1,83,733
1861-62	...	...	...	6,60,352	2,31,712	+ 4,28,640
1862-63	...	...	...	1,82,334	1,75,768	+ 6,566
1863-64	...	...	...	2,43,642	2,04,303	+ 39,339
1864-65	...	...	...	3,30,570	1,95,657	+ 1,34,913
1865-66	...	...	...	3,21,581	2,59,802	+ 61,779
1866-67	...	...	...	3,38,607	2,17,149	+ 1,21,458
1867-68	...	...	...	4,24,184	2,72,840	+ 1,51,344
1868-69	...	...	...	3,91,179	2,69,700	+ 1,21,479
1869-70	...	...	...	4,95,789	2,86,691	+ 2,09,098
1870-71	...	...	...	3,39,762	2,94,860	+ 44,902
1871-72	...	...	...	4,18,882	3,45,717	+ 73,165
1872-73	...	...	...	4,18,767	4,78,147	− 59,380
1873-74	...	...	...	4,49,541	3,53,184	+ 96,357
1874-75	...	...	...	3,64,326	3,97,872	− 33,546

The receipts above shown do not represent the entire return for the charges incurred. There are large plantations, the trees in which have not come to maturity. No data exists for estimating the present value of the plantations.

TRADE AND MANUFACTURES.

Except in Madras, where there is a separate establishment Arrangements for collecting and distributing trade statistics. for compiling trade statistics under the orders of Sea Customs Collectors, the work of compilation in the outports of this Presidency is conducted by the same establishments as are employed in passing goods, collecting duty, &c. When applications are made for exporting goods or clearing those imported, the applicants are required to specify in their applications the quantities and values of the articles with all the particulars required for statistical purposes, and after the applications are passed and the prescribed duty, if any, collected, the information required is compiled from them, tabulated, and submitted to the Collectors daily, where the outports are situated at a distance from the Collector's head-quarters, and monthly where they are close by. From this information the returns required are compiled by the Collectors in certain forms prescribed for the purpose and forwarded to the Board of Revenue, where they are brought together for the whole Presidency and the statements forwarded to the Government of India every month. New forms of statements were brought into use during the year under review. An important feature of the forms is that they are made to exhibit not only the external trade, but also the trade from port to port within the Presidency, which was not hitherto shown in the returns. The following are the principal particulars recorded :—1, the quantities and values of goods, and the value of gold and silver exported or imported; 2, the ports from and to which exports or imports are made; 3, the quantities left in bond and those cleared for house consumption; 4, the amount of duty collected and the articles upon which it is charged; 5, the amount of refunds and drawback allowed; 6, the number of vessels cleared and entered distinguished into steam and sailing, in cargo, and in ballast; 7, the countries from which they enter or to which they clear; and 8, the nationalities and tonnage of vessels. The statistics are reviewed, and any impediments to the progress of trade noticed by the Board annually. In the districts the work is done chiefly by the ordinary establishments, but a clerk has recently been allowed to each district to aid in the work.

The following statement shows the value of exports and Amount of trade. imports for the last twenty-one years at all ports, excluding interportal trade :—

Years.	Value of Imports.			Value of Exports.			Value of Re-exports.
	Merchandise.	Treasure.	Total.	Merchandise.	Treasure.	Total.	Merchandise.
	RS.	RS.	RS.	RS.	RS.	RS.	RS.
1855-56 ...	2,31,33,876	1,37,16,696	3,68,50,572	2,91,70,905	44,18,750	3,35,89,655	6,64,364
1856-57 ...	2,35,25,244	1,70,38,582	4,05,63,826	3,67,26,978	33,33,678	4,00,60,656	7,78,134
1857-58 ...	2,46,85,453	1,86,23,162	4,33,08,615	4,03,65,161	1,17,00,866	5,20,66,027	9,10,155
1858-59 ...	2,93,08,408	1,42,96,207	4,36,04,615	3,37,99,807	57,28,536	3,95,28,343	17,16,376
1859-60 ...	2,99,07,033	1,74,39,684	4,73,46,717	3,87,82,800	45,47,547	4,33,30,347	12,56,494
1860-61 ...	2,16,55,812	2,07,25,887	5,23,81,699	4,45,98,338	62,88,632	5,08,86,970	15,07,146
1861-62 ...	3,44,94,149	2,22,85,900	5,67,80,049	5,42,92,250	39,58,486	5,82,50,736	11,60,099
1862-63 ...	3,03,30,148	3,03,86,890	6,07,17,038	6,35,58,990	61,90,551	6,97,49,541	11,96,496
1863-64 ...	4,02,65,473	3,60,75,985	7,63,41,458	8,77,78,126	2,23,39,284	11,01,17,410	17,35,648
1864-65 ...	4,18,02,487	3,03,13,958	7,21,16,445	8,36,71,790	1,81,50,942	10,18,22,732	10,04,383
1865-66 ...	4,79,87,412	3,66,42,492	8,46,29,904	9,00,15,155	1,26,10,223	10,26,25,378	14,61,719
1866-67 ...	4,16,74,201	1,36,86,606	5,53,60,807	4,45,86,571	1,75,29,881	6,21,16,452	4,86,237
1867-68 ...	5,08,27,573	1,12,93,529	6,21,21,102	5,80,09,230	1,01,55,634	6,81,64,864	4,39,318
1868-69 ...	5,14,00,610	2,25,60,091	7,39,60,701	7,67,50,999	36,81,960	8,04,32,959	14,45,965
1869-70 ...	5,11,84,481	1,76,42,023	6,88,26,504	7,32,45,315	62,22,657	7,94,67,972	18,65,985
1870-71 ...	5,49,93,170	82,68,321	6,32,61,491	6,24,26,649	1,72,12,961	7,96,39,610	26,75,979
1871-72 ...	5,04,11,411	1,04,92,486	6,09,03,897	8,79,57,788	68,99,824	9,48,57,612	21,72,662
1872-73 ...	5,29,04,294	1,19,42,830	6,48,47,124	7,92,95,348	69,92,958	8,62,88,306	20,81,746
1873-74 ...	5,46,45,249	84,69,288	6,31,14,537	8,26,86,748	1,84,09,184	10,10,95,932	25,58,661
1874-75 ...	5,65,69,225	96,01,625	6,61,70,850	8,40,14,312	97,59,965	9,37,74,307	28,04,065
1875-76* {	6,42,27,053	95,62,079	7,37,89,132	8,88,33,445	43,71,537	9,32,04,982	16,74,217
	1,72,59,681	24,09,141	1,96,68,822	1,18,37,969	29,91,753	1,48,29,722	45,34,303

The export trade of the Presidency consists chiefly of agricultural produce, cotton, oil or oil-seeds, grain, coffee, ginger, turmeric, dye-wood, indigo, skins, &c. The imports mostly of piece-goods, twist, metals, liquors, &c. The export and import trade used to be mainly in the hands of European merchants, but native traders are now beginning to conduct their operations direct with Europe, without the intervention of the local houses of agency.

Particulars of trade. The following statement shows in detail the nature of the imports and exports, and the proportion existing between their value in a recent year :—

---

* Upper figures are exclusive of British ports within the Presidency.
Lower figures are those of British ports within the Presidency

Imports.	1875-76, exclusive of British Ports within the Presidency.	Exports.	1875-76, exclusive of British Ports within the Presidency.
	RS.		RS.
Twist ...	1,23,88,399	Coffee ...	1,66,11,109
Cotton piece-goods, grey ...	94,51,950	Cotton wool ...	1,65,28,491
Metals ...	49,96,807	Hides and skins ...	1,08,15,853
Cotton piece-goods not other-		Rice ...	89,00,886
wise described ...	48,66,561	Seeds ...	58,66,899
Railway stores ...	45,95,289	Indigo ...	47,31,631
Paddy ...	20,19,554	Spices ...	40,52,130
Millinery and wearing apparel.	18,10,154	Oils ...	34,42,041
Rice ...	15,53,748	Cotton goods ...	27,80,400
Timber and wood ...	15,17,622	Provisions and oilman's stores.	23,80,652
Silk, raw ...	14,10,365	Sugar and other saccharine	
Spices, including betel-nuts.	13,05,505	matter ...	19,40,827
Spirits ...	10,24,528	Coir, yarn, and rope ...	18,90,966
Wine ...	8,35,741	Cocoanuts ...	11,44,592
Grain of sorts ...	8,21,533	Timber and wood ...	10,45,109
Provisions and oilman's		Tobacco ...	7,32,343
stores ...	7,39,146	Paddy ...	6,84,876
Drugs and medicines ...	6,04,525	Dyes of sorts ...	5,81,326
Malt liquors ...	5,02,455	Grain of sorts ...	3,85,929
Paper ...	4,16,944	Salt ...	3,68,583
Wool, manufactures of ...	3,93,147	Drugs ...	3,12,593
Seeds ...	2,84,125	Horns ...	2,25,914
Glass and manufactures of ...	2,75,639	Fruits and vegetables ...	1,61,080
Silk, maunfactures of ...	2,35,698	Wax ...	1,43,094
Machines and machinery ...	2,14,780	Silk and manufactures of ...	1,37,909
Tea ...	2,14,197	Saltpetre ...	84,829
Coral, unwrought ...	1,76,909	Hemp and manufactures of...	66,349
Wheat ...	1,76,623	Mats ...	57,141
Books ...	1,73,498	Wheat ...	36,292
Stationery except paper ...	1,41,369	Jewellery ...	34,440
Earthenware and porcelain ...	1,19,635	Feathers ...	27,087
Dyeing and coloring mate-		Spirits ...	17,790
rials ...	1,01,068	Ivory and ivoryware ...	11,908
Jewellery ...	70,350	Precious stones ...	5,969
Other articles ...	1,07,89,189	Other articles ...	26,26,407
Total ...	6,42,27,053		
		Total ...	8,88,33,445
£ ...	6,422,705		
Include Government Stores...	34,20,467	£ ...	8,883,344
and Government Salt on the West Coast ...	8,76,961	Include Government Stores...	890

The only official information as to internal trade is obtained **Internal trade.** from the census classification and returns of the different branches of trade. The particular branches of trade are entered in the schedules under eighty-one headings, but the great bulk of traders are described simply as "merchants" (234,531) and "Bazaar-men" (146,182). The following are a few of the chief trading occupations specified: "Arrack-sellers" (14,146), "Bangle-sellers" (7,908), "Fish-sellers" (47,555), "Cloth-

merchants," " Contractors," " Cattle-dealers," " Bankers and
Money-lenders," " Oil-mongers," " Salt-Merchants," " Indigo-
dealers," " Leather-Merchants," " Wood and Charcoal dealers."
A vast majority of the " Merchants " and " Bazaar-men " are
general dealers, and their shops supply the usual requirements
of the community.

Number of traders.

According to the census of 1871 there are 534,662 persons
engaged in trade, or 3·4 per cent. of the male population. All
castes and classes of the people are traders, though certain
branches of trade remain chiefly in the hands of the Chetty or
trading castes. Traders are most numerous in the Northern
Coast districts and the town of Madras and fewest in South
Arcot, Salem, and Trichinopoly. The proportions vary from
7·8 per cent. of the male population in Madras to 2·2 per cent.
in South Arcot. The chief trading caste is the Chetty, of
whose males 42 per cent. are engaged in trade. Next are the
Fisherman and Toddy-drawing castes, who have respectively
about 3 and 5 per cent. of their numbers occupied in trade
and commerce. The mixed class of Mussulmans, known as
Lubbays and Mapilahs, are petty traders to a large extent,
and indeed all the divisions of Mahomedans seem to furnish a
larger number of traders than the Hindus.

Manufactures.

About manufactures again little is known officially except
from the census returns. In 1871 there were 540,061 males
engaged in these occupations, of whom nearly three-fourths were
weavers. About 113,000 persons are " shoe makers," or workers
in skins and leather ; 25,000 were engaged in cleaning and
ginning cotton for export; and about 15,000 were tailors.
The great bulk of the people of India do not indulge in clothing
that requires the aid of a tailor to shape and sew it, but some
of the better classes, of both sexes, wear cut jackets ; hence the
small number of tailors, compared with the numbers engaged in
making shoes, or coverings for the feet. The produce of the
Indian looms is not exported now to any great extent. In
former days the chintzes of Masulipatam enjoyed a great
celebrity abroad. They were celebrated for the freshness and
permanency of their dyes, the colors being brighter after washing
than before. There is still a small demand for these articles
in Burmah, the Straits, and Persian Gulf; but Manchester goods
have nearly beaten the Indian exporter out of the field. The
home-made cloths, however, still hold their own in competition
with British goods.   The working in metals is almost the

exclusive employment of certain divisions of the artisan castes. Of a total of 126,117 males engaged in labor connected with metals, 115,954, or 91·9 per cent. of the whole, are members of the Hindu artisan castes. The metal workers form 0·8 per cent. of the entire male population. Black-smiths or iron workers were in 1871 about 40,566 in number; gold and silver smiths 70,075; brass and copper smiths about 15,000; and workers in tin about 200. There are a few other occupations under this heading, as "engravers," "platers," "wire-drawers," "knife-makers," &c., but the numbers so engaged are insignificant. The simplicity of Hindu domestic life is especially noticeable in the furniture of their houses. As a rule, no house contains either chairs, raised seats or tables, and the people sit and sleep either on the bare floors, or on mats or carpets. Only 71,805 persons are returned as engaged in occupations connected with the manufacture of household goods, or 0·5 per cent. of the males. Of this number, upwards of 50,000 manufacture earthenware pots for holding water and cooking food, while about 16,000 weave baskets and rattan work. In some districts the people use cots of wicker work to sleep upon. The weaving of mats gives employment to upwards of 3,000 persons.

PUBLIC WORKS—GENERAL.

The channel of communication between the Madras Government and the different divisions of the Public Works Department is at the present date, 31st March 1876, the Secretary to Government, Public Works Department; the functions of this officer, as such, proceed no further than the Secretariat. The Examiner of Public Works Accounts acts also as Financial Assistant to the Secretariat, assisting in the present case the Secretary to Government, Public Works Department. The Secretary is also assisted in Secretariat work by the Chief Engineer in charge of one of the main divisions of works, who is gazetted as Joint Secretary for that division. It will be seen from this description that the Secretariat arrangements of the Madras Presidency are not so symmetrical as those obtaining in other Provinces; differing for instance from Bombay, where there is a Secretary to Government and three Deputy Secretaries,

General organization and divisions.

one for each division, and from Bengal, Punjaub, and the North-
West Provinces, where there are three Joint Secretaries, one for
each division. The main divisions of the department are three,
according to the nature of the works to be executed, that is to
say Buildings and Roads, Irrigation, and Railways. The Buildings and Roads division is sub-divided into two branches, the
Executive and the Accounts. At the head of the former is a Chief
Engineer, with an office establishment and an executive staff
consisting of District Engineers, Executive Engineers, Assistant
Engineers, and a subordinate executive. The Chief Engineer
for Buildings and Roads would according to the theory of
the present Madras organization be gazetted as Joint Secretary
also, and as such assist the Secretary to Government in
Secretariat work ; at the present date, however, the Secretary
to Government occupies also the position of Chief Engineer
for Buildings and Roads, so that the Joint Secretaryship lapses.
The Chief Engineer is assisted by a Deputy Chief Engineer
and Under Secretary for Buildings and Roads. At the head of
the Accounts Branch of the Buildings and Roads division is the
Examiner of Public Works Accounts already mentioned, assisted
by a Deputy Examiner for Buildings and Roads, and an office
establishment. The Irrigation division is similarly sub-divided
into an Executive Branch and an Accounts Branch. At the
head of the former is a Chief Engineer, gazetted also as Joint
Secretary, with an office establishment and an executive staff
of District Engineers, &c. The executive staff for Irrigation
is, for economy's sake, identical with that previously mentioned
as belonging to Buildings and Roads. The Chief Engineer and
Joint Secretary in this division is assisted by a Deputy Chief
Engineer and Under Secretary for Irrigation. At the head of
the Accounts Branch is a special Deputy Examiner for
Irrigation acting under the general control of the Examiner
already mentioned, and assisted by an office establishment of
accountants. Here again the office establishment is, for
economy's sake, identical with that employed in the Buildings
and Roads division. It has already been explained that the
executive establishment in the Buildings and Roads and Irrigation divisions is one, being employed that is to say indifferently
in the execution of all works, of whatever nature, which have to
be carried out in the district or range to which they are
attached ; it is proper to mention here that the whole of this
establishment, as an establishment, is under the general
control of the Chief Engineer in charge of Buildings and Roads

or Irrigation who happens to be the senior. At the present date the Senior Chief Engineer is also Secretary to Government. The third main division of the Public Works Department, Railways, is divided, as are the other divisions, into an Executive Branch and an Accounts Branch. The Railways in this Presidency being all guaranteed, there being that is to say no Railways constructed by the direct agency of the State, the officer at the head of the division is called Consulting Engineer. As there are no works to be executed there is no executive staff; but the Consulting Engineer is assisted by two Deputy Consulting Engineers, who aid in office work and inspection. The Railway Accounts Branch is in charge of an Examiner of Railway Accounts with an office establishment of accountants.

The Public Works Department deals with all Engineering Works undertaken by the State, the construction or repair of which has to be carried out under professional superintendence. Detailed designs and estimates for public buildings and other engineering works required by any other department of Government are drawn up by this department, and, after the general arrangements proposed have been approved of, the Public Works Department carries out the works as soon as funds are made available to meet the estimated expenditure. The Public Works Department is thus called upon to plan and execute works for the Government of India; for the Provincial Government; for the various Local Fund Boards; for the Board of Revenue and the Heads of other Departments, as Trustees of certain special funds which they administer; for the Court of Wards; and occasionally for Municipal Corporations. In the absence of State Railways it is evident that there are works to be executed only in the "Buildings and Roads" and "Irrigation" Secretariat divisions. *Nature of work done.*

For the Imperial Government the Public Works Department undertakes the construction and maintenance of the following works. The following classification is the technical one used for statistical purposes:— *Government of India Works.*

(*a.*) *Irrigation*, including all works in connection with Irrigation and River Conservancy.

(*b.*) *Imperial* proper sub-divided into

(1.) *Military*, including all works connected with the army, such as Fortifications, Barracks, Commissariat and Ordnance buildings, Military rest-houses, and Cantonment roads.

(2.) *Other Services*, including all buildings and other works connected with the Postal, Telegraph, and Salt Departments, together with such Mining operations, Light-houses and other Public improvements as may be considered to be rather of Imperial than of Local interest.

To meet the expenditure on these heads, grants are yearly made by the Imperial Government from the ordinary revenues of India and also from loans raised by the Imperial Government for the purpose of constructing reproductive works. By far the most important works carried out by the Public Works Department on behalf of the Government of India are those connected with irrigation and the conservancy of rivers.

Works for Provincial Government. For the Provincial Government, the Public Works Department constructs and repairs all buildings in connection with the Judicial, Revenue, Customs, Police, Educational, Jail, Medical, Marine, and Ecclesiastical Departments, as well as all navigable canals not forming part of a system of irrigation channels. To these may be added a few roads; all works connected with the improvements, water-supply, and drainage of towns other than Municipalities; all works connected with harbours; and all works connected with the light-houses required for the purely local coasting trade. The expenditure from Provincial Funds on Public Works in a great measure takes the form of grants-in-aid to the several Local Fund Boards, which have charge of all the roads in the Presidency, with the exception of a few roads leading up to the hills, considered to be of Provincial rather than of Local importance.

Local and Special Works. The work executed by the Public Works Department on behalf of the Local Fund Boards consists chiefly of the construction and repair of roads, and occasionally of buildings in connection with Hospitals, Dispensaries, School-houses, and Travellers' Bungalows. The expenditure on these works is met by grants from the Local Funds raised under Act IV of 1871, supplemented by the grants-in-aid from Provincial Funds before referred to. Sums to defray the cost of similar works are further allotted to the Public Works Department by the Board of Revenue from special funds administered by the Board itself, such as the Canal and Ferry Fund, Jungle Conservancy Fund, Pound Fund, Irrigation Cess, and other Funds, and also by the Court of Wards from the revenues of the estates under their charge. The Public Works Department also execute various works the cost of which is defrayed from the Port, Educational, Convict Labor, and Police Lodging Funds.

In connection with the Public Works Department are the **Workshops.** Workshops at Madras, Dowlaishweram, and Bezwada. These institutions are self-supporting; the prices charged on the work turned out being sufficient to meet all charges for labor, materials, and supervision, as well as for interest on capital and depreciation of the block.

The Public Works Establishment is divided into two distinct **Establish-** branches, the Executive and the Accounts, the former of which **ment.** deals with the preparation of designs and estimates and with the supervision and execution of the works, and the latter with the control and audit of the expenditure incurred. The Executive Branch consists of (a), the Engineer Establishment of professional Engineers, composed chiefly of officers of the Royal Engineers and of Civil Engineers either trained at one of the Civil Engineering Colleges, or engaged from the Profession at home; (b), the Upper Subordinate Establishment, consisting chiefly of European Artisans, Mechanics, Clerks of works, and others, who have either been apprenticed to some trade, or who have received a professional training at one of the Civil Engineering Colleges; (c), the Lower Subordinate Establishment of native foremen carpenters, masons, and others, who have a practical knowledge of ordinary building work, and some slight knowledge of plan-drawing and surveying; (d), the Petty Establishment of storekeepers, guards, lascars, and other inferior servants; and (e), the Office Establishment of clerks, draftsmen, messengers, and others employed in the various offices. The Accounts Branch is divided into the Control Establishment corresponding to the "Engineer" Establishment, and the "Accountant" Establishment of trained Accountants corresponding to the Upper Subordinate Establishment of the Executive Branch. Further particulars regarding Public Works Accounts will be found under Chapter V. The Public Works Executive Establishment maintained in the districts is employed indifferently in the general execution of all the works entrusted to the Department, the service of each Officer being utilized in the best way practicable in carrying out the works, irrespective of the kind of work to be carried out, or the service for which the work is required. The advantages of having a distinct establishment which would concern itself exclusively with irrigation and thus acquire the efficiency which practice and experience in a limited field of work would give has long been recognized, but the difficulties arising from the small scale of establishments and the large area over which works are spread

has hitherto been considered an insuperable obstacle to such an
arrangement. There is a small special establishment maintained
in connection with Irrigation works, namely the Navigation and
Water Regulation Establishment, the cost of which is a charge
to Imperial Irrigation Funds. This extra establishment is
employed in the distribution of water for irrigation and the
regulation of the supply in canals and channels, the control of
the canal navigation and the record of traffic, the execution of
petty repairs and general conservancy of canals, channels, and
embankments. A grant for temporary establishments employed
on surveys has also been made of late years. These surveys are
required for the purpose of framing the projects for the
completion of the works of the Godavery, Kistna, and Pennair
Delta systems, and also for supplying data for the grouping of
other works of irrigation and their comprehensive treatment in
the way of reform, reconstruction, or repair.

Establishment charges. Apart from the cost of the works themselves, which
includes extra or temporary establishment beginning and
ending with the work and the materials necessary for the work,
there are charges to be met from permanent establishment. The
work of the latter consists in making plans, in supervising
execution by permanent hands, and in accounting and in auditing, and the charges for this are called " establishment charges."
The cost of the whole establishment of the Railway Branch is
borne by Imperial Funds. That of the rest of the general establishment is divided arbitrarily between the several heads of service.
Imperial and Irrigation Funds are charged in each year for Public
Works supervision 25 per cent. on the outlay on works during
the year or on the budget grants, whichever may be the greater.
Local and Special Funds are charged 25 per cent. on the actual
expenditure. The cost of any establishment specially entertained
for particular investigations is charged to the Head of Service
concerned. The balance of the establishment charges, whatever
it may amount to, is charged to Provincial Funds. When works
are carried out by departments other than the Public Works
Department, the latter find the plans and audit the expenditure ;
but no charge is made for establishment on this account.

Tools and Plant charges. Under the Public Works system of account, the estimate
drawn up for a work does not include the cost of the Tools and
Plant required for its execution ; all charges on account of Tools
and Plant being carried to a separate head. At present the cost
of the tools and plant required for the execution of the works
is charged against the different heads of service, Imperial

Irrigation, Provincial, &c., according to the works for which they were intended to be principally used. There is, however, some reason to believe that this arrangement practically leads to an incorrect distribution, and proposals are now under consideration for dividing off the charges for Tools and Plant arbitrarily in much the same manner as those for establishments.

The execution of the Public Works in this Presidency is for the most part carried out either by daily labor under the direction of the Officers of the Department, or by petty contract under the same supervision. A few works, however, after being designed by the Public Works Department, are carried out under the supervision of Officers of the departments directly concerned with the work, special Government sanction being necessary for this in nearly all cases. The employment of large contractors, and especially of European contractors, in the execution of works in this Presidency is extremely rare. The progress of a Public Work from initiation to completion, say of a building required for the Revenue Department, is as follows. When the necessity for the work has been recognized by Government, the District Engineer is called on to submit a plan and estimate, usually through the Collector. When this is sanctioned by Government the work is placed on the list of those which are ready to be carried out when funds are provided. Funds are provided by the Government by sanctioning a specific appropriation for the work in some year's Public Works budget. For the commencement of this work after the funds are provided the sanction of Government is not again necessary. Before beginning the work it will as a rule be necessary for the land to be made over to the Public Works Department; this is done by the Collector, who, if necessary, takes due steps for acquiring the land. The District Engineer then entrusts the work to the Executive Engineer or Range Officer, and the latter either collects labor and materials and builds himself, or gives out the work on petty contract. Funds are drawn by the Executive Engineer from the treasury by cheque on his public account kept there. When this work is done the Collector countersigns a "completion certificate," which has been prepared by the Executive Officer, and the Public Works Department are relieved of responsibility. Repairs to buildings once constructed are made, as occasion requires, by the Public Works Department, under the head of "Repairs" in their budget.

Execution of works.

PUBLIC WORKS—BUILDINGS AND ROADS.

Nature of the division. The Buildings and Roads division in this Presidency includes both of what are known in the Northern Provinces of India as the Buildings and Roads division and the Military Works division. It deals with all questions and works not special to the Irrigation branch, and comprises therefore Military Works ; buildings, &c., connected with the Post Office, Revenue, Telegraph, Ecclesiastical, Educational, and Judicial Departments, and roads, bridges, navigable canals, river improvements, accommodation for travellers, light-houses, mines, and manufactures. Following the classification according to account heads given in the preceding remarks works executed under this division fall necessarily under one or other of the following heads. As a rule the works executed are only of local interest :—

Imperial.	*Provincial.*	*Local and Special.*
Military.	Civil Buildings.	Communications.
Fortifications.	Communications.	Civil Buildings.
Military Buildings.	Miscellaneous Public	Miscellaneous Public
Military Roads.	Improvement.	Improvement.
Miscellaneous.		
Other Services.		
Civil Buildings.		
Communications.		
Miscellaneous Public		
Improvement.		

PUBLIC WORKS—IRRIGATION.

Nature of the division. The Irrigation division of the Public Works Department deals with works in connection with Irrigation and River Conservancy. The expenditure on these works is met partly from ordinary Imperial revenues, and partly from loans. Grants from Loan Funds are made for the construction of such irrigation schemes only as give a reasonable promise that the works will yield a return at least equal to the interest of the money laid out upon them, and for all such works quasi-commercial accounts of capital and revenue are maintained. Works paid for from loans are called Extraordinary Works, and those paid for from current revenue are called Ordinary Works. Outlay from ordinary funds is further sub-divided and accounted for technically under three heads, Capital Ordinary, Revenue, and Ordinary Agricultural. There are therefore in the Irrigation branch four fund heads—(1) Capital Extraordinary, (2) Capital Ordinary, (3) Revenue, and (4) Ordinary Agricultural. This classification is that observed both in the budget estimates and the appropriation and outlay accounts. The notice of works in the yearly Public Works administration reports follows the fund heads, as being the only arrangement practicable. The arrangement however is not so satisfactory under Irrigation as it is under Buildings and Roads, for whereas in the latter division a single work is always carried out from a single fund, in the former the same work is frequently carried out from different funds.

Works under the first head above mentioned are synonymous **Nature of** with Loan Works. All expenditure on construction is regarded **Capital Extraordinary.** as capital outlay and is carried to a capital account. At present only the eight following works come under the category of Loan Works:—

1. Godavery Delta Works.   5. Palar Anicut.
2. Kistna Delta Works.   6. Pelandorai Anicut.
3. Pennair Anicut.   7. Cauvery Delta Works.
4. Chembrambakam Tank·   8. Streeviguntam Anicut.

The Godavery Anicut or Weir was commenced in 1844-45 for **—Godavery** the supply of the canals of the delta, at the head of which it **Delta System.** stands. The river drains an area of about 115,570 square miles. The crest of the anicut is at 38 feet above mean sea level, and it is situated at about 33 miles from the coast. The length of the crest of the weir on the line of which the river is divided into four branches is 3,938 yards. The greatest depth of water which has passed over the weir is 15·25 feet. A short distance below the river forms two main branches with the Central Delta between them. There are three main canals—that of the Eastern Delta has a bottom width of 184½ feet, and when carrying a full supply the water is 8·21 feet deep. That of the Central Delta will be 114 feet wide at bottom with a depth of 7 feet of water. That of the Western Delta varies considerably in width, but where the water is carried in a single channel the bottom width is about 225 feet, and the full depth of water 10 feet. All the principal canals of the delta are navigable. The length of canals now available, or shortly to be ready, for navigation is 450 miles, and many of them have during the last four years been much improved by the construction of additional locks and

the reduction of the current. The total area of the delta is about
2,023 square miles. Extensive drainage works have been undertaken since 1870 in the Eastern and Western Deltas. This
system irrigates about 513,143 acres with an average revenue
of Rs. 15,61,019. The following statement shows the length of
navigable canals open to date :—

Names of Canals.	Proposed Total Length.	Completed and Navigable.	
		Up to 1874-75 inclusive.	Up to 1875-76 inclusive.
	MS. CHS.	MS. CHS.	MS. CHS.
Eastern Delta.			
Main Canal	4 12	4 12	4 12
Samulcotta Canal	32 68	32 68	32 68
Cocanada Canal ...	25 27	25 27	25 27
Bank Canal	37 23	23 40	23 40
Coringa Canal ...	22 27	22 27	22 27
Injeram Canal ...	10 62	10 62	10 62
Mundapetta Canal	13 35	13 35	13 35
Total ...	146 14	132 31	132 31
Central Delta.			
Main Canal	8 0	8 0	8 0
West Bank Canal	44 0	28 0	28 0
East Bank Canal including Billa-curru junction.	45 0	39 0	39 0
Amalapur Canal ...	31 40	27 0	27 0
Bendamurlunka Canal ...	14 0	2 0	2 0
Total ...	142 40	104 0	104 0
Western Delta.			
Main Canal	6 5	6 5	6 5
Kakarapurru Canal	10 29	10 29	10 29
Nursapur Canal ...	29 51	29 51	29 51
Bank Canal	24 40	16 0	21 40
Gostanuddy and Velpur	28 35	14 0	23 40
Ellore Canal	40 27	40 27	40 27
Junction Canal ...	3 43	3 43	3 43
Venkiah and Weyyern ...	29 74	29 74	29 74
Undi Canal	14 73	0 0	5 60
Attili Canal	15 75	15 75	15 75
Total ...	203 52	165 64	186 44
Grand Total ...	492 26	402 15	422 75

—Kistna
Delta System.
The Kistna Anicut or weir was commenced in 1852. The site
chosen is at a point where the river is much narrower than its
normal width, its channel being there confined by rocky hills on
either bank. The length of the crest of this weir is 1,280 yards.
In 1874 the river rose to 19·42 feet above the weir crest, and
this was the highest fresh which has occurred since the anicut
was built. The drainage basin of the river has an area of about

110,000 square miles, and divides the delta into two parts. The Eastern Delta Main Canal will, when completed, have a bottom width of 200 feet, and a depth of water of 8¼ feet. The main canal of the Western Delta will have a bottom width of 230 feet, and a depth of water of 8 feet. The principal canals are navigable and their length so available is at present about 254 miles. Some addition will hereafter be made to the extent of navigation by the extension or improvement of the canals. The area of the two parts of the delta is, together, 2,110 square miles, the irrigated area is 226,226 acres, and the revenue Rupees 8,90,753. The subjoined statement shows the length of navigable canals open to date :—

Names of Canals.	Proposed Total Length.	Completed and Navigable.	
		Up to 1874-75 inclusive.	Up to 1875-76 inclusive.
Eastern Delta.	MILES.	MILES.	MILES.
Ellore Canal	39	39	39
Budaméru	29	29	39
Masulipatam Canal	49	49	49
Pulleru between Head Sluice and Cowtaram.	26	17	17
Bantumilly Canal ...	22	22	22
Polarázkodu Canal ...	17	17	17
	182	173	173
Western Delta.			
Nizampatam Canal ...	42	42	42
Bank Canal	46	21	21
Commamoor Canal ...	50	18	18
	138	81	81
Grand Total ...	320	254	254

The Pennair Delta embraces a comparatively small area ; on the north side of the river there are from 200 to 220 square miles of country in which there are numerous tanks which receive a more or less reliable supply of water, and it has been proposed to improve radically the arrangements ; but hitherto the irrigation is much in the state in which it was found when the district came into British possession. On the south side the area is 150 square miles, and has been provided with a fairly complete system of irrigation. The anicut or weir across the river was commenced in 1855, and was until this year (1875) 527 yards in length, or about one-third of the normal width of the river. It has been lengthened to 677 yards to lessen its liability to damage. In the

—Pennair Anicut System.

flood of 1874, 18.37 feet of water passed over the crest, and much
of the country on both sides of the river was inundated. The
area of the basin drained by the river is about 20,000 square miles.

—Cauvery   The Cauvery Delta has the largest area of irrigation in Madras.
Delta System. About 10 miles west of Trichinopoly, the Aganda Cauvery divides
at the head of the island of Seringham into two branches, the
Coleroon and the Cauvery. Across the Coleroon a weir called the
Upper Anicut was constructed about the year 1834, and was one
of the earliest of the great works planned by Sir Arthur Cotton.
Its effect on the Delta has been very great, and the benefits
conferred on the Government and on the people of the Tanjore
District have more than fulfilled the anticipations of the projector,
by securing a reliable supply of water, and obviating the necessity
for collecting annually or in some seasons several times during
the year several thousands of the cultivators to form temporary
works for the diversion of water down the Cauvery. The head
of this latter river is 1,950 feet wide, and the bed level is regulated
by a dam. After running for some 16 or 17 miles, the Cauvery
divides into two principal rivers, the Cauvery and the Vennaur,
which irrigate nearly equal areas, and which give off numerous
branches : at all the principal bifurcations regulating works have
during the last few years been constructed. The Cauvery was
formerly connected with the Coleroon at the east end of the
island of Seringham, some 20 miles from the Upper Coleroon
Anicut, and across this channel a work called the Grand Anicut
was built by the natives many years before the province of
Tanjore was ceded to the British. This was the first step towards
the improvement of the delta, and its effect must have been
great. In the Northern Deltas the whole of the distribution of
water has been artificially carried out by canals ; but in the
Cauvery Delta the principal distribution was effected naturally by
the numerous branches thrown off by the Cauvery and Vennaur ;
and from these branches innumerable small channels have been cut
to convey water to the lands of the Delta villages. The chief
work to be done under the British Government was to render
the water-supply more reliable, and this was secured by the
upper anicut ; secondly, to regulate the distribution by the
principal rivers towards which something was done formerly by
the regulating works at the head of the Vennaur, and much
more during the last few years by the construction of regulators
at the heads of all the principal branches. It is intended
to bring the Cauvery under complete regulation and to provide
a new head for the Vennaur at the grand anicut, so that

the delta may be entirely protected from excessive floods and that water, which cannot with safety be carried by the various rivers of the delta, may be passed over the grand anicut, into the Coleroon, and thus got rid of. Much useful work has been done in the delta towards regulating the widths of the rivers and improving their alignment. Formerly the river beds varied greatly in width, and the result was that the deep channels changed from year to year, the tendency being to cut away the banks in some places, and to deposit the eroded material elsewhere. The parts of river beds in excess of the width required have been planted up with a tall grass, called nanel or durbah ; this checks the current, causes a deposit of the silt held in suspension, and so gradually reclaims land in a very simple, effectual, and inexpensive manner. The Cauvery rises in the Western Ghauts or mountains, and drains an area of about 28,000 square miles. The area of its delta is about 2,760 square miles. The system irrigates about 835,208 acres with a revenue of Rupees 35,30,336.

The Chembrumbakam tank is a large reservoir about 14 —Chembrum-
miles from Madras, which has been formed by enlarging an old bakam Tank System.
native tank. Before its enlargement it held from 55·61* to 77·80
millions of cubic yards, and had an area of 4,648 acres, or 7·26 square miles. Its present capacity is 102·91 millions of cubic yards, and the water-spread is 5,729 acres, or 8·95 square miles. The old sources of supply have been rendered to a greater extent available by enlarging the supply channel and its head sluice. It is not yet known whether the extension of irrigation will correspond to the expectations entertained when the scheme was sanctioned. Originally it was intended to make the tank large enough to hold 196·87 millions of cubic yards, but a reconsideration of the water-supply available resulted in the alteration of the project to the dimensions above noted.

The Pelandorai anicut gives its name to a system of irrigation —Pelandorai
in South Arcot. The anicut is built across the Vellaur river at Anicut System.
the site which gives the work its name, and a supply channel from the right bank regulated by a head sluice and connected with subsidiary channels conveys water for the irrigation of fifty villages in the Chellumbrum Taluq. The works were commenced in 1870, and are, with the exception of additional storage in tanks, practically completed.

---

* Ordinary.

—Palar Anicut System.

The Palar anicut is thrown across the river of that name at the town of Vellore in the North Arcot District. It is 2,600 feet long, and is the head of a system which irrigates about 37,672 acres. Channels provided with head sluices take off on either bank above the anicut. The original work was constructed about the year 1855. It was damaged and partly carried away in 1874, and has since been restored.

—Striviguntum Anicut System.

The Striviguntum anicut system is of considerable importance. The anicut crosses the Tambrapoorney river in Tinnevelly about 16 miles from the sea, and is the lowest anicut on the river. It provides for the extension of irrigation on both sides of the river, the channels leading from which not only irrigate the land directly but furnish supplies to existing tanks where it is stored. The original estimate of the extent of land to be brought under cultivation was 32,000 acres. The work may be said to be completed.

Nature of Capital Ordinary.

Under the second head mentioned above are comprised works constructed by means of funds appropriated from current revenue. The eight systems of extraordinary works in so far as they have been constructed from Ordinary Capital, belong to this head. There are indeed at present no other works under Capital Ordinary.

Nature of Revenue Head.

Under Revenue are grouped all works connected with minor extensions, improvements and repairs to works in the two heads just mentioned.

Nature of Ordinary Agricultural.

The three heads just mentioned belong to the group of works for which capital and revenue accounts are kept. The term Ordinary-Agricultural is applied to those works for which capital and revenue accounts are not kept. According to present arrangements capital and revenue accounts are kept for the eight systems of irrigation already enumerated, and all other irrigation works are classed as Ordinary-Agricultural. Regarding these works it is necessary to explain that the reason for omitting them from the system of accounts framed to exhibit the returns due to original outlay and to balance the cost of maintenance against revenue is not necessarily that they are unremunerative; but that no such exact conclusion can under the circumstances be arrived at as to make it desirable to prepare for them the elaborate accounts prescribed for the exhibition of the financial results of the systems of irrigation on which Loan funds have been expended. When it is considered that Ordinary-Agricultural Works constitute the bulk of the works of irrigation in the Presidency, and that they irrigate an area of about

3,365,157 acres, yielding a revenue of, approximately, Rupees 1,31,04,126, their importance is manifest; and although the outlay under these works is not at present contrasted or compared in any regular financial statements with the returns in the shape of wet assessment or with the difference between that and the cess on dry land of the same area, the close connection of the works with the land revenue and the intimate sympathy which exists between their condition and the agricultural prosperity of the country must always be borne in mind. The first and most important sub-division of Ordinary-Agricultural works is the head Irrigation. Ordinary-Agricultural irrigation works are widely distributed and exist more or less in every district of the Presidency. They may be divided into two distinctive classes : (1) rain-fed tanks or reservoirs, generally of minor individual importance, each deriving its supply directly from rainfall distributed over an area of land which is called the catchment basin; and (2) channels from rivers and streams providing direct irrigation or supplying tanks, together with the tanks supplied. In the first case the rainfall is caught and retained before it reaches natural drainage lines of any importance. In the last it is diverted from the drainage lines while pursuing its course and led away by artificial means. The second class is the most important, and the works which have been constructed in connection therewith by natives of the country, or by the British Government, whether anicuts or weirs across rivers or channels themselves, are often of considerable magnitude and have a large revenue dependent on them. The following statement in which the number of Ordinary-Agricultural irrigation works in each district is roughly estimated, and in which also the irrigated area in each district is shown, is an index to the geographical distribution of these works throughout the Presidency and to their relative importance in a financial point of view :—

Statement.

District.	Tanks and Irrigation Canals.	Weirs across Rivers or Streams.	Irrigated Area.	Revenue.
1	2	3	4	5
				RS.
Ganjam	3,504	1	287,279	5,15,431
Vizagapatam	392	13	166,846	2,44,098
Godavery	1,602	8	173,089	7,75,540
Kistna	442	...	62,002	2,80,349
Nellore	765	7	208,588	6,78,500
Cuddapah	2,406	...	260,475	9,13,438
Kurnool	654	49	61,791	2,57,656
Bellary	3,493	25	194,380	8,28,462
Chingleput	2,360	7	407,169	12,26,004
North Arcot	3,834	76	271,131	13,21,436
South do.	3,736	179	393,100	18,97,301
Tanjore	...	...	114,525	1,51,696
Trichinopoly	1,489	91	208,665	7,83,290
Salem	2,005	217	113,936	4,85,747
Coimbatore	337	68	102,933	5,99,827
Madura	3,942	373	172,969	6,31,978
Tinnevelly	2,357	98	166,279	15,13,373
Total ...	33,318	1,212	3,365,157	1,31,04,126

NOTE.—The statement as regards the number of works is only an approximate one. The area irrigated as well as the revenue attributable to the systems for which Capital and Revenue Accounts are kept is excluded. Irrigation Works belonging to land-owners are not taken into account.

It has long been understood that, in order to secure a comprehensive treatment of these numerous works, it is necessary that they should be grouped into systems hydrographically connected ; measures have accordingly been taken towards this end. It is obvious that the whole of them can be referred to various natural drainage lines and ultimately to river basins. When this has been done and the particulars of water-supply, revenue and outlay are properly recorded, it will be possible to measure with some accuracy the relation of returns to outlay, and to apportion expenditure with due regard to economy and on sound principles. The other Ordinary-Agricultural sub-divisions coming under the two classes mentioned are River Conservancy, River Embankments, and Miscellaneous, the latter including works not susceptible of being referred to either of the three other classes.

Additional heads and sub-divisions. In addition to the expenditure on new works and repairs for which the Department of Public Works is responsible, there is outlay in other directions. These other heads of account are for the establishment employed in duties of supervision and direction, and for tools and plant used in carrying on the works. The whole outlay may, therefore, be considered under four divisions. Original or New Works, Repairs, Establishment, Tools and

Plant. As regards establishment, since as already remarked the Irrigation Branch is charged with a fixed percentage (25 per cent. on grant or outlay, whichever is the greatest) for general establishment, it is only necessary to notice under this section matters relating to the special establishments which have been described as being attached to the Irrigation Branch. Tools and Plant expenditure have to be considered. In whichever way again outlay under the irrigation branch is treated, it will be necessary to consider under each section the fund heads, Capital Extraordinary, Capital Ordinary, Revenue, and Ordinary Agricultural. These divisions and sub-divisions are attended to in the yearly administration reports.

The revenue dependent on the works existing throughout the Presidency for the purposes of collecting, storing and distributing water for irrigation is, as has already been mentioned, very considerable. The collections from irrigated land amounted in 1874-75, the latest year for which the accounts are compiled, to Rupees 1,95,67,001. On the other hand the receipts actually credited in the Public Works accounts are quite insignificant, accruing not from the sale of water for irrigation but from other incidental sources of profit, such as navigation dues, water-supply of towns, sale of canal produce, such as grass, rent of land, &c. This is due to the revenue system obtaining in the Presidency by which the rent levied on irrigated land is for the most part in the form of a consolidated assessment of which the proportion due to water-supply as distinguished from the claim for the use of the land for cultivation is indefinite. It is only as regards the deltas of the Godavery and the Kistna, and that quite recently, that a settlement has been made distinguishing between land assessment and water-rate, and even here the principle of the settlement has been a consolidated wet rate of which an arbitrary and uniform portion is called the water-rate. In the case of extraordinary works an attempt has been made to estimate profits, and for the irrigation works in the deltas special investigations have already been instituted having for their object on the one hand the summing up of the charges against the works, and on the other the determination of the revenue which is due to the outlay incurred. For five out of the eight extraordinary systems approximate accounts have now been prepared, and the following abstract shows the results temporarily accepted :—

Receipts from Irrigation Works.

Latest year included in this account.	Name of system of Irrigation.	Capital outlay.		Revenue.		Working of expenses.		Net Revenue.		Charges for interest.		Difference between Net Revenue and charges for interest.		Percentage of Net Revenue on capital outlay.
		During the year.	To end of the year.	During the year.	To end of the year.	During the year.	To end of the year.	During the year.	To end of the year.	During the year.	To end of the year.	During the year.	To end of the year.	
1	2	3	4	5	6	7	8	9	10	11	12	13	14	15
		Rs.	Rs.	Rs.	Rs.	Rs.	Rs.	Rs.	Rs.	Rs.	Rs.	Rs.	Rs.	
1874-75.	Godavery Delta* ...	4,41,990	69,10,549	16,23,310	2,29,66,885	1,54,751	54,98,671	14,68,559	1,74,68,216	3,10,974	46,98,602	11,57,585	1,27,69,614	21·25
1874-75.	Kistna Delta† ...	1,56,374	44,93,902	8,90,598	92,16,961	1,94,905	23,50,046	6,95,693	68,66,215	2,02,226	26,46,665	4,93,467	42,19,553	15·48
1873-74.	Cauvery Delta ...	49,844	13,39,641	11,60,713	2,61,75,721	11,204	47,12,266	11,49,509	2,14,63,455	60,294	11,84,754	10,89,225	2,02,78,701	85·81
1872-73.	Palar Anicut‡ ...	538	10,83,714	21,022	11,47,651	10,124	41,149	10,898	11,06,502	48,767	6,26,885	87,869	4,79,617	1·01
1874-75.	Stveignutam Anicut.	65,708	10,60,597	38,779	62,928			38,779	62,928	47,727	1,94,236	8,948	1,31,308	3·65

* Direct income by water-rate is the revenue in this case.

† Direct income by water-rate and Miscellaneous receipts constitutes the revenue.

‡ No information regarding working expenses of this year is available.

Of the departmental receipts referred to above the only items meriting notice are those attributable to the navigation of canals in the Godavery and Kistna Deltas. Licenses to ply on these canals are issued to boat owners, the present rate being 1 Rupee per ton per annum for cargo boats, and from 3 to 6 annas for every square foot of deck space for passenger boats.

The old works of irrigation were almost without exception, **Conservancy of Works of** and a majority of them are still, without adequate means of **Irrigation.** disposing of surplus water and distributing water for irrigation; and an outlay on works, such as weirs, sluices, &c., considerably larger than the present outlay, is required to prevent recurring loss of revenue. It is to be regretted that the responsibility of villagers for the timely execution of petty repairs to tanks and other works belonging to the village have generally been allowed to lapse, but it is doubtful whether there is now a possibility of its revival. The execution of such repairs at the public cost will materially affect the charges for maintenance of irrigation works.

PUBLIC WORKS—RAILWAYS.

The Secretariat arrangements in connection with this branch of **Constitution** the Public Works Department have already been described. All **of the department.** the Railways yet undertaken in this Presidency are under the guarantee system. The design, that is to say, and construction of the railroads are entrusted to joint-stock companies, and the Indian Government guarantees interest on moneys duly raised and paid to Government by these companies, while it controls their expenditure and operations. The principal concessions granted under this agreement are the following:—(1) The Government guarantee interest varying in amount from $4\frac{1}{2}$ to 5 per cent. for a term of years* on all moneys paid with authority into their treasury, and should the profits in any half-year exceed the guaranteed interest, the surplus is equally divided between Government and the shareholders. (2) The Railway Company have the option of demanding repayment, upon their giving six months' notice of their intention to surrender the railway, of the whole of the capital duly expended upon the railway. On the other hand the Government have the option of purchasing the railway at fixed periods (due notice being given) on payment of the value of all shares calculated according to

---

* Madras Railway 99 years, South Indian Railway 999 years.

their mean market-value during three preceding years. The
first opportunity of purchasing the Madras Railway will occur
on the 1st April 1907, and of the South Indian Railway on 1st
March 1890. (3) Government lease to the Railway Company
free of cost for a term* of years all land required for the permanent works of the railway, and further provide all other land
temporarily needed for its construction; land not permanently
needed being returned to Government as soon as possible. In
consideration of the above grants of aid, the Government
have the power to select the line, to define the limits of all works,
to supervise expenditure and operations in England and in
India, to examine accounts, to inspect works and line under or
after completion, to regulate tolls and time-tables, and generally
to control the affairs of the Railway Company. Mails are to be
carried free; troops and Government stores on the usual favorable
terms. The control in England is exercised by an official
Director, who sits at the Boards of all Guaranteed Railway
Companies, and who has the power of passing a veto on their
proceedings. In India the supervision is entrusted to the
Consulting Engineer for Railways, and the following rules have
been laid down for his guidance :—(1) All questions of general
importance shall be referred to Government for decision.
(2) Under the above will be included the general direction of
all lines of railway, the position of stations, and the general
arrangements of the more important stations and works. But
after the general sanction of the Government has been given to
any project, all questions of detail can be disposed of within the
limits of the original sanction by the Consulting Engineer.
(3) All matters of routine, or payments, or acts in accordance
with rule, precedent, or special agreement duly sanctioned, or
undisputed contingent expenditure, may be dealt with by the
Consulting Engineer without reference to Government. (4) All
designs, estimates, and indents, whether for work or for
establishments for carrying into effect objects already generally
sanctioned by Government, may also be disposed of finally by
the Consulting Engineer. (5) The Consulting Engineer may,
without reference to Government, reduce the amount of indents,
or direct designs or proposed operations to be modified if he
thinks it necessary; but the Agent in such cases, if dissatisfied
with the decision of the Consulting Engineer, may always
request that the matter be referred for the final orders of the
Government. (6) When the sanction of the Consulting Engi-

* Madras Railway 99 years, South Indian Railway 999 years.

neer is given to any proposals of the Agent, in which both of
these officers concur, excepting in those matters of great
importance specially excepted above, the sanction so given shall,
so far as the Government is concerned, be considered final.

MADRAS IRRIGATION COMPANY.

The guaranteed Company styled the Madras Irrigation and **History of**
Canal Company was incorporated by an Act of Parliament, dated **Company and**
scope of
the 11th May 1858, for the purpose of constructing and **operation.**
managing works of irrigation and navigation in various parts
of India. An indenture or contract deed was executed on
the 3rd June 1863 between the Company and the Secretary
of State for India, providing for the execution by the Company
of one work to be selected by the local Government, to
cost one million sterling, and on which 5 per cent. return
was guaranteed by the Secretary of State. In pursuance of that
agreement, the so-called Toombudra or Tongabudra project was
adopted. This included a canal for irrigation and navigation
from Sunkesala 17 miles above the town of Kurnool on the
Toombudra to the Kistnapatam estuary on the sea-coast in
Nellore. The Company accordingly undertook that section of
the scheme which extends from Sunkesala to Soomaisweram on
the Pennair river. In 1866 it having been found that the
original estimate was quite insufficient to complete the project,
a further agreement was concluded on the 30th July of that
year. This contract separates the section of the scheme extending from Sunkesala to Cuddapah from the remainder of the
project, and provides for a loan of £600,000 from the Secretary
of State to the Company on the security of debentures issued
by them, the loan to be expended in the completion of the
canal to the Pennair and thence to the town of Cuddapah.
The work was virtually completed in 1871. Hitherto the canal
has been an entire failure in a financial point of view. The
returns from Irrigation and the sale of water generally have
been utterly insignificant when compared with the capital outlay.
They have averaged about Rupees 51,000 per annum, while the
charges against revenue for maintenance and establishment do
not fall far short of Rupees 1,80,000 annually. The causes are
stated to be the unprofitable outlay on works of navigation,
which, owing to the want of capital on the part of the Company,
are not utilized; the scarcity of labor in the district, and the

high rates necessary in order to attract it from a distance for
the construction of the canal, whereby the capital outlay was
increased ; and, the cost of transport of produce to market by the
indifferent roads of the country, and the check thus given to
the extension of irrigation for the growth of rice, which is not
an article of large local consumption.   A general superintendence
over the financial affairs of the Company is exercised by the
Chief Engineer for Irrigation.

POST.

Imperial
Post.

There is no local control of the Imperial Postal Department.

District
Posts—
History.

The District Post existed in this Presidency prior to 1846
solely for the transmission of official correspondence between
Collectors and Magistrates and their subordinate officers.   It
had then no connection with the ordinary Postal Department,
and the dawks were carried by the peons and village servants
belonging to the Revenue Establishment as they could be spared
from other duty.   There were no receipts, and no separate
charges appeared in the accounts.   In 1846 the District Post
was opened to the public on payment of postage in cash, the
agency continued the same, and the district postage, regulated
on a different principle from the post rates of the ordinary Postal
Department, furnished a fund credited to the district in which it
was raised.   A letter passed on from the regular Post to the
District Post for delivery at an outlying village where there
was no regular post office, was charged district rate in addition
to the regular postage, and *vice versa*.   There was no inter-
communication between the two Posts.   It was not at this time
contemplated that the district dawks should be a source of profit
to the State ; consequently it was understood that the Collector
of each district was authorized to expend on the improvement
of the district postal system any revenue which it produced.
The receipts grew very rapidly, and in 1848-49 amounted to
Rupees 21,734.   In 1854 postage stamps were introduced in
lieu of cash payments in the regular Postal Department, and
simultaneously it was arranged that as regards matters of
payment, as far as the public was concerned, there should be no
distinction between this Post and the District Post, the two
forming one system for the public convenience.   From this date
the District Post may be said to have been converted into a
feeder of the Imperial Post.   During the last fifteen years

various improvements have been made in the district dawk in the employment of a special establishment for delivery, in opening new District Post Offices and lines, and in the extension of the system to outlying parts. Under Act XXI of 1866, section 64, the Governor-General in Council is empowered to frame rules, from time to time, for regulating the district dawks, and in exercise of that power sections 25, 27, 35, 42, 43, 44, 45, 47, 48, 49, 50, and 51 of the Act just named have been made applicable to them in this Presidency. As the receipts from postage stamps are now credited to Imperial, and even cash payments incidental to unpaid or insufficiently paid letters sent by District Post are collected by the Imperial Department, while the charges for district runners and gumastahs remain as they were before, it follows that all the receipts in this department go to Imperial while all the charges go to Provincial; the expenditure however is covered by the Imperial grant.

The District Post as now arranged furnishes inter-communi- —Present cation between those parts of the country which are removed arrange-ments. from the General Post line. The taluq stations are the first connected, and between these the delivery is carried out by the ordinary staff of District Post peons. The delivery into outlying villages is carried out by a system called the Rural Delivery. The Rural Delivery establishment consists of a staff of itiner-ating peons, whose beats are so arranged that they shall visit each village in the taluq once, twice, and thrice a week, or daily, according to the importance of the village, its accessibility, and the funds that are available ; and of village receiving-houses or houses of call for the peons. The latter are managed by respectable inhabitants of the village, who in some cases give their services gratuitously, and in other cases are paid a small stipend of Rupees 2 a month. The accounts of the District Post are kept by district post gumastahs at the taluqs. The administration of the District Post is vested in the Revenue Department, but it has been found convenient in the case of most districts to entrust the detailed management to the Postmaster-General, who, in communication with the Collectors, undertakes the practical working of the Post, the Collectors finding the funds in their revenue budgets. Again when a comparison of the District Post charges for any establishment with the Imperial receipts shewn by the postage stamps carried, indicates that in the case of this particular establishment the latter amount covers the former, with a margin of one-fifth, the Postmaster-General is authorized by the Government of India to take over the whole of the charges for that establishment, thus absorbing that portion of the District Post into the Imperial Post. When this takes place Provincial funds get a clear gain of the charges recently incurred, and these savings are utilized in the improvement of the remaining district establishments, especially in the direction of developing the Rural Delivery system. It is difficult to bring about individual solvency in the case of each establishment, and a proposal has been made to the Imperial Department to relax the conditions so as to group establishments and offices for purposes of experiment.

TELEGRAPH.

Imperial Telegraph.

The Government Telegraph Department is imperial, and there is no local control. The following were at the end of 1875-76 the lengths of the Sub-divisions of the Madras Division, excluding wires carried on supports of the Department, but belonging to the Local Government :—

	Miles of Line.	Miles of Wire.
Bezwarrah Sub-division.		
From Masulipatam through Bezwarrah to Hyderabad, Decan, and from Bezwarrah to the right bank of the Kistna. ...	212·5	214
Nellore Sub-division.		
From the right bank of Kistna river to the junction on the Madras Railway 3·5 miles from the Madras Office	260·03	521·62
Paumben Sub-division.		
From Madras to Tallamannar	392·32	425·44
Gooty Sub-division.		
From Madras to Raichore and from Goondacul Junction to Bellary	382·5	911·25
Total ...	1,248·35	2,072·21

The offices open at the end of 1875-76 were :—

Madras.	Nellore.
Pondicherry.	Guntoor.
Negapatam.	Bezwarrah.
Paumben.	Masulipatam.

Telegraphic communication throughout the Presidency is carried out to a great extent by means of the Railway Telegraphs.

SECTION V.

REVENUE, FINANCIAL, AND ADMINISTRATIVE.

THE receipts of this Presidency may be considered under three **Classification** distinct divisions, first those assigned for the general service **of Revenue** **and Finance.** of the Empire, secondly those appropriated for the exclusive wants of the Presidency, and thirdly those appropriated to the exclusive benefit of a particular locality or service within the Presidency. The first division chiefly consists of the revenue derived from taxation of the people, such as Land Revenue, Excise on Spirits and Drugs, Customs, Salt, and Stamps; but includes also some departmental receipts, such as Judicial Fees and Fines, Marine, Postal, and Telegraph collections, Military and Imperial Public Works Receipts, Interest on Loans and Advances made by Government, and sundry miscellaneous items, as gain by exchange and receipts in aid of superannuation. The tribute and peishcush received from the Mysore, Cochin, and Travancore States also appear under this division. The second division, known as Provincial Services, includes at present, besides certain sums annually assigned out of Imperial revenue by the Government of India, the departmental receipts of Jails, Registration, Police, Education, Medical, and Printing; as likewise certain petty items, such as the pilotage collections in the Paumben Channel, and the Uncovenanted Civil Service Examination fees. The third division includes taxes raised by special enactment or ruling, such as Road, Village Service, and Irrigation Cesses, and tolls on roads and canals, these taxes being controlled by the Board of Revenue through the medium of Collectors or of the Local Fund Boards. Under the third division are shown certain Special Funds also, such as Convict Labor, Police Lodging, School Fee, Educational Building, and Port Funds, which are under the control of the Heads of the Jail, Police, Educational, and Marine Departments, respectively. Municipal funds are not treated as State funds, and are therefore omitted from this classification. The distinction in this respect between Municipal funds and Local funds under Act IV of 1871 is somewhat arbitrary. There are however certain technical grounds for a distinction. Thus Local funds under Act IV of 1871 are collected by the ordinary Government agency of the country, and by means of an entry in the usual revenue puttah ; and they are paid invariably into the Government Treasury, and are subject there to Government control and audit. Neither of these conditions can be predicated of funds raised under the Towns' Improvement Act, in the case of which the Town Commissioners are left to collect their own resources, and to bank or not with the Government as they please. Moreover, generally speaking, the interference of Government is less frequently and less directly exercised in the case of Municipal funds than in the case of funds under the Local Funds' Act. The present section will show details of revenue and finance under the heads—

I.—Imperial Services, relating to the transactions described in the first division referred to above.

    (a.) Civil, comprising particular notices of the receipts and charges under several of the heads, and of the administration connected therewith under the following heads :—Abkári, Sea, and Land Customs, Salt, and Stamps.

    (b.) Military.

    (c.) Public Works.

    (d.) Telegraph.

II.—Provincial Services, relating to the transactions described in the second of the divisions referred to above ; and

III.—Local and Special Funds, relating to the third division.

IV.—Monetary arrangements, as under—

    (a.) Cash currency remittances and balances.

    (b.) Paper Currency.

    (c.) Money Orders.

Method of Financial Administration.

All funds, whether falling under the heads I, II, or III given above, are controlled generally by the local Government, and are administered in detail by heads of departments or by the Board of Revenue under the supervision of Government. The Board of Revenue administer in detail the Land Revenue, Forest, Excise, Customs, Salt, Stamps, District Post, District Presses, Local Funds and many of the Special Funds ; while Jails, Registration, Police, Education, Medical, and Marine Services, with a few Special Funds, are administered in detail by the respective heads of those departments. In the case of Military and Public Works, the arrangements are somewhat special. For Telegraph there is no local control. Similarly for Port, one of the heads comprised under civil. In keeping its accounts the Local Government is assisted by Imperial officers, who, though subordinate to the Government of India, are required to conform to all requisitions of the Local Government which may not be opposed to the specific orders of the Government of India. The principal of these officers is the Accountant-General, who, besides his duties connected with accounts and audit, has the duty also of advising the Local Government on all matters of finance. The Accountant-General acts also as general paymaster to the Local Government. He is also appointed Commissioner of Paper Currency.

At a sufficient time in advance of the commencement of each **Budgets.** official year heads of departments place before the Local Government an estimate of the probable income and expenditure of their departments under all heads for that year. The material thus sent in is grouped by the Local Government under the heads I, II, and III mentioned above, or some of their sub-divisions, and budgets are prepared for those heads. The Imperial Services budget goes for final manipulation and inclusion in the general budget for the empire to the Government of India. The details of the others are not manipulated by the Government of India, and the Local Government are therefore competent to dispose of them finally, merely reporting results to the Government of India. Though these two budgets stand thus on a different footing, they go practically to the Government of India in one combined Provincial and Imperial budget.

The mode of dealing with the budgets may be seen by noting **—Preparation** the particular case of the Provincial Services budget, where the **of a Provincial budget.** orders of the Local Government are practically final. In this case District Collectors or other local officers supply the head of the department with approximate estimates of their receipts and expenditure for the ensuing official year. This is done about September in the current year. The subordinate estimates usually contain figures in three columns side by side, showing (1), the actuals of the previous year; (2), the estimate already sanctioned for the current year; and (3), the proposed estimate for the ensuing year. The actuals in the first column are often not the audited figures as finally given by the auditing officer, but for budget purposes this cause of inaccuracy is unimportant. In some cases a "regular estimate" for the current year, consisting of the ascertained actuals of so many months of the current year, added to a newly prepared estimate for the remaining months, is substituted for the budget estimate in column 2 or added as a fourth column. The subordinate estimates prepared in this way are manipulated by the head of the department, in communication, if necessary, with the local officer, and are worked up into a complete budget estimate for that department, and forwarded to the Local Government with remarks and explanations. This is done usually by December in the current year. The Local Government manipulates the departmental budget into a single Provincial budget for the Presidency, which is put on record in a combined form, and forwarded in that form, as above mentioned, to the Government of India for their information. As soon as the whole Provincial budget is arranged, and in some unimportant cases even before that is done, the Local Government send back the departmental budgets separately to the heads of departments with final orders upon them. In some cases the budget is sanctioned as submitted; in other cases the amounts are altered to suit the exigencies of other departments, or for reasons peculiar to that particular budget. The heads of departments in turn transmit the budgets thus received, or portions of them, to the local officers concerned.

—Utilization of a Provincial budget.

A sanctioned Provincial departmental budget indicates to the head of the department and to the auditing officer the limits of expenditure for the year to which it relates. The budget is comprised of various entries, according to the subjects concerned and the sub-divisions or officers composing the department; each appropriation entry is complete in itself, and cannot under ordinary circumstances be exceeded. On the other hand, under certain conditions any expenditure may be incurred during the year up to the amount of that entry. The main conditions are; that the expenditure shall be of a nature such as under an ordinary construction pertains to that head of entry, and in cases where such a restriction is necessary, shall be distributed over the year in a reasonable way suitable to the circumstances, to decide as to both of which is left to the discretion of the spending and auditing officers; again that no more than certain fixed amounts shall be spent without special sanction on any one item, whatever the condition of the funds under the appropriation entry, and that in some cases no expenditure at all shall take place on certain things, for instance new establishments, without special sanction, both of which checks are provided for by standing orders of the local Government. In all these matters the head of the department controls the subordinate officer, and the local Government controls the head of the department. New establishments cannot be sanctioned by any authority lower than the local Government, and general rates of pay and allowances can be altered only on the authority of the Government of India. The transfer of funds from the appropriation entry of one local officer to that of another, or from one "minor head" to another of the same officer's appropriation, can usually be effected by the head of the department but never by any local officer. Similarly, the transfer of funds from one department to another, or from one "major head" to another in the same department, can be carried out by the local Government, but not by any head of department. If an officer finds that the funds under any one of his "minor heads" are exhausted, or are insufficient for his purposes, he applies to the head of the department, who will either provide money from such reserve as he may have at his disposal under the budget-head of "reserve," or will obtain funds from "savings" in one or other of the methods just mentioned. In effecting transfers from "savings," the head of the department ascertains the state of the funds in other branches of his department or under other budget entries of the same branch, either by communication with the local officer himself, or by application to the accounting officer, whose books will give the necessary information. If these measures do not suffice, application must be made by the head of the department to the Government, who will then, if it thinks fit, assign funds from its reserve.

The financial powers of the Board of Revenue are in many respects larger than those of any other head of department; their mention here will at any rate illustrate some of the remarks given above. The officers controlled by the Board are Collectors, the Superintendent of Government Farms, and the Superintendent of Stamps ; Collectors administering nearly all the subjects mentioned above as belonging to the Board. Items on which these subordinate officers can incur no expenditure without previous sanction, whatever the state of funds under the corresponding appropriation entry, are (1), salt works costing more than Rupees 2,000; (2), other petty public works under land revenue and customs costing more than Rupees 100 ; (3), law charges in civil suits ; (4), refunds of unauthorized collections other than law fines after two years have elapsed; (5), office furniture; (6), binding books ; (7), press materials ; and various other less important items. The Board have to go to the

Financial Powers of Board of Revenue.

Government for sanction in the following cases : (1), salt works
costing more than Rupees 5,000 ; (2), other works under land
revenue and customs likely to cost more than Rupees 2,000 ;
(3), purchase of periodicals and books ; (4), office rent; with
various other items. No mention is here made of such conditions as are common to all departments ; for instance, the
prohibition of entertaining new establishments without Government sanction.

Disburse-
ments.

Government money is lodged at the Presidency town with the
Bank of Madras, and at Berhampore, Cocanada, Guntoor,
Negapatam, Tuticorin, Calicut, Cochin, Mangalore, Ootacamund
and Bellary with its agents; at all other places it is left in
treasuries under charge of Collectors of districts. There are
23 district treasuries, besides 333 taluq and subordinate
treasuries; the former are usually under the immediate charge
of Treasury Deputy Collectors and the latter under the
immediate charge of Tahsildars. The funds due from taxation
and other receipts are paid into the various treasuries, and it is
the duty of the Accountant-General to arrange by remittances of
cash and other measures that the funds are duly distributed
over the country in accordance with public requirements.
Remittances from other Presidencies to this Presidency are very
rare. The Accountant-General provides funds for all departments. If a local officer has authority to spend money and wishes
to do so, he draws the sum from the nearest treasury or bank
keeping Government funds. The rules for disbursement vary in
different departments. Generally however it may be said that
an officer wishing to draw cash tenders a bill or claim, and if
the charge is unusual quotes the authority ; if the claim is an
authorized one the Treasury officer pays the money and takes a
receipt from the payee, or if the business of the Treasury be
managed by one of the Banks orders it for payment at the
Bank. At head-quarters the Collector delegates all his powers in
connection with the treasury to the Treasury Deputy Collector ;
the subordinate Treasury officers at the taluqs can ordinarily
make payments only on the authority of the Collector or
Treasury Deputy Collector. In connection with lodgment of
Government funds with treasuries and banks, it should be
mentioned that local officers are authorized to withdraw a certain
small portion of the funds under a permanent advance system
for conducting current expenditure under certain of their budget
heads. The transactions of all taluq and subordinate treasuries
are reported monthly to Collectors, by whom they are

incorporated in the district account and forwarded monthly to
the Accountant-General.

The bulk of the money in the District Treasury is in a chest
under the lock and key of the Collector, only a sufficient sum
being placed in charge of the Cash-keeper for current expenditure.   The amount of money to be left with the Cash-keeper is
not fixed by any rule, but when the balance with the Cash-
keeper in the evening of any day exceeds 10,000 Rupees, the
excess is usually transferred to the Collector's box.   During
the absence of the Collector, the keys are with the Covenanted
Assistant at head-quarters.   The Collector, and, during his
absence, his Covenanted Assistant is personally present when
cash or stamps are taken out of or put into the cash-chest under
his lock and key.   The Treasury is examined monthly by the
Collector, or one of his Covenanted Assistants, and a report is
made to the Board of Revenue as to whether the amount in it
is correct.   The examination is made by the Deputy Collector,
if it is impossible for any of the European officers to conduct
the examination.   Every evening the Deputy Collector signs
the cash-book.   He also examines the balance in the expense
chest with the Cash-keeper, at least once a week.   The periodical
examination of the money in the cash-chest by the Deputy
Collector is always reported to the Collector.   The Taluq
Treasury is under the joint lock and key of the Tahsildar and
Taluq Sheristadar, both the keys being in the sole charge of the
latter when the former is absent from head-quarters.   The
Taluq Sheristadar examines every evening the balance in the
Treasury, and signs the Chitta with a certificate that the balance
has been found to be correct.   The Chitta is countersigned by
the Tahsildar when he is present at head-quarters.   Shroffs
or subordinate Cash-keepers are never placed in charge of the
keys of the Treasury, either in the district or the taluq.   They
are only held responsible for bad coin and over-payments
during the day.   The Tahsildar examines the balance in the
chest not less than twice a month, and every time he leaves
and arrives at head-quarters; and reports having done so to
the Deputy Collector in charge of the Treasury.   Taluq
Treasuries are examined by the Collector or one of his Assistants not less than once every six months, and a report is
made to the Board of Revenue.

The accounts kept by treasuries and forwarded to the
Accountant-General are chiefly records of receipts and disburse-

[margin: Treasury cash arrange- ments.]

[margin: Account and Audit.]

ments, entered in prescribed forms of a more detailed nature
than the budget forms. The principal return is the monthly
Treasury Account Current. Every half-year a set of questions
relating to the internal economy of the treasury is filled in by
the Collector and forwarded to the Accountant-General through
the Board of Revenue. The Presidency books of the Civil
Department are kept by the Accountant-General, those of the
Military Department by the Controller of Military Accounts,
those of the Public Works Department by the Examiner of
Public Works Accounts, and those of the Postal and Telegraph
Departments by the Compilers of those accounts. The accounting officers here mentioned, other than the Accountant-General,
are furnished by the Accountant-General with monthly accounts
of their respective departments, as appearing in the Treasury
accounts in different parts of the country. Such departmental
accounts are, with the exception of Post Office transactions,
treated as remittances in the Accountant-General's books. The
accounts of the local Accountant-General are rendered finally to
the Comptroller-General, by whom they are incorporated in the
Imperial books of the Government of India. Military transactions are accounted for to the Accountant-General, Military
Department, Calcutta, and by him to the Comptroller-General.
Similarly for Public Works and Telegraphs, which go into the
Imperial books through the Accountant-General, Public Works
Department, Calcutta, and the Departmental Accounts branch
of the Comptroller-General respectively. Provincial Public
Works form part of the report of the Examiner Public Works
Accounts, but they come back to the local Accountant-General
for final adjustment. Postal transactions are treated for book-
keeping purposes in the same way as any other receipts and
charges in the Civil Department. The local accounting officers
perform the duties of audit as well. At the Presidency town
itself disbursements of the Civil Department, except those of
the nature of advances, are made after audit by an officer of
the Account Department and on his orders. Elsewhere they are
made in anticipation of the audit of the Account Department.

IMPERIAL SERVICES—CIVIL.

GENERAL.

The general nature of these services has already been suffi-ciently indicated in the first paragraph of the present section. *Nature of the services.* The funds are assigned for purposes which are regarded, artificially at any rate, as having an imperial interest, and in administering them the local Government may be considered as acting in the capacity of agents to the Government of India. The following are the heads of account as usually classified. The figures for 1875-76 are given to furnish an idea of the average amounts in each case. In some instances a comparison can be made between the income and out-goings of the same department. In the divisions next ensuing will be given remarks as to the nature of the entries and the details of administration under the most important of the heads on each side. The treatment is not exhaustive from a financial point of view; and receipts and charges are mentioned together, which is contrary to technical practice :—

Receipts.	RS.	Payments.	RS.
Land Revenue	4,54,50,128	Interest on Service Funds, &c.	4,75,248
Tributes and Contributions ...	34,46,431	Refunds and Drawbacks ...	3,64,303
Forests	4,27,723	Land Revenue	44,48,139
Excise on Spirits and Drugs ...	63,39,011	Forests	4,30,182
Assessed Taxes	481	Excise on Spirits and Drugs...	1,97,035
Customs	30,79,620	Assessed Taxes	...
Salt	1,35,37,890	Customs	1,87,276
Stamps	50,19,708	Salt	18,70,376
Mint	3,000	Stamps	1,36,730
Post Office	9,72,248	Mint	29,307
Law and Justice	4,33,791	Post Office	7,60,301
Marine	12,495	Administration	12,24,436
Interest	2,69,774	Minor Departments	95,392
Receipts in aid of Superannua-tion, &c.	24,42,342	Law and Justice	36,19,583
Gain by Exchange, London ...	99,105	Marine	73,029
Miscellaneous	1,77,898	Ecclesiastical	3,83,140
		Medical	3,12,584
		Political Agencies	1,19,399
		Allowances and Assignments, &c.	24,50,643
		Superannuation, &c., Allow-ances.	15,39,399
		Loss by Exchange, London ...	3,05,638
		Miscellaneous	2,88,340
		Allotments for Provincial Services.	83,55,701
Total ...	8,17,11,645	Total ...	2,77,09,181

The following statement, showing the incidence per head of *Incidence of Taxation.* the population of each head of Imperial taxation roughly calculated with a view to all the circumstances for the same year, will indicate approximately the proportion between the amounts of the taxes :—

	RS.	A.	P.
Land revenue	1	15	2
Excise on spirits, &c. ...	0	3	2
Sea customs on population	0	1	5
Sea customs on Europeans and Eurasians ..	14	13	1
Land customs	0	0	2
Salt	0	6	11
Stamps	0	2	7

LAND REVENUE.

Nature of the entries.   The receipts under this head are revenues of which land is the primary source. They embrace all collections on account of settled demand, the principal items falling under Permanently settled, Ryotwar, Shotriem Jody, and Miscellaneous. The item " Permanently settled " consists of peishcush charged on Zemindaries, ancient and proprietary, Jaghires, Mootahs, and Polliems. " Ryotwary " means settlements made directly with the ryots. " Shotriem Jody " is quit-rent on Shotriem and Inam entire villages. Sale proceeds of waste lands, receipts of all kinds on account of redemption of land Revenue, and all items of Land Revenue which are not included in the annual Revenue Settlement, and which are of a fluctuating character, are shown as Miscellaneous Receipts. Pearl fisheries are included technically under Land Revenue. The gross revenue collected in the districts is brought to account ; and the practice of liquidating stipendiary allowances, or making any other payments, by deductions from the State Revenue, is prohibited, except in cases where the special sanction of the Government has been received. The entire charges on account of salaries of Collectors, and their Deputies and Assistants, including establishments and contingencies ; and the Settlement, Inam Commission, and Revenue Survey charges appear under this head. One-fifth of the cost of the Revenue and Magisterial establishments of Collectors and Deputy and Assistant Collectors is exhibited under " Law and Justice." One-half of the salaries of the Commissioner of the Nilgiris and his Assistant is debited to the present head, and the other half to " Law and Justice." A full description of the Land Revenue system of this Presidency has already been given under Section II.

FOREST.

The receipts here include sale of, and seigniorage on, timber, **Nature of the** including drift and waif wood, rent of sandal-wood farms, sale **entries.** of smuggled wood, &c. Fines under the Forest Law, when levied by Magisterial officers, are credited to " Law and Justice," and when levied by Forest Officers, without the interposition of the Magistrate, are credited to " Forest Revenue." The establishments, contingencies and working expenses of the Forest Department come here as charges. Establishments and contingencies are paid for like any other cash charges ; working expenses are defrayed by cheques drawn by Forest officers, the amounts being charged direct to the Forest grant, and adjusted in due course by detailed bills. Roads made exclusively for the development of Forest revenue are treated as Forest charges. Forest administration has been explained under Section IV.

EXCISE ON SPIRITS, &c.

This head, otherwise called Abkári, exhibits on the receipt **Nature of** side all taxes, duties, and fees levied on the manufacture, **entries.** distillation, or sale of spirituous, intoxicating liquors and drugs. The charges are mainly for establishment and the cost of manufacturing or purchasing liquors in the town of Madras.

The practice of deriving a revenue from a tax upon the sale of **History of** intoxicating liquor has been borrowed from the Mussulman and **Abkári.** Hindu Governments. In the earlier years of the present century there was considerable discussion as to the best mode of collecting the tax. In 1808 the first Abkári Regulation was passed, No. I of 1808 ; but owing to doubts as to the propriety of taxing toddy the operation of this enactment was restricted to taxing the manufacture and sale of arrack, and the sale of foreign spirits. This Regulation provided that the annual rent of the exclusive privilege of selling foreign spirits and of manufacturing and selling arrack should be farmed, and that the places where distillation and sale should take place, as well as the retail prices at which the liquors should be sold, should be determined by the Collectors of districts, in communication with the Board of Revenue. In addition to this system of management Section 17 of the Regulation authorised the licensing of separate stills as an alternative mode, and when the Regulation was sent to the Collectors of districts they were recommended to make a trial of both plans of management. The licensing or out-still system however was adopted in Nellore, South Arcot, and Trichinopoly

only, and there only for a few years; in 1815-16 the renting
system was in force throughout the Presidency, except within
the abkári limits of the town of Madras. The rents, as a rule,
included in practice the exclusive privilege of the sale of
fermented toddy as well as of that of arrack, though there was
no legal sanction for this course; as might have been expected,
therefore, difficulties arose in regard to the realization of the
former portion of the revenue. The Regulation was also found
to be defective, as providing no legal punishment for breach of
license. The amendment of the Regulation was finally resolved
upon in 1819, and in the following year No. I of 1820 was
enacted, which rescinded No. I of 1808, and brought under a
regular Government monopoly the tax on "rum, arrack, or other
fermented liquors," providing that the exclusive manufacture
and sale of these liquors should either be retained under the
direct management of Government, or be rented out by them
to farmers. The new Regulation permitted renters to sub-rent
their farms and to recover their dues from the under-renters by
summary process. Special provisions against the use of noxious
ingredients in the manufacture of liquors and against irregu-
larities in the liquor shops were introduced in this enactment.
It also gave powers to the Board of Revenue to frame rules, from
time to time, as occasion might require, for regulating the sale
of all spirits whether country or foreign, and of toddy or other
fermented liquors ; for determining the places at which stills
and shops should be erected, the retail rates of sale to be
established, and the measures to be used, and generally for
regulating matters relating to the detailed management and
control of distilleries and shops. Passes were required under
the Regulation for any quantity of liquor in transit in excess
of one seer or bottle. The abkári revenue of the mofussil was
managed under this enactment for forty-four years, or until
the present Abkári Act, Madras No. III of 1864, became law.
In 1841 the question whether a higher rate of taxation could not
be imposed on arrack and toddy was considered, but the proposal
was eventually abandoned, the district officers being merely
enjoined to see that no liquor was sold below the minimum
prices prescribed. The immediate cause of the enactment of the
present Abkári law was a ruling of the late Sudder Court to the
effect that foreign imported wines or beer did not come within
the scope of Regulation I of 1820. This difficulty was met in
the new enactment, and a few other amendments of the law were
at the same time made. Among other things, powers were taken

to levy the tax on liquors as an excise duty on the quantity
manufactured, to admit free excise under certain circumstances,
and to suppress the home manufacture of toddy where the
privilege was abused or where it was likely to be used as a cloak
for illicit sales. The abkári of the town of Madras is regulated
by a special enactment Act XIX of 1852, which provides for the
direct management of this revenue by the Collector of Madras
under the orders of the Board of Revenue.

The present sources of the abkári revenue are (1) the tax **Present**
upon the manufacture and sale of country-made spirits or arrack; **sources of taxation.**
(2) the tax upon the sale of date-toddy, palmyra-toddy,
and cocoanut-toddy; and (3) the proceeds of the licenses for the
manufacture and sale of country beer, and for the sale of
European spirits, wines and beer. The revenue is mainly derived
at present from the first two items. The country spirit, which
is in most general use throughout the Presidency, though called
arrack, is, properly speaking, rum, as it is distilled from sugar-
cane-jaggery, palmyra-jaggery, date-jaggery and molasses, or
from a combination of these substances together with a small
quantity of acacia bark. The spirit consumed in every district,
except Kistna, Kurnool, Trichinopoly, Godavery, Malabar, South
Canara, Ganjam, and Vizagapatam, is distilled from these
ingredients. In the first three of the districts just mentioned
the chief portion of the spirits consumed is of this description,
but there is also true arrack or spirits distilled from toddy.
In Kurnool a small quantity of spirit is made from " ippa "
or " mowah " flowers, and in one taluq of Trichinopoly a spirit is
brewed from rice. In Godavery, Malabar, and South Canara spirits
are invariably distilled from toddy. The Ganjam and Vizagapatam
districts are now supplied from Mr. Minchin's Aska Sugar
Factory, and most of the spirits used there is probably rum ; the
manufacture of rice-spirit has, however, recently been undertaken
at this factory. Of the fermented liquors which are assessed to
revenue, the principal is toddy. The most common date-toddy
is the fermented juice of the date palm. The juice is extracted
by making an incision in the bark of the trees and letting it
exude. The average produce is said to be one gallon per tree
every alternate day for three months in the year. It may be taken
at any period of the year, but only for three months out of the
twelve. Date-toddy is largely used in the Bellary district ; it
is also used in Kurnool, Cuddapah, Godavery, Ganjam, and
Vizagapatam, the upper portions of Salem and in parts of

North Arcot. Palmyra-toddy is another description. This is obtained from the palmyra tree by cutting off the ends of the young shoots and squeezing them in a rude apparatus contrived for the purpose. After eight days of this process the juice begins to exude. The male trees produce toddy from January to April, and the female from February to May, and the produce is about two bottles per day during the season. These trees are to be found in almost every district, but they are most plentiful in the southern districts of the Eastern Coast. Cocoanut toddy is obtained from the cocoanut tree by the same process as the palmyra toddy, and the average produce is the same. The liquor may be drawn at any period of the year, but not for more than six months out of the twelve from each tree. Cocoanut toddy is very largely in demand in the Tanjore district, in parts of Trichinopoly and in Canara and Malabar, but in other parts of the country it is not a beverage in general use, as the cocoanut groves are not so thickly spread over the country as to make it easily procurable. There is another fermented liquor in use in the Jeypore Zemindari termed souda which appears to be somewhat similar to the pachwai or rice-beer of Bengal. It is however made from grain, not rice, and is often rendered highly intoxicating by the introduction of which is called a liquor drug. As above stated, the proceeds of license fees for the manufacture and sale of country beer and for the sale of European liquors are comparatively trifling. Under recent orders an excise duty at 4 Annas per gallon has been levied upon the country beer manufactured on the Nilgiri Hills by Messrs. Honeywell and Company, and at Bellary by Messrs. Norton and Company.

Arrack revenue in the Mofussil. The arrack revenue is managed in the mofussil, under Act III of 1864, in two different ways, by the farming system and by the excise system. In each case the system is worked as a monopoly, the exclusive privilege of manufacture and sale within-defined tracts being assigned to the contractors; the provision of the Act admitting free or un-monopolized excise has not yet been utilized. The contracts under the farming system are disposed of at open auction sale. The contractors almost invariably sublet their contracts at a profit; sometimes, however, they adopt the system of entertaining a numbers of sub-renters for outside villages and of retaining the principal town of their tract in their own hands. About 1859-60 efforts were made by Government under the old law to place the farms in the hands of large capitalists by selling entire districts; after ten years' trial however the old system of taluq farms was reverted to, and this still obtains. The excise system was first started in Ganjam in 1860, and afterwards extended experimentally to Vizagapatam, South Areot, Chingleput, and North Arcot, and the system as practised in these five districts still goes technically by the name of the "old excise." Since Fasli 1285 precisely the same system has been in force also in the districts of Salem, Coimbatore, Trichinopoly, Tanjore, Nilgiris, and the Bellary Cantonment, so that about half the arrack revenue is now levied under excise. Under the excise system, as under the farming system, the exclusive privilege of manufacture and sale is assigned to contractors selected on tender made after public notification. Distillation is permitted only at one or two selected places, at which sufficient guard and gauging establishments are maintained at the contractor's expense. The revenue under this system is taken in the shape of an excise duty on each gallon issued at rates defined with reference to strength, and to guard against loss of revenue the contractors guarantee that the excise payments shall if necessary reach a certain amount specified. Payments of excise are made monthly. Under either system the contractors make their own arrangements for obtaining material. The contractors under either system are bound to keep accounts of receipts and disbursements, and of manufacture and issue of liquor, which are to be open to the inspection and examination of the officers of Government; to see that a sufficient number of hydrometers are kept in the shops for testing the strength of the liquor sold so as to check dilution; to sell liquor at only the prescribed strength, and for prices between certain maximum and minimum limits, and to use proper measures and allow inspection of premises by officers of Government. A further restriction provided in the Act is that no greater quantity than one Imperial quart of arrack shall be sold to the public at one sale or put in transit, except on permit given by the Divisional Officer or the abkári renter. The following statement exhibits the consumption of arrack in some of the principal towns in the Madras Presidency as estimated by the Local Revenue officers; it will be seen that it amounts to about $\frac{1}{5}$ a gallon per head per annum, a rate little in excess of the known consumption of the town of Madras which is $\frac{3}{8}$ths of a gallon per head and a little under that of the Nilgiri Hills where it rises to $\frac{9}{16}$ths of a gallon per head.

No.	Madras.	Population.	Consumption in gallons.	Comsumption in gallons per head.
1	Masulipatam	36,168	16,000	½
2	Guntoor	18,033	4,000	¼
3	Nellore	29,922	10,000	⅓
4	Ongole	9,000	3,000	⅓
5	Cuddapah	16,276	19,000	⅙
6	Bellary	51,766	50,000	1
7	Trichinopoly	76,530	30,295	⅖
8	Madura	51,987	10,950	⅕
9	Coimbatore	35,310	24,000	⅔
10	Cochin	13,840	8,300	⅗

Toddy revenue in the Mofussil.   The toddy revenue in the mofussil is also managed under Act III of 1864, but exclusively on the farming system, the rents being put up to public auction. The domestic manufacture of toddy except in a few defined localities is forbidden under Section 28 of the Act. The toddy-rent was formerly in all cases joined with the arrack farms. But of late it has been separated in nearly all districts and given to distinct renters. The toddy-renters obtain toddy from date and palmyra trees on Government waste land free of payment, but they must make their own arrangements with the owners of puttah or inam lands for the use of trees standing thereon.

Abkári in Madras Town.   The abkári of the town of Madras is managed on a system different from that in the mofussil, the revenue from both arrack and toddy being managed directly by Government officers, and being worked under Act XIX of 1852. The area to which it applies is defined as extending eight miles beyond the limits of the town proper or the High Court's original jurisdiction. The arrack system is as follows. Country or puttai arrack is distilled from jaggery and acacia bark under contract on behalf of Government, and the liquor is brought from the contractor's godowns to the Deputy Collector's Office, where it is issued to the shop-keepers. The shop-keepers enter into an engagement called a dowle, wherein they agree to sell or at any rate pay the duty on certain quantities of liquor supplied to them daily from the Government stores. The revenue is obtained by issuing the liquor to the shop-keepers at a price higher than that at which it is obtained from the contractor, and the difference constitutes the duty. Columbo arrack, a superior liquor distilled from cocoanut-toddy, is also sold by Government. This is imported from Ceylon through a contractor, and sold at a profit to the shop-keepers. The duty on Colombo arrack is higher and that on puttai nearly as high within the High Court limits, as the duty on imported spirits; the latter being thus protected. There are at present 48 Colombo and 93 puttai arrack shops. The tract outside the High Court jurisdiction, but within the total circumference, is called the "outside limits" and the tract which is comprised in the High Court's jurisdiction is called the "inside limits." The arrack revenue is administered differently in these two tracts; the prices and excise of liquor being lower, and the interference of Government officers being much less direct, in the outer limits. The forty shops in the outer limits are subordinate to five large depôts or godowns, and the whole rent is divided into five portions only; in the inside limits the Government officers deal with every shop-keeper. Puttai arrack only is sold in the outer limits; in the inner limits both colombo arrack and puttai arrack are sold. In the case of toddy Government do not supply the liquor to the shop-keepers, but the shop-keepers obtain it themselves, under certain conditions imposed to ensure a revenue to Government. Thus each toddy-shop keeper who is licensed by the Government to do so, enters into private engagements with the owners of gardens to draw toddy from the trees situated in those gardens. The Government officers are provided with a list of the gardens and trees which the shop-keeper thus proposes to utilize, and to make sure that no others are used they stamp the trees themselves with marks indicating the season to which they belong or other particulars. When the shop-keeper has decided on the number of trees which he wishes to utilize, the Government fix a corresponding sum which he must pay daily as dowle or duty. As a rule the number of trees employed by a particular shop is constant, and the shops are arranged in four classes indicating the normal number of trees assigned to them. When extra trees are desired by the shop-keeper, these are allowed to be used at fixed rates, or on extra dowle as it is called. Toddy cannot be extracted from any tree until it has been stamped and registered by the abkári officers. Besides the permanent shops for the sale of date-toddy from 100 to 120 shops for the sale of palmyra-toddy are opened in the three months when the palmyra trees yield. The establishment maintained for the management of the Madras Town Abkári costs about Rupees 2,300. Besides the sources of revenue just mentioned a small revenue is derived in Madras from license fees.

Progress of the revenue.

In the year 1800-1801, the amount realized by abkári throughout the Presidency was little over two lakhs of rupees, but in 1807-1808 it had risen to upwards of six lakhs, and during the following three years it rose to nearly nine lakhs. From that year up to 1832-33, when the revenue stood at upwards of 18 lakhs there was a steady annual rise except in 1824-25, which was a year of scarcity, and when a check was received which lasted for the five following years. In 1832-33 the average price of unhusked rice of the second sort rose from 66 seers to 45 seers per rupee, and in the following year to 36 seers. During this period occurred a very serious famine in Guntoor and the other northern districts, and the effects were at once visible on the abkári collections, which fell from 18 lakhs to 16 lakhs, and then to little over 14 lakhs. Though prices fell subsequently to their former rates, the abkári revenue did not recover till the year 1842-43, when it stood again at a little under 18 lakhs. From this year up to 1855-56 when the revenue touched $22\frac{1}{2}$ lakhs there was a regular increase, year by year, except in the two years of scarcity, 1846-47 and 1854-55. The abkári revenue has risen from the $22\frac{1}{2}$ lakhs noted above to upwards of 30 lakhs in 1860-61, to nearly 42 lakhs in 1865-66, and to nearly 60 lakhs in 1869-70. Thus in fourteen years this branch of the revenue increased nearly three-fold. The greater part of the increase is owing to the enhanced taxation on spirituous and fermented liquors resulting from the keen competition among abkári farmers at the different auction sales, but it is also due to increased consumption. Since 1869-70 there has been a slight falling off in the abkári revenue. The annexed statement contrasts the actual revenue in different districts for a recent average year :—

Districts.	Revenue of Fasli 1285 exclusive of Miscellaneous.		
	Toddy.	Arrack.	Total.
	RS.	RS.	RS.
Farming System.			
Godavery	78,965	1,90,941	2,69,906
Kistna	51,430	1,66,867	2,18,297
Cuddapah	14,981	1,98,669	2,13,650
Bellary District	*3,08,818	2,64,795	5,73,613
Kurnool	82,969	1,24,703	2,07,672
Madura	73,999	2,00,874	2,74,873
Tinnevelly	39,511	1,27,023	1,66,534
South Canara	55,258	70,667	1,25,925
Malabar	98,690	1,52,057	2,50,747
Total ...	8,04,621	14,96,596	23,01,217
Excise—Old Excise Districts.			
Ganjam	9,652	65,457	75,109
Vizagapatam	61,619	75,087	1,36,706
Chingleput	1,12,367	85,605	1,97,972
North Arcot	96,635	2,72,880	3,69,515
South Arcot	1,30,000	1,28,833	2,58,833
Total ...	4,10,273	6,27,862	10,38,135
Excise—New Excise Districts.			
Nelloro	16,721	56,968	73,689
Bellary Cantonment	†	1,17,440	1,17,440
Tanjore	3,20,336	1,50,583	4,70,919
Trichinopoly	39,778	1,01,532	1,41,310
Coimbatore	83,208	1,47,496	2,30,704
Nilgiris	‡18,995	80,204	99,199
Salem	98,601	2,73,168	3,71,769
Total ...	5,77,639	9,27,391	15,05,030
Special.			
Madras Town	3,21,494	8,24,214	11,45,708
Grand Total ...	21,14,027	38,76,063	59,90,090

ASSESSED TAXES.

This head is opened for collections under Assessed Taxes **Nature of the funds.** levied imperially. When the income-tax was in force the receipts consisted of collections levied on personal incomes, profits, &c. There are now no imperial Assessed Taxes, and any amounts under this head show arrear transactions. The Income Tax was

* Includes the Collections of Bellary Cantonment.
† Included in the Bellary District.
‡ Excise on country beer.

first introduced in 1860, discontinued in 1865, revived in 1869, and discontinued again in 1872. The rate varied from year to year, and in 1871-72 it was 1 per cent. and affected only incomes exceeding 750 Rupees per annum. The revenue raised in this Presidency between 1860 and 1871 was as shown below. In 1872-73 the tax was levied on incomes exceeding Rupees 1,000 per annum at 2 Pies in the Rupee on $1\frac{1}{24}$ per cent. under Act VIII of 1872. The tax was collected by the land revenue establishments, but a small additional expenditure was incurred every year on account of the salaries of clerks employed for keeping accounts and assisting the Collectors in issuing processes:—

		RS.
1860-61	4 per per cent. on incomes above 500 Rupees and 2 per cent. below that.	5,42,914
1861-62	Do. do.	... 25,48,110
1862-63	3 per cent.	... 23,18,250
1863-64	Do.	... 16,46,522
1864-65	Do.	... 14,65,652
1865-66	... ...	... *6,70,548
1866-67	... ...	*13,911
1867-68	... ...	*215
1868-69	... ...	...
1869-70	$1\frac{1}{2}$ per cent.	... 11,58,531
1870-71	$3\frac{1}{2}$ per cent.	... 22,33,147
1871-72	$1\frac{1}{24}$ per cent. ...	... 9,88,593

CUSTOMS.

Nature of entries. Transit, Import, and Export duties, and Fees, Fines, and Forfeitures in the Customs Department are shown as receipts under this head. It is sub-divided into two sections, Sea Customs and Land Customs; the first including Import and Export duties, and the second Transit and Frontier Duties. The charges exactly correspond.

Sea Customs. Duties on goods imported from and exported to foreign countries are levied under the tariff and rates prescribed in Act XVI of 1875. No duties are collected on goods carried by sea from one British Indian port to another except salt, salted fish, opium, and spirits. The duties are collected by special establishments maintained at each port, and are controlled by the Collectors of land revenue, except at the town of

---

* Arrears.

Madras, where there is a special Collector of Sea Customs. This officer has also charge of the land revenue, &c., of the town, but his chief work consists in supervising sea customs, and his salary is debited to that head. The following is the procedure adopted for the levy of customs duties. As soon as a vessel arrives at a port, the master gives to the officer in charge of the Custom-house a manifest, in which is entered all the cargo he has got on board the vessel, distinguishing goods to be landed at the port; and also the port clearance or any other similar paper granted to the vessel at the port whence she came. A general permit to land the goods as per manifest and import boat-notes for each boat landing cargo are then granted. A register is kept of all permits granted, and consecutive numbers are given to them. A file of boat-notes thus granted is also kept. This acts as a guarantee that no cargo other than what was entered in the manifest is landed, for the permits are checked with the boat-notes, and both with the manifest. After the cargo is landed an application or bill of entry is put in, and on payment of duty leviable the cargo is passed. On application to export goods, a permit is granted accordingly, and boat-notes are given to carry cargo as per permit. Before the vessel sails the master gives an export manifest in duplicate in which the description, quantity, &c., of the cargo he has taken on board for exportation are entered. This document, the permit, the boat-notes, and the application are all checked with each other, and the manifest is signed and returned to the master, the duplicate copy being retained for record.

The customs duty collected during the last fifteen years is **Sea Customs collections of fifteen years.** shown below :—

Years.			Imports.	Exports.
			RS.	RS.
1861-62	...	...	13,63,746	7,07,910
1862-63	...	...	10,71,349	6,82,148
1863-64		...	13,00,505	7,17,286
1864-65	...	...	11,18,870	6,67,535
1865-66	...	...	12,08,080	7,41,280
1866-67	...	...	13,67,250	5,61,180
1867-68	...	...	14,78,360	8,59,980
1868-69	...	...	16,02,130	10,14,790
1869-70	...	...	16,58,390	9,07,880
1870-71	...	...	17,92,484	10,36,885
1871-72	...	...	16,28,128	12,86,629

Years.			Imports.	Exports.
			RS.	RS.
1872-73	...	...	16,34,532	10,90,191
1873-74	...	...	17,48,128	13,71,595
1874-75	...	...	16,80,788	12,25,272
1875-76	...	...	17,84,205	9,75,128

Land Customs.

Land-customs duty is levied only on goods passing by land into or out of the districts and foreign settlements named below :—

Districts.				Foreign Settlements.
Godavery	...	...	...	Yanam.
South Arcot	...	...	...	Pondicherry.
Tanjore ...	...	...	...	Carical.
Malabar ...	...	...	...	Mahé.

The rates of duty charged are the same as those applicable to articles imported from or exported to foreign countries by sea. The duty is collected by establishments posted on the frontiers. The receipts and charges during the last five years were as shown below :—

—			Receipts.	Charges.
			RS.	RS.
1871-72	...	...	2,04,000	12,044
1872-73	...	...	1,96,000	14,267
1873-74	...	...	2,19,000	15,488
1874-75	...	...	2,64,000	15,007
1875-76	...	...	2,85,800	15,144

SALT.

Nature of the entries.

The sale proceeds of salt and of collections therewith connected, including fines and refunds on account of unexpended charges, &c., collected, are shown as receipts under this head. Sea custom duty on salt is also brought to account under the same head. To this head are debited all charges connected with the manufacture and storing of salt and of its superintendence; the salary and allowances of fixed and temporary officers employed in the department, with their establishments and contingences; charges for police gardens; the compensation paid for lands taken up for the manufacture of salt; and other ordinary and extraordinary expenditure arising out of the trade.

The construction and repair of petty works exclusively for the benefit of the department are also debited here.

The Government salt monopoly was created by Regulation I of 1805, which at first applied to the whole of the Madras Presidency with the exception of the districts of Malabar and Canara. Regulation II of 1807 extended the provisions of the law, with certain modifications, to the districts of the west coast. The people are prohibited by these enactments from manufacturing salt except on account of and with the permission of Government. It is made in the coast districts by private individuals under the orders of Government officers, and on the delivery of the salt, which is received by weight, the Government pay manufacturers at rates varying partly on account of the situation and partly on account of private rights in the soil from 3 Annas and 7 Pies to 10 Pies a maund of 82⅔ lbs. The salt is resold to the public at or near the places where it is manufactured at a certain price fixed by law, which at present is 2 Rupees a maund except in the west coast districts and in parts of the Ganjam District. In the west coast districts the price fixed for home-made salt is Rupees 2-2-0, and for salt imported as mentioned below Rupees 2-5-0; in the stations of Ganjam and Itchapur in the Ganjam District the Government selling prices are Rupees 2-4-0 and 2-3-0 respectively. The price fixed at the commencement of the British rule was 9 Annas 4 Pies a maund. The only coast district where no salt is manufactured for sale is Malabar. The supply required for this district and for South Canara, where the salt manufactured locally is insufficient, is brought from Bombay and Goa by private merchants, taken up by public tender by Government, and retailed by Government at their depôts in the same manner as in the other districts. This supply comes eventually from the Bombay ryots, who manufacture on the excise system. Importation by private individuals for sale on their own account after paying an import duty of Rupees 1-13-0 a maund is also allowed. Salt is sometimes exported by sea from this Presidency for sale at Calcutta or Chittagong, Penang, and other places. In these cases it is generally purchased by private individuals and exported by them for sale on their own account, but sometimes it has been exported on indent from the Government of Bengal. In both cases the charge made by this Government is the cost price of the article. Salt is likewise supplied to the French authorities at prime cost for sale at prices similar to

General view of Salt administration.

British prices to the inhabitants of the French Settlements, French manufacture having been put a stop to under certain conventions and in consideration of certain compensation. The whole of Mysore and the greater part of the Nizam's territories and of the southern and eastern portions of the Central Provinces are also supplied with salt taken by private trade from this Presidency. The monopoly is administered by Collectors of districts under the orders of the Board of Revenue, but there is a separate establishment under them to superintend the manufacture and sale, consisting of a Deputy Collector for each maritime district assisted by subordinate officials. There are 68 stations or depôts in the Presidency. Swamp or spontaneous salt, where met with, is destroyed by the Government officials. In the districts of Bellary, Cuddapah, and Kurnool, notwithstanding the salt regulations, the private manufacture of earth salt by lixiviating saline soils was till lately permitted. The practice had grown up gradually and was recognized by Government in consideration of the great distance of these districts from the coast and the hardships that would be entailed on the inhabitants by making them depend entirely on marine salt. A small tax in the nature of moturpha was levied in Kurnool and Bellary, but in Cuddapah the manufacture was free. The concession was, however, found seriously to injure the Government monopoly, and the extension of the railway to these districts having placed marine salt within the reach of the people, it has recently been determined to suppress the manufacture. Arrangements have accordingly been made by which the tax is to be gradually raised until 1879, when it will amount to the full duty paid upon marine salt. Meanwhile inducement has been held out to manufacturers to destroy their modas by the offer of liberal compensation. The manufacture of salt for domestic consumption is now allowed in Malabar and South Canara, the High Court having ruled that Regulation II of 1807 does not forbid it. The execution of petty construction and repair works for the salt department is generally entrusted to the Revenue Department, and forms an important part of its duties.

Details of manufacture of Government salt. Government salt in the Madras Presidency is manufactured exclusively by solar evaporation. The places of manufacture by this process are certain localities along the line of the Coromandel coast, determined on generally as being the old grounds previous to the monopoly, and sometimes fixed with reference to the convenience of the community. It is usually considered more desirable to extend the manufacture at one place, than to open a new ground. The more numerous the localities, the greater the risk of smuggling, and the greater the expense of the establishment. The whole line of coast from Ganjam to Cape Comorin is available for salt manufacture. It is not possible to state the exact extent of land occupied by salt pans, as few of them have ever been measured; but there is no doubt that there is sufficient salt ground to supply the whole of India, if required. The salt is manufactured from the saline water of the backwaters, or salt inlets that abound along the coast. Small channels are cut from the inlet, and the water is baled up by the native picottah into shallow reservoirs made by banking up the ground; when the brine has, after some days, acquired a certain degree of strength or saltness, it is let off into still shallower banked-up enclosures or pans, where the earth has been made hard by stamping. Here it is allowed to evaporate, and the salt scraped off. Brine is then again let in, and another coating of salt is scraped off, and so on for 12 or 15 times as the weather permits. In some few places, pits or shallow wells are excavated in the earth near the sea, and the water is drawn off from these instead of baling it from creeks and inlets. It is not possible to state with certainty the out-turn of sea salt manufactured by solar evaporation on a given area. Every thing depends on the season, and a fall of rain a few days earlier or later may make a difference of two or three hundred per cent in the produce. Soils also differ, some retaining the salt much better than others. The mode of manufacture also is subject to variations. The manufacturers receive so much per garce from Government, and it is probable that they do not exert themselves beyond what is sufficient to find them in what they consider the sufficiencies of life.

The time for commencing the preparation of the pans is the Season. beginning of January. Previous to this the Collector of the district arranges how much salt is required to be made that season, and the pans are apportioned out accordingly, each man engaging to supply a certain quantity. The first scraping of salt takes place some five or six weeks after the commencement of operations in preparing the pans, and successive scrapings take place at intervals till about July, when the rains generally put a stop to the manufacture. The season is occasionally such as to allow the manufacture to be carried on till September.

Storing and Depots.

In the Southern Districts, the scraped salt is heaped up by the side of the salt pans, and when dry is removed to depôts close by. There it is measured and placed on raised platforms, in 10 garce heaps, each covered with thatch. In the Northern Circars the salt is allowed to remain some time in drying yards before storing at the Government cotaurs. In Canara and Malabar, the Bombay-made salt is stored at localities on the coast, and also at depôts a short way up the navigable rivers. In other districts there are no depôts, except those close to the pans; here all the salt manufactured is stored, and here the purchasers must come to buy. At the town of Madras the pans have no roads near them passable for carts, and the sales are so extensive that a large gathering of traders, close to the place of manufacture, would encourage smuggling. The salt from these pans is therefore brought at distances varying from six to ten miles by Cochrane's Canal to the Central Depôt near the south-west wall of Black Town. This arrangement is also more convenient for purchasers, as the salt is sold chiefly to persons who have brought goods from the interior to Madras for sale, and who establish a sort of market close to the depôt. Such purchasers can load their carts as soon as they have completed their sales, without the delay and trouble of going some miles to the salt pans. A second depôt is established close to the beach at Ennore, ten miles north of Madras, for salt purchased by the public for export by sea. This depôt is about three miles from the Ennore pans, and the salt is brought by boats.

Manufacturers.

The persons who manufacture the salt are socially in the same position as the ordinary village ryot, but in general they are, or ought to be, in better circumstances, inasmuch as a salt pan is more valuable property than an ordinary grain land occupancy of the same extent. The labor is entirely voluntary, and the climate of the coast where these people work is healthy. They are the descendants, or heirs, or purchasers of the rights, of the manufacturers who were found so occupied when Government assumed the monopoly. Previous to the monopoly, the salt-producing grounds in the Northern Circars; were armed out or rented like other lands; but in the Carnatic the salt produce or its value in money was divided between the Circar and the cultivator. On first assuming the monopoly the Government recognized in the Carnatic a Meerassee, or private property in the soil, and allowed the salt ryots their share, or Kudivaram, at a much higher rate than they ever had before, and pledged themselves to give compensation in case the pans then at work were discontinued by order of Government, unless the propriety of closing arose from misbehaviour on the part of the Meerassidars, or from their not manufacturing a requisite quantity. In opening new pans, a written agreement is now entered into with the manufacturers, by which they admit the right of Government to close the works when they please without compensation. Every proprietor of a pan is registered under clause 3, Section IV, Regulation I of 1805 ; and when Government extend the manufacture at any one locality, the preference is usually given to the villagers to take up the pans, but if they cannot do so on account of want of capital or other causes, the Government dispose of the pans to whom they please. Persons having pans, but refusing to manufacture or only giving in a quantity far below the proper yield, are liable to have their pans taken away. Under ordinary circumstances, however, a salt pan is recognized as real property, alienable by sale or otherwise. The manufacturers are paid for their salt at the fixed rate per garce as soon as it has been measured in to the Government depôt. Each manufacturer has his quantity brought in separately ; and an individual account is kept of what he has supplied, though each man's supply is not stored separately. All wastage, previous to its measurement at the depôt, is at the loss of the manufacturer. He is not paid for every garce he makes ; but for every garce brought to the depôt.

The rates of Kudivaram have developed considerably, the average **Payments to manufacturers.** having risen from Rupees 0-1-0·0 per maund in 1855 to Rs. 0-1-5·8 in 1875. The maximum present rate is 3 Annas a maund in South Canara. The ryots were relieved in 1862 of the cost of all except the most petty works belonging to the salt operations, which was tantamount to a substantial enhancement of the Kudivaram. An attempt has lately been made to ascertain the extent to which the Kudivaram exceeds the cost of production, and the conclusion arrived at is that the cost and manufacturer's profit, the items representing which under monopoly may be estimated to average 1 Anna 10 Pies per maund for East Coast salt, which might be reduced by competition to the extent of 6 Pies per maund or more.

Taking the East Coast by itself, the cost of the salt to Government, including the charge for general supervision, is 3 Anuas **Cost to Government.** 5·6 Pies, and the excise realized thereon Rupees 1-12-6·4 per

maund; the full duty on the West Coast, except as regards South
Canara indigenous salt, has been secured by Act X of 1875.
The items composing the cost are noted below :—

	Per Maund.	
	A.	P.
Land Assessment	0	0·1
Payment to manufacturers	1	5·7
Works for salt manufacture	0	1·5
Establishment	0	6·5
Contingencies	0	0·6
Police	0	5·8
Miscellaneous	0	3·5
Works for storage and revenue purposes.	0	1·2
Sundry works	0	0·5
Interest on value of salt	0	1·2
Total ...	3	2·6
General supervision	0	3
Total ...	3	5·6

Sale of salt at the depots.
The sale of salt at the depôts is free to every body,
and salt can be bought for cash at the fixed rate in as small
quantities as 5 mercals, or 1½ maunds. The persons who
come to the depôts for salt to supply the neighbouring
districts, are usually people of the country. Those who purchase
salt to convey to a far distance, or to Native States, are usually
Lumbadies or Brinjarries, a wandering race of petty traders
in grain and salt, who possess large herds of cattle, and convey
the salt away on these, or on donkeys. The channels from
the Godavery afford a convenient mode of transport by
boats in the delta of Rajahmundry; and if the Godavery
itself were made navigable, on extensive trade in salt would
probably be opened into the cotton country of Berar. At present
the Nagpore Territory is chiefly supplied from Ganjam, but it is a
scanty trade, owing to the difficult nature of the country. The
Nizam's Territories are supplied chiefly from Guntoor,
Masulipatam and Rajahmundry. In the Town of Madras, the
purchasers of salt for the inland districts are, as before said,
persons who bring goods to Madras, such as cotton, indigo,
sugar, oil, ghee, firewood, &c. Their carts rendezvous at a
locality close to the Salt Cotaur and to the grain market, and
as soon as their goods are disposed of, the dealers load the

return carts with salt; this is nearly the only article for which there is an inland exportation from Madras. In some cases salt is sold wholesale from the Government Depôts, the traders being allowed a credit in this case on the deposit of security. The credit is not allowed to run beyond six months, and the account is not opened for a less sum than Rupees 5,000.

The price at which the Government sell at their depôts to the **Retail prices** dealers has already been mentioned. With regard to the actual **by dealers.** retail price of monopoly salt as sold by the dealers in town and village bazaars, it is of course difficult to give an exact figure ; but probably Rupees 2-9-2 per maund, or $\frac{3}{4}d$. a lb., taking the rupee at two shillings, may be regarded as the price at which on the average the people of this Presidency consume sea salt. The trader's profit may, perhaps, be set down at on the average 3 Annas 10 Pies per maund. The low range of retail prices is attributed to the exceptional advantages as regards facilities of communication which this Presidency possesses ; to the circumstances of the trade, there being but few intermediaries ; to competition ; and to the fact that, owing to there being no interruption to traffic at certain seasons by the periodical rains, the maintenance of large stocks necessitating the sinking of considerable sums is obviated. From the statistics which are available it seems that the general direction of salt traffic is mainly determined by the cheapness of salt, and that the trade is very sensitive to changes affecting the cost. This conclusion shows that the general policy of non-interference with salt after it leaves the Government stores is productive of good results. It must be noticed that the dealer buys from the Government by weight, but sells retail by measure.

The average annual consumption of salt per head in the **Consumption.** Madras Presidency may be estimated by taking the population according to the last census and calculating the amount consumed on the average annual sales of the five years from 1870-71 to 1874-75. Certain tracts beyond the limits of the Presidency partially supplied with salt from Madras depôts must be eliminated, and in the absence of any returns of traffic inland the calculations in this respect must be to a certain extent conjectural. If the exportation to adjoining countries is considered, a rate of 11·38 lbs. is arrived at for the Madras Presidency with Mysore and Coorg ; excluding a population of three millions in the Ceded Districts consuming no sea salt, the rate for the rest of the Presidency with Mysore and Coorg is 12·28 lbs. per head.

Export and Import arrangements.

More salt is usually made than will find a demand at the factitious rate in the open market. This surplus salt is placed by Government at the disposal of traders for purposes of export-ation. Traders receive such salt at a rate which just covers the cost of manufacture, and without the payment of any duty. They take it away and dispose of it in the usual course of trade; it may pay an import duty at other ports or in other countries, but pays no duty at the time of purchase by the traders. Special provi-sion is made by the Government to ascertain the amount of salt available for exportation, and to give public notice to that effect. The Government Gazette contains a notice once a fortnight that so much salt is available for exportation at cost price at such and such stations. Salt for export is usually stored on special platforms. Traders buy at the usual place of sale, and in transit between that place and the ships the salt is watched by Govern-ment officials at the expense of the trader. The importation of foreign salt is a mere matter of ordinary Customs; in some cases however traders are allowed to open a credit for this purpose similar to that opened for the wholesale purchase of Government salt inland.

Statistics.

The following abstract shows the quantity of salt brought to store and of that sold, including exportation together, with the Government price per Indian maund, for the last five years. Miscellaneous receipts, such as proceeds of confiscated salt, on base on earth-salt, &c., are not shown:—

———	1871-72.	1872-73.	1873-74.	1874-75.	1875-76.
	I. MDS.	I. MDS.	I. MDS.	I. MDS.	I. MDS.
Manufactured or imported ...	7,683,610	6,125,054	8,036,134	6,049,187	10,451,248
Home consumption	3,361,508	3,413,289	3,249,151	3,493,154	*3,241,025
Inland do.	3,277,447	3,085,524	3,324,574	3,025,620	3,236,139
Total ...	6,638,955	6,498,813	6,573,725	6,518,774	6,477,161
Exportation	408,052	306,558	291,696	702,482	772,091
Grand Total ...	7,047,007	6,805,371	6,865,421	7,221,256	7,249,255
	RS. A. P.	RS. A. P.	RS. A. P.	RS. A. P.	RS. A. P.
Government price of Salt per Indian Maund.	...	2 0 0	2 0 0	2 4 0	2 5 0
				2 3 0	2 4 0
				2 0 0	2 3 0
					2 2 0
					2 0 0

* Includes 1,881 Indian maunds of salt supplied for curing fish.

The receipts at the commencement of each decade from 1806, when the monopoly was first introduced, have been as shown below :—

—	Revenue.	Monopoly price per maund.		
	RS.	RS.	A.	P.
Fasli 1216 (A.D. 1806-7) ...	19,94,439	0	9	4
„ 1226 („ 1816-17) ...	25,21,199	0	14	0
„ 1236 („ 1826-27) ...	28,30,585	0	9	4
„ 1246 („ 1836-37) ...	36,42,403	0	14	0
„ 1256 („ 1846-47) ...	46,74,928	1	0	0
„ 1266 („ 1856-57) ...	52,67,498	1	0	0
„ 1276 („ 1866-67) ...	115,75,229	1	11	0
„ 1280 („ 1870-71) ...	126,05,009	2	0	0

The abolition of the Government salt monopoly, and the substi- **Proposed Excise System.** tution of a system of excise similar to that in force in Bombay and Bengal, has been debated since the beginning of the century. In 1871 an Act was passed containing provisions for an excise duty, but was not carried into effect. It is probable that the experiment will shortly be tried in Malabar and South Canara, where the circumstances, as has been mentioned, are quite special. In favor of monopoly for the Presidency at large it is to be observed that under it an enormous revenue is easily collected and a fair rate of consumption attained, whilst the people are supplied with a fairly good article, believed to be quite wholesome, at a reasonable price. The advantages claimed for excise consist in a possible improvement of quality and an infinitesimal cheapening of salt to the consumer. The cheapening may be described as infinitesimal, for if the full benefit of the estimated reduction in the cost of production, viz., 6 Pies per maund, is reaped by the consumer, it only amounts to ·037 of a farthing per pound, taking the average retail price at Rupees 2-9-2 per maund and the rupee at two shillings. The change involves the destruction of a system which has existed for seventy years, and is deeply rooted in the prejudices of the people.

STAMPS.

Sale proceeds of Stamps of the Stamp Department, Stamp **Nature of entries.** duties and penalties levied on unstamped or insufficiently Stamped Deeds, together with any other sundry receipts which may be connected with the department, are credited to this head.

Recoveries made for cost of suits *in formâ pauperis*, are credited to Law and Justice. The charges include commission to licensed vendors, and all charges incidental to the department.

History of Stamps.   Stamps, by which is meant not only labels to be affixed to documents, but also blank sheets of paper with stamps impressed in the corner, were first introduced by the British Government. The native rulers did not use this form of revenue. The early stamp laws of this Presidency were contained in Regulations IV, V, VIII, and XVII of 1808; in Section 35 of Regulation VII of 1809; and in Regulation II of 1813; and under these duty was levied by means of stamped papers and stamped cadjan-leaves on the institution of suits, on exhibits, and on summonses issued to procure the attendance of witnesses. By Regulation XIII the law was carried further, and it was enacted that all documents of a certain description, such as bonds, promissory notes, bills of exchange, &c., executed in the provinces should be stamped previous to execution. At the same time a fresh table of fees on the institution of suits and on appeals was substituted for the existing table; and various other steps in the progress of a suit were newly taxed, as the giving of an answer, rejoinder, razeenamah, petition, &c. Under this Regulation a General Stamp Office was established in Madras town with a Superintendent subordinate to the Board of Revenue. All stamped papers required under the Act were to be manufactured by him and counter-stamped at the Government General Treasury. In 1860, the Government of India Act No. XXXVI of 1860 appeared, in which the subject matter of the stamp regulations for Bengal, Bombay and Madras Presidencies, together with several new provisions taken from the English Statutes, was reduced into one enactment applicable to the whole of India. This Act was the first which included the town of Madras, hitherto exempt; by Bengal Regulation XII of 1826 stamp duties were leviable within the town of Calcutta, but down to 1860 no similar law existed for the town of Madras or Bombay. Government of India Act X of 1862 was a mere reproduction with a few unimportant additions of Act XXXVI of 1860. In 1867 Act XXVI repealed Schedule B of the last Act, and the stamp duties on judicial proceedings were increased. The portion of the existing stamp law which related to the stamping of documents other than those for judicial proceedings was down to this date highly obscure, and in 1869 Act XVIII took charge of this part of the subject and aimed at completely reconstructing the law. The Act is still in force. In 1870

Act VII revised the judicial part of the stamp law, diminishing
the rates of 1867 in nearly all cases, and making various
changes in detail. Under this Act the fees in the Original
Side of the High Court and in the Small Cause Court at the
Presidency town were for the first time declared to be leviable
by adhesive stamps in lien of cash. This Act is also still in
force. Act XX of 1870 merely repaired some clerical errors
in Act VII of 1870. A new Act is in preparation.

The Acts at present in operation are XVIII of 1869 Acts in opera-
called the General Stamp Act, for the stamping of documents tion.
other than those indicating steps in judicial proceedings ; and
VII of 1870, called the Court Fees Act, for stamping in the last-
named cases. If a person desires to execute a document
specified in Act XVIII of 1869, he must in most cases either
purchase blank stamped paper, and prepare the document thereon,
or, according to the practice in this Presidency, send his
document prepared but unexecuted to the Stamp Office to have
the stamp impressed. In certain cases however specified in the
Act, an adhesive stamp may be purchased and applied by the
person himself to a document already prepared but not executed.
Again the Act provides that in all cases other than that last named
the Governor-General in Council may authorize the subsequent
application in a speedy manner of an adhesive stamp by Government officials under what is called the " denoting " system to
papers or unexecuted documents brought for that purpose by the
public. Hitherto the Governor-General in Council has only
applied the " denoting " system to a limited number of documents.
Objections have been taken to the Madras practice of subsequently impressing stamps on prepared private papers, and if
this objection is maintained, the state of the case will be as follows.
The public may in certain case purchase adhesive stamps and affix
them previous to execution; in all other cases the usual course
will be to purchase stamped blank paper. In certain cases,
however, out of the number last named the public may take their
documents unexecuted to receive another description of adhesive
stamp at the hands of the Superintendent of Stamps. Under
section 22 and section 24, clause (a) of the General Stamp Act a
person knowingly executing unstamped, and other persons knowingly dealing in certain specified ways with, a document which
is liable to be stamped, can be prosecuted for evasion of the stamp
laws. Such an unstamped document is moreover ineligible as
evidence in Civil Courts, it cannot be registered by the
Registration Department, and it cannot be authenticated by a

public officer. Under Section 20 of the General Stamp Act, Civil Courts can receive unstamped or insufficiently stamped documents, where there is no fraud, on payment of the deficiency with a penalty, and will then endorse on the document that duty has been paid, and constitute it thenceforward valid. Civil and Criminal Courts and public offices can impound documents for evasion of stamp duty, and bring the matter to the notice of the Collector. Collectors are the referees as to stamp duties, and may in certain cases remit penalties. The Board of Revenue may remit penalties in all cases. Stamping after execution is permitted in certain cases to render the document valid, but the process will not absolve the person who executed the document. All stamps under the Court Fees Act are under Notification of the Government of India to be of the adhesive class; this is greatly to the convenience of the public. The law under this Act, as far as it touches the public, relates only to the amount payable on the documents which represent the different stages of the Court's proceedings. The Courts see that they are paid. The working of the stamp laws is being carefully watched, for there is no doubt that they are still too complicated.

Manufacture, supply, and sale. Stamped papers used to be locally manufactured; water-marked paper was received from England on which the value stamp was impressed at the General Treasury, or on the abolition of the latter in 1861, at the Mint, or lastly on the closing of the Mint at the Paper Stamping Department attached to the Accountant-General's Office; the counter-stamp of the Stamp Office was then affixed. The papers so prepared were issued to Collectors, but before they were offered for sale by Vendors, the Collectorate seal had to be affixed. The manufacture of stamped papers locally has been discontinued under the orders of the Government of India. Those now issued to districts for sale are chiefly stamps of English manufacture. The blue and black stamps of local manufacture, of which there is a large number of high value still remaining in store, continue to be used simultaneously until the stock is exhausted. The adhesive stamps used under the General Stamp Act are the ordinary one-anna receipt stamp, the foreign bill stamp, and the share transfer stamp. These and the adhesive stamps under the Court Fees Act are all of English make. The "denoting" process is carried out by the Superintendent by means of a special adhesive stamp of English make. The greater portion of the higher values of Court Fees and special adhesive stamps are under the joint lock and key of the Board of Revenue and the Superintendent of Stamps, but the rest of the stamps of all descriptions, besides Postage and Telegraph stamps, are in the custody of the Superintendent who controls the supply of labels and stamped papers to the provinces. The sales in the Town of Madras are effected by vendors under the control of the Collector of Madras, some of whom are remunerated by fixed salaries and others under the discount system. In the interior of the Presidency the Collectors are in charge of the stock of stamps, which they replenish by indents on the Superintendent of Stamps. Stamps of the value of 50 Rupees and under are sold by a class of vendors who are remunerated by a percentage on their sales ; stamps of greater value are sold by officers of Government only. Frauds are somewhat liable to occur in the use of adhesive stamps, which are easily removed from the documents to which they are applied. The mode of fraud is usually to remove the stamp, and, if it is necessary to cover appearances, to substitute one of inferior value which will resemble it. Section 30 of the Court Fees Act requires that the stamp shall be effaced by punching before the Court can take cognizance of the document. In order to prevent fraud on the part of the ministerial servants who might connive at old punched stamps being introduced, arrangements are made for a second punching in diamond form before the documents are put into the record room ; stamps so punched can hardly be re-introduced. Collectors, under Section 45 of the General Stamp Act, have the power of refunding the value of spoiled stamps when soiled or rendered unfit for use. Similar refunds under the Court Fees Act are governed by the Notification of the Government of Madras, dated 24th April 1872.

Postage Stamps and Telegraph Stamps do not belong to the Stamp Department, but the Superintendent of Stamps is placed in charge of them for custody and distribution. Postage stamps are received direct from England by indents on the Secretary of State for India. Telegraph Stamps from the Stamp Office in Calcutta. Local Depôts are supplied by the Superintendent of Stamps on the indents of the officers in charge. Every Treasury in the Presidency, including those attached to Mysore, Coorg, Hyderabad, and Travancore, is a local depôt for the sale of Postage and Telegraph Stamps of the value of not less than Rupees 5 of labels at one time. A discount of half an anna per rupee is allowed to licensed Stamp-vendors, Postmasters, Deputy Post-masters and others, not being persons employed in a Government treasury, who are required to retail Postage Stamps.

Postage Stamps and Telegraph Stamps.

†

To purchasers other than the above no discount is allowed.
Discount is not allowed on sales of Telegraph Stamps. Half-anna
and one-anna embossed postage envelopes are sold in packets
containing sixteen envelopes, for the value of the stamps borne
on them, portions of a packet not being saleable, under the same
conditions as stamps with the privilege of discount. " Service
Stamps " are sold to Government officials without restriction as
to minimum amount. No discount is allowed on these sales.
The bulk of the Postage and Telegraph Stamps at local depôts
are under the joint lock and key of the Collector or his Treasury
Deputy Collector and the Treasurer.

MINT.

Nature of entries.

The duty on coinage of Silver and the gain on Copper coinage,
including other miscellaneous sources of revenue in this
department, such as the sale proceeds of Silver dross, old annealing
tubes, acids, &c., in the corresponding have hitherto been entered
under this head. The Madras Assay Department was however
closed on 31st March 1876 under orders from the Government of
India. The receipts are now only the sale of old stores and
materials. The charges are cost of remitting copper, and loss on
uncurrent coin withdrawn from circulation.

POST OFFICE.

Nature of entries.

The sale proceeds of Postage Labels, including Remittances
from Deputy Postmasters for Postal collections, &c., made by
them are credited to this head.

LAW AND JUSTICE.

Nature of entries.

The receipts under this head include all Fees, Fines, and
Forfeitures of the Judicial and Magisterial Departments, including those imposed by Judicial officers and officers of other
departments acting magisterially under the Abkári and Stamp
Acts, sale proceeds of unclaimed and intestate property, and
Court fees when realized in cash. The charges comprise the
following :—High Court, including Sheriff of Madras; Law
Officers; Administrator-General; Coroner's Court; Justices of
the Peace; Civil and Sessions Courts; Courts of Small Causes;
Criminal Courts (including the one-fifth charges referred to
under Land Revenue); Special Assistants and Governor's Agents;
and Cantonment Magistrates.

INTEREST.

Under this head are shown interest received on advances and **Nature of entries.** loans to public bodies, Native States, or private individuals; and on arrears of Revenue. There is also a charge head bearing a corresponding name, with charge for interest on Service Funds, Savings' Bank Deposits, and certain local loans on which the Government has agreed to pay interest.

SUPERANNUATION, &c.

Under Receipts in aid of Superannuation are included **Nature of entries.** subscriptions to the defunct Military and Medical Service funds, and contributions for pensions and gratuities made by officers lent for foreign service or employed by the Court of Wards, together with the capitalized value of pensions granted to Local Fund employés; these are the principal items. The charges under the head Superannuation consist simply of pensions and gratuities to Government servants in the several departments.

EXCHANGE.

The heads Gain by Exchange and Loss by Exchange are adjust- **Nature of entries.** ing heads rendered necessary by the fact that the accounts of the Home Government are kept in the English, and those of the Indian Government in the Indian currency. The value of provincial stores, &c., is debited to the proper heads at the fixed rate of exchange, but the per contra credit afforded to the London account is at the rate of 2 shillings per rupee, and the difference between this smaller sum and the debit to Provincial is credited to Gain by Exchange. On the other hand the amount of Secretary of State's bills drawn on India is debited to account with London at the rate of 2 shillings per rupee, the difference between the smaller sum thus obtained and the larger sum actually paid being charged to Loss by Exchange.

REFUNDS AND DRAWBACKS.

Refunds represent repayment of revenue or receipts erroneously **Nature of entries.** collected. The most important at present are Land Revenue and Stamp refunds, and refunds of Magisterial fines ordered by Appellate Courts. Drawbacks represent the portion of Customs Revenue due by law to the exporter or importer for re-exportation or re-importation.

ADMINISTRATION.

This charge head embraces salaries and allowances of the Governor and Members of Council; the household establishment of the Governor; the tour expenses of the Governor; the establishment of the Board of Revenue; the Secretariat establishments of the Government excepting Public Works Department but including Translators' Offices; the establishment of the Offices of Account and Audit, including Money Order Office; the charges connected with the Currency Department; and the payments made to the Bank of Madras for conducting Government Treasury and Savings' Bank business, and for the management of the public debt.

MINOR DEPARTMENTS.

This is a charge head, and comprises the charges of the smaller departments engaged in administration not specified in separate heads. For instance, Meteorology, Public Observatories, Examinations, Emigration, Cinchona and Tea plantations and nurseries, Census, Public Exhibitions and Fairs, Gazetteer, Donations to scientific societies, &c. All expenditure connected with the improvement and development of the resources of the country comes under this head.

MEDICAL.

The charge head Medical in the Imperial section of the public accounts shows the salaries of Civil Surgeons.

ALLOWANCES AND ASSIGNMENTS.

This is the charge head for allowances and assignments under political treaties and public engagements. The sub-heads are Territorial and Political pensions, Inamdars, Pensions in lieu of resumed lands, Compensations, Charitable Allowances, and Miscellaneous.

PUBLIC DEBT.

Public Debt is the generic term for accounts kept (1) of debt incurred by the Government temporarily or permanently, and of debt discharged by the Government; (2) of loans and advances made by the Government and of debts owing to Government; (3) of remittance transactions between the various Governments in India; and (4) of receipts and payments which are recovered under the provisions of the law or otherwise in the public accounts, but which are not payments due by Government or revenue.

LOANS FROM GOVERNMENT.

Corporate bodies having a control of public funds are empowered under Act XXIV of 1871 to obtain money on loan from the local Governments on the security of those funds ; and under the same Act they are precluded from raising money from any persons other than the local Government except with the consent of the latter. The objects for which such loans may be raised are the construction and repair of works of public utility, or the repayment of debts contracted before the passing of the Act for the same purposes ; and it has been ruled that the works must be of a reproductive character, in all cases except where the borrowers are Municipal bodies, in which case a greater latitude is allowed. Loans bear interest at $4\frac{1}{2}$ per cent., and are repayable ordinarily by half-yearly instalments within 20 years. If any of the loan conditions are infringed, the funds of the corporation are liable to attachment by Government. The funds necessary for the issue of these loans are obtained by setting aside at the commencement of each year a certain lump sum from Imperial Services, this sum being fixed on in communication with the Government of India. The loans are given throughout the year out of this lump sum, and are made at the discretion of the local Government except in certain special cases.

Nature of the arrangements.

IMPERIAL SERVICES—MILITARY.

The pay of the Army, whether European or Native, and the pay and cost of military establishments for feeding, clothing, and otherwise providing for troops, are drawn from the ordinary Government treasuries. The sums which are entered as departmental receipts under Military are separately accounted for, and are not drawn against for these purposes. The estimates for military establishments and pay of the troops are made up into a Budget by the Controller of Military Accounts. When this budget is passed by the Government of India the Controller issues cash assignments or letters of credit, in accordance with its provisions. For British Troops the assignments are sent to the Regimental Paymasters, who take up their money require-

Nature of Military Finance.

ments from the nearest Civil Treasury; for Batteries of Artillery, Native Regiments, and military establishments they are sent to the Presidency Paymaster who pays on submission of monthly vouchers. The Accountants-General in the several Provinces where the Madras Army serves are furnished with lists of the annual cash requirement estimates and issue their orders to the several Treasury Officers within their jurisdiction, who hold in readiness the funds necessary to meet the various demands. Detailed accounts of the military expenditure just described are rendered monthly by the Controller to the Accountant-General, Military Department, Calcutta.

IMPERIAL SERVICES—PUBLIC WORKS.

Nature of Finance and Account system.

It has already been explained in Section IV. that the Public Works Department executes works for Provincial and Local Funds as well as for Imperial Funds. A very large proportion of the works are however for the latter and the department is primarily designed for executing these. Moreover the Public Works Account Department is to a certain extent an Imperial Establishment, the superior officers of the department and all newly appointed members of the Subordinate Establishment being available for service in any part of British India. An account will, therefore, here be given of Imperial Public Works Finance and Account, and it will be understood that, except in minor details, the procedure with respect to Provincial and Local Funds is the same.

Budgets.

Two separate budget estimates of Imperial Public Works receipts and charges are prepared annually; one for Irrigation Works, including the embankment and conservancy of rivers, the other for Military, Postal, and Telegraph Works. The irrigation budget is framed by the Chief Engineer for Irrigation in communication with District Engineers. The budget estimate for Imperial Works other than irrigation is prepared by the Chief Engineer, Buildings and Roads, in communication with District Engineers and the heads of the Military, Postal, and Telegraph Departments. Both budgets, after approval by the local Government, are submitted at the beginning of January to the Government of India, by whom they are finally passed. In

these budgets a specific assignment of funds is made for each of
the larger works to be undertaken or continued during the year,
and special establishments are estimated for in detail ; but the
charges for general establishments for administrative and executive purposes are provided for by a percentage on the estimate
for works, and repairs are provided for by lump sums placed at
the disposal of the local officers of the department. Modifications of the budget are made from time to time during the
currency of the year to which it relates. Increases and reductions of the total grants and important transfers can only be
made by the Government of India ; transfers of minor importance can be made by the local Government and by certain
subordinate officers to whom its authority is delegated.

Each budget, when sanctioned by the Government of India, Disburse-
is virtually a letter of credit in favor of the Public Works ments.
Department current during the year to which the budget relates.
At the end of the year the credit lapses. On receipt of a budget,
the local Accountant-General holds the aggregate amount of the
grants at the disposal of the Public Works Department ; and to
the extent of the aggregate amount of all such grants (including
those made in Provincial and Local Fund budgets) he issues credit
orders on the Government Treasuries in favor of the disbursing officers of the Public Works Department, on applications
made from time to time through the Examiner of Accounts.
The Accountant-General regulates only the total issue of credit
orders limiting the total issue to the aggregate of all Public
Works grants ; the Examiner regulates the issue in detail, limiting the credit of each disbursing officer to the aggregate of
assignments made on account of charges to be incurred by him.
All miscellaneous receipts realized by a Public Works Officer are
at once paid into a Government Treasury to a separate account
against which he is not allowed to draw. The expenditure
of each officer is thus strictly limited to the amount of credit
orders granted in his favor ; and the aggregate expenditure of
the department is therefore limited to the aggregate of all
grants made by competent authority. The system of detailed
appropriation prevents expenditure on account of any fund
in excess of the grant made from that fund. The disbursing
officers of the department are the officers in charge of executive
divisions and their subordinates. The executive division is
the recognized unit ; and the officers in charge of these divisions, of which the number is from seventy-five to eighty,
are the responsible disbursers. It is in their favor that credit-

orders are granted on treasuries; and it is they who account to
the Examiner for all receipts realized and expenditure incurred
within their several divisions. They make such advances as
may be necessary to their subordinates, and their subordinates
account to them. They also make payments to officers of other
departments to enable them to carry out such public works as
may be entrusted to them.

As just stated, the subordinate Executive Agents in each
division account to the officer in charge of the division for all
expenditure incurred by them. Their accounts are of the
simplest description, being merely copies of their cash-books.
The classification of receipts and outlay and the compilation of
the accounts of the Executive Officer and his subordinate into
one set of Divisional Accounts is carried out at the head-quarters
of the division; a responsible accountant is attached for this
purpose to each division. Every month the Executive Officer
submits to the Examiner of Public Works Accounts a classified
abstract of his receipts and expenditure supported by
schedules giving such details as are necessary for audit purposes.
Officers of other departments, technically called Civil Officers,
who are entrusted with the execution of public works, account
every month directly to the Examiner for advances received
and outlay incurred by them. The Examiner compiles the
accounts received both from Civil Officers and from Public
Works Officers, and submits to the Accountant-General, with the
Government of India Public Works Department, a monthly
account of the receipts and disbursements of the department,
classified under the following heads :—

RECEIPTS.	CHARGES.
Irrigation.	*Irrigation.*
Receipts on Capital Account Extraordinary—	Capital Extraordinary— Works.
Receipts on Capital Account Ordinary.	Establishment. Tools and Plant.
Receipts on Revenue Account.	Suspense.
Ordinary Revenue Receipts.	Capital Ordinary— Works.
Imperial (other than Irrigation).	Establishment.
Military.	Tools and Plant.
Other Services.	Profit and Loss.
	Suspense.
	State outlay on Guaranteed Irrigation Companies.
	Revenue—
	Extensions and Improvements.
	Maintenance and Repairs.
	Establishment.
	Tools and Plant.
	Profit and Loss.
	Ordinary Agricultural—
	Works.
	Repairs.
	Establishment.
	Tools and Plant.
	Profit and Loss.
	Suspense.
	Imperial (other than Irrigation).
	Military. ⎱ with the same sub-divisions as in the case of Ordinary Agricultural.
	Other Services. ⎰

To the Provincial Accountant-General the Examiner reports monthly the total receipts and expenditure on account of Irrigation and other Imperial funds, distinguishing between Extraordinary and Ordinary.

IMPERIAL SERVICES—TELEGRAPH.

There is no local control of this item of Imperial Finance.   **Telegraph.**

PROVINCIAL SERVICES.

GENERAL.

Nature of the services.
The general nature of Provincial Services has already been indicated in the first paragraph of this Section. They represent that division of the public revenues and charges which, for technical and purely financial purposes at any rate, are regarded as having an interest limited to the Presidency only. They are administered by the Local Government subject only to the criticism and remarks of the Supreme Government.

History of the decentralization measure.
This head of account was first introduced in the year 1871. Under a resolution of the Government of India of the previous year it was decided to make over to each local Government a lump sum from the general revenues, to be administered by them and applied towards the expenses of certain defined departments; the receipts from these departments which had hitherto been credited to Imperial were to be credited in future to the new head of account; and the whole fund so constituted was to be styled the Provincial Fund. In thus decentralizing to a certain extent the fiscal authority no new powers were given to local Governments as regards provincial taxation, for the power of taxing locally for purposes confined to the Presidency had already been possessed and acted upon to a more or less considerable degree by the different administrations. Nor was there any appreciable elasticity in the resources thus placed under the control of the local Government, the assignment from imperial resources being fixed, and the departmental receipts being, as compared with that assignment, insignificant. The operation of the measure was to fix the sum which would thenceforward be contributed by Imperial Funds towards the expenses of the departments specified, and to provide that any additional expenditure in that direction which might be rendered necessary by the growing wants of the country should be met by taxation imposed locally under the legislative powers of the local Governments. This arrangement though constituting an important administrative measure does not at present involve questions of any considerable financial magnitude, at any rate in comparison with similar arrangements in England, in consequence of the small margin which the taxable resources of this country leave to local taxation after the claims of Imperial taxation have been satisfied. The departments transferred under the arrangement just mentioned were (1) Jails, (2) Registration,

(3) Police, (4) Education, (5) Medical Services excepting Medical Establishment, (6) Printing, (7) Roads and Miscellaneous Public Improvements, and (8) Civil Buildings. The sum assigned to this Presidency for the maintenance of these departments and to enable the Government to meet its share of the cost of the proportion of the Public Works Establishment employed on the two classes of Public Works thenceforward to be treated as Provincial, as also to purchase tools and plant, was £739,488 per annum. The total grants for the same services had previously been £876,726; but £81,810, being the sum estimated for the then current year as departmental receipts, was deducted, and the balance only, or £794,916, regarded as the assignment necessary from imperial resources. At the same time, as a measure of relief to Imperial resources, a sum of £350,000 was deducted rateably from the assignments made to all the provinces; in the case of Madras the proportion amounted to £55,428, and this further deduction brought down the sum assigned to the amount above mentioned on £739,488. This was the original arrangement. Additions however have since been made by the Government of India for various minor services transferred from time to time from the Imperial to the Provincial heading, and further changes are in contemplation.

The actual Provincial expenditure on the transferred services **Present** in 1875-76 was £822,910; there was also Local Fund expendi-**Financial** ture on the same services, amounting to £603,255, so that the **results.** total amount spent on these services in 1875-76 was £1,426,165. The Imperial expenditure in 1870-71 on the same objects was £1,222,164; so that a sum of £204,001, being the difference between these two amounts, has been in the present year saved to the Imperial Exchequer and charged to local sources. The amount of local taxation under the Road Fund was in 1870-71 £238,014. The total amount of present local taxation is £376,964, showing an increase of £138,950 in local taxation since the inauguration of the decentralization scheme; it is probable, however, that a great portion of this increase would have taken place in any case.

The balance sheet for 1875-76 is given as showing the heads **Heads of** of receipts and charges, and the general proportion existing **Receipts and** between the different items. **Charges.**

Receipts.				Expenditure.			
			RS.				RS.
Imperial Allotment	...		83,55,701	Refunds	...	...	... 4,601
Departmental Receipts—				Jails	...	...	... 10,57,532
Jails	...	...	2,56,524	Registration	...	...	2,66,563
Registration		...	3,80,530	Police	...	...	... 35,79,908
Police	...	...	37,680	Education	...	...	... 8,75,308
Education	...	...	28,698	Medical	...	...	*5,56,567
Medical	...	...	*31,351	Printing	...	...	2,46,357
Printing	...	...	26,723	Marine	...	...	...
Marine	...	...	25,141	Minor Establishments		...	2,30,831
Miscellaneous Receipts—				Office-rent, Rates and Taxes			85,032
Fees and Fines		...	62,447	Miscellaneous		...	2,31,848
Sundry Receipts		...	51,753	Contributions		...	... 12,22,062
Contributions		...	18,650	Public Works		...	... 11,03,689
Public Works		...	79,669				
	Total	...*93,54,864			Total	...*94,60,298	

LOCAL FUNDS UNDER ACT
IV OF 1871.

Nature of the entries.   A description of the nature of these funds and of the Boards which administer them has been given already under Section III. A general supervision only is exercised by the Local Government, and the funds may be described as funds raised locally, administered locally, and administered for strictly local purposes. The following balance sheet for 1875-76 will show the ordinary heads of receipts and charges. It is not necessary to explain each item.

---

* Excluding the recoveries from Local Funds and Municipal Boards, Rupees 30,862.

Receipts.	RS.	RS.
Allotments from Provincial Services ...	12,33,984	
Special Funds ...	3,57,919	
		15,91,903
Rates and Taxes—		
Cess on Lands ...	36,03,247	
Tax on Houses ...	1,235	
Tolls on Roads, &c.	1,65,163	
		37,69,645
Fees in Schools and Training Institutions ...	...	22,376
Contributions from other Local Fund Circles and Municipalities ...	...	29,530
Receipts of Schools and Endowed Foundations—		
Educational ...	10,634	
Hospitals and Dispensaries ...	22,703	
Choultries, Markets, &c. ...	2,64,798	
Miscellaneous ...	4,614	
		3,02,749
Miscellaneous—		
Miscellaneous Fees, Fines, Rents, Sales, and Contributions ...	85,160	
Public Works Receipts and Refunds ...	1,46,960	
		2,32,120
Advances, &c. ...	...	1,19,100
Loans ...	...	82,237
Total ...		61,49,660

Charges.	RS.	RS.
Public Works—		
Communications ...	35,11,913	
Tolls and Ferries ...	2,795	
Educational ...	18,728	
Sanitary and Miscellaneous ...	2,67,434	
	38,00,870	
Establishment ...	8,41,621	
Tools and Plant ...	37,112	
Refunds of Receipts, &c. ...	24	
Contributions ...	42,413	
		47,22,040
Education—		
Inspection ...	50,241	
Local Fund Schools.	1,89,990	
Grants-in-aid ...	1,80,714	
Contributions ...	1,644	
		4,22,589
Sanitation, Medical Services, and Public and Charitable Institutions—		
Hospitals and Dispensaries and Medical Practitioners ...	1,41,802	
Vaccine Establishments ...	78,952	
Sanitary Establishments and Cleansing Tanks and Wells ...	2,87,298	
Markets, Choultries, &c. ...	2,09,632	
Contributions, &c. ...	80,969	
		7,98,653
Miscellaneous Establishment and Contingencies ...	...	89,273
Advances ...	...	1,12,547
Loans ...	...	17,686
Total ...		61,62,788

SPECIAL FUNDS.

Special Funds are so called from their being formed for special purposes distinct from those to which Local and Municipal Funds are applied, and from those to which assignments from Imperial revenues are made. Though grouped for convenience under the third of the main divisions of finance mentioned at the head of this chapter, these Special Funds are in the extent of their

Nature of the Funds.

application partly Local and partly Provincial. The following is a complete list of the funds. So many changes are going on with reference to them, that it is useless to give figures as to receipts or charges :—1. Jungle Conservancy Fund. 2. Cattle Pound Fund. 3. Surplus Pound Fund. 4. Endowment Fund. 5. Village Service Fund. 6. Irrigation Cess Fund. 7. Cochrane's and Sadras Canal Fund. 8. Canal and Ferry Fund. 9. Nanal Grass Fund. 10. Public Bungalow Fund. 11. Convict Labor Fund. 12. Police Lodging Fund. 13. School Fee Fund. 14. Educational Building Fund. 15. Port Fund. 16. General Fund, under the Customs Consolidated Act VI of 1863. 17. Bearers' Fee Fund. 18. District Road Fund of Bhadrachellum and Rekapally taluqs. 19. District Road Fund. 20. Labor Contract Fee Fund. 21. University Fee Fund. 22. One per cent. Income-tax Fund. 23. Municipal Fund. Each fund is separately administered. Of the above list the first ten are under the control of the Board of Revenue, and the next five under that of the Inspectors-General of Jails and Police, the Director of Public Instruction, and the Superintendent of Marine. The District Road Fund of Bhadrachellum Taluq is worked by the Collector of Godavery, while the transactions under Bearers' Fee and General Customs Funds are confined to only a few districts. The heads " District Road Fund " and " Labor Contract Fee Fund " await certain adjustments for being closed, and the balance under " One per cent. Income-tax Fund " has been transferred to Provincial Services. The mode in which the Municipal Funds are shown in Government Accounts having been changed, the transactions in connection with them are in future to be omitted from the list of Special Funds. The University Fee Fund receipts are adjusted annually by setting them off against a portion of the University expenditure borne on the Provincial Service Account. Of the funds under the control of the Board of Revenue, the Jungle Conservancy Fund of the Nilgiris was merged in the Forest Revenue on 1st April 1875, and the Nanal Grass Funds of Kistna, Chingleput, North Arcot, Madura, Tinnevelly, and Coimbatore have been transferred to Irrigation Revenue, while those of Nellore, Tanjore, Trichinopoly, and Salem await to be so transferred. Notice will be found below of the funds administered by the Board of Revenue.

Jungle
Conservancy
Funds.

The Jungle Conservancy Fund was organized in 1859 for the avowed object of conserving and extending village jungles, which were being rapidly destroyed by the villagers and others in the exercise of ancient prescriptive rights. In order to preserve and improve them, a local tax on firewood cut and charcoal made for sale is levied through the village officers and applied to the formation of plantations and avenues, raising nurseries, &c., it being understood that the prescriptive rights of the ryots to fuel, leaves for manure, and wood for implements intended for their own use and not for sale shall be left undisturbed. The operations of the fund in the several districts commenced in different years ranging from 1860-61 to 1866-67. In 1868-69 the fund was in existence in all but the Madras, Nilgiris, and Malabar Districts. In 1869-70 it was established in the Nilgiris by the transfer of the jungles which were under the conservancy of the Forest Department to the charge of the Commissioner. The jungles were, however, retransferred to the Forest Department from 1875-76. At first the income of the fund was small and the operations necessarily limited. In 1868-69 it was considered that the operations of the fund had become sufficiently extensive to require the preparation of a detailed programme of the work to be done in each year, which was accordingly ordered and carried out from 1869-70, by which system uniformity in the operations has been secured. From 1871-72 the cost of roadside avenues was thrown upon Local Funds and the Jungle Conservancy Fund relieved of the charge. The general rate of seigniorage now in force on fuel is 6 Annas per 1,000 lbs. The rate for charcoal varies from 8 Annas to 2 Rupees, 3 Annas to 6 Pies per 1,000 lbs. In Ganjam and Malabar no seigniorage is levied on charcoal. Besides the tax on fuel and charcoal, the rents of jungles, sale of trees, and sale proceeds of wood contribute towards the receipts.

The Cattle Pound Fund was originally inaugurated under the Imperial Act III of 1857, which was repealed by Act I of 1871. The income of the fund is made up of fines paid on stray cattle and sale proceeds of unclaimed cattle. It is expended in the remuneration of pound-keepers and in the construction and repair of pounds, and the net surplus remaining, which constitutes what is called the Surplus Pound Fund, is applied to the construction and repair of roads and bridges and to other purposes of public utility. Under orders in force a half of the surplus is paid to local and municipal funds for these purposes, and the other half is appropriated to the Government Farms at Sydapet for agricultural education, &c. In 1871-72 four thousand five hundred and ninety-four pounds were maintained, which increased to 5,766 in 1875-76. The pounds are very

Cattle Pound Fund and Surplus Pound Fund.

unequally distributed over the districts, as a condition of the
establishment or retention of a pound is that it shall be self-
supporting. As regards establishment, the head of the village
is by law the ex-officio pound-keeper. In 1875-76 Government
fixed the remuneration of pound-keepers, as to which great
diversity of practice prevailed, at a uniform rate of 50 per cent.
on collections for all districts except the Nilgiris. In 1874
Government allowed the employment of a pound gumastah
on 10 Rupees a month in such of the taluqs of each district in
which one may be considered necessary, and these are now being
gradually entertained.

Endowment Fund.   This fund comprises the endowment of choultries, alms-houses,
and other public foundations not being religious. Most of
the endowed institutions under the control of the Collectors have
been transferred to Local and Municipal Boards, and their receipts
and charges are exhibited in the Local Fund and Municipal
accounts. The institutions now maintained from this fund are
few in number, viz., the Munro chuttrum and dispensary in
Bellary, the lungerkhana in Kurnool, seven chuttrums in
Tanjore, and one chuttrum and one water-pandal in Tinnevelly.
The receipts of these institutions are composed, for the most
part, of fixed allowances granted by Government.

Village Service Fund.   The assets of the Village Service Fund are derived chiefly from
the cess collected with the Land Revenue under Madras Act IV
of 1864 in the districts where the Act has been introduced, from
the deductions from the land revenue made in some districts on
account of village service and which the Government are pledged
to continue for various reasons, and from the sums charged for
the enfranchisement of Village Service Inams. In districts
where the Act has not been introduced, the old merahs or fees
paid by the people as remuneration to the village officers are
collected and credited to the Fund. The object of the Fund
is to improve the pay of the village servants, and to increase
and alter their number so as to meet properly the requirements of the different villages. Act IV of 1864, which is
introduced concurrently with the new settlement in each district, is as yet in operation only in Godavery, Kurnool, Trichinopoly, Salem, and parts of Tinnevelly. The maximum rate
of cess allowed by the law, viz., 1 Anna in every rupee of
assessment, has been levied, and as the cess was collected before
the reorganization of the village establishments, there are
large surpluses in the districts. A portion of the surplus has
been invested in Government securities, but the rate of cess in

Kurnool has been reduced from 1 Anna to 10 Pies in the rupee, subject to report after two years' trial of the whole reorganization of the village establishments recently carried out.

The Irrigation Cess is paid voluntarily by ryots holding lands under certain river channels in lieu of customary labor formerly supplied by them. It existed formerly in Trichinopoly, Madura, and Coimbatore, but is now gradually dying out owing to want of any law to enforce the payment. *Irrigation Cess Fund.*

The Cochrane's and Sadras Canal Fund exists only in the Chingleput District, its income being derived from tolls and license fees on boats using Cochrane's Canal to the north of Madras and the Sadras Canal to the south. The canals were originally Imperial and were made local by the Government of India on an application to that effect from the Government of Madras in 1864. The income is expended on the maintenance of the canals and in payment of the establishment for collecting tolls. The Northern Canal has been extended to within 14 miles of Nellore. *Cochrane's and Sadras Canal Fund.*

The Canal and Ferry is raised under Madras Act I of 1870, and is made up of tolls and license fees on canals, lines of navigation, and ferries. The money is expended on the construction, improvement, repair, maintenance, and extension of the channels and ferries to which the provisions of the Act may be applied. As yet the Act is in operation only as regards certain ferries in the Godavery, Kistna, and Tanjore Districts, and the Salt Canal from Negapatam to Vedaraniem, to which it was extended in 1874-75. *Canal and Ferry Fund.*

The Nanal Grass Fund consists of the sale proceeds of the cuttings from nanal and coray grass and reed plantations grown on tank and channel banks for protection. The collections are expended on the maintenance and the general extension of the plantations. In 1874 Government ordered the receipts to be credited to a new head of account styled "Irrigation Revenue," so that the fund will soon cease to appear under Special Funds. *Nanal Grass Fund.*

Almost all the travellers' bungalows in the Presidency have been transferred to Local and Municipal Boards, District Officers, and other departments of the service. In 1875-76 only two bungalows in Coimbatore remained to be disposed of. These have since been transferred, and the Public Bungalow Fund will shortly become extinct under Special Funds. *Public Bungalow Fund.*

CASH REMITTANCES.

Statistics. The two following statements will show approximately the course of exchange between different parts of the Presidency, and between this Presidency and others :—

STATEMENT I.

Remittances by Cash and Bills received from and sent to the Bank of Madras and other Districts during 1875-76.

Districts.	Remittances from Districts.		Remittances from Bank of Madras to Districts.	Remittances from other Districts to this District.	Remittances from this District to other Districts.
	To the Bank of Madras either in Cash or Bank Transfer.	Supply Bills granted on Payment of Money at Madras.			
	RS.	RS.	RS.	RS.	RS.
Ganjam ...	15,50,000	...	40,000	1,15,000	...
Vizagapatam ...	6,62,980	3,36,700	...	...	...
Godavery	30,00,000	66,680	...	...	1,15,000
Kistna ...	43,00,000	16,380	47,800	...	...
Nellore ...	21,00,100	1,62,580	...	...	...
Cuddapah ...	11,79,220	1,95,800	85,000	...	1,57,490
Bellary ...	26,07,800	...	3,46,690	3,19,490	...
Kurnool ...	10,00,000	6,760	2,45,000	16,000	2,00,000
Madras ...	...	...	...	...	...
Chingleput ...	23,52,510	...	9,00,000	...	...
North Arcot ...	12,70,500	...	4,40,000	...	30,000
South Arcot ...	9,15,980	10,37,080	1,02,000	...	...
Tanjore ...	51,50,000	38,800	3,60,350	40,000	2,00,500
Trichinopoly ...	3,50,000	29,760	7,01,000	12,000	3,00,000
Madura ...	29,84,600	28,410	3,50,000	...	27,000
Tinnevelly ...	26,50,000	1,36,170	2,01,000	27,000	3,00,000
Coimbatore ...	12,81,950	57,000	...	2,44,000	10,57,500
Nilgiris ...	...	...	...	14,78,000	...
Salem ...	15,52,250	1,57,880	1,03,100	...	1,00,000
South Canara ...	15,50,000	...	...	3,00,000	1,00,000
Malabar ...	1,00,000	...	...	4,00,000	6,64,000
Travancore ...	...	...	...	3,00,000	...
Total ...	3,69,38,890	22,70,000	39,21,940	32,51,490	32,51,490

Remittances by Cash and Bills received from and sent to other Presidencies during 1875-76.

Districts, &c.	From other Presidencies.	Sent to other Presidencies.
	RS.	RS.
Ganjam	2,000	11,00,000
Vizagapatam ...	3,000	...
Godavery	...	2,50,000
Tanjore	4,000	...
Tinnevelly	1,000	...
Bank of Madras ...	19,88,840	2,62,27,800
Total ...	19,98,840	2,75,77,800

PAPER CURRENCY.

The Presidency is divided into three Circles of Paper Currency Issue—Madras, Calicut, and Cocanada. The Madras Circle of Issue includes the districts of Nellore, Chingleput, North Arcot, South Arcot, Salem, Cuddapah, Bellary, Kurnool, Tanjore, Trichinopoly, Madura, Tinnevelly, and Bangalore, with the town of Madras as head-quarters for the issue of notes for the circle; the Calicut Circle includes the districts of Malabar, South Canara, and Coimbatore, having Calicut as the office of issue; and the Cocanada Circle embraces the remaining districts, viz., Ganjam, Vizagapatam, Godavery, and Kistna, with head-quarters at Cocanada. In addition to the three head-quarters of issue, a currency agency is established at Vizagapatam to afford facilities to the public for exchanging coin for notes or notes for coin. The Exchange Department at the head-quarters of each circle of issue issues Home notes for coin or other notes, and coin for notes. Other or foreign circle notes are only cashed when there is an available margin for cashing foreign circle notes, which margin is calculated, by deducting from the reserve of silver coin the difference between the circulation account and the fixed minimum for the time being, and the amount of notes held by other offices. At the Head Office at Madras, notes of its sub-circles, Calicut and Cocanada (including its agency at Vizagapatam), are at all times cashed by law. The Exchange Department also issues small silver and copper coin in exchange

Nature of arrangements.

for coin or notes. District Treasuries are supplied with notes by the Accountant-General, through the Treasuries at the head-quarters of each circle of issue, on the receipt of indents from the district treasuries, provided he considers it admissible to do so. Although no person has a legal claim to obtain cash for notes except at the currency office of issue, or in the case of Calicut and Cocanada notes at Madras, notes are cashed freely at Mofussil Treasuries when the Treasury officers are satisfied that no inconvenience can be caused to their treasuries by the encashment. Notes tendered by travellers, other than visitors to hill sanitaria, are cashed to a limited extent, even when the Treasury is unable to cash them to the general public. At every place other than the office of issue notes of the Home circle are a legal tender in satisfaction of any claim against Government, though ordinarily no person is pressed to take notes in part or full of his demand. Payment of Government dues may be made in Government currency notes of any circle of issue. Railway Companies are also required to receive notes of any circle in payment of fares and freight, and the officer in charge of a Treasury into which such company pays its earning is authorized to receive notes so earned.

MONEY ORDER DEPARTMENT.

Nature of Money Order System.

The receipt and payment of money orders is attended to by a paid Agent at the head office at the Presidency and by the Treasury Officers in the districts. The amount of an order cannot exceed Rupees 150, nor is the amount grantable on one day to the same person ordinarily permitted to exceed 500 Rupees. Orders not presented for payment within one year from date of issue are not payable without satisfactory explana-tion of delay afforded to the Comptroller-General. Orders are granted on Europe also under similar rules, but they have to pass through the Accountant-General, Bombay. The rates of exchange is determined by the Comptroller-General from time to time and telegraphed to the Madras Accountant-General.

SECTION VI.

VITAL STATISTICS AND MEDICAL SERVICES.

RESULTS OF LATEST CENSUS.

It has already been mentioned that the Presidency includes Area, &c., of an area of 139,698 square miles; that it is divided into 21 dis- the Presi- tricts, besides the Native principality of Poodoocottah, the latter dency. contributing 1,380 square miles of the total area given above; and that the districts are divided into 156 taluqs, sub-divided into 56,421 villages.

The first census of the Madras Presidency was taken in 1822, History when the population was returned at 13,476,923. The next of early enumeration, within the same territorial limits, was in the year Censuses. 1836-37, when the numbers were returned at 13,967,395, or an increase of only 490,472 in fourteen years, a result doubtless chiefly due to defective census returns, but also attributable in some measure to the epidemic cholera prevailing from 1818 to 1826 or 1827, and to the later epidemic, preceded by famine, which raged in 1833 and 1834. The first of the quinquennial enumerations was taken in 1851-52, when the population was found to have risen to 22,031,697, of which 273,190 belonged to the district of Kurnool which had been annexed after the previous census was taken. An increase of 58 per cent. in fifteen years shows very clearly that one or other of the censuses was extremely inaccurate, and it is now believed that many of the zemindaris were omitted, or their population much under-stated in the returns for 1836-37. The results of the four quinquennial enumerations are shown below:—

.Years.				Population.
1851-52 ...	...	...	...	... 22,031,697
1856-57 ...	...	...	...	... 22,857,855
1861-62 ...	...	...	...	... 24,656,509
1866-67 ...	...	...	...	... 26,539,052

The figures for 1861-62 and 1866-67 are exclusive of North
Canara, which was transferred to Bombay in 1862, with a
population at that time of somewhere about 300,000.

Operations in Census of 1871. The Census of 1871 was taken in accordance with the desire
of the Supreme Government for a general census of the whole
of India. Experience having shown that the circumstances of
the country were such as to render it dangerous to rely on a
census taken on a single day, a preliminary house-to-house
enumeration was resolved on, and full instructions were issued
by the Board of Revenue in September 1872 to all Collectors,
who, as usual, were made responsible for the conduct of the
operations within their respective districts. In the beginning
of January 1871 the preliminary work commenced by the
accountants of each village preparing and transmitting to the
Tahsildars of the taluq a series of statistical returns and
registers of the houses, area, and assessment of their villages,
in order to prepare which the accountants had to proceed from
house to house and affix a number to each in such a manner as
to last till the 15th of November, the day fixed for the final
enumeration. As a rule, these returns reached the taluq offices
in time to permit of returns for each taluq being compiled and
forwarded to the Collectors of the districts by the 15th February,
after which the house registers were returned to the village
accountants for use during the preliminary enumeration, which
commenced on the 15th July, except in South Canara and
Malabar, where it commenced earlier so as to permit of the work
being completed before the outbreak of the south-west monsoon.
Before the end of July, the inmates of every house were
registered and the returns despatched to the local Supervisor,
usually the Revenue Inspector of the range, who tested ten per
cent. of the entries and sent back for amendment such returns
as he found incorrectly prepared, the work of the Supervisors
being again tested by Tahsildars and Divisional Officers. In
municipalities and cantonments the census was conducted under
the supervision of the Municipal Commissioners and Military
Authorities acting in concert with the Collector of the district,
and in such cases the preliminary enumeration was usually
delayed until September or October. The final enumeration took
place on the 15th of November 1871 in all the villages and towns
of the Presidency, except in the district of Tanjore and the town
of Palghaut, where it was thought expedient to defer it for a few
days on account of the occurrence of festivals and the presence of
numerous strangers. The returns prepared on the 15th were sent

to the Supervisors to be tested and then transferred to the Tahsildars, who forwarded them after careful examination to the Collectors, by whom they were transmitted to the Census Office at Madras for final scrutiny and tabulation. The enumerators employed in taking the census were for the most part village officials who received no extra remuneration, but in the larger villages and towns it was necessary to employ paid enumerators in addition. Zemindars usually exerted themselves to assist in obtaining correct results on their own estates, and much assistance was gratuitously afforded in many ways by native gentlemen throughout the Presidency. The number of enumerators employed was 71,641, being about 1 to every 436 of the population. The total charge incurred on this account amounted to Rupees 33,341, or Rupees 1-1-0 per thousand of the population. Naturally the people were somewhat suspicious of the object of the census, but there was little or no active opposition, and any defects in the returns are attributable more to the incapacity or caste prejudices of the enumerators than to anything else. Careful enumerators found little difficulty, as a rule, in overcoming the reticence usually found in supplying information regarding the female population, and in the case of the census of Mahomedan females the difficulty was much less than had been anticipated.

The result of the final examination and tabulation of the returns was to fix the population of the Presidency at 31,597,872, being a gross increase of 5,058,820 over the figures for 1866-67, and a net increase of 4,274,452 after deducting the population in localities not included in the previous census. It has been already stated that previous censuses erred, if anything, in the direction of understating rather than of exaggerating the population. In considering the apparent increase this must be borne in mind. Particulars regarding the distribution of the population are given in the annexed table :— *Gross results of ditto.*

Statement.

Districts.	Area in Square Miles.	No. of Taluqs.	No. of Villages.*	No. of Houses.	Population.	Average No. of Houses to a Square Mile.	Average No. of Houses to a Village.	Average No. of Persons to a Square Mile.	Average No. of Persons to a House.	Average No. of Persons to a Village.	Average No. of Persons to a Taluq.
Ganjam ...	8,313	3	4,562	341,404	1,520,088	41·1	74·8	182·9	4·45	333·2	506,696
Vizagapatam ...	18,344	2	8,581	489,419	2,159,199	26·7	57·0	117·7	4·41	251·6	1,079,599
Godavery ...	6,224	9	2,202	389,712	1,592,939	62·6	177·0	255·9	4·08	723·4	176,993
Kistna ...	8,036	11	2,140	282,358	1,452,374	35·1	131·9	180·7	5·14	678·7	132,034
Nellore ...	8,462	9	2,417	263,820	1,376,811	31·1	109·2	162·7	5·21	569·6	152,979
Cuddapah ...	8,367	11	1,337	339,063	1,351,194	40·5	253·6	161·5	3·98	1010·6	122,836
Bellary ...	11,007	15	2,540	351,943	1,668,006	32·0	138·6	151·5	4·73	656·7	111,200
Kurnool ...	7,358	8	787	205,884	959,640	28·0	261·6	130·4	4·66	1219·4	119,955
Chingleput ..	2,753	6	2,362	141,434	938,184	51·4	59·9	340·7	6·63	397·2	156,364
North Arcot ...	7,139	9	5,292	329,844	2,015,278	46·2	62·3	282·3	6·11	380·8	223,920
South Arcot ...	4,873	8	3,198	228,761	1,755,817	46·9	71·6	360·3	7·67	549·0	219,477
Tanjore ...	3,654	9	3,935	369,981	1,973,731	101·3	94·0	540·1	5·33	501·6	219,303
Trichinopoly ...	3,515	5	1,644	210,690	1,200,408	59·9	128·2	341·5	5·69	730·1	240,081
Madura ...	9,502	6	5,459	413,513	2,266,615	46·7	81·2	238·5	5·11	415·2	377,769
Tinnevelly ...	5,176	9	1,824	403,803	1,693,959	78·0	221·4	327·3	4·19	928·7	188,217
Coimbatore ...	7,432	10	1,575	361,109	1,763,274	48·6	229·3	237·3	4·88	1119·5	176,327
Nilgiris ...	749	1	17	13,922	49,501	18·6	818·9	66·0	3·55	2911·8	49,501
Salem ...	7,483	9	4,021	391,519	1,966,995	52·3	97·4	262·9	5·02	489·2	218,555
South Canara ...	3,902	5	1,288	184,569	918,362	47·3	143·3	235·4	4·97	713·0	183,672
Malabar ...	6,002	10	432	435,462	2,261,250	72·6	1008·0	376·7	5·19	5231·4	226,125
Madras City ...	27	1	23	51,741	397,552	1916·3	2249·6	14724·1	7·68	17284·8	397,552
Total ...	138,318	156	55,636	6,229,954	31,281,177	45·0	111·9	226·2	5·02	562·2	200,520
Puducottah Territory ...	1,380	3	1,279	77,638	316,695	56·2	60·7	229·5	4·07	247·8	105,565
Grand Total ...	139,698	159	56,915	6,307,592	31,597,872	45·2	110·8	226·2	5·01	555·2	198,729

Nationalities.   Of the whole population 28,863,978 were Hindus, 1,857,857 Mahomedans, 490,299 Native Christians, 14,505 Europeans, 26,374 East Indians or Eurasians, 21,254 Jains, 6,910 individuals whose nationality was undistinguished in the returns.   Of these 23,714,578 resided in Government villages or Inam lands, 7,566,599 on permanently-settled estates (zemindaries, &c.), and 316,695 in the State of Puducottah.   The following table shows the distribution of the people according to nationality :—

Districts.	Hindus.	Mahomedans.	Native Christians.	Europeans.	Eurasians.	Buddhists or Jains	Others	Total.
1. Ganjam ...	1,513,673	4,826	679	149	205	45	511	1,520,088
2. Vizagapatam†	2,135,432	21,030	882	378	810	91	576	2,159,199
3. Godavery ...	1,555,981	35,173	585	451	385	39	325	1,592,939
4. Kistna ...	1,365,709	78,941	7,380	77	208	...	59	1,452,374
5. Nelloro ...	1,308,014	65,670	2,653	101	237	...	136	1,376,811
6. Cuddapah ...	1,242,317	103,676	4,608	93	109	4	387	1,351,194
7. Bellary ...	1,534,223	127,783	3,354	1,213	978	327	128	1,668,006
8. Kurnool ...	847,805	107,920	3,644	40	160	2	69	959,640

* The number of villages entered includes those of zemindaries also.

† In the total number of males and females the population of Jeypore (males 168,909 + females 145,579 = total 314,498) is included, but not in the particulars, viz., "children" and "adults."

Districts.	Hindus.	Mahome-dans.	Native Chris-tians.	Euro-peans.	Eura-sians.	Bud-dhists or Jains.	Others	Total.
9. Chingleput ...	899,686	23,192	11,480	2,090	1,571	147	18	938,184
10. North Arcot ..	1,913,020	86,741	6,316	336	666	7,889	310	2,015,278
11. South Arcot...	1,676,462	44,567	30,219	123	370	3,861	215	1,755,817
12. Tanjore ...	1,803,787	102,703	65,262	389	522	239	829	1,973,731
13. Trichinopoly...	1,115,776	32,024	50,822	623	630	143	390	1,200,408
14. Madura ...	2,062,768	132,833	70,445	175	166	13	215	2,266,615
15. Tinnevelly ...	1,506,621	84,753	102,219	197	130	...	9	1,693,959
16. Coimbatore ...	1,715,081	36,026	11,443	153	442	56	73	1,763,274
17. Nilgiris ...	42,451	1,936	2,935	1,339	796	...	44	49,501
18. Salem ..	1,901,060	52,312	12,684	256	377	28	278	1,966,995
19. South Canara..	777,587	83,178	48,938	130	190	8,339	...	918,362
20. Malabar ...	1,637,914	581,609	32,280	2,579	5,409	31	1,428	2,261,250
21. Madras ...	308,611	50,964	21,441	3,613	12,013	...	910	397,552
Total ...	28,863,978	1,857,857	490,299	14,505	26,374	21,254	6,910	31,281,177
Puducottah Terri-tory	296,829	8,506	11,328	8	24	...	..	316,695
Grand Total ...	29,160,807	1,866,363	501,627	14,513	26,398	21,254	6,910	31,597,872

—Hindus. The Hindus formed about 92·3 per cent. of the whole population, inclusive of all aboriginal and mountain tribes, whether having caste distinctions or not. The bulk of these are manifestly not of Aryan extraction, but in South India it is impossible to distinguish the Hindu population in this way with any approximation to accuracy. The proportion of Hindus to the total varied from 99 per cent. in Ganjam to 72 per cent. in Malabar.

—Mahome-dans. The great bulk of the Mahomedan population of the Madras Presidency is of mixed descent, due partly to intermarriages either of the conquering races from the north or of Arab and Persian traders to the Western Coast, partly to forcible conversions in the time of Tippoo, and perhaps still more than either to voluntary conversions from Hinduism, especially on the Western Coast, where the percentage of Mahomedans to the whole population at the time of the census was as high as 25·7 per cent. In Madras, formerly the head-quarters of the Nabob of the Carnatic, the proportion was 12·8 per cent., while in Vizagapatam and Ganjam it was as low as 0·9 and 0·3 per cent.

—Native Christians. Inclusive of Roman Catholics, Syrian Christians, and Protestants, the total Native Christian population of the Presidency amounted to upwards of half a million. The highest percentage, 6·0, was found in Tinnevelly, chiefly owing to the Protestant Missions of later years, while the results of the labors of the earlier Christians and of the Jesuit Missions of the seventeenth century are found most markedly in the districts of South Canara and Malabar on the West Coast, and of Madura, Trichinopoly, and Tanjore in the centre of the peninsula, with a percentage varying from 1·4 to 5·3.

—Europeans.   The more important stations occupied by the Madras Army were not embraced by the census, being situated beyond the civil limits of the Presidency; but the presence of the European troops at the smaller stations contributed in no small measure to bring up the number of the European population to 14,505.

—Eurasians.   The Eurasian or East Indian population amounted to only 26,374, of which 13,584 were in Madras or the neighbouring district of Chingleput, and 5,409 in Malabar, where the Portuguese and Dutch had formerly established extensive settlements.

—Jains and Buddhists.   The Jains and Buddhists were classed together, but probably only a very few, if any, returned themselves under the latter heading. The total amounted to 21,254, of which 11,750 were in the districts of North and South Arcot, and 8,339 in South Canara. The following table shows the numbers of the above classes in each 100,000 of the population of the various districts :—

Districts.	Hindus.	Mahome-dans.	Euro-peans.	Eura-sians.	Native Chris-tians.	Jains.	Others	Total.
1. Ganjam	99,578	317	10	13	45	3	34	100,000
2. Vizagapatam ...	98,899	974	17	38	41	4	27	100,000
3. Godavery ...	97,679	2,208	29	24	37	3	20	100,000
4. Kistna	94,033	5,435	5	15	508	...	4	100,000
5. Nellore	95,003	4,770	7	17	193	...	10	100,000
6. Cuddapah ...	91,942	7,673	7	8	341	1	28	100,000
7. Bellary	91,978	7,661	73	59	201	20	8	100,000
8. Kurnool ...	88,346	11,246	4	17	379	1	7	100,000
9. Chingleput ...	95,897	2,472	223	167	1,223	16	2	100,000
10. North Arcot ...	94,926	4,304	17	33	313	392	15	100,000
11. South Arcot ...	95,480	2,538	7	21	1.722	220	12	100,000
12. Tanjore ...	91,386	5,206	20	27	3,307	12	42	100,000
13. Trichinopoly ...	92,950	2,668	52	52	4,234	12	32	100,000
14. Madura	91,007	5,860	8	7	3,108	1	9	100,000
15. Tinnevelly ...	88,941	5,003	11	8	6,036	...	1	100,000
16. Coimbatore ...	97,267	2,043	9	25	649	3	4	100,000
17. Nilgiris	85,758	3,911	2,705	1,608	5,929	...	89	100,000
18. Salem	96,648	2,660	13	19	645	1	14	100,000
19. South Canara ...	84.671	9,057	14	21	5,329	908	...	100,000
20. Malabar ...	72,434	25,721	114	239	1,428	1	63	100,000
21. Madras	77,628	12,819	909	3,022	5,393	...	229	100,000
Total ...	92,273	5,939	46	84	1,568	68	22	100,000
Puducottah Territory.	93,727	2,686	2	8	3,577	...	...	100,000
Grand Total ...	92,287	5,907	46	84	1,587	67	22	100,000

As might naturally be expected the density of the population **Density of**
was greatest on the sea-board and in the more highly irrigated **population.**
districts, such as Tanjore and Trichinopoly, and most sparse in
the hill ranges and the forest tracts adjoining the Eastern and
Western Ghauts.   The average number of persons to a square
mile throughout the Presidency was 226·2, the maximum per
district being 540·1 in Tanjore, and the minimum 66 on the
Nilgiri Hills.   Excluding the Nilgiri the thinnest population of
all the districts was found in Kurnool, Cuddapah, and Bellary.
The highest town population was 98,732 per square mile in the
2nd division of the town of Madras.

The house accommodation for the population was as below **Houses.**
noted, showing an average of five persons to a house.   On the
night of the census 371,960, or six per cent. were returned without inhabitants, being either shops or simply empty houses.   The
average number of persons to a terraced house was 5, to a tiled
house 6, to a thatched house 4·9, and to a house undefined 5·1.
Taking the Presidency as a whole, the terraced house is probably
a superior class of building, but this is not necessarily the case
in some districts, such as Bellary, Kurnool, and Cuddapah
where the prevalent high winds render it a more suitable style
for general adoption, while on the other hand the heavy rainfall
on the Western Coast leads to its almost complete absence in the
districts of Malabar and South Canara.

Terraced	...	...	...	...	492,279
Tiled ...	...	...	...	...	447,420
Thatched	...	...	...	...	5,180,146
Unspecified	...		...	...	110,109
			Total	...	6,229,954

Allusion has been made above to the difficulty in obtaining **Proportions**
correct returns of the female population having been got over **of the sexes.**
more successfully than had been anticipated, but internal
evidence shows that it still, in some measure, affected the relia-
bility of the census, as the female population, which is usually in
excess of the male in other parts of the world, appeared in the
returns as such only in the case of the eight districts noted
below :—

1. Tanjore.	5. Coimbatore.
2. Trichinopoly.	6. Salem.
3. Madura.	7. Madras.
4. Tinnevelly.	8. Puducottah Territory.

If the proportion shown for these districts, viz., 103·6 to 100, had prevailed in the other, the total female population would have been increased by 721,010. As it is, the proportion for the whole Presidency according to the returns was 99 females to 100 males. The lowest proportion, 93·9 females to 100 males, was found in Bellary, and the highest, 108·4 to 100, in the Pudu-cottah territory. If the returns of the various classes of the population be examined it is found that the defect was almost entirely confined to the Hindus, including Native Christians, Jains, and Buddhists, as the disproportion in the case of Europeans was obviously the result of the peculiar circumstances of their position in the country :—

	Total.	Males.	Females.	Proportion of Females to every 100 Males.
Hindus (including Native Christians and Jains).	29,669,296	14,909,056	14,760,240	99·0
Mahomedans	1,880,720	938,750	941,970	100·3
Europeans	14,561	9,957	4,604	46·2
Eurasians	26,450	13,091	13,359	102·0
Others	6,845	3,381	3,464	102·4
Total ...	31,597,872	15,874,235	15,723,637	99·0

The following table shows the proportions in the various districts :—

Divisions.	TOTAL.			
	Total.	Males.	Females.	Proportion of Females to every 100 Males.
1. Ganjam	1,520,088	779,112	740,976	95·1
2. Vizagapatam ...	2,159,199	1,110,034	1,049,165	94·5
3. Godavery	1,592,939	803,603	789,336	98·2
4. Kistna	1,452,374	737,495	714,879	96·9
5. Nellore	1,376,811	707,392	669,419	94·6
6. Cuddapah	1,351,194	693,400	657,794	94·9
7. Bellary	1,668,006	860,173	807,833	93·9
8. Kurnool	959,640	490,883	468.757	95·5
9. Chingleput	938,184	475,968	462,216	97·1
10. North Arcot	2,015,278	1,020,678	994,600	97·4
11. South Arcot ...	1,755,817	885,922	869,895	98·2
12. Tanjore	1,973,731	953,968	1,019.763	106·9
13. Trichinopoly... ...	1,200,408	588,134	612,274	104·1
14. Madura	2,266,615	1,112,066	1,154,549	103·8
15. Tinnevelly	1,693,959	836,515	857,444	102·5
16. Coimbatore	1,763,274	874,975	888,299	101·5

Divisions.	TOTAL.			
	Total.	Males.	Females.	Proportion of Females to every 100 Males.
17. Nilgiris	49,501	27,192	22,309	82·0
18. Salem	1,966,995	975,502	991,493	101·6
19. South Canara ...	918,362	459,729	458,633	99·8
20. Malabar	2,261,250	1,134,889	1,126,361	99·2
21. Madras	397,552	194,676	202,876	104·2
Total ...	31,281,177	15,722,306	15,558,871	99
Pudncottah Territory ...	316,695	151,929	164,766	108·4
Grand Total ...	31,597,872	15,874,235	15,723,637	99·0

The want of an accurate knowledge of their ages among the people, and their consequent readiness to adopt round numbers renders the usual quinquennial grouping unsuitable for India. The following statement shows the ages in decennial groups, exclusive of the Puducottah results :— **Ages of the people.**

Ages.	Males.	Females.	Persons.
0 to 10	5,113,672	5,036,151	10,149,823
10 to 20	3,063,170	3,031,720	6,094,890
20 to 30	2,757,350	2,944,728	5,702,078
30 to 40	1,960,508	1,818,485	3,778,993
40 to 50	1,294,445	1,233,393	2,527,838
50 to 60	795,887	798,095	1,593,982
Above 60	482,697	501,052	983,749
Unknown ages	254,577	195,247	449,824
Total ...	15,722,306	15,558,871	31,281,177

In the table given below the percentage of population at each decennial period of age is compared with the proportions found at the British Census of 1861 :—

Ages.	10.		20.		30.		40.		50.		60.		Above 60.		Unknown.	
—	Males.	Females.	Males.	Females.	Males.	Females.	Males.	Females.	Males.	Females.	Males.	Females.	Males.	Females.	Males.	Females.
British Census, 1861 ...	25·0	24·4	20·6	19·6	16·3	17·5	12·8	13·2	10·2	10·3	7·06	7·08	7·04	7·7	...	...
Madras	32·5	32·4	19·5	19·5	17·6	18·9	12·5	11·7	8·2	7·9	5·06	5·1	3·07	3·8	1·6	1·2

The result of the comparison is to show that the proportion of young children below ten years of age is very much greater in

Madras than in England, and that this excess continues, though in a decreasing ratio up to the age of forty. At fifty the excess is the other way, and at ages above sixty the Madras proportion is not half that of the British. The number of children and adults in the various districts is shown below :—

Districts.	CHILDREN.		ADULTS.		TOTAL.	
	Boys under 12 Years.	Girls under 10 Years.	Males.	Females.	Males.	Females.
1. Ganjam	309,609	251,443	469,503	489,533	779,112	740,976
2. Vizagapatam* ...	370,235	306,506	570,890	597,080	1,110,034	1,049,165
3. Godavery	310,898	256,223	492,705	533,133	803,603	789,336
4. Kistna	271,008	233,490	466,487	481,389	737,495	714,879
5. Nellore	248,362	213,811	459,030	455,608	707,392	669,419
6. Cuddapah	237,325	205,334	456,075	452,460	693,400	657,794
7. Bellary	299,477	255,059	560,696	552,774	860,173	807,833
8. Kurnool	175,358	148,269	315,525	320,488	490,883	468,757
9. Chingleput	183,370	165,662	292,598	296,554	475,968	462,216
10. North Arcot ...	385,495	345,292	635,183	649,308	1,020,678	994,600
11. South Arcot ...	344,384	310.306	541,538	559,589	885,922	869,895
12. Tanjore	355,990	317,259	597,978	702,504	953,968	1,019,763
13. Trichinopoly ...	219,777	197,754	368,357	414,520	588,134	612,274
14. Madura	430,264	380,984	681,802	773,565	1,112,066	1,154,549
15. Tinnevelly	311,876	273,981	524,639	583,463	836,515	857,444
16. Coimbatore	338,298	302,560	536,677	585,739	874,975	888,299
17. Nilgiris	9,032	7,734	18,160	14,575	27,192	22,309
18. Salem	382,087	343,524	593,415	647,969	975,502	991,493
19. South Canara ...	165,322	137,470	294,407	321,163	459,729	458,633
20. Malabar	436,982	355,789	697,907	770,572	1,134,889	1,126,361
21. Madras	56,678	47,211	137,998	155,665	194,676	202,876
Total ...	5,841,827	5,055,661	9,711,570	10,357,631	15,722,306	15,558,871
Puducottah Territory ...	55,644	50,861	96,285	113,905	151,929	164,766
Grand Total ...	5,897,471	5,106,522	9,807,855	10,471,536	15,874,235	15,723,637

Religions of the people.　The numbers of each great religious class were as follows :—

Hindus	...	...	...	... 28,863,978
Mahomedans	...	...	...	... 1,857,857
Christians	...	...	...	... 533,760
Jains and Buddhists	...	...	...	21,254
Other religions		...	...	... 4,328
			Total ...	31,281,177

* In the total number of males and females the population of Jeypore (males 168,909 + females 145,579 = total 314,488) is included, but not in the particulars, viz., " children" and " adults."

The numbers returned under the four great divisions of Hindus —**Hindus.** were—

Sivaites	...	...	...	...	16,159,610
Vishnavaites	...	...	...	...	11,657,311
Lingayets	...	...	...	...	154,989
Other Hindus (including hill tribes) ...					892,068

Total ... 28,863,978

In the Northern Districts the Sivaites were in the minority. In the Ganjam District they were as one to ten of the Vishnavaites ; in Vizagapatam as one to four ; in the Godavery as one to three and a fraction ; and only when the Kistna District was reached did the Sivaites approach in number to the Vishnavaites. In Nellore, Cuddapah, Bellary, Kurnool, Chingleput, North Arcot, and South Arcot the proportions of these two great divisions of the Hindu people were nearly equal, while in the districts to the south the Sivaites constituted the major portion of the Hindu population. In Tanjore they were nearly seven to one of the Vishnavaites ; in Trichinopoly and Coimbatore about four to one ; in Tinnevelly and Madura more than five to one ; and in Salem two to one. On the Western Coast they were in the proportion of two to one in Canara, and about sixty-seven to one in Malabar. In connexion with the above proportions, it is to be borne in mind that in modern times all demon-worshippers, who seek to appease the power of evil, are included under the head of Siva-worshippers. The Lingayet sect dates from the twelfth century, and owes its origin to Basava, the son of a Sivaite Brahmin, and prime minister of the king of Kalyanapura, a town on the Western Coast, about forty miles north of Mangalore, and at that time the capital of Karnataca. Its distinctive tenets are the unity of the godhead represented by Siva, the absence of caste distinctions, and the necessity of respecting women. The Lingayets or Jangams do not appear to have spread beyond the south and south-west of India, and they are now numerous only in the west of Mysore.

The numbers of the different divisions of the Mahomedans —**Mahomedans.** were as follows :—

				Population.	Per Cent.
Soonees	...		...	1,654,529	89·0
Shias	...	...	...	69,302	3·7
Wahabis	...	...	...	3,954	0·2
Unspecified	...	...	...	130,072	7·1
		Total ...		1,857,857	100·0

The Soonees abounded in all the local and national divisions of the Mahomedan community, but principally among the Moplahs of the Western Coast, of whom 95·8 were returned as Soonees. The largest proportion of Shias was found amongst Mahomedans of Pathan or Mogul descent, in each of which classes about 13 per cent. of the whole were Shias. Outside the town of Madras the Wahabis were few in number.

—Christians.   The Christian population of the Madras Presidency in Southern India, exclusive of 11,360 in the Puducottah territory, was made up as follows :—

Europeans and East Indians	... ...	40,879
Natives of India	...	490,299
Nationality unspecified	...	2,582
	Total ...	533,760

Nearly one-fifth of the whole Christian population was found in the Tinnevelly District, and next to this they were numerically strongest in Madura, Tanjore, Trichinopoly, South Canara, and Malabar. Christianity has been known in Southern India for many centuries. A Pehlevi inscription in the ancient church of the Little Mount near Madras indicates a settlement of Manichæans or Persian Christians on the Eastern Coast as well as on the west, and tradition speaks of the preaching of St. Thomas in the districts of Madras, Tinnevelly, and Malabar. The adherents of the Syrian Church in Malabar, Travancore, and Cochin are the most ancient Christian community in Southern India ; and after these come the Roman Catholics. The Protestant Churches only date from about the commencement of the century, but their progress since that time has been considerable. The following table shows how far the various castes and nationalities had contributed to the formation of the Native Christian community :—

	Roman Catholics.	Protestants.
Brahmins	3,658	39
Kshatriyas	4,535	565
Chetties	3,414	375
Cultivating Castes	35,742	6,147
Shepherd Castes	2,462	395
Artisan Castes	5,215	399
Writer Castes	143	25
Weaver Castes	5,027	595
Agricultural laborers (Vunnias)	90,852	11,411
Potters	622	110

		Roman Catholics.	Protestants.
Mixed Castes (Satani)	...	6,861	1,586
Fishermen	... ...	14,459	278
Shanars	... ...	26,724	36,470
Barbers	... ...	906	420
Washermen	... ...	1,840	348
Other Hindus	... ...	49,389	3,369
Pariahs	... ...	131,367	30,164
Mahomedans	... ...	17	5
Nazaranies (wrongly classed Mussulmans)	...	13,808	527

It will be observed that 3,697 were of Brahmin origin. A large —Jains and majority of these were Roman Catholic Christians of South Canara. Buddhists. The Buddhists are practically extinct in Southern India, but an offshoot, or perhaps heretical branch survives in the Jains, who numbered 21,254 chiefly in the districts of North Arcot (7,889), South Arcot (3,861), and Canara (8,339). Communities also exist in Western Mysore. The leading tenets of the Jains are denial of the divine origin and infallibility of the Vedas; reverence for sanctified or deified ascetics; and veneration for animal life.

The number of persons classified in the census returns as Castes— Brahmins was 1,094,455, of whom 547,027 were males and Brahmins. 548,418 females, the proportion of the latter to the former being 100·3 to 100 males. The distribution of this important caste is not a little curious, and shows very conclusively that the Aryan colonization of the south could never have been the result of the conquest and subjugation of the aboriginal races. The Brahmins were most numerous in Canara and in the northern districts of the Presidency. In Canara they were 13 per cent.; and in Ganjam 6·9 per cent. of the Hindu population. In the Godavery District 5·8 per cent.; in the Kistna 7·2 per cent.; in Nellore 4·9 per cent.; in Chingleput 3·6 per cent.; in South Arcot 1·9 per cent. In the Tanjore District, still further south, there was a sudden rise to 6·8 per cent. In Trichinopoly again the proportion diminished to 2·7 per cent.; in Madura they were only 1·8 per cent.; in Tinnevelly, the most southern district, 3·5 per cent. They were rare in Coimbatore and Salem, where the proportions were 1·6 and 1·5 per cent. respectively. In the remaining districts they averaged from 2·3 to 3·6 per cent. of the Hindu population. For the whole Presidency the average proportion of Brahmins as 3·7 per cent. of the Hindu population. The unequal distribution of the Brahmin population is probably the result of the occupation of favorite sites by the Aryan people in ancient times.

—Present occupations of Brahmins. The male Brahmin population of the Presidency was 547,027, and of these 338,934, or 61·9 per cent., were entered in the occupation columns, and thus accounted for :—

Major Heading.	Minor Heading.	Number employed.	Proportion in 100.
Professional ...	Government Civil Service...	8,837	1·6
	Military or Police Service...	747	0·1
	Learned Professions ...	18,499	3·4
	Minor do. ...	55,504	10·2
Domestic ...	Personal Service	19,584	3·6
Commercial ...	Traders	12,910	2·4
	Conveyors	969	0·2
Agricultural ...	Cultivators	132,443	24·2
Industrial ...	Dress	165	0·03
	Food	1,778	0·3
	Metals	20	0·003
	Construction	55	0·01
	Books	40	0·007
	Household Goods	16	0·003
	Combustibles	11	0·002
Indefinite and unproductive.	Laborers	5,384	1·0
	Property	64,545	11·7
	Unproductive	15,529	2·9
	Others	1,898	0·3
		338,934	61·9

—Divisions of Brahmins. The principal divisions are the Pancha Dravida and Pancha Gauda, sub-divided as follows :—

Dravidas.	*Gaudas.*
1. Andhra or Telinga.	1. Kanójia.
2. Mahratta.	2. Saraswat.
3. Dravida.	3. Gauda.
4. Karnataca.	4. Utkala.
5. Garjar.	5. Mathila.

When the Mahrattas overran the south and established a kingdom in Tanjore, the Brahmins settled wherever they could obtain lands. The Andhra or Telinga were mostly found in the Northern Districts, and the Dravidas in the Tamil country. In Malabar the Namburi Brahmins were most prominent. The origin of the latter is not very clear, but tradition tells of their ancestors being a race of fishermen. Karnataca Brahmins were most numerous in Bellary and Canara.

—Kshatriyas. The census returns showed only 190,415 persons of the Kshatriya caste, the majority of which were in Vizagapatam,

Godavery, Nellore, Cuddapah, North Arcot, South Canara, and the Town of Madras. The principal sub-divisions of the caste found in the Presidency are—

Arasar (Tamil).	Pandyakulam.
Oorya Kshatriya.	Rajavar (Telugu).
Bondiliar.	Nandamandalam Rajulu.
Bhat Rajah.	Murikinati Rájah.
Manu.	Suryavamsapu Rájalu.

Of these, the Bondiliars and the Bhat Rajahs were the most common.

Throughout the Presidency 714,712 persons, or 2·4 per cent. —The of the Hindu population, were returned as belonging to the Trading Castes. various trading castes. The greater part of these were classified as "Chetties" or "Beri Chetties" and "Komaties." Besides these, there were Banyias, Márwáries, Oilmongers, and Kásikkárá or bankers. Many of the above wear the sacred thread and claim to be Vaisyas. Some are clearly foreigners, and others, not of recent immigration, shew signs of Aryan origin. A large number however are clearly of aboriginal descent, and, in many cases, of Sudra origin. The Trading Castes are more numerous in proportion to other classes in Kistna, Nellore, Cuddapah, Kurnool, Madura, Coimbatore, and, most of all, in the Town of Madras. The Chetties are few in number in Canara only, where the trade of the country seems to have fallen into the hands of Brahmins, Mussulmans, and others.

The Vellalars may be taken as a type of the agriculturists in —The Agricultural the Tamil country. They speak a pure Tamil and no other Castes. language, and are chiefly the ryots or farmers of the district they inhabit. Those who are well to do, do not work with their own hands, but like the Brahmins, employ persons of inferior castes to do their menial work. They are mostly Sivaites, but their chief worship is that of the village gods. In some districts they have adopted the title of Pillai, which is also used by the shepherd and accountant classes. The Velama castes in the Telugu country are practically the same as the Vellalars in the Tamil District. They held formerly on military tenures. The cultivators of the Ceded and Central Districts are called Kápus or Kápalu. In the Northern Districts they are known as Kápus or Naidus, Kammavárs, aud Kammás. In Canara they are called Bants and Nadavars. In Malabar the Nairs are the corresponding class of land-owners or occupiers, and these appear formerly to have had a military tenure of their lands. The sub-divisions of the cultivators are too extensive for enumeration here. The number of the population classed as belonging to the agricultural castes was 7,826,127, or 26·6 of the entire Hindu population. They were most numerous in the districts of Vizagapatam, Cuddapah, and Coimbatore ; but in South Arcot, Canara, Trichinopoly, and Tanjore, their place seems to have been taken in a great part by the Brahmins on the one hand and the Vunnian or Pully castes on the other.

—Shepherd and Pastoral Castes. The principal Tamil representatives of the Shepherd and Pastoral castes are the Idaiyars. The Telugu term is Golla. The numbers at the time of the census were 1,730,681, or 5·9 per cent. of the Hindu population. They were most numerous in the inland districts where the country is hilly and mountainous, or from the nature of the climate unadapted for cultivation. In Bellary and Kurnool they numbered 14·1 and 11·3 per cent. of the Hindu population, but in Canara and Malabar only ·1 and ·2 per cent., the climate there being inimical to sheep and goats, and the breed of cattle inferior. The shepherd castes were also comparatively few in the fertile and fully cultivated deltas of the Godavery and Cauvery. A large proportion of the members of these castes have now adopted occupations other than their original caste pursuits. In religion, they are chiefly Vishnavaites, but there are a few Sivaites or demon-worshippers.

—The Artisan Castes. The artisan castes in Southern India have always maintained a struggle for a higher place in the social scale than that allotted to them by Brahminical authority. They are known by the Tamil name of " Kámálar " and the Telugu " Kamsála " or " Panchála." They numbered at the last census 785,085, or 2·7 per cent. of the Hindu population, being most numerous in Canara, Malabar, Vizagapatam, and Madura. Of the whole number nearly one-half were employed in occupations connected with metals, and the majority of the remainder as carpenters, builders, &c. A very small proportion of these castes are Vishnavaites, the bulk calling themselves Sivaites, but in reality worshipping either Kali or the village deity and burning their dead.

—The Writer or Accountant Classes. The caste name of the writer or accountant class in Tamil is " Kanakkan," in Telugu " Karnam." They numbered only 107,652 persons and were very irregularly distributed, being almost unknown in some districts where their hereditary occupation appears to have been usurped by Brahmins or Vellalars.

The term "Conicopillay" applied to agents, purveyors, &c., is a corruption of "Kanakkanpillai," a writer or accountant, "pillay" being a title of respect usually accorded to them as well as to the agricultural and shepherd castes.

—Weaver Castes. The weaver castes formed at one time an important section of the community, but at the last census their number was only 1,071,781, or 3·7 per cent. of the Hindu population. They were distributed all over the country, but were most numerous in the cotton-producing districts of Vizagapatam, Godavery, Kistna, Cuddapah, Bellary, Coimbatore, Salem, and Tinnevelly. The Tamil weaving castes are—

Kaikalar.	Jendraver.	Sedan.
Seringar.	Sáliyar.	Silupan.
and the Telugu		
Sále.	Padmay Sále.	Dévángalu.
Jendrar.	Thokat.	

As usual in castes of this grade, the Sivaites bury and the Vishnavaites burn their dead. Many of the weavers have adopted the Jangam or Lingayet religion. Their occupation is mainly confined to the original calling of the caste.

—Agricultural Laboring Castes. The Vannias or Pullies are the great agricultural laboring class of the southern districts. The term Naick is usually affixed to the name of the Vannias, and the Naicks of Madura and Tinnevelly were great men not very long ago. There are about thirty sub-divisions or branches of the laboring castes, the most important of which are the Marawars or Kallans, formerly turbulent tribes, addicted to thieving and general lawlessness. The Marawars were most numerous in Madura and Tinnevelly, and the Kulluns in Madura, Trichinopoly, and Tanjore, the Rajah of Puducottah being the acknowledged head of the tribe. The Oddars or Wadavars are a laboring tribe of Telugu origin, great at tank-digging, well-sinking, and road-making. The Upparava, a sub-division of the Vunniah caste, are chiefly engaged in the manufacture of salt on the sea-coast and the saltpetre in the inland districts. In the whole Presidency the agricultural laboring castes numbered 3,944,463, or 12·6 of the entire population. In the Telugu country they formed only about three per cent. of the population, but were more than thirty per cent. in South Arcot, Tanjore, and Trichinopoly. In religion they called themselves Sivaites, and occasionally Vishnavaites, but in reality they are demon-worshippers.

—Potter Castes.

At the last census the Potter castes numbered 250,343 persons or about ·9 per cent. of the Hindu population, distributed all over the country, but being most numerous in Kurnool, Madura, Nellore, and Canara. The majority still follow their caste occupation of pottery.

—Mixed Castes.

Classes of persons bearing about 200 different designations were classified in the returns under the head of "Mixed Castes," as it was found impossible to classify them with any of the recognized and defined orders of the people. The principal of these were the "Satanis," the followers of "Chaitanya," a reformer of the fifteenth century, or of his disciple Sanatana. The number grouped in these mixed castes in the census returns was 714,233, or about 2·4 per cent. of the Hindu population. The Satanis were really very few in number, and the bulk of the mixed castes were a nondescript people, devoted to religion or temple service.

—Other Castes.

The remaining numerically important castes are the fishing and hunting castes, called in Tamil "Sembadaven," and in Telugu "Besta." They numbered 971,837, or 3·3 per cent. of the Hindu population. In the coast and jungle districts most of them get their living by hunting and fishing, but large numbers are now engaged in cultivation and other pursuits. The palm-cultivator castes are numerous only in the districts in which the cultivation is practised. They are called Shanars in Tinnevelly and the South, Tiyars in Malabar, Billawars in Canara, and Idiyars in the northern or Telugu districts. They numbered 1,664,862 at the last census, or about 5·7 per cent. of the Hindu population. They are clearly an aboriginal people, and, as a rule, demon-worshippers. The barber caste is called "Ambattan" in Tamil, and "Mungala" in Telugu. Their numbers were 340,450 distributed pretty equally throughout every district. Of the male members of the barber caste, 42·6 per cent. followed the original calling.

—Hill and Wandering Tribes.

The number of persons unclassified according to castes amounted to 2,666,890, or about 9·1 per cent. of the Hindu population. In the settled and cultivated portions of the country the proportions were lower, but in the hilly districts of Ganjam and Vizagapatam, Kurnool, Nilgiris, South Canara, and Malabar they varied from 54·2 per cent. in the Nilgiris, and 31·4 in Ganjam, to 7·4 in Kurnool. Numerically speaking, the Khonds and Sowras of the Northern Districts are the most important of the hill tribes. South of the Kistna are found the

Yanadis, Yerakalas, and Chentsus, practically the same people as those further north, but in some parts partially civilized and engaged in settled occupations. Further south and west, in Salem and the neighbouring districts, are found a tribe of hill people called "Malayalies" not engaged as cultivators and shepherds. In Coimbatore, Malabar, and Canara the Mulcers and Kaders live by the products and the chase and on roots and herbs requiring no special cultivation. On the Nilgiris the Badaghers, who are employed in cultivation, have evidently moved up from the plains. The Todas, a stalwart and rather fine-looking race with a Jewish cast of feature, are peculiar to the high elevations of the Nilgiris, and are exclusively a pastoral people, worshipping local deities or demons, and addicted to polyandry. They are now dying out, having numbered only 693 at the last census. All over the country there are wandering tribes of carriers known as Brinjaries, Lambadies, &c. The religious beliefs of the aboriginal tribes have been modified to a great extent by the prevailing phases of Hinduism, and they are often called Vishnavaites or Sivaites. Practically, however, they are worshippers of local deities, generally females with power to do harm, and required to be propitiated by bloody sacrifices. The following list contains the names of some of the principal hill and wandering tribes :—

Budubudukar...	A class of mendicants.
Badaghers	...	Cultivators in the Nilgiris.
Gadala	...	A sub-division of Jat tribe.
Irulars	...	Hill tribe of the Nilgiris.
Jetti	...	Boxers, wrestlers, shampooers.
Jógis	...	Beggars and mendicants.
Koravars	...	A wandering tribe common in many districts of the Carnatic, addicted to thieving, &c.
Kótars	...	Artisans of the Nilgiri tribes.
Kumari	...	Jungle cultivators.
Lambadi	...	A gipsy tribe, carrying salt and grain.
Malayalies	...	Inhabitants of hills.
Mulcers	...	Tribes of the western jungles.
Pyclavar	...	Jugglers.
Pambattar	...	Snake-charmers.
Tombiravan ...	Jugglers.
Villi	...	A jungle tribe.

Yénadi	...	A wild tribe of the Eastern Coast districts.
Dommora	...	Juggler tribes.
Brinjaries	...	Gipsies and grain-carriers.
Chentsu	...⎫	Hunters and forest races.
Yerakala	...⎭	

—Pariah or Outcaste Tribes.

There is no part of the country in which the Pariah or out-caste are not to be found under various designations. In Tamil they are called Pariahs ; in Telugu, Mala ; in Canarese, Holia ; in Malayalum, Poliyar ; and Dheda in Mahratti. They are everywhere the menial servants of the country, and in times prior to the British rule were the slaves of the superior castes. Their numbers at the census were 4,761,503, or 16·2 per cent. of the Hindu population, four times as numerous as the Brahmins. The proportions in the different districts varies from 8·6 in Vizagapatam to 26 per cent. in Chingleput and South Arcot. As regards their occupation, the Pariahs do not now materially differ from any other class of the community. In religion they are nominally Sivaites or Vishnavaites, but practically worshippers of village idols and demons.

—Mahomedans.

The Mahomedans were classified as follows in the census returns :—

1. Labbay.	5. Syud.
2. Mapilah (Moplahs).	6. Pathan.
3. Arab.	7. Moghul.
4. Sheik.	8. Other Mahomedans.

The origin of the Labbays cannot now be definitely ascertained. The word is used to signify the descendants of foreign traders (Arabs and Persians) and women of the country. Beyond their customs and dress, there is now nothing to distinguish them from the other people of the country. They numbered 312,088, or 16·7 per cent. of the total Mahomedan population, and were nearly all found in the districts south of Madras. The Mapilahs or Moplahs are confined almost exclusively to the districts between the Western Ghauts and the sea. They were originally of Arab extraction, but their number has been greatly added by conversions, forcible and otherwise, among the people of the country. At the last census they numbered 612,789, or 32·7 per cent. of the Mahomedan population, 549,912 being found in Malabar and 65,641 in Canara. They are usually a hardworking, plodding, and frugal people, but

under the influence of religious excitement they have often been
a source of danger to the public peace. A few Mahomedans,
2,121 in all, chiefly in the Trichinopoly and Tinnevelly Districts,
returned themselves as " Arabs." A large proportion of the
Mussulman population of the Presidency consists of the
descendants of converts who at the time of their conversion
assumed the name of Sheik or Syud. The number of " Sheiks "
returned at the census was 511,112 and of Syud 89,219. The
term " Pathan " is applied to Mahomedans of Affghan descent.
They numbered 70,943 chiefly in Ganjam, Coimbatore, and
Salem. The Moghuls are the reputed descendants of Tartar
chiefs who followed Tamerlane into India, and are found chiefly
in the Northern and Ceded Districts and in Salem. The
following abstract shows numbers in each division and their
proportions to the whole Mahomedan community :—

Divisions.	Males.	Females.	Total.	Proportion of Females to 100 Males.	Proportion to the Gross Mahomedan Population.
Labbays	146,493	165,595	312,088	113·0	16·7
Mapilahs ...	307,321	305,468	612,789	99·4	32·7
Arabs	922	1,199	2,121	130·0	0·1
Sheiks	260,817	250,295	511,112	96·0	27·3
Syuds	45,883	43,336	89,219	94·4	4·8
Pathans	36,115	34,828	70,943	96·4	3·8
Moghuls	6,329	6,078	12,407	96·0	0·7
OtherMahomedans.	130,835	130,700	261,535	99·9	14·0
Total ...	934,715	937,499	1,872,214	100·3	100·0

The number of persons classified as following some occupation was 9,930,012, or 63·1 per cent. of the whole male
population to which the classification was confined, as the
inclusion of females leads to fallacious results owing to the
practice always prevailing under such circumstances of entering
females as following the occupation of the head of the family.
The number of males engaged in the classified occupations was
as follows :—

*The occu-
pations of
the people.*

Statement.

—	Number.	Proportion of each Sub-Division.	Proportion of Major Groups.
1. Government Service, Civil	57,251	or 0·4	} 2·0
2. Do. do. Military & Police ...	54,827	„ 0·3	
3. Learned Professions	37,249	„ 0·2	
4. Minor do.	172,116	„ 1·1	
5. Personal Service	519,350	„ 3·3	3·3
6. Trade and Commerce	534,662	„ 3·4	} 3·7
7. Conveyance of men, animals, and goods ...	48,108	„ 0·3	
8. Cultivators	4,878,890	„ 31·1	81·1
9. Employments connected with dress or textile fabrics.	510,061	„ 3·4	
10. Employments connected with food, drink, and stimulants.	335,287	„ 2·1	
11. Workers in metals	126,117	„ 0·8	
12. Workers in constructive works, buildings, &c.	121,036	„ 0·8	} 7·72
13. Employments connected with paper and books.	3,421	„ 0·02	
14. Household goods	71,805	„ 0·5	
15. Combustibles	13,189	„ 0·1	
16. Laborers for hire (unskilled)	2,071,602	„ 13·1	13·1
17. Persons subsisting on property, or of independent means.	176,580	„ 1·1	
18. Unproductive, such as mendicants, strollers, &c.	103,778	„ 0·7	} 2·2
19. Persons unclassified under any of the foregoing heads.	64,683	„ 0·4	
Total ...	9,930,012	„ 63·1	...

Education. ¶ All that the census professed to ascertain in regard to the education of the people was the number of persons, male and female, of each religion able to read and write; and of the whole population only 1,530,150, or about 5 per cent., possessed these qualifications, the proportion being rendered unusually small by the almost total absence of education among the females. The northern districts were the most backward, and in the south also the district of Salem showed a proportion of only 2·8 per cent. Outside the Presidency town female education has made the greatest advance in Tinnevelly, owing to the labors of the Protestant Missions in that district. While the general average of males able to read and write is 5 per cent., the Hindus have only 4·8 per cent., the Mahomedans 4·9, Native Christians 7·4, Europeans and East Indians 53·3, Jain 12·9, and "Others" 18·4 per cent. The following table shows the numbers and proportions of the population able to read and write in the several districts :—

Districts.	Population.	Number of Persons able to read and write.	Percentage of Columns 3 to 2.	Districts.	Population.	Number of Persons able to read and write.	Percentage of Columns 3 to 2.
1	2	3	4	1	2	3	4
Ganjam ...	1,388,976	35,362	2·5	Madura ...	2,266,615	134,567	5·9
Vizagapatam...	1,844,711	42,449	2·3	Tinnevelly ...	1,693,959	138,074	8·2
Godavery ...	1,592,939	47,202	3·0	Coimbatore ...	1,763,274	63,213	3·6
Kistna ...	1,452,374	58,173	4·0	Nilgiris ...	49,501	3,990	8·1
Nellore ...	1,376,811	55,588	4·0	Salem ...	1,966,995	55,133	2·8
Cuddapah ...	1,351,194	44,179	3·3	South Canara.	918,362	31,905	3·5
Bellary ...	1,668,006	69,576	4·2	Malabar ...	2,261,250	119,071	5·3
Kurnool ...	959,640	35,918	3·7	Madras ...	397,552	72,865	18·3
Chinglepnt ...	938,184	74,492	7·9				
North Arcot ...	2,015,278	109,038	5·4	Total ...	30,835,577	1,530,150	5·0
South Arcot...	1,755,817	93,920	5·3	Puducottah			
Tanjore ...	1,973,731	173,349	8·8	Territory ...	316,695	19,857	6·3
Trichinopoly ...	1,200,408	72,086	6·0				
				Grand Total ...	31,152,272	1,550,007	5·0

The number and proportion of boys and girls at the time of the census were :—

Population ...

- Males under 20 ... 8,176,842
- Females under 12 ... 5,584,364
- Total ... 13,761,206

Schools ...

- For Boys 3,922
- Mixed 296
- Girls 163
- Total ... 4,381

Pupils ...

- Boys 122,141
- Girls 10,781
- Total ... 132,859

Proportion of pupils to 100,000 children.

- Boys ... ... 1493·7
- Girls ... ... 191·9
- Total ... 965·04

The above table, however, only includes schools brought under the inspection of the officers of the Educational Department, and takes no notice of the great majority of the indigenous village schools scattered all over the country. The following list of matriculated students shows the extent to which the various classes of the community have availed themselves of the means introduced of late years for the higher education of the people :—

Europeans and East Indians	...	...	424
Brahmins	...	...	2,058
Hindus, other than Brahmins	...	...	856
Native Christians	...	...	294
Mahomedans	...	...	61

Total ... 3,693

Infirm persons.

In the following table the infirmities of the general population are given as returned in the census. Persons of unsound mind appear to number about 0·45 per 1,000. In the "deaf or dumb" return persons deaf by age are included. The blind are about 1·9 per 1,000, most of them being aged. Leprosy appears to be less common inland than on the coast, and the proportion in the several districts ranges from 0·2 to 1·0 per 1,000 :—

Infirm.	Males.	Females.	Total.
Insane	4,088	3,447	7,535
Idiotic	3,491	2,991	6,482
Deaf *or* Dumb ..	21,373	19,596	40,969
Blind	27,984	32,369	60,853
Leprous	9,240	4,607	13,847

General comparative vital statistics.

The following table gives at a glance the most general results in the Presidency statistics, comparing them with those of the whole of India, and in some cases with those of England :—

—	England.	British India.	Madras Presidency.
Total population, excluding feudatory States.	...	190,563,048	31,281,177
Total area, square miles, excluding feudatory States.	...	904,049	138,318
Average population per square mile.	422	211	226
Average number of houses per square mile.	73	41	42
Average number of persons per house.	5·33	5·14	5·60
Total population, including feudatory States.	...	238,830,958	33,308,225
Total area, including feudatory States, square miles.	...	1,450,744	148,128

—	England.	British India.	Madras Presidency.
Population of largest town... {	London. 3,254,000	Calcutta. 795,000	* Madras. 398,000
Proportion of Hindus to total population.	...	73·07	92·27
Proportion of Mahomedans to total population.	...	21·45	5·94
Proportion of Christians to total population.	...	·47	† 1·71
Number of persons employed in professions and Government service.	...	2,404,855	289,676
Number of persons employed in agriculture.	...	37,462,220	6,215,847

SANITARY.

The only purely sanitary officer in this Presidency is the Sanitary Commissioner. This officer is the adviser of Government in its Civil and Military Departments, of Local Fund Boards, and of Municipalities on all questions relating to the prevention of disease and the preservation of health. He possesses no executive power, and his functions are confined to the collection of sanitary information and to inspection and report. He receives weekly returns of sickness and mortality from military hospitals and annual reports of cantonments, monthly returns and annual reports from Central and District Jails, and monthly returns of births and deaths from Districts, Municipalities, and Cantonments; and during the prevalence of cholera he receives daily returns of attacks and deaths from District Officers. Civil hospitals do not send returns to the Sanitary Commissioner. The information thus collected is recorded and tabulated; and abstracts of the cholera returns are supplied daily to the Quartermaster-General, the Surgeons-General of the Indian Medical and British Medical Departments, and the Sanitary Commissioner with the Government of India. Budget estimates of Local Fund Boards are submitted to the Sanitary Commissioner before being forwarded for the sanction of Government,

Sanitary Commissioner.

---

* Slightly more than in Manchester and Birmingham, each of which towns has about 350,000 inhabitants.

† The Christians in Madras form thus five-sixths of the whole number of Christians in British India.

in order that he may express an opinion upon the sufficiency
of the proposed provision for sanitary wants. From Municipalities the Sanitary Commissioner receives an annual sanitary
report. In tours the Sanitary Commissioner inspects jails, of
which he is an official visitor, Municipal towns and villages, for-
warding to the responsible authorities such suggestions for the
improvement of their sanitary condition as may occur to him.
Notes of these tours of inspection are printed in his monthly Proceedings. In the same Proceedings, which are supplied to all
Local Fund Boards and Municipalities, are published replies to
references on sanitary subjects and sanitary papers communicated by Government to the Sanitary Commissioner. In this
manner each local body is made aware of the sanitary improvements which are being carried out in other parts of the
Presidency and of India. The Sanitary Commissioner holds a
somewhat ambiguous position with reference to the Civil and
Military Departments of Government. The original Sanitary
Commission and its successor, the Sanitary Commissionership,
were instituted chiefly with a view to military requirements, and
they were at first connected with the Military Department and
communicated with Government through the Military Secretary.
The civil portion of the Commissioner's duties however gradually
assumed larger proportions, and it was decided in 1869 that he
should be thenceforward, as in Bengal, under the orders of the
Civil Department, and that all expenses connected with the
appointment should be transferred to the Civil Budget. The
duties of the Sanitary Commissioner lie now mainly in the civil
branch of the administration. One result of the double position
occupied by the Sanitary Commissioner is that he has a different
local jurisdiction in the two capacities. Thus the garrisons in
Burmah, Secunderabad, the Mysore country, and the Central
Provinces are all under inspection by the Sanitary Commissioner
for the Madras Presidency; in civil matters however he has no
jurisdiction beyond the Presidency limits. Under instructions
from the Secretary of State for India the Sanitary Commissioner
includes in his yearly report a detailed account of the health, &c.,
of British and Native troops; as however this differs in no
material respect from the account furnished on the same subject
by the military medical authorities, and as an abstract of the
latter has usually been given in Chapter III of the yearly
Administration Report under the section headed "Military," it
is not customary to introduce the Sanitary Commissioner's Army
statistics in Chapter VI of that Report. There are differences

between the statistics of the two offices just named. Thus the Sanitary Commissioner embodies in his statistics only such regiments as are actually serving in Madras commands, including British Burmah, while the returns from the Surgeon-General's office exhibit the vital statistics of all Madras regiments irrespective of their being within or without the limits of the Madras Presidency. The method of tabulation from returns is also different in the two offices. A third cause of discrepancy is that the Sanitary Commissioner deals with corps according to the station in which they may have been quartered, but the Indian Medical Department accepts results irrespective of location. Thus it may happen that a corps has spent ten months of the year in Bangalore and two in Cannanore; under such circumstances the Sanitary Commissioner records one series of results for the time passed at Bangalore and another for that passed at Cannanore. In the Surgeon-General's office on the other hand each regiment is looked upon as a unit and its health statistics are projected in general totals and averages irrespective of locality. The former plan is adopted with a view to sanitarian and the latter with a view to medical purposes. Still the net result in the two sets of statistics is much the same, and for the purposes of the yearly administration reports there is no necessity to introduce both; as the medical statistics are made up for the official year, these are preferred in that publication. As regards the relations between the Civil Medical Department and the Sanitary Department of the Government, it may perhaps be pointed out that while it is the business of the former to treat disease and to promote medical science, it is the business of the latter to act in the direction of preventing disease, and to collect vital and mortuary statistics as a guide to sanitary measures and as a test of sanitary progress.

The machinery of birth and death registration differs in **Mode of registering Births and Deaths.** town and country. In the districts generally it is simple and inexpensive, but not on the other hand as accurate as could be wished. The Curnam or Village Accountant records the births and deaths which occur in his village, obtaining his information in the former case from the village dhoby or washerman and in the latter case from the village taliary or watchman. A monthly abstract of his records, which in the case of deaths includes particulars as to age and cause of death, is forwarded to the Collector through the taluq authorities. The returns are tabulated in the Collector's office, and transmitted by him to the

Sanitary Commissioner. It is the duty of the Revenue Inspectors, a class of subordinate Revenue officials, to supervise the registration as far as they have opportunities for doing so. There is no law compelling persons to report births or deaths to the village officers. In municipal towns special Registrars are appointed, sometimes for purposes of registration only, and sometimes for this in conjunction with other sanitary duties. The law makes compulsory the registration of births and deaths occurring within municipal limits, relatives being bound to report within 20 days. Payment of Registrars by results has in some cases been attempted, but the plan has been abandoned. It is believed that under ordinary circumstances birth registration in this Presidency may be regarded as obviously defective when the registered rate falls below 2·5 per cent. of population. The English birth-rate is understood to be 3·51, and the French birth-rate 2·63 per cent. ; the corresponding death-rates being 2·25 and 2·36 respectively.

Mode of ascertaining public health. The machinery for birth and death registration, involving as it does registry of the ages at death and presumed causes of death, constitutes at present the only means of testing the public health which can be described as of a scientific nature. The organization of a separate Health Department has been at various times contemplated, but financial difficulties have prevented the plan from being carried out. The particulars regarding public health usually given in the yearly Administration Reports are taken from the returns of the Sanitary Commissioner. It is to be noted however that the Government obtain health returns from Collectors of districts through the Board of Revenue, and from medical officers in charge of stations through the Surgeon-General, Indian Medical Department; and that these sources of information, though not professedly of a scientific or statistical nature, are still on general questions as valuable, and in the present state of birth and death registration perhaps as accurate as the more formal returns of the Sanitary Department.

Distribution of practical sanitation. Practical sanitation is undertaken chiefly by Local Fund Boards and by Municipalities. Municipal sanitation is not checked in detail by Government. Sanitary expenditure by Local Fund Boards is divided technically into three classes : (*a*) improvement of water-supply, (*b*) enlargement or improvement of village sites, and (*c*) conservancy of towns and villages. The main source of income of Local Fund Boards is the land-cess, two-thirds of which is necessarily devoted to Communications. The remaining third is available for other objects.

and, though there are some other minor sources of income, may be taken roughly as the income available for miscellaneous expenditure. This third is divided amongst four claimants, Education, Medicine (Hospitals and Dispensaries), Convenience, and Hygiene (the last including Vaccination). The ratio of distribution is decided in each case on its merits. The sanitation of jails and in the two armies engages the separate attention of Government.

EMIGRATION.

The population of Southern India is drained to some extent by emigration of the laboring classes to neighbouring countries, and especially to Burmah and Ceylon. British Burmah contains a large area of uncultivated land, and there is a migration of population from the Telugu districts, especially from the ports of Coringa and Cocanada to Burmah, but no account is kept of the numbers so migrating. The movement is voluntary and unaided by the Government. A number of women emigrate from the northern districts to Burmah for the purpose of prostitution in the Burmese sea-ports. They usually return to their own country after a few years of absence, or when they have saved money. A temple was recently built at Coringa by a woman of this class at a cost of Rupees 30,000, or £3,000. The emigration to Ceylon is on a larger scale, the greater part of the labor required on the coffee estates in Ceylon being furnished from Southern India. At certain seasons of the year, when labor is in demand, the laboring classes of the southern districts travel across to Ceylon; and, when they have saved a little money, return again to their native villages. The cooly traffic between the south ports and Ceylon is constant and mutually advantageous to the people of India and to Ceylon. The high wages offered by the planters enable the people to save, and ultimately to take the position of small farmers in their own villages, while the planters in Ceylon can always obtain as much labor as they want by offering sufficient inducements. The Ceylon Government undertakes to see that the coolies are properly housed, fed, and provided with medical attendance, and the migration to and from the coffee districts is entirely voluntary. About 70,660 persons go over to

Nature of South Indian Emigration.

Ceylon every year from the southern districts, and of these about
54,000 return to India.   The others settle more or less permanently in the island.   The following table shows the migration
of the Madras population to and from Ceylon for ten years prior
to the date of the last census :—

—	To Ceylon.	From Ceylon.
1862	68,896	41,915
1863	70,718	61,765
1864	81,800	62,276
1865	89,597	64,539
1866	88,528	49,229
1867	42,769	45,996
1868	51,033	37,061
1869	58,689	54,316
1870	65,114	55,082
1871	89,529	68,310
Total ...	706,673	540,519
Mean of 10 years ...	70,667·3	54,051·9

This table shows that the great check to coffee speculation in
1867 immediately affected the labor market.   In that one year
more coolies returned from the island than went over.   But the
great industry of Ceylon, under the stimulus of high prices, has
been reviving, and in 1871 the cooly migration was as great as
in the years 1864 to 1866, when much capital was expended in
opening out new estates.   In the ten years ending with 1871
the southern districts of India lost 166,154 persons by migration
to Ceylon.   The greater part of the survivors of these places
are probably doing better for themselves in the land of their
adoption than they could hope to do in their native land.   They
are free to return whenever they please, and that they do not
come back must be taken as an indication that they are content
to remain.   Emigration goes on also to the more distant countries
of Mauritius, Bourbon, and the West Indies under regulations
defined by law; but the numbers proceeding to those places are
comparatively few.   The following abstract shows the number
of emigrants and of returned emigrants to and from Mauritius,
Bourbon, and West Indies for the ten years ending 1871 :—

—	From Madras Ports.	Returned Emigrants.
1862	6,804	542
1863	5,118	614
1864	5,229	...
1865	7,133	1,261
1866	7,317	1,192
1867	12,339	851
1868	1,426	768
1869	3,084	1,696
1870	3,816	667
1871	3,308	1,293
Total ...	55,574	8,884
Mean of 10 years ...	5,557·4	888·4

The legal provisions regarding emigration are the same **Nature of** throughout India. The Government take no account of emi-**Government protection.** gration other than that to Ceylon ; to the British Colonies of Mauritius, Jamaica, British Guiana, Trinidad, St. Lucia, Grenada, St. Vincent, Natal, St. Kitts, and Seychelles ; to the French Colonies of Réunion, Martinique, Guadaloupe and its dependencies and Guiana ; and to the Danish Colony of St. Croix. Emigration to these places, excepting Ceylon, is regulated or provided for by Act VII of 1871, and contracts regarding emigration proper to any other places have not the force of law. The Ceylon emigration is regulated, as far as the Ceylon Government is concerned, by the Ceylon ordinance as 11 of 1865 ; on the part of the Madras Government, the number of emigrants is checked by the Collectors of the southern districts. This movement of labor, though practically emigration, inasmuch as many of those who go are lost to the country, and though representing the greater number of so-called emigrants, is not of a kind to require much technical interference on the part of the local Government. As has been said, emigration to Burmah and the Straits Settlements goes on from this Presidency, but it is informal and is not checked. For the British Colonies named above a machinery of protection is provided under the Act specified. Each Colonial Government concerned nominates its agent and recruiters for the Presidency and establishes its depôt for the reception of emigrants at the town of Madras ; the Protector of Emigrants on the other hand, assisted by a Medical Inspector, represents the local Government. The emigrant enters into an engagement with the recruiter in one or other of the districts for service in the colonies under certain conditions as to time of service, pay, rations, free passage

both on the way to the colony and return home, and hours and
day of work in the colony. The time of service is usually five
years. In the case of the Mauritius the pay ranges from 5 to
10 Rupees according to service in the colony, and in other
colonies the pay is usually 5 Rupees. The emigrants have
generally to work six days in the week and nine hours in the day.
Emigrants when licensed by the recruiter are registered in the
mofussil by Magistrates and at the Presidency town by the
Protector. The recruit is brought before the Magistrate or
Protector as the case may be, and if he is found to understand the
terms of the engagement, and to be willing to emigrate, he is
registered and sent to the depôt belonging to the colony concerned,
where he remains under the care and responsibility of the
recruiter till he embarks. Previous to embarkation the vessel
intended to carry emigrants is surveyed by competent marine,
officers and certified to be fit to carry emigrants, and the Protector
personally superintends embarkation. The stock of provisions
and medicines, and the accommodation to be afforded, is prescribed by standing orders. The Protector is empowered to stop
the embarkation of such emigrants as seem to him unfit to
undertake the voyage. The Protector inquires into the treatment experienced by them in the colony and during the voyage
and a report is made to Government. Anything worthy of
notice and requiring remedy is communicated to the Colonial
Government concerned. The return emigrants, or immigrants as
they are sometimes called, can only land at the port of Madras,
and their numbers are there registered. The only British
colony at present represented in this Presidency is the Mauritius,
but the establishment of an agency and depôt for Natal is in
contemplation. For the French colonies, in which case a special
convention secures to the French Governments similar advantages to those enjoyed by British colonies, the procedure is
very much the same; there are however three ports of embarkation and three depôts, viz., at Madras, Pondicherry, and
Karikal. The interests of the local Government are represented
at Madras by the Protector of Emigrants, and at the two
French ports by two special officers styled British Consular
Agents. For the Danish colony mentioned in the Act no provision
is made.

MEDICAL RELIEF.

Operations under this title consist of the operations undertaken **Nature of** by Government, or by Local Boards in towns and rural circles **relief.** acting under the orders of Government, for the medical relief of the population. This is done in the case of the Army by Military Hospitals attended by officers of the two Medical Departments, and in the case of the general public by a system of civil hospitals, dispensaries, and asylums. Officers of Government are medically attended by officers of the Indian Medical Department. The information and statistics regarding public health given in the yearly administration report of the Government are those obtained from the observations of sickness taken exclusively in connection with the Civil Hospitals, Dispensaries, and Asylums.

The British Medical Service is the portion of the Army Medical **British** Department serving in the command with European troops. The **Medical Service.** establishment sanctioned for the Madras Presidency and Burmah includes 1 Surgeon-General, 3 Deputy Surgeons-General, 26 Surgeons-Major, and 48 Surgeons, making in all a total of 78. Each officer comes to India on a tour of foreign service, returning to England on its conclusion. The ordinary period of this tour is five years, but in special cases it may be prolonged beyond that limit. The routine duties of the department are exclusively in connection with British troops. The Surgeon-General is in communication with Government through the Military Secretary, with the Commander-in-Chief through the Adjutant-General and Quartermaster-General, and War Office in London through the Director-General of the Department. He conducts the duties of his office at the seat of Government. The Deputy Surgeons-General are in charge of circles or divisions, and are responsible both to the General Officer in command of their particular district and to the Surgeon-General. These officers perform yearly inspections of barracks and hospitals occupied by British troops. The Surgeons-Major and Surgeons are in professional charge of officers and soldiers and their families, and are available during their tour of duty in this Presidency to be sent wherever British troops are stationed.

To the Indian Medical Department are allotted medical duties **Indian** connected with the Native Army and the civil administration of **Medical Service.** the country; its members are also occasionally employed by

Government on scientific and other extra-professional duties. The department consists of Commissioned and Subordinate grades, and its officers are specially engaged for service in India and other Eastern Dependencies. The Subordinate Medical Establishment consists of two classes, viz., the Apothecary or Warrant and the Hospital Assistant class. In addition to the ordinary and Military Medical Subordinates there are at present under training two classes of Medical Subordinates intended for employment under Government in Provincial Hospitals and for service in the Hospitals of Municipalities and of Local Fund Boards. These officials are to be designated respectively Civil Apothecaries and Civil Hospital Assistants, and to be purely civil officers not amenable to military discipline or available for military duty. The Surgeon-General at the head of the department is entrusted with the control and superintendence of Military Hospitals and Medical Establishments connected with Native troops; and of Lock Hospitals, Medical Store Depôts, Civil Hospitals and Dispensaries, and Medical Establishments attached to the Judicial, Revenue, Police, and other Civil Departments. In matters connected with the Native Army this officer is subordinate to the Commander-in-Chief. There are six Deputy Surgeons-General, to each of whom is assigned a circle of superintendence.

Civil Medical Relief.

The agencies for the relief of the sick poor in this Presidency are annually increasing under the operation of the Towns Improvement and Local Fund Acts. According to the latest information there were 134 hospitals and dispensaries in operation throughout the Presidency, the medical staff of which consisted of 48 Commissioned Officers, 4 Honorary Surgeons, 62 Officers of the Warrant grade, and 81 Hospital Assistants, making a total of 195 Medical Agents. These institutions are open to all classes of the community applying for relief. Of the 134 institutions 99 are hospitals having wards for in-patients, and 35 may be classed as dispensaries, inasmuch as they at present only afford relief to out-patients. Since the passing of the Towns Improvement and Local Fund Acts in 1871, the cost of maintaining hospitals and dispensaries has, under sanction of the law, been thrown on Municipalities and Local Fund Boards, and at the present moment the entire cost of all up-country civil hospitals and dispensaries is met by those Boards, with the exception of the pay of the Medical Officers when of the Commissioned grade or of the grade of Honorary Surgeon. In the case of a Native Surgeon, Warrant officer, or Hospital

Assistant holding charge of a civil hospital along with police or jail duties one-fourth of his pay becomes a provincial charge in virtue of the latter duties. In most cases the local hospital is a joint charge on the adjoining Local Fund Circles and the Municipality in which it is situated, the expenses being divided equally between them. At the Presidency town the General Hospital, on account of its being a clinical school for the College students, and four other special hospitals are entirely supported by Government. The cost of the Civil Lock Hospital in Madras is also partly borne by Government, but the maintenance of the other hospitals is purely a municipal charge. At Mofussil stations Government support two Lunatic Asylums and a Lazaretto, together with Civil Dispensaries at the three large military stations of Secunderabad, Kamptee, and St. Thomas' Mount. The cost of the Civil Hospitals on the Nilgiris is also partly met from provincial funds. The cardinal principle, however, of the existing system of medical relief for the masses in this Presidency is its maintenance by local taxation, consequently its extension depends chiefly on the action of the ratepayers. So far the new arrangement has proved no obstacle to the extension of medical relief, but would appear on the contrary to have given it a fresh impetus; dispensaries have multiplied rapidly under Local Boards, and the increase in their number would have been still greater had the Medical Department been in a position to provide the requisite number of medical men to take charge of the new institutions. The provision of medical men, and their education and training, has up to the present moment been undertaken by the Government. The Contagious Diseases Act, No. XIV of 1868, is administered by a Health Officer specially appointed.

CHEMICAL EXAMINER.

—

The duties of the Chemical Examiner to Government are **Duties.** chiefly to examine and report upon substances submitted to him for investigation by Magisterial and Police Officers, in cases where poisoning is suspected, and to examine weapons and other articles for blood-stains. He is also required to analyse potable waters used by troops and public establishments; and to examine Government stores of all kinds, soils, limestones, salts, liquors, and other substances submitted by the various departments of the service.

VACCINATION.

Nature of Department.   The Department of Vaccination consists of an Inspector, Superintendents, First and Second class Vaccinators, and Volunteers, the last being more properly candidates preparing for admission into the department. The general supervision of the department devolves on the Inspector who is a Commissioned Medical Officer. The Inspector visits all parts of the Presidency, and subordinate supervision is maintained by the Superintendents, of whom there are one or more in each district, and who are all in direct subordination to the Inspector. The actual work of vaccination is done by the Vaccinators, whose pay varies according to grading and local arrangements. The Vaccinators themselves are under the orders of the Local Boards. As a general rule each works in his own Municipal town or taluq, but in some cases the plan has been adopted of working in bodies which itinerate from village to village. With a few exceptions the whole cost of the Department of Vaccination is borne by Local Fund Boards and Municipalities. Government however contributes the pay and allowances of the Inspector and entertains at its own expense two or three Cantonment Vaccinators. Down to the beginning of 1875-76 vaccination was treated as a branch of the Medical Department, and the principal officer was styled Superintendent-General; it is now treated as a branch of the Sanitary Department, and the officer just named is styled Inspector of Vaccination. The following list shows the different classes of vaccinators at work, and the relative results attained by each as shown by the figures of a recent year :—

	Total of Operations.
Vaccine Districts and Vaccine Depôt ...	291,493
Military Cantonments	5,323
Private Vaccinators	5,940
Temporary Vaccinators	12,677

	Total of Operations.
Local Fund Vaccinators	14,671
Medical Subordinates	11,032
Municipalities	29,115
Zemindaries	4,245
Civil Dispensaries	408
Hospital Assistant, Pulney Hills and Amindivi Islands.	51
Railway Apothecaries	
Chuttrum Vaccinators	1,189
Result-system Vaccinators	5,268
Total ...	831,421

SECTION VII.

INSTRUCTION.

EDUCATIONAL DEPARTMENT.

Historical retrospect —1826 to 1855. In 1826 Sir Thomas Munro appointed a Board of Public Instruction to organize a system of public instruction with authority to establish two principal schools in each collectorate and an inferior school in each taluq. Fourteen collectorate schools and eighty-one taluq schools were accordingly set on foot, together with a central school at the Presidency; but the scheme proved a failure, and all the schools established in the provinces were abolished. In 1836 the Board of Public Instruction was superseded by a new Board styled the "Committee for Native Education," who were directed to organize a Normal school for training teachers for the eventual establishment of English schools in different parts of the country. This body was in its turn replaced by the University Board which was constituted by Lord Elphinstone for the government of an institution to be styled the Madras University, and to consist of a high school and college upon the plan followed by the Scottish Universities. The high school was opened in April 1841, but it was not until January 1853 that the standard was considered by Government sufficiently advanced to justify the establishment of a Collegiate Department. In 1853 and 1854 Provincial schools were opened at Cuddalore, Rajahmundry, Combaconum, Calicut, and Bellary. The educational operations of the Madras Presidency were at this period on a very small scale compared with those of the other Governments. The entire expenditure in 1852-53 amounted to only Rupees 45,556-13-4. In the provinces scarcely any thing had been done. In addition to the Provincial schools just mentioned, there was nothing but a small industrial school at Negapatam, a few elementary schools for the instruction of the Khonds of Gumsur and Chinna Kimedy, some Vernacular schools in the

delta taluqs of the Godavery District, two Vernacular schools
in South Arcot, and a small school at Pulicat originally
founded by the Dutch Government. A monthly grant of
Rupees 350, known as the Schwartz grant and dating from the
commencement of the present century, had been given to certain
Protestant schools in Tanjore and Ramnad. Certain Yeomiahs
granted by the former Mahomedan Government for the instruction of Mahomedan children in the Koran had been continued in
Nellore and North Arcot, and just at the close of this period a
grant of Rupees 5,000 was given to the Madras Training Institution, which was established in 1853 to train male and female
teachers for employment in Christian schools.

In March 1855, Mr. Alexander Arbuthnot, the Secretary of the —Establish-
University Board, was appointed Director of Public Instruction, ment of pre-
and during the course of the year sanction was given for the ment Depart-
appointment of four Inspectors of Schools, twenty Assistant ment.
Inspectors, afterwards styled Zillah Visitors and now known as
Deputy Inspectors, and sixty Sub-Assistant Inspectors called
Taluq Visitors. The Madras University was remodelled and
received the name of the Presidency College. A Law Class was
established as a branch of this institution, and provision was made
for a Normal school for training teachers, four Provincial and
eight Zillah schools, a hundred Taluq schools, a depôt for school-
books, Educational Presses, and Rupees 12,000 for scholarships.
To carry out these measures occupied several years, and some
changes were made from time to time in the details of the plan
originally sketched out. Thus the full number of taluq schools
was never established, and schools of a somewhat higher grade
known as Anglo-Vernacular schools took the place of some of
the taluq schools. The Madras Normal school was supplemented by Normal schools of a more elementary type in the
provinces. A special school for Mahomedans known as the
Madrasa-i-Azam was remodelled in 1859. The Provincial school
of Combaconum grew into a College and was formally recognized
as such in 1867. The Madras Medical School established in
1835 was constituted a College in 1851 and transferred to the
Educational Department in June 1855. The School of Ordnance
Artificers, established privately in 1840, was in 1855 constituted
a Government institution. At about the same time a School of
Arts opened privately in 1850, and a School of Industry similarly established in 1851, became Government institutions and
were amalgamated under the designation of the School of Industrial Arts. The Survey School originally attached to the Board

of Revenue and afterwards to the Chief Engineer's Office was constituted the Civil Engineering College in 1858.

—Private Schools.

Although Government had up to 1855 done but little, educational operations had been carried on in different parts of the Presidency by private societies and individuals, and in some districts on a very extensive scale. In these operations the various Missionary Societies had taken a leading part. The two chief Societies of the Church of England, the Church Missionary Society, and the Society for the Propagation of the Gospel in Foreign Parts, had established a considerable number of Village Boarding schools and Day schools in the Southern Districts, but principally in Tinnevelly. The Scotch Free Church Mission had large schools in Madras, at two of the principal towns in the neighbouring district of Chingleput, and at Nellore. The efforts of this Mission were then as now mainly devoted to education. The Mission connected with the Established Church of Scotland, the London Mission, and the Wesleyan Mission had also large schools in Madras. In Vizagapatam and Masulipatam schools had been established by the London Mission and by the Church Missionary Society, and on the Western Coast a similar institution was in operation at Mangalore founded by the German Mission. Exclusive of the indigenous village schools the number of schools supported other than by Missionary Societies was comparatively small. The chief of these was Pachiappah's Institution, a large school in Madras established from the proceeds of a bequest left for charitable purposes by Pachiappah Moodelliar and in connection with which smaller schools had been established at Conjeveram and Chellambrum. At Nursapore and Coimbatore schools had been established partly supported by native subscriptions, but their establishment was mainly due to the influence and aid of European officials.

—Grants-in-aid to Private Schools.

The first Government Grant-in-aid Rules, that is to say rules for regulating State aid given to private schools, were published in 1855, simultaneously with the arrangements above mentioned for the establishment of a purely Government Department. The rules were couched in very general terms, but embodied some important principles. They provided that the grants were to be for specific purposes, mostly for teachers' salaries, and that they were not to exceed in amount the sum contributed on the part of the school itself, that is to say from fees, endowments, &c. Except in the case of Normal and Female schools they were to be confined to schools in which school fees were levied. Every aided school was to be under Government inspection, and no teacher was to receive a grant until his qualifications had been reported on by a Government Inspector. Experience showed that more definite rules were needed, and in 1858 a new code appeared. It was to a large extent an adaptation of the old English Code. Its main feature was an elaborate system of Teachers' certificates in connection with the salary grants. Nine standards of qualification were laid down for schoolmasters and five for schoolmistresses, and for each standard there was a departmental examination. To each class of certificate a specific grant was attached, which represented one-third of the teacher's salary. These rules were superseded by a third code which came out in 1865, and which with some modifications is in force still. In this code the number of grades for schoolmasters was reduced to five, and for schoolmistresses to three. The maximum grants claimable under these rules were made much higher than they had been before, representing one-half instead of one-third of the salaries of teachers. The University B.A., F.A., and Matriculation Examinations were substituted for the departmental examinations for the three higher grades, the departmental examination in these grades being confined to a paper in method and teaching a class in the presence of an Inspector. Grants again were made claimable under the code for various purposes besides salaries, such as the erection and repair of buildings and the purchase of furniture, school apparatus, and books. Grants could also be claimed as an alternative in elementary schools on the payment for results system, but the standards for native schools were pitched so high, that this portion of the code remained at first inoperative. A new set of Results Rules came out in 1868 and are at the present moment in force. These are avowedly framed for elementary schools and are of a more elementary character even than the results rules in force in Great Britain, there being only four instead of six standards. In many respects they are well adapted to the educational requirements of this Presidency. Large numbers of indigenous as well as Mission schools in every district have been improved with the aid of these rules, and the results grants system has almost entirely superseded the salary grant system in elementary schools of all classes. Schools aided on the results grant system generally receive no aid except a result grant once a year. A still further modification of the original grant-in-aid system has of late been allowed to grow up in the form of what is known as the " combined " system,

consisting of part fixed salaries and part results grants under
the rules.   The arrangements for carrying out this system are
at present treated as special cases in each instance, but in view
to the utility and popularity of the plan it is in contemplation
to draw up fixed rules.   The three main systems of aid
are then the salary-grant system, the results-grant system,
and the combined system.   The pure results-grant system is
considered to be chiefly adapted for the promotion of education
in backward parts of the country and among the ruder classes,
where the advantages of a less mercenary and purer method of
State aid would meet with no appreciation.   The salary grant
system is regarded as the most suitable where public opinion is
active and where confidence placed in teachers will meet with
response.   The combined system occupies in principle a ground
intermediate between the other two, and may probably be relied
upon for all intermediate acts of circumstances.   The description
of the different forms of State aid given to private schools will
not be complete without mentioning that in a few cases lump grants
and special grants are given by Government; these, however, are
quite exceptional.   In speaking of State aid in this paragraph it
must be understood that the term includes the aid given by
various Municipal and Local Fund Circle Boards, which are in
fact quasi-Government institutions.   The grant-in-aid rules were
originally drawn up to regulate aid given by the Government
itself, but the Boards just mentioned have been required to
adopt the Government rules.

—Act VI of
1863.

After the grant-in-aid system of 1855 had been in force for
some years, it became apparent that however useful it might be
in improving higher and middle class schools, it had been doing
up to that date very little for elementary education in consequence
of the limited number of applications made from elementary
schools.   In 1863 the Madras Education Act was passed.
The object of this measure, which was based on the Municipal
Act XXVI of 1850, was to provide a proper machinery for the
collection and management of a rate, by which certain village
schools in the sub-division of the Godavery District were
supported, and to furnish the inhabitants of towns and villages in
other parts of the Presidency with the means of raising permanent funds for the establishment of new and the improvement of
existing schools and of availing themselves of the grants-in-aid
which Government were prepared to give.   The Act provided
that if the majority of the rate-payers in the Godavery District
did not petition against the continuance of the schools within

two months from a given date, the schools should be continued for five years, and that a similar procedure should be observed at the end of every recurring period of five years. In any district the inhabitants might petition for an order declaring the Act in force in any town or village, and the order was to be issued if, after inquiry, a sufficient majority of the inhabitants was found in favor of the application. When however the Act came to be worked, it was found to be ill-adapted to rural communities. The Godavery Commissioners were inexperienced ryots, who knew little or nothing about the management of schools. The collections fell in arrears and the teachers remained unpaid for long periods. In the other districts very few schools were established, and in many cases after the Act had been put in force with the apparent assent of the inhabitants, it was found necessary to close the schools or to abandon the attempt to establish them. At the end of seven years the Act had been brought into operation in only nine out of nineteen districts, and the total number of rate schools was only 104. In the Godavery District the number had dwindled down to fifty-nine, in the other districts it ranged from two to seventeen. Among these were two important schools of the higher class at Palghaut and Sydapet. Except in the Godavery District, the other schools were almost entirely middle-class schools. Thus the experiment of extending an interest in education by means of a voluntary rate met with little general success.

The only alternative was a compulsory cess. So far back as —Acts of April 1859 the attention of the Government of India and of the ¹⁸⁷¹. several Local Governments had been drawn by the present Earl of Derby, who was then Secretary of State, to the expediency of imposing a compulsory rate to defray the expenses of schools for the rural population. The measure did not at that time find favor at Madras, the Government, at the head of which Sir Charles Trevelyan, being opposed to any compulsory taxation for educational purposes. In May 1868 the Government of India pointed out that Act VI of 1863 had entirely failed in the main object for which it was passed, and suggested for consideration the introduction of an education cess on the model of the one which had proved so successful in Northern and Western India. The necessity for supplementing Imperial revenues by local taxation had long been felt in this Presidency, and various local Acts were already in operation under which the conservancy of the principal towns and the formation and maintenance of district roads had been provided for by local taxes. The embarrassed condition of the finances of India, which became known in the following year, although it was not, as was popularly supposed, the immediate cause of the enactment of the Towns Improvement Act III of 1871, the Local Fund Act IV of 1871, and the Madras Municipal Act V of 1871, rendered it impossible to defer this class of legislation any longer, and those Acts were accordingly passed, providing among other things for the promotion of education in town and country. The provisions of the Acts and the nature of the taxation levied under them have been fully described under Section III. The description of education to which Local and Municipal Funds were applicable was purposely left undefined in the Acts. Government have however since decided that these funds shall be mainly appropriated to the maintenance and improvement of " elementary " education. The exceptions which have been allowed are the rate schools of the higher and middle class established under the Madras Education Act, institutions for medical and technical training, and certain schools which have been dealt with as exceptional cases. It was originally intended that one-fourth of the cost of all Government Normal schools should be debited to Local and Municipal Funds, but it was found that some of these schools supplied few or no teachers to elementary schools, and it was considered inequitable to throw any portion of their cost on Local or Municipal Funds. This part of the scheme was therefore carried out only with reference to a few Normal schools and circumstances occurred which rendered it of very short duration even in this limited form. In the years 1871-72 and 1872-73 three hundred and twenty-three Local Fund schools had come into existence, and the house-tax under the Local Funds Act had been imposed in a corresponding number of villages or groups of villages. But the imposition of this tax encountered in several instances such extreme hostility, that Government determined that it should proceed no further. As the effect of this order was to leave charges for sanctioned " Union " schools unprovided for to an aggregate amount of Rupees 1,10,000, a special grant was made from Provincial Funds to the circles concerned to supply such deficiency as could not be met from the unallotted balance of the General Fund of each circle. Since 1873-74 Local Fund Circle education has been developed without the aid of a house-tax. It was calculated at the end of 1873-74 that, including the one-third land-cess, the General Local Fund might be estimated at about $14\frac{1}{4}$ lakhs, of

which 5¾ lakhs were allotted as an additional contribution to
the Road Fund, and three quarters of a lakh was given as a
contribution towards the pay of the Deputy Inspectors and the
cost of Normal schools. From the commencement of 1874-75 it
was resolved that no contributions should be made from the
one-third land-cess to the Road Fund until the requirements of the
other purposes to which the General Local Fund might by law be
applicable had been fully met and that all charges on account of
Deputy Inspectors and Normal schools should be resumed
in toto as a provincial charge. The general effect of these
measures was to place about eight lakhs and a half at the disposal
of the Local Fund Boards for elementary education. In December 1874 the Local Fund Boards and Municipalities were further
relieved of all charges connected with female education, and a
few girls' schools which had been maintained or aided by them
were constituted Government institutions.

During the last five years the progress has been satisfactory, —Recent
whether in State schools, in Local Board schools, or in private progress.
schools aided by the State and Local Boards. There has been a
great development of elementary education and female education. Colleges and higher-class schools have also been increasing
in numbers and efficiency. The Central Institution of the Free
Church of Scotland, the Doveton Protestant College, and the
S.P.G. High school, Tanjore, are now fully developed Colleges
educating up to the B.A. degree. The rates of school fees have
been twice raised, and many of the higher-class schools are
beginning to pay half and even a larger proportion of their cost
by means of school fees. Middle-class education is in a less
satisfactory state. The higher-class schools are stimulated and
improved by the University examinations. The lower-class
schools come under the influence of the examinations for results
grants. Middle-class schools suffer from the absence of a
middle-class examination. The expediency of establishing such
an examination has been recently suggested by the Government
of India and is now under consideration.

The Department of Public Instruction is administered by an Controlling
officer styled the Director of Public Instruction, aided by six Agency
Inspectors of Schools, under whom are two distinct grades of
Subordinate Inspectors called Deputy Inspectors and Inspecting
Schoolmasters. The Inspectors travel in their divisions for
eight months of the year, and examine each year every higher and
middle class school and a certain number of the elementary
schools situated in them. The examination of aided schools is

more cursory and less complete than that of Government schools.
The Inspector has the general charge of all Government schools
in his division and aids the Presidents of Local Fund Boards and
Municipalities with his advice in the management of Local Fund
and Municipal schools. Thirty-eight Deputy Inspectors have
up to date been sanctioned. Besides aiding the Inspectors in
their examinations of higher and middle class schools these officers
have the immediate supervision of the Anglo-Vernacular and
Taluq schools, and in some districts of a few Government
girls' schools. They are also largely employed in superintending
Municipal and Local Fund schools, and nearly all the work
of examining schools for results grants is done by them.
As members of Local Fund Boards and Municipalities, they
have to advise and vote on local educational questions, and
it is their duty to report and remark on any shortcomings in the
Educational Budgets of their circles. There are at present
115 Inspecting Schoolmasters. Their duty mainly consists in
travelling about slowly from village to village and teaching the
masters of indigenous schools how to prepare their pupils for
examinations under the rules for results grants. They show the
masters how a school should be organized by dividing the pupils
into classes, by the adoption of time-tables, by the introduction
of printed books and maps, and by keeping registers of attendance. They do not conduct examinations for results grants.
Most of the Inspecting Schoolmasters are paid entirely from
Local Funds, but four are at the present date paid by Municipalities, and one in the Bhadrachellum and Rekapully Taluqs
is paid from Provincial Funds. In the Hill tracts of Ganjam,
there is an officer of nearly the same standing as an Inspecting
Schoolmaster, who is styled the Superintendent of Hill Schools,
but he is under the orders of the Special Assistant Agent, who
has the general management of the Hill schools. In some
districts the Inspecting Schoolmasters visit Local Fund schools.

Classification
of Educa-
tional Insti-
tutions.

Omitting for the moment the Madras University, such
institutions as deal with special or professional instruction, and
certain private institutions which although under inspection do
not require aid from public funds, the remainder of the
institutions in connection with the educational department may
be divided, according to the mode in which they are supported,
into three classes as follows :—(a) Public institutions under
the direct management and control of the Educational Department and maintained from Provincial Funds, supplemented
in a few cases by endowments, and in most cases by fees, which

are paid into the treasury and credited either to Provincial
Funds or the School Fee Fund; these are called Government
institutions : (b) Public institutions under the direct management of Local Fund Boards and Municipalities, (" Local
Fund Schools" and "Municipal Schools") or of Committees
acting under the control of Government, and mainly supported from Public Funds, Local, Municipal, or Provincial,
but in which the fees if any are credited to the local body and
not to Government : (c) Private institutions receiving from
Government or local Boards (i) salary grants, (ii) results grants,
(iii) lump grants, or (iv) aid on the combined system, supplemented in most cases by fees from parents, and in some cases by
private subscriptions and endowments; these are called " aided
schools."

Government institutions for general education falling under —Govern-
class (a) may be sub-divided into Colleges, Provincial schools, ment Institu-
Anglo-Vernacular schools, Taluq schools, and schools for special tions.
classes of the community. In Colleges, Provincial, Zillah, and
Anglo-Vernacular schools the following classification prevails,
but no institution contains all the classes enumerated :—College
Department : Tenth or B.A. Class, Ninth or Preparatory B.A.
Class, Eighth or F.A. Class, Seventh or Preparatory F.A.
Class. Upper School : Sixth or Matriculation Class, Fifth or
Preparatory Matriculation Class. Middle School : Upper Fourth
Class, Lower Fourth Class, Third Class. Lower School : Second
Class, First Class. There are at present only two Government
Colleges for general education, the Presidency College and the
Provincial College of Combaconum ; both of these contain a
complete College Department, and the lowest class in the former
is the lower fourth, in the latter the upper fourth. There is a
Law Class attached to the Presidency College which prepares
students for the B.L. examination. There are four Provincial
schools at Rajahmundry, Calicut, Mangalore, and Bellary. The
highest class in all is the eighth ; the lowest the lower fourth,
except at Bellary, where the lowest is the third class. There are
eight Zillah schools in which the highest class is the sixth ; the
lowest is generally the second, but a first class exists at Kurnool,
and an Ooriya first class at Berhampore. There are nine Anglo-
Vernacular schools. At Cannanore there is a fifth class from
which pupils occasionally matriculate. The others are middle-
class schools which ought to have an upper fourth class ; few
of them however go beyond the lower fourth, and in some the
highest class is the third. There are forty-nine Taluq schools.

Hitherto these schools have had a classification of their own,
the fifth or highest class about corresponding with the lower
fourth, and the first class being a vernacular class, which does
not exist in Zillah schools. In future the classes will be
numbered according to the Zillah school standard and the
vernacular class will disappear. Few of the Taluq schools have
reached the standard prescribed for them, and some of them
have no middle department at all. The Madrasa-i-Azam and
Anglo-Vernacular school, Mylapore, are special schools for
Mahomedans at Madras. In the former, the highest class is the
lower fourth ; in the latter, the third class. There are also ten
elementary schools for Mahomedans at Rajahmundry, Ellore,
Masulipatam, Adoni, Cuddapah, Kurnool, Vellore, Arcot, Trichi-
nopoly, and Nagore. There are sixteen Elementary schools for
Ooriyas and Khonds in the Hill tracts of Gumsur and Chinna
Kimedy, five Elementary schools for boys in the Rekapally and
Bhadrachellum Taluqs, transferred to the Godavery District
from the Central Provinces, a school for the half-savage
Yenadies of Sriharicottah, now temporarily closed, and an
Elementary mixed school for the children of European
Pensioners at Tripassore.

—Quasi-
Government
Institutions.

The Lawrence Asylum at Ootacamund is the only institution
which is managed by a Committee, working under the control
of Government. There are two higher-class schools falling
under class (b). These are the Local Fund schools at Palghant
and Sydapet, which correspond with Zillah schools. There
are forty middle-class Local Fund schools and six middle-class
Municipal schools. Most of these correspond with Anglo-
Vernacular and Taluq schools, but a few are purely Vernacular
schools. There are also 654 Local Fund schools of the lower
class and forty-one Municipal schools. Most of the Local Fund
schools are Vernacular schools in which the highest class corresponds with the third results standard. It is optional with the
Local Fund Boards to allow English to be taught or not, but
most of the schools are vernacular schools. Girls are not
excluded from these schools, but the number in attendance is
insignificant. Theoretically these schools are managed by the
Local Fund Boards with the aid of the Inspector of the division,
in practice the tendency of the system is to throw all administrative details into the hands of the Deputy Inspectors. A few
of the Municipal schools are schools for special classes, such as
Mahomedans, East Indians, Silk-weavers, &c., but the majority
of them are for all classes, and in large towns they act as feeders

to the more advanced schools, and do some of the work which used to be formerly done in the primary departments of those schools. The attendance in some of these schools is tolerably large, ranging between one and two hundred, and a few of the best schools are beginning to realize a fair income from school fees. It is a matter for regret that so few Municipal schools have been as yet established, the Boards preferring to utilize the results system. In the Town of Madras this is exclusively the case. English is taught in a good many of the Municipal schools, which thus act as feeders to more advanced schools.

Under class (c) there are three Private Colleges, four Collegiate **—Aided** schools, and thirty-eight Higher-class schools aided on the salary **Institutions.** grant system from Provincial Funds. All Middle-class schools which receive salary grants are also aided from Provincial Funds. Salary grants are rarely given now to Lower-class schools, but if given they are paid from Local or Municipal Funds. Grants earned under the results system are at present paid from Provincial Funds if the school is certified by the Inspecting Officer to belong to the Middle class, and from Local or Municipal Funds if it is certified to belong to the Lower class. The line of demarcation between these two classes of schools will be explained further on. Certain rate schools originally established under the Madras Education Act and afterwards transferred to Local Fund Boards and Municipalities, and certain Middle-class schools which had been aided on the salary grant system previous to their transfer to the Local Fund Boards, receive lump grants from Provincial Funds. Since the adoption of the house-tax, lump grants have also been given, not only to individual schools, but also to certain Local Fund Circles. These grants are not in any way regulated by the ordinary rules. Certain aided schools are worked by Local Boards on the combined system already mentioned. This was originally applied to the Middle-class Local Fund schools of Malabar. According to this plan a proportion of each Teacher's fixed salary was taken and made to depend on the result of the annual examination of the school. His regular salary was reduced, but if he exerted himself, he might eventually get something more than he would have otherwise drawn. In May 1873 this scheme in a somewhat different form was applied to the Elementary Local Fund schools of Malabar. The indigenous teachers were in this case to be trained and to receive a monthly stipend of Rupees 4 with full results grants in addition to such school fees as they could collect. In July 1874 a somewhat similar scheme was sanctioned for the Middle-class and Elementary schools of South Canara, but under this arrangement the indigenous Schoolmasters were to receive Rupees 6 instead of Rupees 4 a month. Various other schemes on the combined system, differing not only in their details, but in their fundamental principles, have been since sanctioned or proposed for different parts of the Presidency. In some districts full results grants are given in addition to salaries of varying amounts; in others only half results grants are given; in some the amount drawn as salary is deducted from the result grant, and is thus a mere advance to be eventually refunded. In some districts the fees belong to the teachers, in others to the Local Fund Boards. In some districts buildings and furniture are provided by the Boards, in others by the teachers. There is generally at present no condition that the teacher shall be trained, or even that he shall be certificated. In some districts schools on the combined system are regarded as Local Fund schools, in others as private schools. It has already been mentioned that all these details are under consideration, with a view to the framing of general rules. The following statement shows the growth of the Grant-in-aid system during the last ten years. It does not include building grants :—

Years.	Payments made by Government.	Grants sanctioned for Lower-class Schools under the Results System.	Total.	Years.	Payments made by Government.	Grants sanctioned for Lower-class Schools under the Results System.	Total.
	RS.	RS.	RS.		RS.	RS.	RS.
1866-67 ...	1,21,271	...	1,21,271	1871-72...	2,50,333	79,446	3,29,779
1867-68 ...	1,54,985	...	1,54,985	1872-73...	2,59,483	1,18,664	3,78,147
1868-69 ...	2,41,549	...	2,41,549	1873-74...	2,74,883	1,69,555	4,44,438
1869-70 ...	3,07,881	...	3,07,881	1874-75...	2,57,787	1,94,470	4,52,257
1870-71 ...	3,35,394	...	3,35,394	1875-76...	2,64,818	2,20,450	4,85,268

Female Education.

Female education was for many years almost entirely in the hands of the Missionary Societies. Of late years secular schools have been springing up in various parts of the Presidency, among which may be specially named several large schools established by the Maharajah of Vizianagram at Madras and in various parts of the Northern Circars. None of the Maharajah's schools receive any aid from the State, and some of them, although under inspection, furnish no returns. In December 1874, the Local Fund Boards and Municipalities, as has been already mentioned, were relieved of all salary and results grants which they had been previously paying on account of girls' schools and mixed schools of boys and girls,

and a few girls' schools which had been entirely supported by
them became Government institutions. This policy has not
however been strictly adhered to, and several Municipalities have
been recently permitted to open Municipal girls' schools. The
only girls' school of the higher class is the Doveton Girls' school.
There are at present ten Government girls' schools and five
Municipal girls' schools. Most girls' schools are aided on the
salary grant system, but results grants are given at rates 50 per
cent. higher than those allowed for boys, and a capitation grant
of a Rupee a-head is allowed on the average attendance throughout the year. Results grants are also given for needle-work at
rates ranging from 1 Rupee to Rupees 4.

The University of Madras was established on the 5th **Constitution**
September 1857. It is constituted on the model of the University **of the Madras**
University.
of London and is purely an examining body, conferring degrees
in Arts, Law, Medicine, and Civil Engineering. The Senate,
which consists of a Chancellor, a Vice-Chancellor, and not less
than thirty Fellows, is divided into the four Faculties just
mentioned, and has power, subject to the approval of Government, to make bye-laws and regulations. The executive
government of the University is vested in the Syndicate. This
body appoints Examiners, regulates examinations, keeps the
accounts, and carries on the correspondence of the University,
with the aid of the Registrar, who is an officer appointed once
in two years by the Senate. There is no limit of age for any of
the University examinations. In the Faculty of Arts there are
four examinations: the Matriculation, First Arts, B.A., and
M.A. examinations. In the Faculty of Laws examinations are
held for the degrees of Bachelor of Laws and Master of Laws.
The Faculty of Medicine has the degrees of Licentiate in Medicine
and Surgery, Bachelor of Medicine, and Master in Surgery.
Candidates who have obtained the degrees of B.A. and M.B.
and C.M. are permitted to proceed to the degree of M.D.
without examination on producing a certificate of having been
engaged two years in the practice of their profession. Previous
to the institution of the University medical diplomas were
conferred by the Medical College. The only examination in the
Faculty of Civil Engineering is that for the degree of Bachelor
of Civil Engineering. The table given below shows the number
of degrees conferred since the establishment of the University :—

B.A.	...	...	...	...	...	...	463
M.A.	...	...	...	...	...	...	11
B.L.	...	...	...	...	...	...	108

M.L.	...	...	...	...	...	3
L.M.S.	...	...	...	...	...	1
M.B. and C.M.		...	...	...	...	6
M.D.	...	...	...	...	...	3
B.C.E.	...	...	...	...	...	14

Fees ranging from Rupees 10 to Rupees 50 are levied for the
various examinations of the University, and these nearly suffice
to cover the payments made to the Examiners. The salary of
the Registrar, the cost of his establishment, and the expense of
stationery, furniture, printing, and other miscellaneous charges
are at present borne entirely by Government. The net cost of
the University in 1875-76 was Rupees 12,684-6-4, but the
question of making the University entirely self-supporting is
now under consideration.

**Special
Institutions.**

The School of Agriculture has already been described under
Section IV. The Madras Medical College, the Civil Engineering
College, the Madras School of Industrial Arts, and the Lawrence
Asylum will be separately noticed hereafter. The only other
institution of a special nature is the Law Class of the Presidency
College. The Law Professorship, after being in abeyance for
three years, was revived in 1873. The majority of the students
are persons who are following various avocations other than that
of law.

**Normal
Schools.**

Two different systems have been tried in the Normal schools
of this Presidency. Originally the students were kept under
instruction for long periods and were prepared for successive
Certificate and University examinations. On admission they
were required to execute an agreement binding themselves
to serve as teachers in a Government or aided school for five
years, and during the whole period of their training they were
supported by a scholarship, which they were bound to refund in
the event of their failing to fulfil the agreement into which they
had entered. Under this system the attention of both masters
and pupils was far too much directed to success in the examinations, and the training became a secondary consideration. The
Educational Department being unpopular, the best men generally
held aloof from the Normal schools, and even those who accepted
the scholarships and signed the agreements, often did so without
any real intention of becoming teachers, their object being
to pass the University examinations, and to get employment in
the Revenue or Judicial Departments. This system has been
to some extent abandoned. No preparation for University

examinations goes on now in any way of the Normal schools. Students who have already passed such examinations are trained for nine or ten months, but are not required to enter into any engagements and are not guaranteed employment in the Educational Department. The Madras Government Normal school is now entirely on this footing and trains graduates, First Arts men, and matriculates, who receive scholarships of Rupees 15, 12½, and 10, respectively. The other Government Normal schools in the mofussil are conducted in the main on the principle just mentioned. The Government Female Normal school at Madras prepares six East Indians or Europeans, eight Native Christians, and sixteen Hindus for the first, second, and third grades of the school mistresses' Teachers' Certificate examination. The course extends over four years, during which the scholarships rise from Rupees 6 to Rupees 12. There are four aided Normal schools for males at Masulipatam, Dindigul, Palamcottah, and Sawyerpuram, and one for females at Palamcottah.

A Government examination for Teachers' certificates in connection with the salary grant-in-aid rules already described is held in July or August. Normal students and all female candidates, whether Normal students or not, are at present admitted to this examination without paying any fees. Other candidates are charged a fee of Rupees 5. It has been recently determined to restrict the fifth or lowest grade examination to Normal students. Persons who are not Normal students will not be admitted to this examination, but will receive a fifth-grade certificate if they pass the Uncovenanted Civil Service Examination, Vernacular Branch, and satisfy the Inspecting Officer in giving a lesson to a class. Persons who have passed the University examinations obtain a certificate after passing in Method and teaching a class before an Inspector. *[Teachers' Certificates.]*

There are at present four kinds of Government stipendiary scholarships, that is to say (1) scholarships awarded on the result of the University examinations ; (2), scholarships given to Ooriya pupils in the taluq schools of the Ganjam District ; (3) scholarships held by Normal students ; and (4) scholarships tenable in the Medical College, the Civil Engineering College, and the School of Arts. *[Government Scholarships.]*

Fifteen superior officers of the department, including the Director of Public Instruction, the Inspectors of Schools, the Principals of the Presidency College and Provincial College *[Financial System of Government Department.]*

of Combaconum, and the Professors of the Presidency College,
are graded in classes, and their salaries rise by annual increments
from the minimum to the maximum prescribed for their class.
The Principal and Professors of the Medical College, who belong
to the Indian Medical Department, and the Principal of the
Civil Engineering College, who is an officer of the Corps of
Royal Engineers, are subject to special regulations. The
principle of giving salaries rising by increments has been
recently sanctioned in the case of the Head Masters of Zillah
schools, the Head Master of the Madrasa-i-Azam, and the
masters of Anglo-Vernacular and Taluq schools. Masters and
Deputy Inspectors, who are paid from Provincial Funds, have the
same claim to pension as other members of the Uncovenanted
Civil Service, but masters who are paid from the School Fee
Fund are not on the same footing as the others. The School Fee
Fund is a general fund to which are credited all fees received in
Government schools except the fees of the Presidency, Medical,
and Civil Engineering Colleges, the Madras Male and Female
Normal schools, and the Madrasa-i-Azam, which are credited to
Provincial Services. The School Fee Fund was formerly
devoted exclusively to charges connected with Government
schools, such as salaries of School Assistants, servants, library
and prize allowances, rent and contingent expenses ; but, as the
receipts have increased, while the charges have remained nearly
stationary, the School Fee Fund is now largely indented on
to supplement the grants given from Provincial Funds to aided
schools. Although the Medical College is under the control of
the Director of Public Instruction, no charges connected with
this institution fall on the Educational Budget. The salaries of
the Principal and major Professors, who are all officers holding
various medical appointments, and the stipends of the Military
Hospital Apprentices appertain to Imperial Services. The
salaries of the minor Professors and all the other items belong to
the medical branch of Provincial Services. The Educational
Building Fund was originally formed from the surplus balance
of the Devasthanum Funds. Under the orders of the Court of
Directors this amount was set apart for educational buildings
and was subsequently considerably augmented by a transfer of
the unexpended portion of the annual grant of Rupees 50,000
given for native education from 1828-29 to 1854-55. A
4 per cent. Treasury note was issued in the same year for Rupees
10,00,000, afterwards reduced in 1868 to Rupees 8,00,000. The
interest upon this note, after meeting charges incurred in

connection with educational buildings, was credited to the
Educational Building Fund and continued to accumulate until
July 1861, when the Secretary of State directed that no
further additions should be made by the accumulation of
interest, and that, whenever the building charges fell below the
interest, the balance should be applied towards defraying
general educational expenditure. Sums raised by private contributions and subscriptions for the construction of school-houses
are credited to this fund. All charges on account of educational
buildings are met from it and are divided into charges on
account of original buildings and repairs of Government colleges
and schools and building grants to aided colleges and schools.
These charges have of late years greatly exceeded the annual
receipts from interest and local contributions, and it has been
necessary from time to time to divert considerable sums from
capital. The Presidency College, the Senate-house, and the
Provincial College of Combaconum have largely contributed to
the depletion of this fund, which was reduced on the 31st
March 1876 to Rupees 4,29,500.

The undermentioned scale of monthly school fees has been **School Fees.**
required since the 1st September 1871 in Government schools
and schools aided by Government :—

Classes.	Government Schools.		Schools aided by Government.	
	Madras.	Mofussil.	Madras.	Mofussil.
	RS. A. P.	RS. A. P.	RS. A. P.	RS. A. P.
B.A.	5 0 0	4 0 0	3 8 0	2 12 0
F.A.	4 0 0	3 0 0	2 12 0	2 0 0
Matriculation or VI ...	3 0 0	2 8 0	2 0 0	1 12 0
V and IV	2 8 0	2 0 0	1 12 0	1 8 0
III	1 8 0	1 0 0	1 0 0	0 12 0
II	1 0 0	0 12 0	0 12 0	0 8 0
I	0 8 0	0 8 0	0 8 0	0 6 0

Only 5 per cent. of the whole number of pupils in any school
are allowed to be free scholars. Besides these fees an entrance
fee is charged when a pupil first enters a school at the rate of
Rupees 3 in the Matriculation class, Rupees 2 in the fifth and
fourth classes, and Rupee 1 in the other classes. Mahomedan
and Ooriya pupils pay only half the above rates. No rules have
been laid down with regard to school fees in girls' schools,
and the fees in the Practising Departments of Normal schools
are not regulated by the above scale. No school fees are levied

in the hill schools of Gumsur and Chinna Kimedy and some
of the other elementary schools maintained by Government for
special classes. The rules relating to school fees have been
declared not to be in force in schools aided on the results system,
and in schools supported directly by Local Fund and Municipal
Boards it is left to the Boards and Commissioners to decide
whether any, and if so what, fees shall be levied.

Outlay on Education.

The following percentage statement shows the proportionate
amount spent from all sources on the different branches of
education, as shown by the figures of a recent year :—

Superintendence	9·51
General Instruction { Superior Instruction	5·37
Secondary do.	27·77
Primary do.	43·71
Miscellaneous	5·77
Special Instruction. { Superior Instruction in Law, Medicine, and Civil Engineering.	·30
Secondary Instruction in Professional Colleges and Technical Schools.	3·85
Normal Schools	3·05
Scholarships	·62

Technical classification of Educational Institutions.

The classification of colleges and schools given in the
above remarks has been made with reference to the sources
from which those institutions are supported. In the reports
of the Educational Department, the order followed is that
of educational standard, and the subjects generally reported on
run as follows :—Madras University, Arts Colleges, Collegiate
schools, Higher-class schools, Middle-class schools, Elementary
schools, Girls' schools, and Mixed Boys' and Girls' schools,
Professional Colleges and Technical schools, Normal schools
and Teachers' Certificate Examinations, and General Statistics.
The definition of the term "elementary" as applied to education has been found necessary in connection with the duty
imposed on Local Boards as mentioned above, to provide for
instruction answering to that description. The rules for results
grants having been framed for elementary schools, the fourth
or highest standard under those rules would seem to be the
natural limit of elementary education. It was however
decided in 1871 that the line of demarcation between elementary
and middle-class education should be drawn at the third
standard which does not go beyond the second book of lessons
in the vernacular, writing from dictation, the compound rules

and reduction, the rudiments of grammar, the geography of the district, English reading as contained in the first book, and writing easy words in large hand. The fact of two or three boys passing under the fourth standard was however not to be regarded as taking a results school out of the list of Middle-class schools. This year a more definite rule has been adopted and a results school is not ranked as a Middle-class school unless it passes six boys in five heads of the fourth standard, arithmetic being one of the heads. The fourth standard includes reading from the third book in the vernacular, writing from dictation, moderately easy questions in vulgar fractions and proportion, a general knowledge of vernacular grammar, the geography of the Madras Presidency, and a general knowledge of the geography of Hindustan, the second book of lessons in English, writing English from dictation and the etymology and syntax of simple sentences. The distinction between Middle and Higher-class education is not necessary except for purely technical purposes. Middle-class education may however be regarded as extending to a limit about two years below the Matriculation standard of the University, after which will come Higher-class education. Schools which have a Matriculation class or a Preparatory Matriculation class are classed as Higher-class schools. Still higher instruction is given in Collegiate schools, which educate up to the F.A. standard; and in Colleges which educate up to the B.A. degree. There are no institutions in which M.A. classes exist. This degree is attained by private study.

BOOK REGISTRATION.

Act XXV of 1867, which provides for the preservation of copies of all books printed in British India and for the registration of such books, came into operation in the Madras Presidency with effect from the 1st July 1867 under the late Director of Public Instruction, who was appointed to act as the first Registrar of Books. On the 1st January 1868 this officer was relieved of the Registrarship at his own request, and a separate Registrar was appointed. The work of collecting, cataloguing, and preserving book works printed in the Presidency town belongs to the Registrar of Books; similar duties are performed in the districts by the District Registrars of Assurances, who are in communication

Nature of the system.

with the Registrar of Books at Madras and transmit their collections to him.   Printers are compelled to furnish Registrars with
three copies of each of their publications within a month from the
date of issue from the press, together with a memorandum of
particulars regarding each work as laid down in the Act ; and, to
induce a general compliance with the provision of the law, and to
encourage the punctual delivery of books, their published prices
are paid to the presenters.   It has not yet been found necessary
to enforce the penal provisions of the Act.   The Registrar of
Books compiles for publication in the Fort St. George Gazette
quarterly catalogues of all registered works with a short statement of the contents of such of them as do not carry the information in their titles or as otherwise deserve distinction, copies
of the works themselves being despatched to Government once
a month for transmission to the Government of India and the
Secretary of State.   He further submits an annual analysis and
review of the published literature of this Presidency and other
periodical reports called for by the Government of India and the
local Government.   In this way a tolerably correct acquaintance
is obtained by the Administration with the progress of literary
effort during each year, and with the tendency of the published
works.   The registration of copyright is optional with the
proprietors of books.

GOVERNMENT BOOK DEPARTMENT.

**Constitution
of the Book
Department.**
The Government Book Department, the work of which lies in
the supply and distribution of English and Vernacular books
for the use of Government and other schools, has now been in
operation for twenty years.   The Book agency consists of a
Central Depôt in Madras under charge of a Curator, and
subordinate to this depôt are 19 branch or district depôts at the
principal up-country stations managed by local agents who are
styled District Curators.   The curators are paid by a commission
in addition to fixed salaries.   Up to the year 1871 the whole
cost of the Book Department was included in the Annual
Educational Budget, but in the beginning of that year a change
was made and salaries only were left to be provided for by the
Educational Department.   The printing and purchase of books
and other operations of the Book Department are carried on
now by means of advances made by Government, who recoup

themselves from the sale proceeds of books. This system has been successfully worked for nearly six years, and the department has become fully self-supporting, leaving in fact a surplus after the payment of all charges including the salaries provided for in the Educational Budget. The selling prices of books are fixed on the following system :—In the case of English books imported an addition of 20 to 25 per cent. is made to the published price. In the case of Indian books locally purchased, 10 per cent. is added to the published price, taking no account of the discount allowed by the publishers. With regard to books printed for the department, 25 per cent. is added to the cost price in the case of editions of new books, and this margin is worked up to 50 per cent. by reducing the cost of printing in the case of fresh editions of old books. The former charge includes the amount paid to the author or compiler, while the latter secures a margin of profit without any addition to the price first fixed.

MISCELLANEOUS LITERARY.

Book Translator. A Tamil Translator on a fixed salary of Rupees 70 is employed under the supervision of the Professor of Vernacular Literature in translating books required for the Government Book Department, in revising old editions, and correcting proofs of new editions published for sale.

Madras School Book and Vernacular Literature Society. The Madras School Book and Vernacular Literature Society has hitherto received an annual grant of Rupees 2,000 from Government. In September 1875 the grant for 1876 was reduced to Rupees 1,500. The Society's Magazine, the Janavinodini, which is now published in Telugu as well as in Tamil, is very popular. A good Telugu Dictionary for the use of students being a desideratum, the Committee have agreed to pay Rupees 5,000 for a dictionary, and the work is now going through the press. The publication of this work will necessarily be a heavy drain on the resources of the society. Such profits as the society makes are derived from reprints of school books, many of which are likely to be superseded. Besides reprints of school books, interesting articles from the Janavinodini are reprinted and sold in the form of tracts at prices ranging from 1 Pie to 3 Pies.

Library of Oriental Manuscripts.   The Library of Oriental Manuscripts is under the charge of the Professor of Sanscrit in the Presidency College.   When this officer assumed charge of the library on the 4th November 1872 he found it in bad order.   Since then the manuscripts have been nearly all catalogued and placed in substantial teakwood glass cases.   The Professor of Sanscrit was directed in 1868 to carry out certain orders issued by the Government of India in regard to the discovery and preservation of the records of ancient Sanscrit literature.   He was to take such measures as might be necessary for commencing the printing of all procurable unprinted lists of Sanscrit manuscripts in the Native Libraries. He was also to arrange for the examination of the manuscripts named in the Native catalogues printed as above described, for the discovery of new manuscripts, for their purchase, and for the employment of copyists to transcribe codices which were unique, extremely old, or otherwise desirable, but which the possessors refused to sell.   He was to make occasional short tours for these objects and was to take advantage of every opportunity of inquiring for and procuring any ancient manuscripts in the vernacular languages which he might consider to be of historical or literary value.   All these undertakings are in course of execution.

MADRAS MEDICAL COLLEGE.

Nature of the institution.   The Madras Medical College was established in 1835 for the instruction in Medicine and Surgery of persons entering the medical branch of the public service.   The benefits of instruction have been since thrown open to the community at large, but the students are still for the most part of the class just mentioned. The Medical College is under the general control of the Director of Public Instruction, the Surgeon-General, Indian Medical Department, being *ex-officio* visitor. The pupils in attendance at the College consist of—(1.) Pupils of the Senior Department, comprising candidates for the University Degrees of M.B. and G.M., and Licentiate in Medicine and Surgery; the only qualification for entry being that candidates must have passed the general educational standard laid down by the University. (2.) Pupils of the Second Department, comprising Military Hospital Apprentices qualifying for employ as Military Assistant Apothecaries, and Civil Hospital Apprentices qualify-

ing for employ as Civil Apothecaries under the Government or
Local Boards; the test for entry being a competition examination in the former case and the University Matriculation
examination in the latter. (3.) Pupils of the Junior Department, comprising Military Native Medical Pupils qualifying for
employ as Military Hospital Assistants, and Civil Medical Pupils
qualifying for employ as Civil Hospital Assistants under the
Government or Local Boards; the test for entry being a
competitive examination in either case. (4.) Female students
qualifying for a certificate of fitness to pursue the medical
profession. The students of the Second and Junior Departments
mentioned above spend the earlier part of their course attached
to Military and Civil Hospitals, and the latter part of their
course as pupils at the College itself. The technical course of
education consists of Anatomy, Botany, Chemistry, Pharmacy,
Physiology, Materia Medica, Surgery and Practice of Medicine,
Hygiene, Midwifery and Diseases of Women and Children,
Diseases of the Eye, Comparative Anatomy, Medical Jurispru-
dence, Pathology, Clinical instruction in Medicine, Surgery, &c.
The lectures on Chemistry, Botany, Physiology, Medical Juris-
prudence, and Hygiene are open to the public.

CIVIL ENGINEERING COLLEGE.

The old Government Survey School was established in 1834 **Nature of the**
for the purpose of training men as Surveyors under the Revenue **institution.**
Department. In order to supply the wants of the Department
of Public Works the curriculum of instruction was extended
and the Survey School merged in the Civil Engineering College.
When first established the College had for its object the training
of men as subordinates only, that is to say, as Overseers and
Sub-Overseers in the Department of Public Works; but in 1861
a Special Class for Drawing and Estimating was formed, and in
March 1862 a First Department was established for the purpose
of training Military Officers and under-graduates of the Madras
University holding the F.A. diploma for the position of Assistant Engineers. In December 1862 an Officers' Surveying Class
was added. The Civil Engineering College therefore now
consists of a First Department, Officers' Surveying Class,
Second Department, Special Survey Class and Drawing Classes.

The educational staff consists of a Principal; two masters for mathematics and engineering; four masters for surveying, drawing, and estimating ; and two Munshis for vernacular languages. The number of students has risen from 46 in 1859 to 152 at the close of 1875-76. The First Department is open to officers of Her Majesty's British and Indian Armies and Civilians, Europeans and Natives. The Second Department consists of European Non-commissioned Officers and Soldiers of Her Majesty's British and Indian Forces, and Civilians (Europeans, Eurasians, and Natives).

MADRAS SCHOOL OF ARTS.

Nature of the institution. The School of Industrial Arts was established privately by Dr. Hunter in 1850, and was supported till 1855 by fees from pupils, by payments for drawings, engravings, and work turned out in the school, and by small contributions from the public. In 1855 the school was taken up by Government, and a committee, in communication with Dr. Hunter, laid down rules and a course of instruction. Owing to the difficulties in finding competent technical instructors and a suitable class of students, the method of the school has somewhat fallen away from the intention of Government as then expressed. Of late, however, the institution has engaged the particular attention of Government, and efforts are being made to extend its usefulness. The school is divided into a Drawing Academy and an Industrial Department. The course of instruction at the former is very similar to that adopted at South Kensington ; all attempts at high art are discouraged, and efforts are made to introduce an accurate standard of free hand. A girls' branch has been opened in the Drawing Academy and promises to be successful. As the pupils in the Drawing Academy show aptitude, endeavours will be made to apprentice them to skilled workmen in the industrial department, enabling them thus to work at drawing and one of the crafts together. In the industrial department the pupils are paid for their labor, and it forms in fact a kind of Government workshop for carrying out art experiments. No difficulty is found in providing an outlet for the work produced in the industrial department, but care is taken to avoid competition with local trades by introducing only arts which are not practised outside. The work done in the industrial department has of late been considerably extended. Thus to pottery, engraving, wood-cutting, and plaster-moulding, have been added recently glass-painting (enamels), stone-carving, wood-carving, different kinds of metal work, and wall decorating. This institution is now under the charge of Mr. R. F. Chisholm.

OOTACAMUND LAWRENCE ASYLUM.

Sir Henry Lawrence in 1856, after having established the **Origin and** Hill Asylums for the children of the British soldiers at Sunawur **object.** and Mount Aboo, offered a donation of Rupees 5,000 if a similar institution could be founded on the Nilgiris. The proposal was warmly received by the residents at Ootacamund, but the project fell through owing to a want of unanimity in regard to the religious basis upon which the Asylum was to be founded. Two years later, in 1858, after Sir Henry Lawrence's death, the matter was again brought forward and the present asylum was established. The object in establishing the asylum was twofold :—1st, To do honor to the memory of Sir Henry Lawrence ; and 2ndly, to benefit the children of the European soldiery, by providing a refuge from the debilitating effects of a tropical climate and the demoralizing influence of barrack life.

The asylum consists of two branches, male and female. **Constitution** Owing to the want of a separate building for a hospital, the **and funds.** number of boys is limited to 330. The number of girls is limited to 60, as the building in which they are located is not capable of accommodating more than that number. The management of the institution is placed in the hands of a committee of nine members, four of whom are appointed by Government. The Commander-in-Chief and the Bishop of Madras are the patrons of the institution. The Principal of the Asylum must be a clergyman of the Church of England, and his appointment is subject to the approval of the Governor in Council. In September 1871, after many years of corre-spondence and delay, the children of the Madras Military Male Asylum were transferred to the Nilgiri institution. The asylum receives a grant-in-aid from Government of Rupees 4,000 per mensem, 66 per cent. of which is placed to the credit of the male branch and the remaining 34 per cent. to that of the female branch. The funded capital of the male branch belonging originally to the Military Male Orphan Asylum is Rupees 4,89,200, the interest and Government donation on which amount to Rupees 38,828 per annum. The Asylum Press contributes a liberal grant of about Rupees 10,000 a year. Another source of income is the sum obtained on account of military pay and orphan allowance to which children and orphans of soldiers are entitled. At present this averages about Rupees 1,000 per mensem. The other sources of income are variable.

COMMITTEE FOR EXAMINATION OF ASSISTANTS.

Functions. The Committee for the Examination of Assistants took the place in 1854 of the old College of Fort St. George. It now consists of a President and a certain number of members *ex-officio* and special. The President who is always the Second Member of the Board of Revenue, the Tamil, Telugu, Canarese, Malayalam, and Hindustani and Persian Translators to Government, the Sub-Secretary to the Board of Revenue, and the Registrar of the High Court, Appellate Side, are members *ex-officio*. Other Members of the Committee are appointed at the pleasure of Government. At present the special members are the Collector of Madras and one of the Judges of the Small Cause Court. In conjunction with District Committees appointed by Government, the Committee conducts the technical quarterly examinations of Covenanted Junior Civilians under what are called the first and second standards. They conduct also examinations in Tamil, Telugu, Canarese, Malayalam, and Hindustani for Covenanted Civil Servants and for the following officers :—*Candidates in the Service :* 1, Chaplains ; 2, Public Works Department Officers ; 3, Farm Superintendents ; 4, Forest Officers; 5, Jail Superintendents ; 6, Medical Officers ; 7, Military Officers ; 8, Police Officers ; 9, Postal Officers ; 10, Revenue Survey Officers ; 11, Revenue Settlement Officers ; 12, Telegraph Officers ; 13, Uncovenanted Officers. *Candidates not in the Service :* 14, Agents and Accountants of the Madras Bank ; 15, Railway Officers. For the vernacular examinations the Committee is divided into sub-committees, each sub-committee consisting of the President or a Member and a Translator to Government.

For the High Proficiency and Honors Examinations, under the special rules for the encouragement of the study of oriental languages, a scholar of reputation, outside the Committee, is appointed as an extra member by Government. The Committee is expected to conduct examinations in other languages, but cases have not yet arisen. When a candidate has passed the High Proficiency Examination, the Committee grants a special certificate. When the Honors Examination is passed a certificate is granted by the Governor in Council. The Committee also examine Police Officers and Cantonment Magistrates in law.

UNCOVENANTED CIVIL SERVICE EXAMINATIONS.

These examinations owe their origin to the Educational Despatch from the Court of Directors of the East India Company to the Governor-General of India, dated 19th July 1854. This despatch authorized the Government of India to establish a liberal system of education throughout India, and approved of the institution of examinations for testing the fitness of candidates for offices under Government. The discussion of details occupied considerable time, but a scheme of examination for all Government appointments in this Presidency above the grade of peon was at last promulgated in March 1858, when for the purposes of the examination the Uncovenanted Service was formed into two divisions, the first including all appointments the salary of which exceeded Rupees 50 per mensem, and the second all appointments below that grade and above the grade of peon. The examination standards of the various departments are given in full in Appendix F of the Madras Educational Report for 1858-59. The examinations just mentioned were for a short time held under the direction of the late Board of Examiners with the following total results :—Passed for the 1st Division, English Department, 65 ; for the 1st Division, Judicial Department, 2 ; for the 1st Division, Revenue Department, 4 ; for the 2nd Division, English Department, 336 ; and for the 2nd Division, Revenue and Judicial Departments, 646, making a total altogether of 1,053 passed candidates. No fee was required for the old test examinations, and the consequence was that more examinees came forward than could be provided

Former Test Examinations.

with proper accommodation. Copying and other malpractices could not be prevented; and in order to reduce the number of examinees to more manageable proportions the Government, in an order of the 11th October 1860, authorized several modifications to be made in the examination scheme, amongst which were the exemption of all appointments of Rupees 25 per mensem and under from the operation of the rules, and the exaction of a fee. In consultation with the then Director of Public Instruction, the management of these examinations was at the same time transferred to a Commissioner, and the tests became what is now known as the "General Test."

Present General Test Examinations. The rules for the General Test at present in force were published as a notification, dated the 26th April 1861, in the Fort St. George Gazette. According to the most recent orders appointments of Rupees 20 per mensem and under are exempted, but in the case of all other appointments the candidate for office must have passed this examination; in the case of the special appointments, a very large class, for which "special tests" are provided, the qualifications are of course more severe. The present General Test is an elementary examination in Language, Hand-writing, Spelling, Arithmetic, Indian History, and General Geography. The General Test is divided into three branches, according as the candidate elects to pass hand-writing, composition, and orthography in English, or in a vernacular language, or in both. The appointments in the public service are similarly roughly classed in a corresponding manner (though there is no schedule giving a precise definition) into English, Vernacular, and Anglo-Vernacular appointments; the candidates for any of these appointments must have passed in the corresponding branch. Fifteen of the examinations have been held, and 2,582 candidates have been declared qualified for the public service according to the Anglo-Vernacular Branch, 3,267 according to the English Branch, and 2,908 according to the Vernacular Branch of the test.

Present Special Test Examinations. The present Special Test Examinations were instituted for the purpose of testing the fitness of candidates for particular situations demanding special qualifications, and the first examination of this nature was held in March 1863 in subjects relating to the Judicial and Magisterial Departments. The Revenue Tests came into force in 1864. The original rules bear date the 4th February and 30th May 1862; later on these were revised, and the rules were again superseded by those published under date the 29th July 1869. The latter remain in force with certain slight alterations. Under the rules no persons are admitted to any of the Special Tests except those who have passed the General Test or the University Entrance Examination, but exceptions are sometimes made under the authority of Government. The result of the Special Test Examinations from their commencement in declaring candidates eligible for particular offices is as follows:—

	No. passed.
Principal Sadr Amins, District Munsifs, and Pleaders in Civil and Sessions Courts, Principal Sadr Amins' Courts, and Courts of Small Causes	558
Pleaders in District Munsifs' Courts ...	784
Court Sheristadars	260
Deputy Collectors and Magistrates ...	317
Nazirs in Civil and Sessions Courts and Principal Sadr Amins' Courts	61
Sub-Magistrates, 1st Class	530
Uncovenanted Assistants and Sheristadar of the Revenue Board Office	165
Superintendents and Assistant Superintendents, Salt Department	84
Superintendents of Sea Customs	65
Huzur Sheristadars ... ... ⎫	
Abkári Superintendent, Deputy Superintendent, ⎬	157
Madras ... ... ⎭	
Tahsildars and 2nd-Class Sub-Magistrates, Taluq Sheristadars, Deputy Tahsildars, &c...	677
Sub-Collector's Sheristadar and Head Assistant's Head Clerk	164
Superintendents, Clerks, and Accountants in the ⎫ Accountant-General's Office	
Accountants in the English Department of Collectors' Offices drawing a salary of Rupees 30 and upwards	
Accountant in the Board's Office ... ... ⎬	191
Accountant, Deputy Accountant, and Book-keeper in the Mint and Assay Office ...	
Accountant, Marine Office	
Do. Sea Customs Office	
Do. Stamp Office	
Do. Office of the Conservator of Forests. ⎭	

	No. passed.
Translators, High Court and Civil and Sessions Courts	
Interpreter, Court of Small Causes, Madras ...	139
Do. Office of the Commissioner of Police.	
Do. Police Courts	
Translators, Office of Government ...	
Do. Revenue Board	
Do. Revenue Settlement Office ...	2,070
Do. Collectors' Offices	
Chief Clerk or Manager, Royapettah Police Court	40
Head Clerks, Police Courts	
Assistant Head Clerk, Royapettah Police Court.	
English Record-keepers, Collectors' Offices ...	909
Head Writers, Civil and Sessions Courts and Principal Sadr Amins' Courts	
Head Clerks, Small Cause Courts	
Appointments in Public Offices for which Précis-writing alone is prescribed as a test ...	2,631

ARTS AND SCIENCES.

MUSEUMS.

Nature of Government operations.   The efforts of Government to establish Museums in this Presidency commenced, under authority of the Court of Directors, in 1851. In that year the Madras Literary Society presented to Government a collection of geological specimens, and this, with the duplicates left after despatching the articles for the "Great Exhibition," formed the nucleus of what is now the Government Central Museum. Subsequently, in 1855, subordinate Museums were established at Bellary, Cuddalore, Mangalore, Rajahmundry, and Ootacamund for local purposes and with the object also of serving as feeders for the Central Museum; these were not successful, and with the exception of the one at Rajahmundry were closed in June 1861. In case of Ootacamund the allowance of Rupees 100 per mensem withdrawn from the Museum was transferred to the Public Library there and continued till 1875, in which year the grant for the Rajahmundry Museum was also discontinued. In 1855 the formation of a Zoological Garden in connection with the Central Museum was sanctioned, and the animals were retained there till 1863, when they were transferred to the Madras People's Park. The Government continued to meet the cost of feeding the collection till the close of 1875, when it became a Municipal charge. The Central Museum has been always open to the public free of charge, and the large numbers which daily frequent it show that the boon is appreciated.

ARCHITECTURE.

With a view to the improvement of architectural and struc- **Nature of** tural designs in Government buildings, the Madras Government **Government** **operations.** have for some years entertained a Consulting Architect, to whom all projects for important buildings are sent, and from whom designs for various purposes are called for. In nearly all cases the design merely is called for, and the execution is handed over to the Public Works Department, subject to general superintendence by the Consulting Architect. Works at the Presidency town, however, are usually put under direct charge of the Consulting Architect, who then executes them with Public Works subordinate agency. The main objects kept in view by the Consulting Architect's Department are a comprehensive consideration of the capabilities of the various materials, the suppression of ornament serving no useful end, the careful arrangement of apartments with a view to economy, the thoughtful distribution of parts and masses to avoid ugliness, and the development of ideas and forms suitable to the climate and country. Among the more important buildings constructed during the past few years are the Presidency College, Madras; the Lawrence Asylum, Ootacamund; the College, Combaconum; the Public Library, Madras; the Revenue Board, Madras; and the Senate House, Madras (in progress). Among the works of restoration and adaptation are Teroomal Naick's Palace, Madura; the old Palace at Trichinopoly; and the new Palace at Royapettah, Madras. With the exception of the Presidency College, Madras, and the Lawrence Asylum, Ootacamund, the whole of these buildings have been constructed in

oriental styles with oriental ornamentation; the introduction
of European taste has been as much as possible avoided, with
a view to giving every advantage to the development of arts
indigenous to the country, and with a view to avoiding the
necessity for using European ornamentation which it is impossible to imitate and difficult to import. The incumbent of the
post since its institution has been Mr. R. F. Chisholm.

ARCHÆOLOGY.

**Archæologi-
cal remains
in the Presi-
dency.**
No archæological department as yet exists in this Presidency.
A general list of the principal objects of antiquarian interest in
each of the districts in charge of the Revenue Department is
here given pending the appearance of the complete series of
District Manuals. To the list must be added Terumala Naick's
Palace at Madura, which is now in course of reconstruction by
the Department Public Works, and is in charge of that department. There are also of course very numerous public monu-
ments, buildings, including all pagodas and mosques still used
as places of worship, which are in the hands of private individuals or corporations, and which there are no means of
cataloguing :—

District.	Taluq.	Village.	Name or Description of Building.
Ganjam ...	Berhampore.	Jagoda ...	Rock engravings exhibiting the Asoka tablet said to be more than 2,300 years old.
Kistna ...	Guntoor ...	Undavalli ...	The rock caves at Unda-valli.
	Satianapalli.	Amaravati ...	The remains of the Amara-vati tope.
	Palnad ...	Pedugural ...	The mound at Pedugural.
	Gudivada ...	...	A colossal figure of Buddha in the enclosure of a choultry at Gudivada.
	Bezwada ...	...	Buddha images (stone and copper) in the library at Bezwada.
	Vinucondah...		The mantapam in Vinu-condah used by the Post Office.
	Narsarowpett.		The Fort at Kondavied.
	Bezwada ...		Do. at Kondapally.
	Sattenapalli...		Do. at Bellumkonda.
	Nandigama ...		The carved stone of the Ramireddipulli Hill.

District.	Taluq.	Village.	Name or Description of Building.
Cuddapah ...	Voilpaud ...	...	Old palace at Gurrumkondah with upstairs.
	Madnapalli ...	...	Pagoda at Sompalli. Carved monolith in front with fine carvings. Fresco paintings.
	Cuddapah ...		Four buildings formerly occupied as palaces of the Nawab of Cuddapah.
	Jammalmadugu.	...	Two temples constructed about 700 years ago and one mosque built about 400 years ago situated at Gundicola hill.
Bellary ...	Hospett ...	...	Stone-posts and stone car belonging to the Vojia Vittaldevor temple in Venkatapur, said to be in ruins.
	Huvinbadgalli.	Magalam ...	Temple of Vainogopaulsawmy.
	Hospett ...	Anantasawyanagudi.	Temple of Anantasawmy.
		Malpangudi ...	Temple of Iswara.
		In the limits of Kamalapur.	Temple of Pattabhirama. Temple of Kumbara. Mattam of Chandrasikara. Rock cut room or hall. Temple of Yellamma. A tower the top of which is in the shape of a lotus. Another tower (dark). Another tower called Bangalada. Palace with spiral steps. Anisalumantapam, or elephant stables. Nowbuthkhana. Penalarama mantapam. Gymnasium of Achuta Row. Agasaquith Mahal, *i.e.,* Washerman's palace. Temple of Hajar Ramachendra. Nelamani, *i.e.,* a house in the ground. Maharavani Dedhba or Simhasanam or throne. Vokalihonda or Bath. Bhimanabagalu, *i.e.,* Bhima's gate. Gaujetti Temple, *i.e.,* of Oilmongers.
		Khaderampuram.	Mantapam near Uddana Varabhudra's temple.
		In limits of Kristnapuram.	Ugra Narasimha's temple. Badali Linga temple. Krishnapuram temple. Vokalihonda temple.
		In the limits of Humpi.	Sasivikulu Benakappa. Mantapam of Hemakootam. Kadlikal Benakappa. Mantam of Nija Linga. Manmatha Muda. Lokaparanum. Temple of Edura Basappa.

District.	Taluq.	Village.	Name or Description of Building.
Bellary— (*Continued*).		In Venkatapur.	Mathangi Hill. Bazaar and temple of Atchutapuram. Temple of Rungasawmi. Temple of Yentradaraka. Temple of Rama. Sittia-sarovaram. Kalum temple. Varaha temple. Malyanantha Ragoona-thasawmy. Temple of Goddada Simmappa.
Chingleput ...	Sydapet ...		" Puncha Pandova Malay " close to Palaveram.
	Chingleput ...	...	Mahabalipuram or "Seven Pagodas." There is a small shrine cut out of a single rock in the village of Vallam.
North Arcot...	Choodragheri.		1. Rajah Mahal or Rajah's palace of Chendragheri. Built by the Telugu kings. Rajah Sreeranga Rozer of that dynasty is said to have signed the Treaty granting the settlement of Madras to the English in the centre room in 1640. The mahal is unique for strength and pecu-liarity of architecture; built almost entirely of granite, no wood being employed. 2. Rani Mahal, a smaller build-ing adjoining.
	Arcot ...	...	Delhi Dorwaja.
South Arcot...	Cuddalore ...		1. The garden house. Built about 1738; was more than once captured by the French. During the period from 1746 to 1752, when Fort St. David was the chief settlement on the Coromandel Coast, this building is said to have been the Governor's residence. 2. The forts of Gingee, Thiatgur, Perumagul, Valdoor, and St. David. At Fort St. David some remains of the subterra-neous gallery which ran round the fort under the glacis and of the mines leading off from it were not long ago discovered and opened up. 3. An obelisk to the memory of Major Stevens, Chief

District.	Taluq.	Village.	Name or Description of Building.
South Arcot— (*Continued*).			Engineer in the Army under Sir H. Munro, killed at the siege of Pondicherry in 1778. 4. Some old tombs in an ancient grave-yard at Cuddalore. 5. An old grave-yard near Fort St. David. 6. A cenotaph at Trickalore.
Tanjore ...	Tanjore ...		The palace of the late Rajah of Tanjore in charge of the Government Agent and occupied by the relatives of the late Rajah.
Trichinopoly...	...		1. Nawab's palace. 2. Main Guard gate.
Madura ...	Madura ...		Tamakam Bungalow. Said to have been built by the ancient kings as a stand whence to witness the fights of wild beasts.
Tinnevelly ...	...		The rock carvings at Kolugumalai.
	Tuticorin ...	...	A colossal stone Jain image, about six feet high, now preserved in Tuticorin.

MADRAS OBSERVATORY.

The Madras Observatory was instituted in the year 1792, and the present Government Astronomer, Mr. Norman Pogson, was appointed in 1861. The work of the observatory consists in observations of stars, the preparation of catalogues and maps, and the conducting of scientific experiments connected with astronomy; besides the usual attention to all casual phenomena, such as eclipses, transits, occultations, phenomena of Jupiter's Satellites, &c. From the years 1841 to 1861 systematic hourly records of magnetical and meteorological instruments were made. The publication of the results of these registers is still in progress; the observations themselves having been continued only upon a reduced scale, consisting of three observations per day.

Nature of the institution.

METEOROLOGICAL DEPARTMENT.

Nature of the department. The Meteorological Department of Madras was established in the year 1867 with a view to securing a better knowledge of the climatic conditions of various parts of the Presidency. Observations of undoubted excellence had been made at the Madras Observatory ever since the close of the last century, and for a shorter term of years at Bombay, Calcutta, Trevandrum, and Simla, but no reliable records with properly compared instruments had been made generally over India. Meteorological Superintendents were accordingly in that year appointed for Madras, Bombay, Bengal, the Central Provinces and the North-West Provinces, with Assistants in the various up-country stations, in correspondence with the Meteorological Superintendents, but acting under the immediate orders of the local medical officer. At the end of 1874 a Meteorologist to the Government of India was appointed at the head of the whole establishment. The stations of the Madras Presidency are at present twelve in number, Bangalore, Bellary, Cochin, Coimbatore, Kurnool, Madura, Masulipatam, Negapatam, Salem, Secunderabad, Trichinopoly, and Wellington. The Madras Observatory meteorological observations are made available for the purposes of the Meteorological Department, but do not strictly belong to it, being still under the sole control of the Government Astronomer, and being maintained out of his Budget estimates. Monthly mean and extreme results of the twelve stations in the Madras Presidency are printed in the Fort St. George Gazette for current use.

SECTION VIII.

MISCELLANEOUS.

ECCLESIASTICAL.

THE Madras Ecclesiastical Establishment proper consists of a Bishop, an Archdeacon, 39 Chaplains, and a Registrar. The Chaplains are divided into two classes, senior and junior, promotion to the senior class being attained upon the completion of ten years' service. Chaplains are required to serve twenty years for a full pension, and seventeen of those years must have been spent in actual service; but smaller pensions are granted on retirement enforced through sickness. Retirement is compulsory on the completion of twenty-five years. The appointment of Chaplains to the different stations is made by Government. At every station where there is Government Church property a Church Committee is appointed consisting of two Lay Trustees, the Chaplain acting as President. The churches for European congregations are with rare exceptions the property of Government. Outside the regular establishment is a considerable body of European and Eurasian Clergymen, some serving with European congregations not entitled to the services of a resident Government Chaplain, and the rest engaged in ordinary Missionary work. The former of these receive their salaries either from one of two Societies for providing additional Clergy, or from local contributions, or from both; the Government in all cases allowing a grant-in-aid. The Missionaries, as such, are not connected with Government, but are wholly maintained by the two leading Missionary Societies. In addition to these Native Clergymen, Tamil, Telugu, and Malayalum, constitute a third and continually growing class. The affairs of the Native Churches, in matters not spiritual, are managed by Councils composed chiefly of native clergy and laity, and by the Committees of the Missionary Societies. The native church councils are of two kinds; the smaller or district councils, and the larger or provincial.

Nature of the establishment, &c.

51

REGISTRATION OF MARRIAGES.

Procedure of Marriage Registrars. The office of Marriage Registrar was created by Statute 14 and 15 Vict., Cap. XL, entitled an "Act for Marriages in India," which was extended to this Presidency by the Government of India Act No. V of 1852. There have been three repealing Acts since then—Act XXV of 1864, Act V of 1865, and Act XV of 1872; "The Indian Christian Marriage Act," the last named Act, being the law now in force. The duties of Marriage Registrars are set forth in Part V of the latter Act. When a marriage is to be solemnized one of the parties gives the Marriage Registrar notice, as per Schedule I. On receiving the notice, the Registrar affixes a copy in some "conspicuous place" in his office. If one of the parties is a minor he sends a copy to each of the other Marriage Registrars (if any) in the same district for publication. He files all notices received by him, and enters a true copy of each in a book called the "Marriage Notice Book," which is open for inspection by the public at all reasonable times without fee. When the party giving notice of the marriage has made the oath required by Section 42 of the Act, and requests the issue of the certificate (Schedule II), the Registrar issues under his hand a certificate of such notice having been given, and of such oath having been made, provided that there is no lawful impediment; that its issue has not been forbidden by any person authorized in that behalf by the Act; that four days have expired since receipt of notice; and further, when one of the parties is a minor, that fourteen days have expired. In the latter case, if both parties are residing at Madras, and are desirous of being married in less than fourteen days, they may apply by petition to a Judge of the High Court for an order directing the Marriage Registrar to issue his certificate before the expiration of fourteen days. Any person whose consent to the marriage of a minor is necessary may enter a protest against the issue of the Registrar's certificate by writing at any time before its issue the word "forbidden" opposite to the entry of the notice in the "Marriage Notice Book," and subscribing his or her name thereto. Every such person is liable for the costs of all proceedings in relation thereto and for damages, if the grounds of protest be found to be frivolous. When a protest has been entered, the Marriage Registrar withholds the issue of his certificate until satisfied that the protest ought not to obstruct its

issue, or until the protest is itself withdrawn by the person
who entered it ; or the Registrar may himself apply by
petition stating all the circumstances of the case and pray
for an order and direction of Court.   If the person whose
consent is necessary is insane, or unjustly withholds consent,
the parties interested may petition a Judge of the High Court
or of a District Court to examine the matter, and if upon such
examination it shall be declared that the marriage is proper, the
declaration is as effectual as if the person whose consent was
needed had consented to the marriage, and the Registrar issues
his certificate.   Should, however, a Marriage Registrar himself
refuse to issue a certificate the parties concerned may petition
as above, and the decision of the Judge of the High Court or
of the District Court in the case is final.   After the issue of the
certificate by a Marriage Registrar, the marriage is solemnized
according to such form and ceremony as the parties think fit to
adopt.   The ceremony invariably takes place in the presence of
two or more credible witnesses, and in a part of the ceremony
each of the parties declares that he or she knows of no lawful
impediment to the union.   When a marriage is not solemnized
within two months after receipt of the notice, the notice and the
certificate and all other proceedings thereupon are considered
void.   After the solemnization of a marriage, the Registrar
registers it in a Marriage Registrar's Book (Schedule IV), and
also in a certificate attached to the book as a counterfoil.
The entries in the Register are signed by the Registrar, by the
parties married, and by the two credible witnesses in whose
presence the ceremony takes place.   The certificate attached to
the book is sent by the Registrar to the Secretary to the Local
Government.   The book itself is kept by the Registrar until it
is filled, when it is also sent to the Government.   In the Rules
published in the Fort St. George Gazette, dated 14th March 1874,
the Government have, under the provisions of Sections 82 and 83
of the Marriage Act, authorized the levy of certain fees, and
have prescribed the manner in which they shall be disposed of.

STATIONERY.

The Stationery Office is in charge of a Superintendent **Nature of the**
supported by a small establishment.   Stationery of all descrip- **department.**
tions required for office use and for drawing purposes is issued

annually by the department. In addition to this, school
books, color boxes, and mathematical instruments are supplied
to Army and Regimental schools and Survey classes. The
Government Printing Presses are supplied with ink, flannel,
and rollers. Bibles and Prayer Books are issued for the use of
Churches, Military and Civil Hospitals, and to the Drummers of
Native Regiments, theodolites, levelling instruments, compasses,
and level and survey books, to the Public Works Department,
and ecclesiastical forms are supplied to all Marriage Registrars.
The Ordnance Atlas Sheets received from the Surveyor-General
are sold to private parties, but supplied free to Government offices.
All public offices both in the Presidency and at out-stations
are supplied with stationery free of charge, as also are Regimental
schools, Veterinary Surgeons, Garrison Instructors, Instructors
of Musketry, Military and Civil Hospitals, the Bishop of Madras,
and the Senior Chaplain of the Church of Scotland. Stationery
is also supplied on payment to the Mysore Commission, Municipal
Commissions, Adjutants of Regiments of Infantry, Staff Officers,
Wing Officers, and Commandants of Batteries of Artillery, the
Principal of the Presidency College, Curator of the Government
Book Depôt, and to the Inspector of Normal Schools.

GOVERNMENT PRESS.

**Establish-
ment, and
nature of
work.**   The Government Press, including a branch at the Penitentiary,
is under charge of a Superintendent assisted by a staff of upwards
of 600 persons employed in various printing operations. One
of the Under Secretaries to Government acts as Supervisor to the
Press, and exercises a general control. With the exception
of the Compositors, who are paid by piece-work, all the Press
employés receive fixed monthly salaries, and these range
from Rupees 2 upwards. The rate of remuneration to
the Compositors for their work is 2 Annas per 1,000 ens or
letters, including composition, distributing, and correcting all
proofs but author's, for which latter 2 Annas an hour are paid.
To facilitate the operations of the Press it is sub-divided into
departments, viz., Public, Public Works, Military, Revenue,
Revenue Board, Gazette, Book, Job, Vernacular, and Binding,
each of which is in charge of a Foreman. In the printing
department 16 machines and 39 hand-presses are constantly

employed, and the work turned out comprises Government Proceedings, the Proceedings of the Board of Revenue, the Gazette, Vernacular Acts in five languages, Selections from Government Records, monthly returns, annual and other reports, District Manuals, and a large number of forms and miscellaneous job-work for official use in the Public Offices throughout the Presidency. At the Penitentiary branch, where about 77 adult and 22 juvenile prisoners are employed, Land Revenue, Magisterial, Judicial, and other forms, averaging in amount upwards of 22,000,000 during the official year, are turned out for use in the Mofussil.

LAWRENCE ASYLUM PRESS.

The Lawrence Asylum Press in Madras is a quasi Government institution, the general management being entrusted to a Committee appointed by Government, though the persons employed in connection with it are not eligible to pension under the Uncovenanted Service Civil Pension Code. The connection between this Press and the Government depends on the fact that the former is really a part of the Ootacamund Lawrence Asylum institution, the stability of which is ultimately guaranteed by Government, although the necessity for assuming the charge on State funds has not arisen and is not likely to arise. The Press was originally attached to the Madras Military Orphan Asylum, and the latter has been amalgamated with the Lawrence Asylum. The major portion of the work turned out by the Press is surplus work which cannot be done at the Government Press, and would otherwise find its way to private Presses. Twelve lads apprenticed from the Lawrence Asylum are boarded and clothed at the expense of the Press, and any profit accruing is paid over to the Principal of the Lawrence Asylum for the benefit of the school.

Nature of the institution.

DISTRICT PRESSES AND GAZETTES.

District Presses were first established in pursuance of an order of Government passed in 1855. In the previous year the Collector of North Arcot employed a small printing establishment

District Presses.

which he worked at his own cost as an experiment. About the same time one of the Assistant Collectors in the same district set up a small lithographic press of his own to print the ordinary correspondence of the Rajahmundry Collector's office. The successful working of these presses and their utility being brought to the notice of Government, they ordered that a press should be set up at the Huzoor station of the most important Collectorates, and fifteen districts were shortly afterwards supplied. By March 1859 every district was furnished with its own press, and labor is now greatly economized by the printing of numerous papers, such as puttahs, forms of account, circulars, Proceedings of Government, of the High Court, and of the Board of Revenue, &c., which formerly had to be copied in manuscript. The presses are worked under the orders of the Collectors and managed by a Supervisor or Head Compositor receiving a salary of Rupees 50 per mensem. In 1873-74 Mr. Keys, Superintendent of the Government Press at Madras, was deputed to inspect and report upon the working of the several District Presses. He brought to light several abuses which have been since rectified and prepared a manual for the guidance of the press establishment. The subjoined statement shows the annual value of work done and the receipts and charges during the last ten years :—

Years.	Estimated value of the work done.	Receipts.	Charges.
	RS.	RS.	RS.
1866-67 ...	1,56,260	17,975	61,510
1867-68 ...	1,89,126	24,261	54,731
1868-69 ...	2,33,461	26,643	60,724
1869-70 ...	2,28,883	29,292	55,783
1870-71 ...	2,41,291	25,092	57,982
1871-72 ...	2,23,000	18,994	58,905
1872-73 ...	2,33,574	22,169	72,768
1873-74 ...	1,43,028	20,556	67,964
1874-75 ...	1,40,315	19,815	67,117

District Gazettes.

With the establishment of presses commenced the publication of District Gazettes, which were issued for the first time in 1856-57. The District Gazettes are published in each district fortnightly. As a rule, everything is in diglott. Two regular supplements are published, one the Police Sheet, containing matters of special interest to the Police Department, and the other a sheet containing the Standing Orders of the Board of Revenue. When Acts, Bills or other lengthy papers are published in the

Gazette, these are also put into a Supplement, so that they may
be filed consecutively. The following are the principal statements
published :—the calendar ; a statement showing arrival and
departure of vessels ; the cultivation and rain-fall and price list ;
demand, collection, balance statement ; statement of business in
the taluqs ; salt sales and manufacture statement ; statement of
exports and imports ; vaccination statement; and statement
showing the working of the dispensary. The Gazette
contains also all orders of a general nature ; notice of offences
committed ; of appointments ; promotions ; leaves of absence ;
returns from leave ; dismissals ; suspensions ; punishments ;
deaths ; resignations, &c., among the District servants ; abridg-
ments or brief notices of orders of Government or Acts of the
Legislatures, and other matters of general or official concernment,
such as Rolls of unclaimed sums in Regimental Cash Chests ;
sales of land and notices of Abkári rents ; sale notices, &c.
There are also Circulars issued by the Local Authorities when of
the nature of Standing Orders ; Circular Orders of the Board of
Revenue and of the High Court ; the result of criminal trials ;
lists of stolen property ; description of escaped convicts ; and
offers of reward for their apprehension ; changes in postal rules ;
the progress of the Railway and other public works ; the
proceedings connected with local exhibitions ; advertisements
inviting tenders for contracts ; notices of the dates of preliminary
and other hearings in the Civil Courts; decisions of the Civil
Courts, whether for Plaintiff or Defendant ; place where the
Collector will hold his Cutcherry during the ensuing week, and
similar items of intelligence. The advertisements and circulars
of the Officers of the other Public Departments are published free
of charge. Editorial articles, mere news or correspondence on
any subjects, or comments on the proceedings of the Courts or
Cutcherries have no place in the Gazettes. Private advertisements are published on payment. The District Gazette is
supplied gratis to certain officials and persons, but the subscription of other persons is 3 Annas a month. Village servants and
officials drawing less than Rupees 25 per mensem are supplied
with the Gazette, post free, for a subscription of 2 Annas per
mensem.

REGISTRATION OF JOINT STOCK COMPANIES.

Nature of Government control.   Joint-Stock Companies are either registered under the Indian Companies' Act, 1860, or formed under some other Act or constituted by Royal Charter or Letters Patent. In the two latter cases the Companies are subject to the terms of the special enactment, charter, or letters patent, under which they are respectively constituted. Most Companies, however, are registered under the Indian Companies' Act of 1866, and under this enactment are controlled by a Registrar appointed by Government. The accounts of such Companies are audited and rendered yearly, and the documents relating to them, which are kept by the Registrar, are open to the public on payment of a fee. The Registrar sees that the Memorandum and Articles of Association are in accordance with the Act, and that the documents required to be furnished to him are duly sent in.

MONEGAR CHOULTRY.

Nature of the institution.   The Monegar Choultry in Madras is an institution which affords shelter, food, and clothing to native poor and infirm persons without reference to caste. It was founded in the year 1808. Besides a Choultry or Pauper Asylum, it contains also an infirmary and a special asylum for foundling and stray children. The institution is supported by public contributions aided by the Government. The management is placed under the supervision of a Committee selected annually by the Government.

TRIPLICANE LUNGHERKHANA.

Nature of the institution.   This is a poor-house of considerable antiquity, and was taken over by the Government from the Carnatic Sirkar in 1857. Charity is dispensed to out-door and in-door paupers to the extent of Rupees 400 monthly, which is the amount of the

Government endowment. The institution is managed by the Deputy Commissioner of Police for Madras.

SULPHUR LICENSES.

Over a hundred tons of sulphur is annually expended or sold in this Presidency, and dealers are licensed to have in stock over two hundred tons. The sulphur is chiefly used in making gunpowder and fire-works and in blasting operations, and to some extent in bleaching ginger. A little sulphur is employed in medicine, and it has in some instances been used as a disinfectant. The manufacture of sulphur and its traffic are regulated by the Arms and Ammunition Act, XXXI of 1860, under the provisions of which no one can manufacture or deal in sulphur except under a license. Magistrates may be empowered under the Act to grant licenses to sulphur dealers; but the rule in this Presidency is for the Government to give the sanction on the recommendation of District Magistrates. The premises, books, and stock of licensed sulphur dealers are periodically examined by the Assistant Magistrates, and in the Presidency town by the Deputy Commissioner of Police; annual returns are submitted by District Magistrates of the number of dealers and the business carried on by them.

Nature of arrangements.

GOVERNMENT WORKHOUSE.

The "Strangers' Home" at Madras, which had existed since 1867 as a private charitable institution, was in 1870 taken over by Government as a Government Workhouse. The institution is now managed by a Governor and a Committee, of which the President is the Commissioner of Police for Madras. It is used exclusively in connection with the Vagrancy Act, No. IX of 1874, for the temporary housing of vagrants according to the provisions of that enactment. The annual budget grant for the expenses of the institution is Rupees 20,000.

Nature of the institution.

MONEY, WEIGHTS, AND MEASURES.

Money.   There is no separate Mint in Madras. The currency is Imperial and consists in silver of rupees, half and quarter rupees, and double annas; and in copper of single, half, and quarter annas, and single pies. The following are the amounts used in this Presidency for accounts:—

$$\begin{aligned}
3 \text{ Pies} &= 1 \text{ Paisa or } \tfrac{1}{4} \text{ Anna.} \\
12 \text{ Pies} &= 1 \text{ Anna.} \\
16 \text{ Annas} &= 1 \text{ Rupee.} \\
15 \text{ Rupees} &= 1 \text{ Gold Rupee.} \\
16 \text{ Rupees} &= 1 \text{ Gold Mohur.} \\
1,00,000 \text{ Rupees} &= 1 \text{ Madras Lakh.}
\end{aligned}$$

The sovereign is a legal tender for 10 Rupees. The nominal value of the Rupee in English money is two shillings. Accounts were formerly kept in Madras in Star Pagodas, Fanams, and Cash, and the practice still prevails in some parts of the Presidency. The values of these coins are as under :—

$$\begin{aligned}
80 \text{ Cash} &= 1 \text{ Fanam.} \\
42 \text{ Fanams} &= 1 \text{ Star Pagoda.}
\end{aligned}$$

The Star Pagoda, when current, was made of gold $19\frac{1}{2}$ carats fine, and was nominally worth in English money about 7s. 5d.

Weights.   The original unit of weight in Southern India was the gold pagoda coin of $52\frac{1}{4}$ grains Troy weights ; 32 " Red Seeds " made one pagoda weight, and 10 pagoda weights made 1 pollum. A more stable ponderary unit however, and one still in universal use, is the Tola, a weight which is practically equivalent to the weight of a single silver rupee. The following is the table of weights in use in most Government operations in this Presidency :—

$$\begin{aligned}
180 \text{ Grains} &= 1 \text{ Tola.} \\
3 \text{ Tolas} &= 1 \text{ Pollum.} \\
40 \text{ Pollums} &= 1 \text{ Viss.} \\
8 \text{ Viss} &= 1 \text{ South Indian Maund.} \\
20 \text{ South Indian Maunds} &= 1 \text{ Barum or Candy.}
\end{aligned}$$

The following table gives approximately the equivalents in English measures :—

Madras Weights.		Avoirdupois.			Troy.		
		lbs.	oz.	drs.	lbs.	oz.	dwts.
	1 Tola ...	0 ·	0 ·	6·582⁹	0 .	0 .	7½
3 Tolas	1 Pollam ...	0 ·	1 ·	3·7·18½	0 .	1 .	2⅝
40 Pollams	1 Viss ...	3 ·	1 ·	5·942½	3 .	9 .	0
8 Viss	1 Maund ...	24 ·	10 ·	·15·512⁹	30 .	0 .	0

The various maunds or muns used under other Administrations differ from the South Indian maund considerably. In salt measure the following Imperial table is adopted, the maund being equivalent to 82⅔ lbs. Avoirdupois the tola and seer remaining the same:—

80 Tolas = 1 Seer.
40 Seers = 1 Imperial Maund.

The Imperial seer, which it was the object of Act **XXXI** of 1871 to introduce, (= 2·2046 lbs., or 85·7344 tolas) has not yet been applied to this Presidency.

In linear measure the English foot and yard are superseding **Linear** the native measures, but the latter deserve notice. A table is **Measure.** given below based on a combination of the native measures with the English yard; this is in general use and may be taken as approximately correct with reference to the equivalence of the English and native measures :—

4 Ungulums or Thumbs = 1 Hand.
3 Hands = 1 Span.
2 Spans = 1 Cubit or Moolum.
2 Moolums = 1 Yard.
2 Yards = 1 Fathom or Thundum.
2,000 Thundums = 1 Coss.
4 Coss = 1 Kadum (10 miles).

The basis of linear measure in the South of India is the moolum given above, which is the distance from the elbow to the tip of the middle finger of a full-sized man.

In square measure the use of the English Acre is encouraged, **Square** but the following table holds its ground, the native Cawny taking **Measure.** the place of the Acre :—

144 Inches = 1 Square Foot.
2,400 Square Feet = 1 Mannie or Ground.
24 Mannies = 1 Cawny.
484 Cawnies = 1 Square Mile.

The Cawny is in proportion to the English acre as 121 to 160.

　　　　　MISCELLANEOUS.

Measure of Capacity.

In the greater part of the Presidency there are no actual dry and liquid measures of capacity, these measures depending in reality on the weight of different commodities used in connection with them; thus the seer measure is understood to be a measure which when "heaped" will contain a seer weight of rice. In the neighbourhood of Madras however and in some of the Southern Districts, the ordinary grain measure is a "puddy" which, though variable, does not represent any weight. The following table is used in Government transactions, the Ollock being equivalent to 12½ cubic inches :—

> 8 Ollocks = 1 Measure or Puddy.
> 8 Puddies = 1 Marcal.
> 400 Marcals = 1 Garce.

A parrah of chunam consists of 5 marcals. It will be seen that 20 Ollocks are equivalent to 1 English Gallon. The Imperial measure of capacity, which it was the object of Act XXXI of 1871 to introduce (= a measure containing one Imperial seer of water at its maximum density, weighed in a vacuum), has not yet been applied to this Presidency. The following table shows in greater detail the exact dimensions of the Madras measures :—

Measures.	Depth and Diameter inside, in Inches and Tenths.	Size for practice, in Inches and Tenths.		Capacity in Cubic Inches.	Weight of Rainwater contained by each Measure, the water being at 80° of Fahrenheit's Thermometer, in lbs. Avoirdupois.			
		Diamr.	Depth.		lbs.	oz.	drs.	grs.
	Cylindric.	Square.						
Parrah	17·2050	20 × 20	× 10	4000	144 ·	0 ·	5 ·	0
		Cylindric.						
Marcal	10·0616	10·3	9·6	800	28 ·	12 ·	13 ·	22
½ do.	7·9859	8·2	7·6	400	14 ·	6 ·	6 ·	24
¼ do.	6·3384	6·3	6·4	200	7 ·	3 ·	3 ·	13
Measure (Puddy)...	5·0308	5·0	5·1	100	3 ·	9 ·	9 ·	20
½ do.	3·9930	4·0	4·0	50	1 ·	12 ·	12 ·	23
¼ do.	3·1692	3·2	3·1	25	0 ·	14 ·	6 ·	12
Ollock	2·5154	2·6	2·4	12½	0 ·	7 ·	3 ·	6
½ do.	1·9965	2·0	2·0	6¼	0 ·	3 ·	9 ·	17
¼ do.	1·5846	1·6	1·6	3⅛	0 ·	1 ·	12 ·	22

Comparison of local food measures.

For the purposes of the returns of food prices sent to the Government of India as mentioned in Section IV, a thorough comparison was four years ago made of the local food measures in use, taking the form of a conversion of capacity measures into weight measure. In each locality it was ascertained what

was the recognized measure of capacity used for selling grain
and salt, what was the capacity of this measure in cubic inches,
and how much weight of ordinary rice it contained in terms of
the tola or rupee weight. The ratio between the weight of
ordinary rice and that of other grains and of salt having then
been arrived at by two independent methods, similar results
were established for the other commodities. In establishing the
ratio between grains and rice one ratio for the whole Presidency
was decided on ; in the case of salt however the variations in
different districts, owing to reduction of weight by transport to
places distant from source of supply and other causes, were so
considerable that several ratios had to be taken for the whole
Presidency. The Board of Revenue, who made these calculations,
are acquainted thereby with the weight of each principal
commodity contained in each of the local measures ; and when
the bi-monthly returns showing the number of measures of each
commodity sold for a rupee reach them from the districts, they
are in a position to issue tables showing their price lists in terms
of a single common weight. At present the unit of weight
adopted for the price lists is the seer of 80 tolas.

A small fee is collected from shopkeepers, grain merchants, Stamping
and others wishing to have their weights and measures tested Weights and
and stamped in proof of their being of the proper standard. Measures.
The fee varies from 4 Pies to 6 Annas for each measure tested
and stamped, and from the proceeds a small establishment is
maintained for doing the work. The fee is not collected under
any law, but the benefit of the arrangement is appreciated by
the people, and many come of their own accord from long
distances to have their measures tested and stamped. The
receipts and charges up to 1873 were assigned to the general
revenues, on the understanding however that the charges should
never exceed the receipts, but they were then transferred to
Provincial Funds. The receipts and charges usually average
Rupees 10,000 and Rupees 5,000 respectively.

PRESIDENCY GAZETTEER, &c.

The Madras scheme of District Manuals and Presidency District
Gazetteer was inaugurated before the appearance of the scheme Manuals and
for a statistical survey of the Indian empire put forward by Gazetteer.

the Government of India, and does not exactly tally with it.
In the Madras Presidency the different districts produce their
own manuals, each at a different time, at a separate cost, and,
to a certain extent, on a separate plan.   The Presidency
Gazetteer is to be a distinct publication, prepared hereafter from
these manuals.   On the plan adopted for the rest of India, no
separate District Manuals are published, but the Gazetteers or
" Statistical Accounts " of each province consist of a series of
" District Accounts " placed side by side in one publication;
the District Accounts are in this case on one uniform plan, and
are prepared in a central office from rough material supplied
by the districts, while the cost is confined to that of the
central office.   The Madras District Manuals thus correspond to
the district sections in the Statistical Accounts of each of the
other Administrations ; the differences above mentioned are
however too considerable to admit of their playing the same
part in the compilation of the Imperial Gazetteer, and special
arrangements will have to be made in Madras in the direction
of supplying material for that publication.

The following list shows the writers of the different manuals :—

District.	Writer of the Manual.	Remarks.
1. Vizagapatam ...	Mr. Carmichael	Finished.
2. Madura	„ Nelson	Do.
3. Nellore	„ Boswell	Do.
4. Bellary	„ Kelsall	Do.
5. Cuddapah ...	„ Gribble	Do.
6. Coimbatore ...	Messrs. Rice and Mackenzie·	Do.
7. South Arcot ...	Mr. Garstin	In the Press.
8. Godavery ...	„ Morris	Do.
9. Chingleput ...	„ Crole	Do.
10. Trichinopoly ...	„ Moore	In progress.
11. Ganjam	„ Maltby	Do.
12. Kistna	„ Leman	Do.
13. Tinnevelly ...	„ Bird	Do.
14. Nilgiris	„ Grigg	In the Press.
15. Salem	„ Le Fanu	In progress.
16. Malabar	„ Logan	Do.
17. Kurnool	M.R.R. G. Kistna Chetty ...	Do.
18. South Canara ...	Not yet arranged ...	Not yet begun.
19. Tanjore	M.R.R. Venkasawmy Row.	In progress.
20. North Arcot ...	Not yet arranged ...	Not yet begun.

**Translitera-
tion.**   The transliteration of native proper names in the District
Manuals is conducted in the main on the system of Sir William
Jones as finally authorized by the Government of India for
the purposes of the Imperial Gazetteer in February 1870.   Sir
William Jones' system may be described as the system of
spelling according to continental vowel sounds, with an arbitrary

transliteration of consonant sounds ; being opposed in the former particular to the system of Dr. Gilchrist, which proceeded more phonetically in its rendering into English of native vowels, and to the common usage of Europeans, which may be said to be a mixture of the phonetic principle and tradition. The system as authorized by the Government of India for the Imperial Gazetteer is understood to be arbitrary only as regards the twelve ordinary vowel sounds, leaving the consonant sounds, which vary much in the different languages of India, to be variously represented. Systematic transliteration has not hitherto been attempted in this Presidency in the publication of Government Proceedings and other official papers ; but it is in contemplation to take measures in that direction.

APPENDIX.

53

APPENDIX TO SECTION II.

(1) *Statement showing the Taluqs under the charge of Divisional Officers on 1st February 1877.*

District.	Designation of Office and Head-quarter Station.	Taluqs, Zemindaries and other separate Tracts forming the Charge.	Area in Square Miles.	Population.	Land Revenue.	Remarks.
					RS.	
Ganjam.	1. Collector, Chetterpore.	*Government Taluq.*				
		1. Gumsur	$277\frac{3}{4}$	157,960	1,95,763	A portion of the Magisterial charge of Gumsur Taluq is under the Senior Assistant.
		Zemindaries.				
		2. Surada	46	15,324	4,000	
		3. Attigada ...	$149\frac{3}{8}$	77,228	60,000	
		4. Palur	$16\frac{5}{16}$	4,173	553	
		5. Humma	5	2,754	1,171	
		6. Beridi	$14\frac{3}{4}$	10,960	4,500	
		7. Kallikotta ...	84	42,589	19,000	
		Total ...	$593\frac{3}{16}$	310,988	2,84,987	
	2. Principal Assistant Collector (First Asst.), Chicacole.	*Government Taluq.*				
		1. Chicacole ...	$279\frac{1}{4}$	200,655	2,48,698	
		Zemindars' Estates.				
		2. Sreekurmana of Vizianagaram in Vizagapatam.	$17\frac{3}{4}$	16,927	...*	* The revenue is included in that of Vizianagram in the Vizagapatam District.
		3. Karakavalasa ...	$9\frac{1}{16}$	7,795	4,048	
		4. Mungatavalasa ...	$5\frac{3}{4}$	3,695	4,048	
		5. Gottipalli ...	$6\frac{1}{4}$	4,351	4,049	
		6. Takkali Estates ...	$61\frac{9}{16}$	58,054	49,088	
		7. Tarla	$28\frac{3}{4}$	24,639	4,000	
		8. Chackipalli ...	$\frac{3}{4}$	1,018	869	
		9. Konsalacottur ...	$\frac{1}{4}$	674	393	
		10. Tarlepatta ...	$\frac{3}{4}$	388	256	
		11. Chinnatangam ...	$\frac{3}{8}$	395	424	
		12. Peddatangam ...	$\frac{6}{16}$	564	424	
		13. Tallavalasa ...	$\frac{3}{8}$	347	424	
		14. Jarangi	$2\frac{3}{4}$	2,336	1,002	
		15. Yellamanchilli ...	1	643	654	
		16. Beddam	$1\frac{3}{4}$	217	69	
		17. Belamarapalava-lasa.	$2\frac{1}{2}$	855	1,043	
		18. Gopalapuram ..	5	5,165	3,699	
		19. Chittivalasa ...	$7\frac{7}{16}$	5,698	2,074	
		20. Parlakemedi ...	$451\frac{1}{2}$	252,391	82,139	
		21. Urlam	$14\frac{1}{2}$	11,061	13,582	
		22. Dauta	$4\frac{1}{16}$	3,220	2,309	
		23. Tilaru	$15\frac{3}{4}$	6,180	3,654	
		24. Towdam ...	$2\frac{1}{4}$	1,030	686	
		25. Akkayavalasa ...	1	788	278	
		26. Santalaksimipu-ram.	$7\frac{1}{16}$	485	1,192	

(420)

(1) *Statement showing the Taluqs under the charge of Divisional Officers on*
1st February 1877—(Continued).

District.	Designation of Office and Head-quarter Station.	Taluqs, Zemindaries and other separate Tracts forming the Charge.	Area in Square Miles.	Popula-tion.	Land Revenue.	Remarks.
					RS.	
	2. Principal Assistant Collector (First Asst.), Chicacole. (*Continued*).	27. Talasamudram ...	$1\frac{3}{4}$	923	2,383	
		28. Lusaram ...	$\frac{3}{4}$	320	332	
		29. Rajapuram ...	$\frac{3}{16}$	266	76	
		30. Seddibeharakut-tur.	$\frac{1}{4}$	109	103	
		31. Jonnupadu ...	$1\frac{6}{16}$	138	93	
		32. Malgam	$1\frac{0}{16}$	916	572	
		Maliahs.				
		33. Parlakemedi Maliah Tracts.		19,201	...*	* Area not known. The revenue is included in that shown for the Par-lakemedi Zemin-dary above.
		Total ...	$925\frac{11}{16}$	631,344	4,32,681	
		Government Taluq.				
		1. Berhampore ...	399	243,685	3,19,322	The Magisterial charge of a por-tion of the Ber-hampore Taluq is to remain with the Collector.
		Zemindaries.				
		2. Daraskota ...	$50\frac{1}{4}$	31,262	25,000	
		3. Seerghar ...	$20\frac{3}{4}$	9,595	5,500	
		4. Chinnakemedi ...	$55\frac{3}{16}$	29,849	20,000	
		5. Aska	$3\frac{9}{16}$	7,712	4,857	
		6. Davabhuny ...	4	3,539	5,188	
	3. Senior Asst. Collector (Second Asst.), Berhampore.	7. Kurla	$3\frac{3}{4}$	5,457	5,455	
		8. Peddakemedi ...	$78\frac{7}{16}$	40,810	23,500	
		9. Chicati	$64\frac{1}{2}$	40,789	34,000	
		10. Surangi	$14\frac{3}{4}$	12,919	3,500	
		11. Jarada	9	5,813	2,000	
		12. Jalantra ...	$25\frac{1}{2}$	18,450	7,000	
		13. Barwa	$10\frac{1}{4}$	8,454	7,800	
		14. Mandusa ...	$35\frac{3}{4}$	34,508	14,000	
		15. Budarasinghi ...	$4\frac{1}{4}$	3,244	500	
		Maliahs.				
	Do. ...	16. Peddakemedi, Surange, Budara-singhi, Jarada, and Mandusa Maliahs.		26,937		
		Total ...	$779\frac{1}{16}$	522,023	4,77,622	

Ganjam—(*Continued*).

(1) *Statement showing the Taluqs under the charge of Divisional Officers on 1st February 1877*—(Continued).

District.	Designation of Office and Head-quarter Station.	Taluqs, Zemindaries and other separate Tracts forming the Charge.	Area in Square Miles.	Popula-tion.	Land. Revenue.	Remarks.
Ganjam—(Continued).	4. Special Asst. Collector (Third Asst.), Russelkonda in the low country. Beeligoodu in the Maliahs.	*Maliah Tracts.* 1. Gumsur Maliahs... 2. Chockapad, Chali, Pasara, and Gatigudu of the Gumsur Taluq. 3. Surada and Kuttingia Maliah and the portions of Chinnakemedi Maliahs. 4. Chinnakemedi and Bodigada Maliahs.	...	28,364 7,202 73,551 ...	RS.	Area and revenue not known. Revenue not known. Population of these Maliahs is included in that of the Zemindaries to which the Maliahs belong.
		Total ...	...	109,127	50	
		Grand Total ...	2,297	1,464,355	11,95,340	
Vizagapatam.	1. Collector, Vizagapatam.	*Zemindaries.* 1. Vizagapatam ... 2. Bimlipatam... ... 3. Serungavarapu-kota ... ... 4. Chepudipalli ...	216 243 318 615	90,467 113,079 130,362 162,827	... ...	
		Total ...	1,392	496,735	...	
	2. Principal Asst. Collector First Asst.), Narasipatam.	*Zemindaries.* 1. Golakonda ... 2. Sarvasiddi ... 3. Viravalli ... 4. Anakapalli ... 5. Hill tracts of Golcondah and Viravalli.	874 960 688 597 500	26,720 129,185 166,184 143,549 15,880	1,02,374 1,90,595	
		Total ...	3,619	481,518	2,92,969	
	3. Senior Asst. Collector (Second Asst.), Vizianagaram.	*Rented.* 1. Palconda... ... *Zemindaries.* 2. Parvatipoor... ... 3. Vizianagaram ... 4. Gajapatinagarum ... 5. Bobilli ... ... 6. Salur ... ... 7. Ganapur ... ... 8. Royagadda ...	432 402 333 276 333 222 2,000 1,000	191,908 123,830 149,920 121,758 140,739 77,006 63,127 59,780	... ...	
		Total ...	4,998	928,068	...	

(1) *Statement showing the Taluqs under the charge of Divisional Officers on 1st February 1877*—(Continued).

District.	Designation of Office and Head-quarter Station.	Taluqs, Zemindaries and other separate Tracts forming the Charge.	Area in Square Miles.	Population.	Land Revenue.	Remarks.
					RS.	
Vizagapatam—(Continued).	4. Special Asst. Collector (Third Asst.), Korapat.	*Zemindaries—Jeypore.* 1. Kirapad ... ... 2. Kolupa... ... 3. Navarangapore ... 4. Malkangiri	8,500	132,655 80,034 87,363 12,801	...	
		Total ...	8,500	312,853	...	
		Grand Total ...	18,509	2,219,174	2,92,969	
			...	...	11,02,022	Zemindari revenue, for which Taluq-war particulars are not known.
		Total ...	...	...	13,94,991	
Godavery.	1. Collector, Cocaunda.	*Zemindaries.* 1. Pittapore ... 2. Cocaunda ... 3. Coringa ... *Government Taluq.* 4. Ramachendrapur..	188 168 507	79,606 66,944 24,916 203,583	3,41,627* 8,34,842	* Including the revenue of Tuni.
		Total ...	863	375,049	11,76,469	
	2. Sub-Collector (First Asst.), Rajahmundry.	*Government Taluqs.* 1. Rajahmundry ... 2. Poddapoor ... *Zemindaries.* 3. Tuni ... ... 4. Badrachellum and Rakapalli.	2,058 505 376 885	128,901 111,189 50,201 27,695	1,57,303 2,35,551 ... 21,090	Zemindari revenue included in that of Cocaunda and Coringa.
		Total ...	3,824	318,286	4,13,944	
	3. Head Asst. Collector (Second Asst.), Elloro.	*Government Taluqs.* 1. Elloro ... .. 2. Ernagoodam ... 3. Tanuku	729 1,249 366	136,875 145,715 167,491	2,19,794 1,95,217 6,16,189	
		Total...	2,344	450,081	10,31,200	

(1) *Statement showing the Taluqs under the charge of Divisional Officers on 1st February 1877*—(Continued).

District.	Designation of Office and Head-quarter Station.	Taluqs, Zemindaries and other separate Tracts forming the Charge.	Area in Square Miles.	Popula-tion.	Land Revenue.	Remarks.
Godavery—(*Contd.*)		*Government Taluqs.*			RS.	
	4. General Depy. Collector, Narasapoor.	1. Narasapur ...	450	177,876	5,74,821	
		2. Bhimaveram ...	416	92,457	4,36,216	
		3. Amalapoor ...	437	206,885	5,79,471	
		Total ...	1,303	477,218	15,90,508	
		Grand Total ...	8,334	1,620,624	42,12,391	
Kistna.	1. Collector, Masulipatam.	*Government Taluqs.*				
		1. Gudivada ...	533	87,138	4,49,508	
		2. Bandar	687	164,525	3,10,021	
		Total ...	1,220	251,663	7,59,529	
	2. Sub-Collector (First Asst.), Guntoor.	*Government Taluqs.*				
		1. Bapatla ...	694	143,629	5,90,405	
		2. Guntoor ...	500	126,997	4,07,008	
		3. Sattanapalli ...	621	101,728	3,69,704	
		4. Repalli	622	169,912	6,45,838	
		Total ...	2,437	542,266	20,12,955	
	3. Head Asst. Collector (Second Asst.), Bezwada.	*Government Taluqs.*				
		1. Nandigama ...	599	106,452	2,04,247	
		2. Bezwada	406	83,081	1,57,092	
		Zemindaries.				
		3. Nuzvid	561	107,465	1,08,221	
		4. Virsanapetah ...	257	55,662	20,829	
		Total ...	1,823	352,660	4,90,389	
	4. General Depy. Collector, Vinnucondah.	*Government Taluqs.*				
		1. Narasarowpettah...	682	120,619	3,40,585	
		2. Palnad	1,095	120,658	3,31,703	
		3. Vinnucondah ...	561	64,508	1,47,204	
		Total ...	2,338	305,785	8,19,492	
		Grand Total ...	7,818	1,452,374	40,82,365	

(1) *Statement showing the Taluqs under the charge of Divisional Officers on
1st February* 1877—(Continued).

District.	Designation of Office and Head-quarter Station.	Taluqs, Zemindaries and other separate Tracts forming the Charge.	Area in Square Miles.	Popula-tion.	Land Revenue.	Remarks.
		Government Taluqs.			RS.	
	1. Collector, Nellore.	{ 1. Nellore* ... ... 2. Gudur	627 813	179,769 147,141	3,20,805 3,23,604	* The Magisterial charge under the Head Assistant Collector.
		Total ...	1,440	326,910	6,44,409	
		Government Taluqs.				
		1. Ongole ... ... 2. Kandukur ... 3. Kanigiri	710 722 695	195,068 138,375 127,258	3,27,151 2,86,834 69,442	
Nellore.	2. Sub-Collector (First Asst.), Ongole.	*Zemindaries.*				
		4. Darsi Division ... 5. Podile do. ...	488 405	73,139 62,934	... ...	} Revenues included under Venkatagiri.
		Total ...	3,020	596,774	6,83,427	
		Government Taluqs.				
	3. Head Asst. Collector (Second Asst.), Nellore.	1. Kavali ... ... 2. Udayagiri ... 3. Atmakur ...	533 595 608	81,336 100,985 103,802	1,72,639 67,196 1,61,927	
		Total ...	1,736	286,123	4,01,762	
		Government Taluqs.				
	4. General Depy. Collector, Naidoopet.	{ 1. Rapur ... ... 2. Venkatagiri ... 3. Polur Division ...	541 229 184	63,885 52,258 50,861	1,32,003 3,79,045 ...	
		Total ...	954	167,004	5,11,048	
		Grand Total...	7,150	1,376,811	22,40,646	
	1. Collector, Cuddapah.	} 1. Cuddapah ...	1,207	163,013	2,35,064	
Cuddapah.		*Government Taluqs.*				
	2. Sub-Collector (First Asst.), Madanapalli.	{ 1. Royachoti ... 2. Kadiri ... 3. Voilpaud .. ... 4. Madanapalli ...	649 1,442 708 631	128,162 140,948 145,591 135,468	1,59,013 1,55,760 1,91,157 2,10,648	
		Total ...	3,430	550,169	7,16,578	

(1) *Statement showing the Taluqs under the charge of Divisional Officers on 1st February 1877—(Continued).*

District.	Designation of Office and Head-quarter Station.	Taluqs, Zemindaries and other separate Tracts forming the Charge.	Area in Square Miles.	Popula-tion.	Land Revenue.	Remarks.
Cuddapah—(Continued).		*Government Taluqs.*			Rs.	
	3. Head Assistant Collector, (Second Asst.), Ontimittah.	1. Jammalmadugu ...	670	109,965	2,03,116	
		2. Proddatur ...	343	102,744	1,89,005	
		3. Pulivendla ...	579	110,405	1,72,855	
		Total ...	1,592	323,114	5,64,976	
		Government Taluqs.				
	4. General Depy. Collector, Cuddapah	1. Budwail	704	93,051	1,38,389	
		2. Sidhout	508	76,667	1,17,940	
		3. Pullampet ...	609	145,180	2,06,424	
		Total ...	1,821	314,898	4,62,753	
		Grand Total ...	8,050	1,351,194	19,79,371	
Bellary.		*Government Taluqs.*				
	1. Collector, Bellary.	1. Bellary	985	182,244	2,97,582	
		Government Taluqs.				
	2. Sub-Collector (First Asst.), Gooty.	1. Adoni	805	181,583	2,60,907	
		2. Alur	677	98,230	2,76,953	
		3. Gooty	1,014	144,568	2,21,631	
		4. Tadpatry	772	117,211	1,76,153	
		5. Anantapore ...	789	102,761	1,40,779	
		Total ...	4,057	644,353	10,76,423	
		Government Taluqs.				
	3. Head Assistant Collector, (Second Asst.), Pennacondah.	1. Pennacondah ...	654	88,754	1,28,020	
		2. Hindupam ...	481	87,859	1,40,273	
		3. Madakasira ...	439	79,458	1,22,625	
		4. Dharmaveram ...	1,226	120,608	1,65,333	
		Total ...	2,800	376,715	5,56,251	
		Government Taluqs.				
	4. General Depy. Collector, Harpanahalli.	1. Huvanadgalli ...	623	89,538	1,42,731	
		2. Harpanahalli ...	592	85,729	1,15,472	
		3. Hospett	540	93,424	1,56,398	
		Total ...	1,755	268,691	4,14,601	

(1) *Statement showing the Taluqs under the charge of Divisional Officers on 1st February* 1877—(Continued).

District.	Designation of Office and Head-quarter Station.	Taluqs, Zemindaries and other separate Tracts forming the Charge.	Area in Square Miles.	Popula-tion.	Land Revenue.	Remarks.
Bellary—(Continued).	5. General Deputy Collector, Bellary.	*Government Taluqs.* 1. Kudlighi ... ... 2. Raidroog	864 890	93,228 87,779	RS. 1,12,609 1,57,367	
		Total ...	1,754	181,007	2,69,976	
		Grand Total ...	11,351	1,653,010	26,14,833	
Kurnool.	1. Collector, Kurnool.	*Government Taluqs.* 1. Nandikotkur ... 2. Ramalkota ...	1,186 836	101,866 146,195	2,21,277 1,81,541	
		Total ...	2,022	248,061	4,02,818	
	2. Head Assistant Collector, (Second Asst.), Cumbum.	*Government Taluqs.* 1. Cumbum ... ... 2. Markapur ...	885 1,039	123,042 92,065	1,66,686 1,01,160	
		Total ...	1,924	215,707	2,67,846	
	3. General Deputy Collector, Nandial.	*Government Taluqs.* 1. Nandial ... ... 2. Sirwell	777 487	107,320 71,066	2,05,527 1,66,462	
		Total ...	1,264	178,386	3,71,989	
	4. General Deputy Collector, Koilkuntla.	*Government Taluqs.* 1. Pattikondah ... 2. Koilkuntla ...	1,190 637	173,434 98,844	2,35,429 2,33,544	
		Total ...	1,827	272,278	4,68,973	
		Grand Total ...	7,037	914,432	15,11,626	
Chinglepat.	1. Collector, Sydapet.	*Government Taluq.* 1. Trivellore ...	308	186,404	2,52,984	

(1) *Statement showing the Taluqs under the charge of Divisional Officers on 1st February 1877—(Continued).*

District.	Designation of Office and Head-quarter Station.	Taluqs, Zemindaries and other separate Tracts forming the Charge.	Area in Square Miles.	Population.	Land Revenue.	Remarks.
		Government Taluqs.			RS.	
	2. Sub-Collector (First Asst.), Chingleput.	1. Chingleput ...	474	132,328	2,22,376	Altered with reference to G.O., dated 17th July 1877, No. 2,321.
		2. Madurantakum ...	635	197,308	4,22,563	
		3. Conjeveram ...	447	168,036	4,05,905	
		Total...	1,556	497,672	10,50,844	
		Government Taluqs.				
	3. Dy. Collector, Sydapet.	1. Sydapet ...	...	...	...	
		2. Ponneri ...	312	104,210	2,11,403	
		Total ...	...	...	...	
		Grand Total ...	2,619	938,184	17,96,425	
	1. Collector, Chittoor.	1. Chittoor* ...	965	213,045	2,52,348	* The taluqs of Chittoor and Chendragiri are usually placed under the charge of an Assistant Collector, and if he leaves the district temporarily the Collector retains charge of the Chittoor Taluq, the Chendragiri Taluq being placed under the Head Asst. Collector.
		2. Palmanair ...	664	60,211	79,537	
		3. Chendragiri* ...	553	99,628	99,952	
		Zemindari.				
		4. Poonganoor Zemindari.	524	109,282	66,859	
		Total ...	2,706	482,166	4,98,696	
		Government Taluqs.				
	2. Sub-Collector (First Asst.), Vellore.	1. Arcot ...	379	157,391	3,23,685	
		2. Vellore ...	281	179,156	1,91,972	
		3. Gudiattum ...	443	162,980	2,48,216	
		Zemindari.				
		4. Kangundy Zemindari.	179	52,047	22,959	
		Total ...	1,290	551,574	7,86,832	
		Government Taluq.				
	3. Head Asst. Collector (Second Asst.), Ranipet.	1. Wallajah ...	516	216,204	3,82,549	
		Zemindaries.				
		2. Calastry ...	602	135,104	1,76,816	
		3. Karvattinuggur ...	634	289,894	1,80,495	
		Total ...	1,752	641,202	7,39,860	

(District column: Chingleput—(Continued); North Arcot.)

(1) *Statement showing the Taluqs under the charge of Divisional Officers on 1st February 1877—(Continued).*

District.	Designation of Office and Head-quarter Station.	Taluqs, Zemindaries and other separate Tracts forming the Charge.	Area in Square Miles.	Popula-tion.	Land Revenue.	Remarks.
North Arcot—(Continued).	4. General Dy. Collector, Gudiyathum.	*Government Taluqs.*			RS.	
		1. Wandewash ...	413	153,507	3,56,291	
		2. Polur ...	330	109,150	2,01,450	
		Zemindari.				
		3. Arni Jaghire ...	170	77,679	5,933	
		Total ...	913	340,336	5,63,674	
		Grand Total ...	6,661	2,015,278	25,89,062	
South Arcot.	1. Collector, Cuddalore.	*Government Taluq.*				
		1. Cuddalore ...	459	284,849	4,04,793	
	2. Sub-Collector, Tindevanum.	*Government Taluqs.*				
		1. Trinomalay ...	990	164,657	2,98,648	
		2. Tindevanum ...	810	239,754	5,53,798	
		3. Villapuram ...	611	236,108	4,70,541	
		Total ...	2,411	640,519	13,22,987	
	3. Head Assistant Collector), Virdachellam.	*Government Taluqs.*				
		1. Virdachellam ...	566	178,504	3,37,577	
		2. Chedambaram ...	393	239,133	6,70,712	
		Total ...	959	417,637	10,08,289	
	4. General Dy. Collector, Trikalore.	*Government Taluqs.*				
		1. Trikalore ...	500	216,246	4,02,020	
		2. Kallakurichi ...	607	196,566	3,24,441	
		Total ...	1,107	412,812	7,26,461	
		Grand Total ...	4,936	1,755,817	34,62,530	

(1) *Statement showing the Taluqs under the charge of Divisional Officers on 1st February 1877*—(Continued).

District.	Designation of Office and Head-quarter Station.	Taluqs, Zemindaries and other separate Tracts forming the Charge.	Area in Square Miles.	Popula-tion.	Land Revenue.	Remarks.
					RS.	
	1. Collector, Tanjore.	......				
		Government Taluqs.				
	2. Sub-Collector (First Assistant), Negapatam.	1. Negapatam ...	242	200,733	3,98,251	
		2. Nannilam ...	294	207,407	7,02,225	
		Total ...	536	408,140	11,00,476	
		Government Taluqs.				
	3. Head Assistant Collector (Second Asst.), Combaconum.	1. Tanjore	635	344,339	5,95,456	
		2. Combaconum ...	341	341,034	7,66,649	
		Total ...	976	685,373	13,62,105	
Tanjore.		*Government Taluq.*				
	4. Asst. Collector, Tanjore.	1. Pattukotta ...	945	237,423	1,87,003	
		Government Taluqs.				
	5. Dy. Collector, Mayaveram.	1. Mayaveram ...	276	219,358	5,65,963	
		2. Shealli	170	107,459	2,72,933	
		Total ...	446	326,817	8,38,896	
		Government Taluqs.				
	6. Dy. Collector, Manargudi.	1. Manargudi ...	300	161,264	4,05,235	
		2. Tritrapoondy ...	536	154,714	3,39,658	
		Total ...	836	315,978	7,44,893	
		Grand Total ...	3,739	1,973,731	42,33,373	
Trichinopoly.		*Government Taluq.*				
	1. Collector, Trichinopoly.	1. Trichinopoly ...	519	306,461	4,60,429	

(430)

(1) *Statement showing the Taluqs under the charge of Divisional Officers on 1st February* 1877—(Continued).

District.	Designation of Office and Head-quarter Station.	Taluqs, Zemindaries and other separate Tracts forming the Charge.	Area in Square Miles.	Popula-tion.	Land Revenue.	Remarks.
					RS.	
Trichinopoly—*(Continued)*.	2. Head Assistant Collector (First Asst.), Museri.	*Government Taluqs.*				
		1. Museri	931	257,174	3,44,411	
		2. Kulatalai	667	228,313	2,30,525	
		Total ...	1,598	485,487	5,74,936	
	3. Dy. Collector, Keelapalore.	*Government Taluqs.*				
		1. Perambalore ...	690	170,567	2,40,960	
		2. Oodiarpoliem ...	777	237,839	2,36,144	
		Total ...	1,467	408,460	4,77,104	
		Grand Total ...	3,584	1,200,408	15,12,469	
Madura.	1. Collector, Madura.	*Government Taluqs.*				
		1. Periacolum ...	446½	231,418	3,17,851	
		2. Melur	514½	128,983	2,53,247	
		Total ...	960¾	360,401	5,71,098	
	2. Sub-Collector (First Asst.), Dindigul.	*Government Taluqs.*				Altered with refer-ence to G.O., dated 6th July 1877, No. 2,235.
		1. Dindigul	1,108¾	324,366	3,77,211	
		2. Palani	988¾	184,831	2,62,142	
		Total ...	2,097½	509,197	6,39,353	
	3. Head Assistant Collector (Second Asst.), Ramnad.	*Zemindaries.*				
		1. Ramnad	2,351	504,131	3,38,686	
		2. Shevagunga ...	1,557	434,253	2,88,317	
		Total ...	3,908	938,384	6,27,003	
	4. Dy. Collector, Madura.	*Government Taluqs.*				
		1. Madura	1,200	217,418	2,65,063	
		2. Terumangalum ...	618¼	241,215	3,69,192	
		Total ...	1,818½	458,633	6,34,255	
		Grand Total ...	8,784¾	2,266,615	24,90,240	

(1) *Statement showing the Taluqs under the charge of Divisional Officers on 1st February 1877—(Continued).*

District.	Designation of Office and Head-quarter Station.	Taluqs, Zemindaries and other separate Tracts forming the Charge.	Area in Square Miles.	Popula-tion.	Land Revenue.	Remarks.
					RS.	
		Government Taluqs.				
	1. Collector, Palamcottah. {	1. Tinnevelly ...	346	184,109	3,53,173	
		2. Sankaranainarkovil	609	182,018	2,50,565	
		Total ...	955	366,127	6,03,738	
		Government Taluqs.				
	2. Sub-Collector (First Asst.), Tuticorin.	1. Ottapidaram ...	...	...	...	
		2. Teukarai	463	156,862	2,13,717	
			533	176,954	3,28,845	
		Total ...	...	...	...	
		Government Taluqs.				
Tinnevelly.	3. Head Assistant Collector, (Second Asst.), Shermadavi.	1. Nangunery ...	337	122,001	2,46,372	Altered with refer-ence to G.O., dated 18th July 1877, No. 2,339.
		2. Ambasamudram...	303	163,215	4,23,403	
		3. Tenkasi	...	...	...	
		Total ...	640	285,216	6,69,775	
		Government Taluqs.				
	4. General Dy. Collector, Kovilpatti.	1. Srivilliputtoor ...	...	...	...	
		2. Sattoor	604	178,078	3,84,445	
		Total ...	...	...	...	
		Grand Total ...	4,815	1,693,959	30,38,855	
		Government Taluq.				
	1. Collector, Coimbatore. }	1. Coimbatore ...	625	243,995	3,09,270	
Coimbatore.		*Government Taluqs.*				
	2. Sub-Collector (First Asst.), Erode.	1. Caroor... ...	564	175,659	2,70,264	
		2. Dharapuram ...	775	217,493	3,36,121	
		3. Bhowany... ...	582	102,813	1,09,808	
		4. Erode	595	233,564	3,95,510	
		Total ...	2,516	729,529	11,11,703	

(432)

(1) *Statement showing the Taluqs under the charge of Divisional Officers on 1st February 1877—*(Continued).

District.	Designation of Office and Head-quarter Station.	Taluqs, Zemindaries and other separate Tracts forming the Charge.	Area in Square Miles.	Population.	Land Revenue.	Remarks.
					RS.	
Coimbatore—(*Continued*).	3. Head Assistant Collector (Second Asst.), Pollachy.	*Government Taluqs.* 1. Oodumalpett ... ... 2. Palladam ... ... 3. Pollachy	365 741 428	123,650 237,808 167,546	1,98,675 3,76,266 2,14,984	
		Total ...	1,534	529,004	7,89,925	
	4. General Dy. Collector, Sattiamungalum.	*Government Taluqs.* 1. Collegal ... ... 2. Sattiamungalam.	738 966	90,830 169,916	86,345 3,24,742	
		Total ...	1,704	260,746	4,11,087	
		Grand Total ...	6,379	1,763,274	26,21,984	.
Nilgiris	1. Commissioner, Ootacamund.	1. Nilgiris	1,000	49,501	46,049	Assistant Commissioner is District Magistrate and has Magisterial charge.
Salem.	1. Collector, Salem.	*Government Taluqs.* 1. Salem ... ... 2. Athur	993 798	393,805 164,006	4,56,871 2,21,393	
		Total ...	1,791	557,811	6,78,264	
	2. Sub-Collector (First Assistant), Oossoor.	*Government Taluqs.* 1. Oossoor ... ... 2. Kistnagiri ... 3. Darampuri ...	1,169 658 998	193,037 170,233 190,626	1,93,902 1,73,923 1,92,215	
		Total ...	2,825	553,896	5,60,040	
	3. Head Assistant Collector (Second Asst.), Tripatore.	*Government Taluqs.* 1. Tripatore ... 2. Uttengarai ...	805 808	190,800 153,801	1,65,528 1,29,081	
		Total ...	1,613	344,601	2,94,609	

(1) *Statement showing the Taluqs under the charge of Divisional Officers on 1st February* 1877—(Continued).

District.	Designation of Office and Head-quarter Station.	Taluqs, Zemindaries and other separate Tracts forming the Charge.	Area in Square Miles.	Population.	Land Revenue.	Remarks.
Salem—(*Continued*).		*Government Taluqs.*			RS.	
	4. General Deputy Collector, Namakal.	1. Namakal	743	261,009	3,62,558	
		2. Trichengode ...	632	249,678	3,67,202	
		Total ...	1,375	510,687	7,29,760	
		Grand Total ...	7,604	1,966,995	22,62,673	
South Canara.		*Government Taluqs.*				
	1. Collector, Mangalore.	1. Mangalore ...	865	242,779	3,67,135	
		2. Uppenangadi ...	1,047	107,722	1,44,267	
		Total ...	1,912	350,501	5,11,402	
		Government Taluqs.				
	2. Head Assistant Collector (Second Asst.), Kundapur.	1. Udipi	892	231,570	3,25,100	
		2. Kundapur ...	525	113,713	2,07,882	
		Total ...	1,417	345,283	5,32,982	
		Government Taluq.				
	3. Assistant Collector (Third Assistant), Mangalore.	1. Kassergode ...	1,064	222,578	2,43,195	
		Grand Total ...	4,393	918,362	12,87,579	
Malabar.		*Government Taluqs.*				
	1. Collector, Calicut.	1. Calicut	360	189,768	1,28,975	
		2. Cochin	3	19,826	18,679	
		Total ...	363	209,594	1,47,654	
		Government Taluqs.				
	2. Sub-Collector (First Asst.), Tellicherry.	1. Cherikal	671	257,377	2,13,652	
		2. Kottiam	460	143,561	99,948	
		3. Kurambranad ...	527	243,751	2,09,306	
		Total ...	1,658	644,689	5,22,906	

(434)

(1) *Statement showing the Taluqs under the charge of Divisional Officers on 1st February* 1877—(Continued).

District.	Designation of Office and Head-quarter Station.	Taluqs, Zemindaries, and other separate Tracts forming the Charge.	Area in Square Miles.	Popula-tion.	Land Revenue.	Remarks.
					RS.	
		Government Taluqs.				
	3. Head Assistant Collector (Second Asst.), Palghaut.	1. Palghaut	681	325,855	2,77,905	
		2. Ponani	450	374,756	3,08,853	
		Total ...	1,131	700,611	5,86,758	
Malabar—*(Continued).*		*Government Taluqs.*				
	4. Special Asst. (Second Asst.), Malapuram.	1. Ernaad	997	287,936	2,00,555	
		2. Valluvanad ...	932	292,482	2,47,229	
		Total ...	1,929	580,418	4,47,784	
		Government Taluq.				
	5. Dy. Collector, Manantoddy.	1. Wynaad	1,115	125,938	1,11,279	
		Grand Total ...	6,196	2,261,250	18,16,381	

(2) *Statement showing the Particulars of the Estates under the charge of the Court of Wards at the end of Fasli 1285.*

District.	Name of the Estate.	Name of the Ward.	Sex of the Ward.	Age of the Ward.	Date of Assumption of Charge.	Date when the Estate will probably be restored.	Demand for Fasli 1285.
							Rs.
Ganjam	Parlakemedy	Virapratapondra Gajapathi Narayana Deo.	Male	46	July 1830	Not known ...	3,69,333
	Jalantra	Ramakrishna Chokroya Deo	Do.	16	November 1860.	13th May 1881.	28,453
	Barwah	Chandramurupathy	Do.	19	August 1859	13th Feb. 1874.	8,297
	Seerghur	Lakshmi Narasimha Sing Deo	Do.	14	Do. 1872	27th April 1883.	18,414
						Total ...	4,24,497
Vizagapatam	Bezwada	Vasanthavas Venkata Lakshmi Narayana Vishnu Row Puntulu.	Do.	15	March 1869	20th Oct. 1882...	5,888
	Salur	Rajah Jagunatha Narayana Ramachandru Raj Pedda Baliyar Simbala Bahadur Garu.	Do.	18	October 1869	25th March 1879.	1,02,902
	Meringhi	Setrucherla Jagannad Raj Babadur.	Do.	8	Dec. 1869	1st Feb. 1889	43,794
	Chemuda	Narasangami Pattamahadevi	Female.	46	17th July 1875...	Not known ...	12,086
						Total ...	1,64,670
Godavery	Nallamillapadu	Pasupalete Jaganathamma	Do.	19	18th Jan. 1866.	June 1878	611
	Kapoleswarapuram	Balasu Ramalakmanamma	Do.	14	27th Sept. 1869.	June 1883	37,619
	Gopaulpore	Sri Raja Vupyalapathi Venkata Vizia Gopala Raz Garu.	Male.	12	8th Oct. 1874 ..	1st Feb. 1885	61,985
						Total ...	1,00,215
Nellore	Chunda	Raja Ankappa Narayanum Garu	Do.	18	9th March 1871.	October 1879	55,274
North Arcot	Naraganti	Venkatachelapathi Nayanivaru	Do.	16	January 1867	1st August 1881.	21,758
Chinglepnt	Soorunjeri	V. S. Krishnasomi Iyengar	Do.	12	Sept. 1875	April 1885	5,150
Tanjore	Agharagurayangudi	Alagasundram Pillay	Do.	20	April 1869	1st Jan. 1874	3,734
	Shealli	Sandanathanni	Femal.	20	Do. 1870		43,574
	Vettangudi	Nallanayaga Pavutnunda Nayanar.	Male.	19	September 1873.	September 1877.	9,101
						Total ...	56,449

(2) *Statement showing the Particulars of the Estates under the charge of the Court of Wards at the end of Fasli 1285—(Continued).*

District.	Name of the Estate.	Name of the Ward.	Sex of the Ward.	Age of the Ward.	Date of Assumption of Charge.	Date when the Estate will probably be restored.	Demand for Fasli 1285.
							Rs.
Trichinopoly	Peramur	Madhava Row	Male.	28	14th Dec. 1868.	Not known	8,962
	Ramnad	Bhaskarasami Setupathe	Do.	8	15th Mar. 1873.	October 1889	7,83,985
	Bodinaickanur	Kumararaj Pandia Naick	Do.	18	12th Feb. 1863.	9th Oct. 1879	62,307
	Guntamanuickanur	Tirumala Guntama Gondala Nagiah Ramakrishnasami Naick.	Do.	9	4th Nov. 1867	24th Jan. 1888.	55,498
Madura	Sandyur	Gopalakrishna Amnal	Female.	54	16th Nov. 1871.	Not known	10,256
	Othappanaickanur	Tirumala Muthulinga Thumbia Veliasami Othappa Naick.	Male.	18	14th Jan. 1866.	14th Jan. 1879.	9,629
						Total	9,21,605
Tinnevelly	Maniachi	Subramania Talaver	Male.	15	March 1866	June 1882	9,176
	Sungampatti	Thonnatho Pulimalakutti Siva Subbramania Tevor.	Do.	16	April 1867	January 1881	21,099
	Urkad Zemindary	Kotilinga Seturayor	Do.	16	July 1872	September 1881	39,945
	Do. Partible Property	Sivanaiga Perumal Setu Rayer	Do.	19	November 1869	July 1878	1,856
	Ettiapuram	Muttu Jagavira Ramakumara Ettiappa Naickar.	Do.	19	January 1872	September 1878.	2,90,376
						Total	3,62,452
Coimbatore	Samattur and Kottamputty.	Kolandasami Vanavaraya Gounden	Male.	19	1st Oct. 1866	4th Aug. 1878.	10,620
Salem	Yerunaputty and Paliapoliun.	Kamatchi Ammal	Female.	25	22nd June 1874.	Not known	16,159
South Canara	Brahmavar Estate	Sarvothama Raw	Male.	6	October 1875	December 1891.	4,246
	Srinivasa Row's Estate	Srinivasa Raw	Do.	15	May 1875	August 1882	1,654
						Total	5,900
Malabar	Kavalapara	Parvathi Natheiyar	Female.	10	July 1872	May 1887	28,231
						Grand Total	21,81,902

INDEX VERBORUM.

INDEX VERBORUM.

www.ingramcontent.com/pod-product-compliance
Lightning Source LLC
Chambersburg PA
CBHW031819270326
41932CB00008B/468